The Quebec Connection

New World Studies
Marlene L. Daut, Editor

# The Quebec Connection

## A Poetics of Solidarity in Global Francophone Literatures

Julie-Françoise Tolliver

University of Virginia Press
Charlottesville and London

University of Virginia Press
© 2020 by the Rector and Visitors of the University of Virginia
All rights reserved
Printed in the United States of America on acid-free paper

*First published 2020*

9 8 7 6 5 4 3 2 1

Library of Congress Cataloging-in-Publication Data
Names: Tolliver, Julie-Françoise, author.
Title: The Quebec connection : a poetics of solidarity in global francophone literatures / Julie-Françoise Tolliver.
Description: Charlottesville ; London : University of Virginia Press, 2020. | Series: New World studies | Includes bibliographical references and index.
Identifiers: LCCN 2020010014 (print) | LCCN 2020010015 (ebook) | ISBN 9780813944883 (hardcover) | ISBN 9780813944890 (paperback) | ISBN 9780813944906 (epub)
Subjects: LCSH: French-Canadian literature—Québec (Province)—History and criticism. | African literature (French)—History and criticism. | Caribbean literature (French)—History and criticism. | Césaire, Aimé—Criticism and interpretation. | Aquin, Hubert, 1929–1977—Criticism and interpretation. | Mongo Beti, 1932–2001—Criticism and interpretation. | Imperialism in literature. | French language—Political aspects.
Classification: LCC PQ3917.Q3 T65 2020 (print) | LCC PQ3917.Q3 (ebook) | DDC 840.9/714—dc23
LC record available at https://lccn.loc.gov/2020010014
LC ebook record available at https://lccn.loc.gov/2020010015

*Cover art:* MabelAmber/pixabay

The University of Virginia Press gratefully acknowledges the American Comparative Literature Association Helen Tartar First Book Subvention Award, which provided funds toward the publication of this book.

of unborn baby in, 77, 78, 96–108, 116, 216; author's presence in, 84, 94; elements of Césaire's work and biography in, 76; *entrelacs* trope, 78, 85–88, 106–7, 117; literary ventriloquism trope in, 78, 81–84; oscillation between concrete and abstract in, 117; play "White Baby" and, 108–16; race thematicized in, 76, 81–84, 96–108, 115–18, 248n29; structure of, 77–78; tropes in, 78; unreliable authorship and text in, 93–96, 101–2, 103–5; violence against women in, 77, 78, 82, 85, 86, 88–93, 101–6, 175, 216, 218

Trudeau, Margaret (née Sinclair), 169, 253–54n9

Trudeau, Pierre-Elliott, 162, 253–54n9

Tshombe, Moïse, 53

Tunisia, 19, 216–36

Um Nyobé, Ruben, 151

*Une saison au Congo* (Césaire), 23, 25, 52–61; failed solidarity in, 52–61; personification of historical forces in, 52–53, 57; Sanza Player in, 56–57, 60

*Une tempête* (Césaire), 23, 25, 47–52, 72; intra-black solidarity, 48–51, 74–75; solidarity as mutual destruction in, 48, 49–50

Union des populations du Cameroun (UPC), 122–24, 135, 140, 151–52, 157, 161, 163

Urry, John, *Mobilities*, 257n7

Vallières, Pierre: Mouvement de libération populaire founded by, 133; *Nègres blancs d'Amérique*, 2, 5–7, 63–64, 98, 190–91, 238nn12–13

*vie africaine, La*, 246n5

Vietnam, 150, 173, 254n12

Vigneault, Gilles, "Les gens de mon pays," 226

violence against women trope, 77, 78, 82, 85, 86, 88–93, 101–6

Wall, Anthony, "Prisonnier dans ce trou, ce Trou de mémoire," 97, 101

Wallerstein, Immanuel, 237n6

Walsh, John Patrick, *Free and French in the Caribbean*, 242n15

War Measures Act, 226

Warren, Jean-Philippe, "L'opération McGill français," 145

water metaphors, 37–39

Webster, David, "Foreign Policy, Diplomacy, and Decolonization," 162

White, Hayden, *Tropics of Discourse*, 7, 239n20

"White Baby," 78, 108–16, 248n29

Wilde, Lawrence, *Global Solidarity*, 239nn18–19

women, francophone solidarity and, 19–20, 216–36

Yacoubi, El Hassan, "L'autofiction comme alternative à l'autobiographie chez les écrivains marocains," 204, 255–56n26

Yanacopoulo, Andrée, 108

Zaire, 151, 152, 159

Zand, Nicole, "Entretien avec Aimé Césaire," 24

RECENT BOOKS IN THE SERIES
# New World Studies

*Comrade Sister: Caribbean Feminist Revisions of the Grenada Revolution*
Laurie R. Lambert

*Cultural Entanglements: Langston Hughes and the Rise of African and Caribbean Literature*
Shane Graham

*Water Graves: The Art of the Unritual in the Greater Caribbean*
Valérie Loichot

*The Sacred Act of Reading: Spirituality, Performance, and Power in Afro-Diasporic Literature*
Anne Margaret Castro

*Caribbean Jewish Crossings: Literary History and Creative Practice*
Sarah Phillips Casteel and Heidi Kaufman, editors

*Mapping Hispaniola: Third Space in Dominican and Haitian Literature*
Megan Jeanette Myers

*Mourning El Dorado: Literature and Extractivism in the Contemporary American Tropics*
Charlotte Rogers

*Edwidge Danticat: The Haitian Diasporic Imaginary*
Nadège T. Clitandre

*Idle Talk, Deadly Talk: The Uses of Gossip in Caribbean Literature*
Ana Rodríguez Navas

*Crossing the Line: Early Creole Novels and Anglophone Caribbean Culture in the Age of Emancipation*
Candace Ward

*Staging Creolization: Women's Theater and Performance from the French Caribbean*
Emily Sahakian

*American Imperialism's Undead: The Occupation of Haiti and the Rise of Caribbean Anticolonialism*
Raphael Dalleo

CPSIA information can be obtained
at www.ICGtesting.com
Printed in the USA
LVHW100456220422
716875LV00005B/939

# Contents

| | | |
|---|---|---|
| | Acknowledgments | vii |
| | Introduction: Toward a Francophone Poetics of Solidarity | 1 |
| 1. | "Interior Geographies": Solidary Locations of Aimé Césaire's Poetics | 23 |
| 2. | Interlace, Interrace: Anticolonialism and White Babies in Hubert Aquin's *Trou de mémoire* | 76 |
| 3. | Publishable Offense: Simile, Solidarity, and Mongo Beti's Quebecois *Main basse sur le Cameroun* | 118 |
| 4. | As through a Canadian Fog: *Mort au Canada* and Other Moroccan Mysteries | 165 |
| | Coda: Francophone Nostalgias and the Afterlives of Independence-Era Solidarity | 215 |
| | Notes | 237 |
| | Bibliography | 259 |
| | Index | 271 |

# Acknowledgments

THIS PROJECT has been many years in the making. I began it at the University of Pennsylvania under the deft supervision of Lydie Moudileno, to whom I owe more than I can express; what I learned about being wary of all essentialisms I learned from her. Gerald Prince, Kevin Brownlee, Maurice Samuels, and Caroline Weber in French also provided welcome guidance, and Julia Verkholantsev, Kevin Platt, and Peter Steiner in Russian offered the balance of an outside perspective. David Kazanjian, in his support of the student union and in his Marxism and American Studies seminar, provided a model of scholarly activism. I always felt anchored in our otherwise centrifugal comparative literature program because of then program directors Rita Copeland and Liliane Weissberg—and also because of JoAnne Dubil, who was the heart of the office and of our communal experience.

I would not have begun thinking about solidarity had it not been for my experiences both in the graduate-student unionizing movement at Penn and in the gypsy-funk band the Blazing Cherries. GET-UP taught me the *work* of solidarity; I think fondly of conversations and collaborations with Shonni Enelow, Walt Hakala, Stefan Heumann, and Tatjana Scheffler. Peter Gaffney especially but also Esther Alarcón, Anna Frangiosa, Nicola Gentili, Tom Kelso, Rolf Lakaemper, Michael Schupp, and the rest of the Blazing Cherries musical and artistic constellation helped me imagine solidarity as both a practice and a vision.

My graduate-school colleagues in CompLit and in the Francophone Reading Group brought me challenging discussions and stimulating exchanges; Paul Carranza, Adrian Daub, Daniel DeWispelare, Nicole Eddy, Burcu Gursel, Stephen Hock, Ben Huberman, Ilinca Iurascu, Sarah Kerman, Grace Lavery, Edward Lybeer, Keith Poniewaz, Thangam Ravindranathan, Jessica Rosenberg, Rebecca Sheehan, Andre Soares, viii *Acknowledgments*

Lucy Swanson, Sayumi Takahashi, Jamie Taylor, Hervé Tchumkam, Ellen Welch, Emily Weissbourd, and Michael Wiedorn were in turn inspiring and hilarious, helping me keep my work in healthy perspective. Chris Hunter and Jen Jahner continue to be cherished friends and guides.

At Hamilton College, where I taught for two years, I saw my exceptional former professors (I also graduated from Hamilton) transform into supportive colleagues: John Bartle, Heather Buchman, Françoise Davis, Martine Guyot-Bender, Lydia Hamessley, Marianne Janack, Rob Kolb, Bonnie Krueger, Joseph Mwantuali, and Franklin Sciacca. Nancy and Peter Rabinowitz and Doug Raybeck continue to answer my phone calls when I encounter both major obstacles and minor dilemmas. I also appreciated the support of new colleagues: Michael Nieto Garcia, John Lytle, Peggy Piesche, Charlotte Rogers, Aurélie Van de Wiele, and many others. Hamilton was a great place to study, to teach, and to write; thank you.

The University of Houston has proved a warm and welcoming site to continue writing. U of H supported my work with a Small Grant and several travel grants. In addition, I appreciate the colleagues who sustained me along the way: Jeanna Abbott, Richard Armstrong, Francesca Behr, Jason Berger, Marie Boinot, Alessandro Carrera, Sreya Chatterjee, Amelia Chin, Jim Conyers, Jacqueline Couti, Kerry Creelman, Daniel Davies, Hildegard Glass, Maria Gonzalez, Elizabeth Gregory, Casey Dué Hackney, Marie Theresa Hernandez Ramirez, Marie-Céline Johnson, J. Kastely, Julia Kleinheider, Kairn Klieman, David Lake, Jean-Michel Lanskin, Auritro Majumder, Andrea Malone, David Mazella, Keith McNeal, Nelly Noury, Maya Panchang, Alex Parsons, Rachel Pope, Annalisa Quaini, Rachel Afi Quinn, John Roberts, Caryn and Ben Tamber-Rosenau, Antonio Tillis, Nina Tucci, Xiaohong Wen, Jennifer Wingard, Sunny Yang, Robert Zaretsky, and Lauren Zentz. Claudine Giacchetti especially served as a shining model for conducting serious research in a sea of administrative duties.

The cities of Houston and Ottawa were ideal places to write. Innie Chen, Rebecca Danard, Helena Forbes, Beryl Forrest Mazella, JD Pluecker, Melissa Rivero, Kathy Shine and Brenda Jacoby, Emily Thorn, Carolina and Claudia Villarroel, Lisa and Leonie Wall, and their families provided friendship and welcome support. I also appreciate the companionship of the good people at Fioza Café, Bank Street Second Cup, Meyerland Hot Yoga Plus, and Big Power Yoga Montrose who encouraged either the writing or the stretching that inevitably followed.

I benefited tremendously from the structure of the Faculty Success Program (and its alumni variant) provided by the National Center for

Faculty Development and Diversity, paid for by an award from the University of Houston. Coach Naomi Hume and members of my small group, especially Aditi Chandra and Brianne Kothari, have been incredibly supportive; I value the accountability they offer and continue to learn from the examples they set.

Eric Brandt, director in chief at the University of Virginia Press, has been most helpful in bringing this work to fruition. The late J. Michael Dash and Marlene Daut, former and current series editors, generously supported the inclusion of my project in New World Studies. I am also deeply grateful to the anonymous peer reviewers who volunteered their time and energy to provide me with comments and suggestions, to Morgan Myers for managing the process of publication, and to Joanne Allen for her thorough and insightful editing of the manuscript.

The panels on solidarity organized by Anna Bernard for ACLA 2018 and by Tony Alessandrini for ACLA 2019 represent treasured moments of dialogue and questioning about the nature, practice, critique, and future of solidarity. All the participants' work, our ensuing conversations, and the International Solidarity Action Research Network (isarn.org) nurtured my understanding of solidarity and shaped the final production of this book. Part of the coda was published in *Contemporary French Civilisation* 43.1 (2018) under the skillful editorship of Leslie Kealhofer-Kemp and Michael Gott. The article grew out of a paper written for a most productive conference on *cinéma-monde* organized by Leslie and Michael in 2016.

It would not have been possible for me to write *The Quebec Connection* without the generous support of the National Endowment for the Humanities, which awarded me a fellowship for 2017–18. Jim Turner at the NEH was particularly helpful in navigating the grant process. At the risk of sounding banal, I will state that receiving the NEH has completely changed my career and my life. Having a full year to focus on writing without teaching or administrative duties taught me how to be a researcher. The NEH, which in my case figured as a sort of miraculous fairy godmother, more generally constitutes a national treasure as a bastion defending the humanities. In addition, I am grateful to the American Comparative Literature Association, which supported the publication of this book with the Helen Tartar First Book Subvention Award. It is an honor to have my work linked to the memory of Helen Tartar.

Many friends and colleagues have read sections of *The Quebec Connection* and provided invaluable suggestions. The two writing groups to which I belonged were instrumental in helping me think through my project and bring it to completion: Hosam Aboul-Ela, Margot Backus, Audrey Coulombe, Sarah Ehlers, Karen Fang, and Kavita Singh gave hours of their brilliance to help me advance my work. Asma Al-Nasser, Ann Christensen, Erin Hurley, Duy Nguyen, Bhavya Tiwari, and Lynn Voskuil also offered vital feedback. Katherine Aid read and helped mold the entire manuscript into a single narrative. Ambroise Kom and Fernando Lambert graciously agreed to be interviewed; Denis Provencher and Hélène Tissières were generous with their advice. For many years, Monica Popescu has been a dear friend and an exceptional interlocutor. Her vast knowledge and her keen insights have provided a phenomenal sounding board not only for this project but also for many of my other endeavors.

My family has supported my work both in ways they understand and in ways they cannot begin to imagine. The Georgia Tollivers—Gwendolyn, Cedric, Nikki, Joel, Aunt Barbara, Grandma Luvenia—champion our research from afar. Louann and Rob Shaner asked all the right questions, especially the difficult ones, offering marvelous hospitality that fed the mind and the body. My many aunts and uncles, in particular Marie-Claude Jean and Sylvain Leduc, offered conversations that helped further my thoughts—or that helped free me from my thoughts when I needed to be freed. My brother, Thomas Kruidenier, and my sister-in-law, Yuko Mitrovic, provided fascinating windows into other domains of learning and ways of working. My parents, Hélène and Bastian Kruidenier, babysat for weeks at a time when I needed to bury myself in the archives or in my manuscript; they never doubted the importance of my writing. My children, Éloïse and Emy, are learning, growing, asking, and laughing in ways I find astoundingly beautiful. Finally, Cedric Tolliver has been my steady *compagnon de route* and my go-to for ideas and advice through all these years.

Many others have helped along the way; I am grateful for your solidarity and encouragement, which have made this project conceivable.

# The Quebec Connection

# Introduction
## Toward a Francophone Poetics of Solidarity

> Une image poétique peut être le germe d'un monde, le germe d'un
> univers imaginé devant la rêverie d'un poète.
> —Gaston Bachelard, *La poétique de la rêverie*

IN 1965, a young woman from Quebec smuggled explosives from Montreal to New York City to help the Harlem-based Black Liberation Front dynamite the head and torch-bearing arm of the Statue of Liberty. Conceived as an act of symbolic vandalism, and subsequently revealed to have been partly an FBI setup, the planned explosion was preempted by the arrest of all the conspirators and so faded into obscurity. And yet the surprising fact remains: a young, French-speaking, white Quebecois woman, who was a successful television announcer to boot, identified with African American militancy to such an extent that she conspired with an underground Black Power organization in Harlem. This instance of *identification with*, moreover, was not an isolated one.[1] The intellectual events that led to this unexpected alliance form but one of many parallel solidarities that illuminated the French-speaking world in the period between 1950 and the late 1970s, structuring French-language texts and delimiting political imaginaries.

Retracing the steps that made a Montreal-Harlem connection possible leads to anticolonial movements in francophone Africa and the Caribbean. As intellectuals from these regions imagined alternatives to colonialism and neocolonialism, their texts—essays, manifestos, novels, plays—became blueprints for thinkers in other parts of the world who also sought solutions to social and economic inequity. For Quebecois intellectuals, a militant sympathy with anticolonial struggles produced the radical transformations that occurred in the 1960s with the Quiet Revolution.[2] This sympathy took the form of identification, a solidarity primarily constructed in texts and through reading practices. The attempt to join the Black Liberation Front in defacing the Statue of Liberty was an enactment, however misled, of the solidarity Quebecois thinkers felt with African Americans when they adopted the designation *nègres blancs d'Amérique* from the title of Pierre Vallières's 1968 autobiography.

*The Quebec Connection* examines the ways French-language texts of the 1950s, 1960s, and 1970s manipulated a language whose expansion was directly linked to France's imperial history to construct anticolonial solidarities of this sort.[3] Specifically, I examine the transnational and transracial[4] ties that linked French-language writers from Quebec to those in the Caribbean and Africa during a period when independence represented a buoyant ideal in all these regions. Quebec, whose racial demographics and geopolitical situation are somewhat anomalous in the fields of francophone and postcolonial studies, features here as a site for the articulation of anticolonial and postcolonial imaginaries. This book does not focus exclusively on Quebecois literature but rather interrogates how Quebec figures in the expression of the francophone solidarities that ushered in and followed the dusk of French empire.

The idea of solidarity is intricately linked to the fact of French imperialism. Indeed, the adjective *solidaire* appeared in French usage in 1584,[5] coinciding with the years of early exploration and settlement in New France, now Canada. First an economic term defining the connection created by debt or financial obligation, the word *solidaire,* and its noun counterpart, *solidarité* (which entered usage in 1693), points to the transformation in social relations within the context of the advent of French imperial mercantilism.[6] Even as it was devised in France to define French legal developments, the concept of solidarity developed out of the need to represent financial exchanges and obligations across vast expanses of time and space, linking entities beyond any single duchy, region, or continent. *Solidarité,* then, is the term necessary to describe the transatlantic network of investment and economic exchange that developed from the late sixteenth century onward. And yet the very trajectories of solidary exchange that supported and made empire profitable also fostered the means of resistance to that same empire. This paradoxical relationship recalls Marx's description of capitalism producing its own gravediggers: factories brought together workers to produce commodities and simultaneously enabled these same workers to become conscious of their class belonging and of their potential for revolution. Thus, too, transatlantic networks of financial exchange brought into contact people who imagined alternative relations to those of empire. The second definition of *solidarité* is connected to this alternative vision: the imagination of a community of interests bound by a moral obligation of support. Through elaboration of a new financial vocabulary and through its extension in the social realm, the emergence of the term *solidarité* therefore coincides with the emergence of a mercantilistic imperial system whose reach extended (and in some ways still extends) from Europe to North America, the Caribbean, and Africa.

*The Quebec Connection* resists easy readings of solidarity as too idealistic, as a utopic feeling that can and perhaps should be dismissed as inconsequential and intellectually insufficient. Scholars like the geographer David Featherstone have shown that solidarity constitutes a powerful social force worthy of critical study. In his influential 2012 monograph titled *Solidarity: Hidden Histories and Geographies of Internationalism*, Featherstone defines solidarity as "a relation forged through political struggle which seeks to challenge forms of oppression" (5), locating solidarity in a range of collaborative actions that dramatically shaped global exchanges. This book emphasizes that these collaborative actions must be articulated through language, as indeed Patrice Lumumba's 1959 speech at the Congress for Liberty and Culture in Ibadan demonstrates. When Lumumba spoke to African leaders and intellectuals of the *esprit de solidarité* that he hoped would unite independent African nations, he made it clear that "spirit" was not a mere feeling: "La solidarité africaine doit se concrétiser aujourd'hui dans les faits et dans les actes" (Lumumba 29). The first concrete policy that Lumumba then proposes to facilitate solidary support among African nations is a *linguistic* policy: "Pour favoriser les échanges culturels et le rapprochement entre les pays d'expression française et ceux d'expression anglaise, il faudrait rendre l'enseignement du français et de l'anglais obligatoire dans toutes les écoles d'Afrique. La connaissance de ces deux langues supprimera les difficultés de communication auxquelles se heurtent les Africains d'expression anglaise et ceux d'expression française lorsqu'ils se rencontrent" (Lumumba 29). Lumumba's focus on language indicates the fundamentally communicative nature of solidarity. Moreover, his willingness to use the languages of empire as the most expedient tools to foster anticolonial community suggests how workable he considered these languages to be in terms of subverting and breaking down empire.

*The Quebec Connection* proposes to investigate the work done on the French language by authors intent on forging anticolonial solidarity through texts. These authors' writings show that writing solidarity constitutes a complex gesture mixing fervent feeling with a rational understanding of its own limits and limitations. Indeed, as francophone writers nurtured and tried to express solidarities defined by broadly leftist politics, they had to give serious consideration to the interregional, interracial, and interclass differences that defined the French-speaking world. I argue that the French-specific tropes authors used to express unity across these differences[7] reveal both gaps and unexpected connections in the francophone political imaginary. To analyze the abecedary of these tropes, then, is to bring to light a poetics of solidarity that both defines a foundational moment in French-language world literatures and interrogates the intersection of solidarity with literature, asking how each grew from the other. Solidarity in this book is a desire for unity-in-difference, a search for commonality despite distance and disparity, which is materialized in written linguistic articulation. I call this articulation a *poetics* because it relies on the techniques of literary expression. This introduction uses illustrative vignettes to suggest how the mechanism of tropes constructs francophone textual solidarities as an asymptotic and abstract concept that nevertheless proved influential in defining an era and a geography in which independence circulated as a dominant idea.

## Tongue Ties: French-Language Connections

While francophone anticolonial intellectuals were "tied" to one another linguistically through their use of the French tongue, their connection was also constricted ("tied") by the inherent qualities of a language that had been shaped by the material practices of colonization and of anticolonial opposition.[8] On the one hand French was, from the sixteenth century on, an imperial language marked by a chasmic racism that defined humanity according to racialized constructions; the Code Noir's infamous statement "Déclarons les esclaves être meubles" is emblematic of this type of usage. On the other hand, by the 1950s French was also well established as a language of abolitionism, of resistance to colonization, and of anticapitalist struggles. As Nick Nesbitt argues in *Caribbean Critique,* "The continuously renewed concern for abstract, universal concepts first articulated [in French] following the fall of the Bastille in 1789 and the powerful potentials they hold to transform the actual, specific lived experience of a multitude of non-identical subjects" (292n2) make francophone thought of particular interest for investigations into liberatory discourses. The Jacobins under Robespierre "asserted the then-novel human right to life" (37) and articulated (and attempted to institute) popular sovereignty and justice as equality. The Abbé Grégoire's pamphlets arguing for the emancipation of slaves offer an early example of the use of French to imagine racial equality;[9] Toussaint Louverture disrupted the discourse of the "colonial family romance" by removing himself from the position of child/pupil and reimagining himself as a father/teacher,[10] offering another early model of resistance to a racialized hierarchization of humanity. The 1848 Slavery Abolition Decree, whose composition was overseen by Victor Schoelcher as leader of the provisionary government's emancipation committee, similarly marked the French language by extending human dignity to slaves and by assigning to French colonial territory the same emancipatory status as held by France itself ("le sol de la France affranchit l'esclave qui le touche"). The Paris Commune of 1871 nurtured anticapitalist discourses that then resurfaced in the twentieth century through syndicalism and anarchist movements. The interwar years saw the formation in France of anticolonialist leagues and associations, such as the Comité de défense de la race nègre, which sometimes worked with the Parti communiste français in articulating anti-imperialist demands.[11] All these discourses, for and against slavery, colonialism, and capitalism, shaped the French language. The writers who found connections with one another in French during the independence era had to negotiate this complex politico-linguistic history, and their choices in deploying the language reflect those negotiations.

I discuss this linguistic boundedness by using as an example the 1968 manifesto-autobiography *Nègres blancs d'Amérique,* mentioned above, written by the revolutionary Quebecois sovereigntist Pierre Vallières from prison.[12] The actual content of the autobiography narrates francophone solidarity explicitly, as Vallières recounts his transformative French-language encounters with Martinican Marxist militants (part 4, chapter 4). The title, however, problematizes this interracial solidarity, specifically by using a figure of style, a trope, to suggest the complicated, as yet unexpressed difficulties of Vallières's position in a structure of solidarity. The title is an oxymoron: a *nègre* cannot be *blanc,* and yet he suggests by juxtaposing the two terms that these categories are unstable and need to be questioned. The title is provocative: the term *nègre* has a history of and continues to be redolent with French imperial and colonial racism, and Vallières's title is racist both in its use of the term and in its white appropriation of the inequalities the term implies. The historian Fernande Roy writes critically in 2009, "On ne peut pas simplement se dire que toute comparaison est boiteuse. Ici, la comparaison est odieuse. Elle révèle, à mon avis, une bonne dose d'ignorance et même de nombrilisme" (Roy 34). Moreover, as David Austin reminds us in his study of black Quebec, Vallières's appropriation erases actual black people living in Quebec. Vallières's intention, however, was not racist.[13] As Fernando Lambert, professor emeritus of French at Laval University in Quebec City, explains in a 2018 email to the author,

> Vallières fait du Nègre, c'est-à-dire de l'homme noir et de sa condition dans l'histoire, un prototype de l'homme dominé et nié en quelque sorte par la colonisation, la situation du Québécois ayant à certains égards des traits communs avec la figure du Nègre, sans valeur péjorative ou dépréciative de l'homme noir. En quelque sorte, cette figure joue le rôle de miroir: comprendre cette image ou figure, c'est à la fois sympathiser avec les victimes et aussi prendre conscience que l'on a tenté de nous réduire à une figure semblable dont il faut s'émanciper. Et comme le groupe de la Négritude, il faut redécouvrir son identité et l'affirmer, la proclamer fièrement.

Lambert's experience of the term *nègres blancs* suggests that for at least some Quebecois intellectuals Vallières's title represented a sympathizing, solidary gesture, one that adopts *négritude* writers and artists as role models in self-liberation. And yet it is impossible to divorce language from its history; if *négritude* writers found such power in revindicating the label *nègre,* it was precisely, of course, because of the abuse with which French usage had laden it.

Pierre Vallières, by appropriating the term, dredges up its racist imperial history, yes. But by juxtaposing it to *blanc,* he also problematizes this history by expanding its signifying potential with a trope that tries to articulate something as yet unfamiliar: a position of white colonial victimhood in solidarity with blackness.[14] His tropological experimentation with language in some ways distorts the racial categories that language helped erect and safeguard, creating linguistic and conceptual space for a new way of being *in French* and *in relation to* other French speakers.

In addition, the title *Nègres blancs,* for all its insensitivity, specifically exposes the race and class differences that characterize the French-speaking world: the term *nègre* was used interchangeably with the word *slave,* for example, during the era of the slave trade and referred (refers) as much to class as to race. So Vallières's decision to use *nègre* to describe a white, francophone Quebecois underclass brings to a head the very race and class divisions that gave the term its meaning. French-language solidarity therefore participates in constructing race and class categories even as it seeks to overcome them: the oxymoron *nègres blancs* functions precisely by reasserting the subjugation of black people, the perpetual oppression of *négritude,* even as it places white Quebecois people in solidarity with black downtroddenness. Vallières's solidarity does much more than simply usurp victimhood from French-speaking black people. The oxymoron Vallières uses in fact underscores the tensions latent in his solidary appropriation; *nègres blancs* draws attention to the racist structures that invented and distilled the term *nègre* in all its racist and classist implications, and it calls for an examination of possible solidarities (including Vallières's own solidarity) within this racist context. The title *Nègres blancs d'Amérique* thus makes solidarity inseparable from critique.

Vallières's title stands as an example of the stylistic gestures used by francophone authors to portray and problematize solidarity and the new imaginaries it can engender. Stylistic figures, or tropes, are the stuff of textual solidarity. They are the linguistic acrobatics that allow writers to invent the expression of something that they have felt and acted on but that has nevertheless left them uncomfortable or inexpressive because they have understood or glimpsed its limitations. It has been of primordial importance to certain authors to express their solidary feelings despite that discomfort, because such feelings were vitally true to the intellectual dawn those authors were living; a trope "is always not only a deviation *from* one possible, proper meaning, but also a deviation *towards* another meaning, conception, or ideal of what is right and proper *and true* 'in reality,'" Hayden White asserts (2, emphases in original).[15] Vallières and other French-language writers were linguistically striving to articulate the truth of a new, unfamiliar relation; each poetic image they invented represented "le germe d'un monde, d'un univers imaginé," as Gaston Bachelard aphorizes in *La poétique de la rêverie*. The solidarities invented by independence-era writers through novel poetic images—through figurative language—represented visions of possible new worlds. For Édouard Glissant in *Traité du tout-monde,* literature represents "ce mouvement désentravant, qui mène de notre lieu à la pensée du monde" (248). Poetics for Glissant *is* Relation, the attempt to open ourselves to the other without relinquishing our identities, and this process is one of solidarity: "*La Relation,* c'est-à-dire en même temps la Poétique . . . qui nous hausse en nous-même et la solidarité, par quoi nous manifestons cette hauteur. Tout réseau de solidarité est en ce sens une vraie Poétique de la Relation" (249).[16] Poetics is thus linked together with solidarity as the elevated mode of being that makes possible our constantly novel opening to the world. As J. Michael Dash writes, "Tropes are the basic units of discourse and *tropics* is the vital process that renders the unfamiliar familiar" (26). New modes of relation and fresh alliances in the historically charged field of France's former empire demanded, and still demand, these tropological linguistic experimentations precisely *because* they represent a step into unknown desire—a desire for shared anticolonial understanding across race, class, and region. This book offers an examination of the tropics that constitutes independence-era literary solidarity, the set of tropological paradigms that made it possible for writers to incorporate new, unfamiliar connections within the familiar, hackneyed practices of the French language, loosening the "ties" of established usage while reinforcing the "ties" of mutual comprehension in a single tongue.

**In the Breach: Solidarity as Asymptotic Unity**

Tropes are essential to expressing solidarity not only because of the incongruity of the new connections stretching the bounds of the old language but also because of the nature of solidarity itself. If Quebecois writers identified with Caribbean and African anticolonial discourse, they felt they had something in common with it; and yet identification[17] implies specifically that there are two separate elements that are, in one or more aspect(s), straining toward similarity or sameness. This is also the nature of the solidarity that drove the desire to "identify with." Solidarity is always incomplete: it is always in the process of imagining correspondence in spite of difference and/or distance. Solidarity works by abstracting some commonality over and above the disintegrating, separating, isolating impulse of infinite difference. Logically, any project of uniting difference is in its very essence destined to fail. Failure is constitutive of solidarity's desire to reach across insurmountable difference, because an abstract commonality can never map precisely onto an infinite number of specificities. In a way, then, solidarity's yearning for unity is *asymptotic;* solidary unity exists as an unreachable horizon. The idea that "their fight is our fight" (Alessandrini) constitutes an asymptotic statement. It exists, it works, it is locatable as a gesture or direction (like a mathematical curve), but it can never be what it proclaims to be: "our fight" can only ever approach "their fight." And yet solidarity exists, it performs *in the breach* between its desire for unity-in-difference and the impossible state of unity-in-difference.

My metaphorical application of the mathematical figure of the asymptote is new to solidarity studies, but the asymptote has figured in other fields to symbolize similarly complex ideals. I turn briefly to political philosophy, a field abounding with asymptotic ideals, many of which are imagined as social ideals. Walter Benjamin, for example, criticized the German Social Democrats for idealizing Marx's idea of a classless society: "Once the classless society had been defined as an *infinite task,* the empty and homogeneous time was transformed into an anteroom, so to speak, in which one could wait for the emergence of the revolutionary situation with more or less equanimity" (Benjamin 402, emphasis added). The principle of a classless society as Benjamin criticizes it—in the form of an infinite task representing an asymptotic ideal—discourages revolutionary action rather than motivating it. Similarly, speaking of the impossibility of completely doing away with war and revolution, Victor Hugo wrote, "La paix universelle est une hyperbole dont le genre humain suit l'asymptote. Suivre cette asymptote, voilà la loi de l'humanité" (*Le Rhin*, Conclusion XVII). Philip Rorty, with *Contingency, Irony, Solidarity*, extends these intellectual experiments in understanding an asymptotically idealized social state to solidarity itself. For him, solidarity in its utopic fullness should include all of humanity, and in his "liberal ironic" perspective free of universal truths, he imagines the work of solidarity as a creative process, one of gradually understanding the suffering of more and more people, building toward the impossible but highly desirable horizon of a full, total, global human solidarity (xvi). Rorty's utopia represents the idealized concept of total mutual comprehension. His theorization hopes for but also sees the impossibility of absolute, total inclusion: the term *utopia* could well be replaced by *asymptote*.[18] Rorty's form of solidarity thus resembles Benjamin's classless society or Hugo's universal peace: they are goals, ends in themselves. For Rorty, solidarity is therefore (as are classless society and universal peace) a form of social idealism, asymptotic because it is impossible to get all people to mutually understand one another. My project differs slightly from these sociopolitical applications of asymptotic ideals because it focuses on the way language articulates the breach between ideal and practice.

Solidarity has been a missing piece in conceptualizing francophone studies. Françoise Lionnet's work stands out as a notable exception, however. Her article "Continents and Archipelagoes: From 'E Pluribus Unum' to Creolized Solidarities" performs an interesting shift from solidarity as a social goal to solidarity as a method for achieving more democratic and ethical global relations. She theorizes "creolized solidarities" as a way of resolving racial and ethnic imbalances in the context of French national policies of color-blind assimilation, policies that, Lionnet shows, only reinforce a racist status quo ("Continents and Archipelagoes" 1511–12). She articulates her theory as a question—"Can a renewed understanding of the internal—creolized—multiplicity of language, culture, and identity help transform twenty-first-century civic culture?" (1511)—emphasizing the incompleteness of the project in which solidarity-as-method participates.

For Lionnet as well, then, creolized solidarity shimmers as an asymptotic mode of relation, an idealized concept that might transform but can never realistically replace the model of French civic belonging in which a singular ideal of French citizenry is held up to the "many" as assimilative paradigm.

I follow Lionnet's lead in considering solidarity as a method rather than a goal, applying it not to a national civic context but rather to a transnational literary one. In this context, I analyze solidarity as a *set of tools* and a *condition of striving,* asymptotic because it is impossible to match the desire for solidarity to the articulation of it. This model of solidarity is always contingent and therefore ephemeral: a particular solidarity is contingent on a particular abstract commonality existing in the context of a particular set of struggles. Once the context changes, there is no expectation that solidarity will outlive it, whereas classless society, universal peace, and Rorty's solitary utopia are idealized as eternal rather than ephemeral goals. Solidarity, therefore, is an asymptotic linguistic or modal form that indicates striving toward, a particular subjunctive mood that indicates not subjectivity but rather subjective desire for unity.

Thinking solidarity asymptotically helps us understand the spatiality and temporality of solidarity. The curve (the expression of or desire for unity-in-difference) continually approaches the asymptote (unity-in-difference, or solidarity) but does not meet it at any finite distance. In other words, the curve can be considered to meet the asymptote at infinity; solidarity is a concept of infinity. Abstraction can only finally, fully express infinite difference at infinity, a nonexistent point in both space and time, which makes each moment and place where solidarity is yearningly expressed an approximation of a perfect but impossible unity. This asymptotic nature of independence-era literary solidarity can be illustrated by analyzing a few lines from a song by the sovereigntist Quebecois author, composer, playwright, and singer Georges Dor. In "La chanson difficile" Dor sings about the power of song to reach across difference and distance: "Quand je chante, je deviens chanson!/. . ./Quand je marche, je marche vers toi,/Toi l'autre à l'autre bout du monde." The singer's metaphorical transformation into song ("je deviens chanson") allows for radical movement across absolute difference, even as "l'autre à l'autre bout du monde" remains a hyperbole of otherness and distance, projecting the world as somehow having "ends" that might be the points furthest from one another. Only by imagining the singer *as song* can Dor reach asymptotically across infinite distance and difference. Solidarity in this lyric is a movement always "toward," an incompletable proposition, and yet it is performed with the resolute conviction of a march. The music's momentum (2/4 time) suggests the transformative power of song, as does Dor's metaphor of becoming song, but the image of "marching toward" persists as one of impossibility, of eternal striving: "l'autre à l'autre bout du monde" remains inalterably other, and the distance to this other does not disappear or shorten.

Time does not shorten any more than space: the song ends with the lines "Quand je vous dis je vous aime,/Je deviens le verbe aimer/À tous les temps!" These lines bear witness to the same hyperbolic transformation: language, the spoken phrase "je vous aime" (in the sense of *l'amour du prochain*—a plural *vous*), represents the asymptotic desire of eternal love, past and present and future. In this light, solidarity becomes endlessly transposable, both translocally and transtemporally; it can be endlessly recovered, borrowed, imitated. This endless repetition, then, is constitutive of solidarity in the same way that asymptoticness is; the feeling of impossible infinite belonging, multiplied across space and time, is an essential part of the powerful exhilaration of solidarity. In solidarity, we rub shoulders as much with infinity as with one another, that is to say, not at all but almost. This is what writers of solidarity try to express.

Solidary love, here, is also elliptically metaphorized as a memory of grammar exercises (conjugating verbs in all tenses) to suggest precisely that it is the abstract quality of *language* that makes these asymptotic dreams possible—as aspirations. Dor's song imagines solidarity as the asymptotic relationship between a linguistic articulation and the desire, which that articulation attempts to express, for overcoming difference ("l'autre"), distance ("l'autre bout du monde"), and time ("à tous les temps"). The asymptotic nature of solidarity, in fact, begins to explain its curiously simultaneous existence as a feeling *and* as an articulation of that feeling. The authors whose work is examined in *The Quebec Connection* consciously tried to work through the differences and inequalities of the French-speaking world that formed the terrain on which they had to construct any kind of relation. This "working through" of inequality happened in linguistic expression, and it was inspired by solidarity at the same time as it tried to articulate solidarity. Acts of solidarity therefore appear to be motivated by a feeling of solidarity even though neither the feeling nor the act in isolation can be termed *solidarity*.[19] Solidarity seems both to precede its own articulation and also to exist only through its articulation, with a time-lapse effect (feeling then action) that collapses into simultaneity. Not only does solidarity constitute an asymptotic desire for unity-in-difference, then, but it also stands in a kind of asymptotic relation to the moment of its own articulation, affectively preempting itself even as it comes into linguistic being.

Paradoxically, moreover, even as failure is constitutive of solidarity, solidarity itself cannot fail (or succeed, for that matter). We can speak of a solidary movement failing, of a solidary gesture being misunderstood, of a solidary cause being betrayed, but the solidarity itself stands apart from the failure. Solidarity is a concept that forms a conjuncture of relations, feelings, actions, ideological perspectives, and hopes, any of which can be considered to fail or succeed without the conjuncture itself being in that same jeopardy. Solidarity may fail to do something, to accomplish a goal, but in its straining toward an impossible union, it establishes itself as a thing whose structural failure renders any kind of "real" failure (or success) a moot point. For this reason, it is more productive to investigate how solidarity functions as asymptotic desire than to try to assess its success in the world.

The key to understanding the asymptotic desire for solidarity, I argue here, lies in the language used to express it. Language both expresses the breach and tries to bridge it, and literary language in particular possesses fabulous tools to exploit the breaches in language that mimic, critique, and explain solidarity's asymptotic nature. The mechanics of solidarity as asymptotic modal form (or, to put it differently, the words used to express the vector of desire for unity-in-difference) are tropes: writers use figurative language to introduce or make noticeable a gap between words and the significance these words hold, and this productive gap (a tropological *différance*) allows for the insertion of solidary desire. And tropological, symbolic expressions bring solidarity itself into the realm of possibility. Kristin Ross similarly examines post–Paris Commune metaphors used to imagine a more positive outcome to the Commune, writing that "without these 'merely symbolic' gestures of relationality and correspondence the possibility of solidarity or of refashioning an internationalist conjuncture at any moment in the near future is increasingly remote" (61). Correspondingly, the *nègre blanc* is an impossible being, but the juxtaposition of the words simultaneously shows and invents a desire for that being's solidary existence; solidarity emerges as the desire for this impossible creature to exist. *The Quebec Connection* proposes to analyze the tropological gaps, which I collectively call a *poetics,* that create openings for solidarity in French-language independence-era dramatic and narrative texts: plays, novels, essays, and a film.

## Solidarity as Abstraction

Tropes are important to the articulation of solidarity because solidarity necessarily performs a kind of abstraction across real, practical differences, and language is the medium that must accommodate this gap between the ideal of solidary unity and the reality of infinite difference. The francophone authors I study, struggling with this gap, turn to a poetics precisely to try to express the solidarity that both unites and divides them: the techniques of poetics—tropes—allow them the flexibility to express a feeling or political position that is both unifying (through a common anticolonialism) and isolating in its revelation of material distance and difference. Tropes work well to articulate solidarity because they too straddle abstraction and specificity; a metaphor, for example, compares objects based on an abstract similarity, in spite of the objects' literal differences. If solidarity is a culling of abstract similarities from a pool of infinite difference, then, metaphors underscore resemblances that exist in spite of variance. Solidarity abstracts commonality from dissimilar human lives; literary language uses abstracting tropes to express significant correspondences that mark the human experience.

In other words, solidarity functions in a way that is parallel to how literary representation (figurative language or poetics) functions: both are balanced between a space/time of absolute specificity (my colonized circumstances, your colonized circumstances; the wording, the specific articulation of a text) and an abstract position that can be applied across a multitude of specificities (the abstract experience of "colonialism"; the symbolic application of a text beyond its narrow articulation to larger "truths"). I will here illustrate this process of abstraction by briefly analyzing Ousmane Sembene's 1960 novel *Les bouts de bois de Dieu: Banty mam yall,* which recounts the successful 1947–48 strike that united West African railway workers against the railway's French owners and managers. Although the novel introduces the expression *bouts de bois de dieu* as a brand-new trope in French, it explains that in Wolof this is a common idiom: the phrase *banty man yall* (the novel's subtitle, meaning "god's bits of wood") represents a way of labeling people while counting them so as not to endanger their souls. Reflecting a belief in the uncountability of human life, the expression *banty man yall* metaphorizes people who need to be counted into inanimate objects (pieces of wood) touched by the divine. The expression's neologistic translation into French drags this metaphorical baggage into the context of the colonial language and of global capitalism. In French, the abstraction of workers as inanimate bits of wood erases the differences between the colony's (and the world's) black and white workers, focusing on their countability—the numerability of their cumulative unity—in the face of colonial and global exploitation. Indeed, Sembene dedicates the novel "À VOUS, BANTY MAM YALL, à mes frères de syndicat et à tous les syndicalistes et à leurs compagnes dans ce vaste monde," which suggests that the *bouts de bois de dieu* of the title is a category with global application. Of course, by writing in French Sembene draws on a long legacy of French syndicalist solidarity; and indeed, during his time as a docker in Marseille he himself was a member of the Confédération générale du travail. Syndicalism is part of the French language's configurations, but Sembene reconfigures both the language and the concept by inserting a new tropological unit into them to identify an innovative, unfamiliar concept (global anticolonial syndicalism originating in West Africa). The process of creating this figure of speech is a process of abstraction, which allows for the existence of both difference (in the understanding that people are not entirely alike, that they are really not as like one another as bits of wood are like one another) and unifying solidarity (they are all similar in that they count themselves against imperial capitalism). The French-language trope works the same way as Sembene's imagined solidarity works, by abstracting (metaphorizing) a unifying feature while allowing space for difference to exist.

The content or focus of solidarity and of literature's mechanisms of abstraction can differ. In the formulation of solidarity, the abstraction relates generally to a shared resistance to oppression, meaning that the abstract similarity is part of a power relation. But solidarity's abstraction of resistance is more complex than this single dimension in its formulation; otherwise, it would be simply the same as resistance. The mutuality implied in solidarity (its "sharedness") requires delicate articulation because, as I have shown above, no sharing is absolute; it is always a negotiation of similarities and differences. Because the valence of literature's mode of abstraction is flexible, literature constitutes a privileged mode for attempting to define the dimensions of solidarity that go beyond resistance. A literary trope, for example, *can* expose and demand analysis of the power relations revealed in a literary text (indeed, postcolonial literature tends to begin with this gesture), but the text, in its complexity, always allows for other readings. Literary solidarities can be analyzed and explained, but they remain irreducible, irreproducible through other means than the ones found by their authors to express, with poetic abstraction and economy, each particular nexus of connection and division.

The *master tropes* of solidary literature thus build on solidarity's abstracting function.[20] As this book shows, there are trends across authors' attempts to articulate solidarity; most commonly, these authors call on metaphors and similes to do the work of abstracting shared traits, while allowing space for difference to flourish. Metaphors and similes become uniting factors across the various versions of independence-era solidarity examined here, but the different implementations of these models and their conjunction with a variety of other tropes, such as irony or wordplay, animate a plurality of attempted textual solidarities.

These tropes are lodged in French-language texts that differ widely in origin and style but that share certain formal similarities. On a micro level, as I have explained, they rely on literary figures of style to express new solidarities. On a macro level, these tropological experiments are located in forms conducive to exploring the development of a theme over time. The texts studied in this book belong to specific genres—the novel, the play, the essay, and the film—because these genres sustain a representation of reality that includes temporal development, a chronology of events (even if not presented in chronological order) allowing for the progressive elaboration of solidarity. The authors' tropological experiments are thus cocooned within forms suited to the description, narration, or dramatization of sequential transformation, allowing for the potential development of the trope in an imaginary world resembling reality enough to make the experimental connection meaningful.[21] *The Quebec Connection* looks at plays and lectures by the Martinican writer and politician Aimé Césaire, a novel by the Quebecois author Hubert Aquin, a long essay by the Cameroonian writer and publisher Mongo Beti (together with its prefaces), novels by the Moroccan French author Driss Chraïbi, and a film by the Tunisian director Nouri Bouzid from a later decade, placing each author's tropological experiments with solidarity within the context both of the work in which it appears and of the reality this work purportedly imitates.

## An Era and a Geography Constructed through Solidary Texts

The texts analyzed in this book, gathered together because they are structured by tropes expressing solidarity in the French-speaking world, unexpectedly subvert the regional and racial boundaries that sometimes limit the discipline called francophone literature and also redefine the era of francophone literature from the 1950s through the 1970s. I call this literary epoch the *long independence era*. Conceptualizing independence as a twenty-year period is unusual; typically, the period of independence comprises exclusively the African independences, which took place in the years immediately preceding and following 1960. Considering a longer period, however, allows us to address previously neglected connections between the various regions of the francophone world that together or sequentially yearned for self-determination. Whether that hope was realized (and arguably betrayed) with the creation of independent nations, as on the African continent, whether it was made more complex by departmentalization, as in French Caribbean territories, or whether it was eventually defeated by vote, as in Quebec, the idea of independence circulated among these regions and transformed each region's texts and political possibilities. It is important to note that I speak here of *hope for,* and not actual, independence. The actualization of Gaullist neocolonial independence on the African continent, for example—what the Cameroonian author Mongo Beti disdainfully called "la bamboula de l'indépendance" (*Main basse 66*)—proved to be a disappointment of preindependence hope. But the idea of independence played an inspiring role throughout the period.

Of course, this era is not uniformly coherent across the French-speaking world. Because at different times francophone regions were either in a colonial state of preindependence, in a phase of neocolonial postindependence as nation-states, or in the limbo of perpetually deferred independence, the "long independence era" remains a messy and uneven classification. This complex temporal and geographical structure was, in a very real sense, constructed through a network of interlocking texts, the length of the independence era resulting directly from the solidary reading that inspired copycat or secondary independence struggles and animated postcolonial resistance to neocolonialism. In a language delimited by a history of imperialism—French—the textual exchanges I study sought to understand and express independence as a solidary network of anticolonial projects, relying on poetics to transform the language into a tool for constructing new political and poetic imaginaries. The temporality and geography of this poetics of solidarity fuse in a strange spacetime that blends anticipation for change, a transnationally oriented retrospection on bygone hopes, and a reaction against both colonial pasts and neocolonial presents.

The long independence era can be seen as the crucible of *francophone literatures,* the moment when they flourished at a rate never before approached in the non-European French-speaking world. I want to explain why I use the plural term *francophone literatures* rather than the singular *francophone literature,* preferred by the US academic discipline.

The plural, while it does not fully avoid the amorphous category "francophone literature," which lumps all the French-language writers outside metropolitan France into a single undifferentiated mass,[22] at least points to the vastness and variety of literary production in French. Conceptualizing francophone literatures in the plural also diversifies French-language literary production, implying multiplicity rather than uniformity. I use the word *francophone* because it makes sense for the time period and the geographical focus of *The Quebec Connection*. Indeed, the period of the 1950s through the 1970s straddles the end of the French empire, and it represents a time when French was still spoken as a lingua franca among the colonized and formerly colonized (as well as settlers, as in Quebec). And with the book's focus on Quebec, where the French language represented a point of cultural and identitarian revindication, *francophone* is apt and productive.[23]

I also use the term *francophone* because it continues to invite criticism even as it remains widely used in academic discourses and taxonomies.[24] This book's intervention inscribes itself in the wake of Françoise Lionnet and Shu-Mei Shih's *Creolization of Theory*, whose introduction argues that the US discipline of "francophone studies" or "francophone literature" derives from impulses similar to those that shaped ethnic studies: it is "racially marked" (13). Essentially, Lionnet and Shih argue, the term *francophone studies* is an obfuscating misnomer for "non-white French studies"; *francophone* as a label for a literary corpus or a field of studies masquerades as a linguistic definition, whereas it in fact delineates a racial (or ethnic) distinction. I call this double movement the *linguistic trick*, locating it at the convergence of the concepts of the linguistic turn and what David Kazanjian terms the *colonizing trick*.[25] The term *francophone* stages an elision, a universalizing euphemism of sorts—euphemistic in the sense of a universalism that "assimilates within itself all forms of cultural diversity into a concept of Culture [and thus] hides geographic, racial, and other differences," in the words of Lionnet and Shih (*Creolization* 15). Ultimately, the *francophone* of *francophone studies* or *francophone literature* performs the double gesture of bringing attention to a literature that has been considered marginal compared with hexagonal literature while simultaneously masking the fundamental power relations (defined in racial terms) that structure hexagonal literary centrality and privilege. In other words, francophone studies features "marginal" literature and yet, by suppressing the specifics of racial difference, hides the mechanisms that have marginalized it.[26] The recourse to language, to the "French sounds" encoded in the word *francophone*, appositely describes (at least one of) the language(s) of composition of the writers and intellectuals labeled "francophone,"[27] but it also leaves unspoken one of the characteristics that structures the racially determined field of francophone studies; it tricks us into sublimating questions of race and racial power relations into a question of language.[28] This racial inequality across French-speaking spaces is precisely what the authors I study were at pains to make evident in their solidary inter-writing.

The same linguistic trick that overdetermines francophone literature in the American academy leaves Quebec in a kind of limbo. Perceived as a white space, Quebec does not appeal to the same theorizing motivations as non-majority-white regions where French is spoken—namely, Africa, the Caribbean, and Asia. This book examines the eccentric position of Quebec within francophone studies by analyzing the tropological virtuosity that independence-era French-language writers used to understand and accommodate Quebecois anticolonial solidarity.[29] The first chapter examines the Martinican writer Aimé Césaire's plays (published between 1956 and 1973) as a sequence of tropological experiments with French-language solidarity. It compares Césaire's plays with the 1972 lectures he gave in Quebec City, where he used poetic excerpts to articulate a functional solidarity with the Quebecois public, who had, much to his surprise, adopted him as a symbolic father in their quest for cultural affirmation and political independence. The second chapter reads the Quebecois Hubert Aquin's 1968 novel *Trou de mémoire* with an eye to the latent mixed-race future resulting from an interracial solidarity that the novel expresses as metaphorical instability. The third chapter considers the 1974 Quebecois publication of a text censored and seized in France in 1972—the essay *Main basse sur le Cameroun: Autopsie d'une décolonisation,* by the Franco-Cameroonian author Mongo Beti—and focuses particularly on the similes and analogies that structure the solidary paratexts surrounding it. The fourth chapter traces the shift in the Moroccan author Driss Chraïbi's genre and style back to his year spent in Quebec and, zeroing in on its Canadian similes, situates his famous 1972 novel *La civilisation, ma mère!* . . . in the context for which it was originally commissioned: as a French-as-a-second-language textbook for Canadian anglophones. Locating *La civilisation* in this original framework decontextualizes French as a language of conquest in the Maghreb and reconceptualizes it as a language of resistance in Quebec.

The main authors whose texts are examined here are all men. There are several reasons for this. I address this particularly in the chapter on Hubert Aquin, but it bears explaining here. On an abstract, discursive level, independence-era solidarity, as it emerged from anticolonial reflexion and resistance, was haunted by empire's own masculine structures. For example, "virgin" territories were explored and appropriated by men, whose discourse relied on gendered, sexual metaphors of penetration and possession; colonial subjects were feminized as they were subjugated and controlled.[30] For some men who were colonial subjects, rebellion against imperial discourse thus became a reclamation of their masculinity. Of course, women also rebelled and imagined alternatives to empire; Annette Joseph-Gabriel's *Reimagining Liberation: How Black Women Transformed Citizenship in the French Empire* (2020), for example, examines such instances.

But an examination of *solidarité* must contend with the fact that the very vocabulary of solidarity in French tends to be gendered. As the texts analyzed in *The Quebec Connection* make explicit attempts at articulating transnational, transracial solidarity, they work within a tradition that has metaphorized solidarity as *fraternité* or as *filiation,* a tradition where the absent vocable for "solidary person" is frequently *frère*. Mireille Rosello has remarked on the gendered nature of metaphorical language defining Aimé Césaire's influence, for example, pointing out that if Césaire is considered a father figure, his descendants are invariably sons: "The gender-specific allusion to male offspring seems to dominate" (Rosello 78). Moreover, the transnational solidarities analyzed here are associated with macropolitical models that are overwhelmingly represented as masculine exchanges, in contrast to "the nation writ small," as Susan Andrade's brilliant title terms women authors' insights into national politics through family metaphors. The other domain on which these independence-era solidarities drew is labor, and as Sembene's above-quoted dedication suggests, this was generally a masculine field—"à tous les syndicalistes et à leurs compagnes," writes Sembene, suggesting a paradigm in which men work and women accompany. Sembene's pointed inclusion of syndicalists' *compagnes* is part and parcel of the feminist agenda that defines his work,[31] and yet it also reveals the typically gendered nature of labor and of union solidarity at that time and in that context.

The overwhelming masculinity of independence-era French-language solidarity emerges as a flaw, as chapter 2 makes clear. I return to this failing in the coda, which considers the question of what happened to textual francophone solidarity after the independence era, analyzing muted vestiges of that era appearing in the Tunisian filmmaker Nouri Bouzid's 1997 film *Bent familia*. The film, which contemplates the ideals of independence with nostalgia, critiques some of the limitations of independence-era

20   The Quebec Connection

solidarities (e.g., their hypermasculinity) and attempts to nurture some of the period's old hopes.

Through an analysis of tropological articulations of solidarity in these texts (Césaire's, Aquin's, Beti's, Chraïbi's, and Bouzid's), *The Quebec Connection* offers a model for understanding the workings of independence-era solidarity in francophone literatures. These texts bear witness to a broader solidary movement, and while their idiosyncrasies may reveal differences as much as similarities, they represent a pattern of attempts at solidary expression that defined the period. The poetics of solidarity this book examines offers precise and eloquent evidence of both the possibilities and the limits of shared language as a site for transnational political agency.

## On Solidary Reading

If the act of writing solidarity requires sustained experimentation with figurative language's ability to establish (inexact) likenesses, then reading solidarity means interpreting those figures. I would like to conclude this introduction by framing solidarity as a kind of ur-trope for literary analysis and proposing the concept of solidary reading. It is particularly productive to consider solidary reading as offering a dialectical counterpoint to the destructive impulses of criticism, what Paul Ricoeur termed the *hermeneutics of suspicion*. Solidarity's oscillation between sincerity and suspicion becomes a useful metacritical position to adopt especially in understanding the types of texts *The Quebec Connection* addresses, texts that explicitly thematize solidarity. This is because solidary reading parallels the linguistic work of the authors studied in this book, authors who use language simultaneously to imagine solidarity and to show its flaws or impossibilities. A solidary critique, then, must likewise operate in two directions at once: it must be sincerely attuned to the real possibilities alive in the texts for creating better political imaginaries or better modes of being in community,[32] while at the same time maintaining the distance represented and made necessary by the linguistic nature of any intervention. Given the asymptotic nature of solidarity, of course, formulating or understanding the solidary possibilities and universes latent in texts remains an approximative gesture. This kind of critical position is not new, but I propose that consciously articulating it as a solidary dialectical oscillation between embrace and suspicion will prove useful.

Let us imagine a solidary reading of the symbolic implications of the 1965 attempt to dynamite the Statue of Liberty, the plot that united the

Quebecois sovereigntist revolutionary with Harlem's Black Liberation Front. For the conspirators, the Statue of Liberty functioned as a multisymbolic object. For members of the Black Liberation Front, it would have represented an American conception of "liberty" based, among other things, on the enslavement, exploitation, and incarceration of black bodies. But the Statue of Liberty is also a nineteenth-century French construction; in this light, and particularly for the Quebecois revolutionary, it would have represented a French ideal of "liberty" based, among other things, on the French imperial/colonial occupation of Africa, Asia, and the Caribbean. So the American "liberty" against which the Harlem revolutionaries rebelled was conjoined—symbolically, through gift giving, and historically, through economic and political ties—to a French colonialist/imperialist *liberté* that likewise excluded the exploited bodies of slaves and colonized peoples. The statue stands as a commemoration of a nineteenth-century alliance of Western hegemony, euphemistically labeled "liberty" to better mystify the massive inequalities on which it rested. The transnational revolutionaries' decision to try to blow up the statue represents, therefore, a solidary Black Power act but also a symbolic action against France, against the French colonial powers of the nineteenth century and their present-day effects. The preempted explosion would have been a gesture against French (actual and cultural) imperialism as well as an attack on (white) America. Solidary reading seeks out these parallels and, above all, works to perceive the desired world that any solidary text, action, or expression has hoped to accelerate into being.

Of course, an attempted act of symbolic vandalism also deserves (and receives, when it receives any attention at all) a critical reading conducted through the channels of exclusive suspicion. In light of the much more recent attack on New York City, it even begins to resemble terrorism. The suspicious aspect of solidary reading too must account for the violence and material damage intended or done in the attempt to bridge the gap between present desire and idealized future. A solidary reading merely vouchsafes the possibility of interpreting an act that has become despicable *also* as a desire for revolutionary solidarity against Western capitalist hegemony and as an imagination of alternative futures. Our solidary reading restores to the vandalism-that-wasn't "le germe d'un univers" (Bachelard 1), which its perpetrators had imagined would blossom from the obliteration of the symbol of a tainted liberty.

# 1 "Interior Geographies"
## Solidary Locations of Aimé Césaire's Poetics

PERHAPS NO literary figure emblematizes transcontinental francophone fellow feeling better than the Martinican poet, essayist, playwright, and politician Aimé Césaire. This chapter examines Césaire's plays, which dramatize independence either directly (*La tragédie du roi Christophe, Une saison au Congo*) or address anticolonial resistance more broadly (*Et les chiens se taisaient, Une tempête*), and compares them with the essays Césaire gave as lectures in 1972 in Quebec City, in which he responds to Quebecois hopes for independence.[1] Thematically, Césaire's plays and Quebec City lectures span centuries and continents, questioning francophone solidarity's moorings in the Caribbean, Africa, and North America by investigating the colonial end times that shaped three distinct moments in which after-colonial imaginaries gained material purchase: the Haitian Revolution and independence, Congolese independence, and Martinique and Quebec's deliberations on national determination.

While Césaire's political position with regard to Martinique was not sovereigntist,[2] the plays and Quebec City lectures show that independence nevertheless remained a serious concern of his through the long independence era. Moreover, these texts' iterative attempts at imagining transnational liberatory solidarity suggest that for Césaire the question of independence is closely linked to that of tongue ties—of connections to French-speaking spaces across the globe—articulating an unusual mixture of hope for and doubt about the possibilities of French-language solidarity. Paradoxically, the dusk of empire represents a moment for Césaire when the French tongue was positioned to serve as a global linking tool even as France's imperial role waned. His texts return again and again to the possibility of solidarity as an antidote to the French empire's radically unequal modes of human relation, but this possibility remains asymptotic, without reaching a conclusive and fully coherent model for solidarity.

At the heart of these textual investigations into the solidary possibilities afforded by the French language lies the issue of race: to what extent is solidarity an outgrowth or a form of *négritude?* To what extent is *négritude* defined by attempts at solidarity? Césaire's conception of *négritude* oscillates between mooring itself in racial identity, specifically in blackness or in African roots, and designating a power-relation abstraction articulated through race, as when Césaire affirms that self-designated Quebecois "white negros" "had understood what negritude was all about" (*Discours . . . suivi de Discours sur la négritude* 81). In his plays, Césaire experiments with multiple tropes that present solidarity as simultaneously a hopeful necessity and an impossible ideal; the plays figure solidarity as a desire that can only ever be tropologically expressed, an aspiration that takes shape through the abstraction of poetics. These plays, the adoption of Césaire's theories by white Quebecois intellectuals, and Césaire's use of abstraction to respond to that solidary appropriation in his Quebec City lectures illustrate that a shared poetics is the necessary ingredient that enables French-speaking people to formulate interracial solidarity as an "interior geography," affectively uniting distant and racially distinct locations.

The concept of "interior geography" is repurposed from an interview Césaire gave the journalist Nicole Zand in 1967: "L'Afrique, même si je ne la connais pas bien, je la sens. Elle fait partie de ma géographie intérieure" (Zand 13). If, for Césaire, "interior geography" constitutes an affective link ("je la sens") connecting the diaspora to the African continent, this chapter pluralizes the term to suggest the multiple locations of francophone solidary imaginaries. The French-speaking continents form the landscape in which Césaire attempts to ground solidarity. Césaire returns over and over to certain tropes—bodies becoming land and metaphors of landscape, water, and animals—that show his attempt to territorialize solidarity, on a figurative or abstract level. This chapter suggests that these tropes form the intercontinental "interior geographies" of possible solidarities, or rather, of hopes and nostalgias for solidarity.

Solidarity, at times interracial and at others intraracial, emerges from Césaire's historically deep, discursively imagined map of the French language as simultaneously necessary (multiply sought and imagined), impossible (unfeasible under the circumstances structuring each text), and transcendent, in that solidarity can exist beyond the diegesis of each text, in the potential for performance. Each of Césaire's plays and Quebec City lectures forms an incisive critique of solidarity, recognizing its fantasies and insisting on its contingency; and yet they perform a relentless desire for it, underscoring Césaire's ongoing investment in exploring how solidarity might redress historical violence and inequity.

Products of this exploration, the works analyzed in this chapter track race as always already intertwined with the problems of slavery, colonialism, and capitalism as they defined and shaped the French-speaking world. I focus especially on the four plays—*Et les chiens se taisaient, La tragédie du roi Christophe, Une tempête,* and *Une saison au Congo*—that narrate the foundational moments of francophone anticolonial solidarity: the Haitian Revolution, its aftermath, and the independence era. Theater emerges, for Césaire, as a creative domain located between reality (politics) and poetry, a genre in which to attempt to understand historical events imaginatively. As Romuald Fonkoua establishes in his magisterial intellectual biography of Césaire,

> Le théâtre apparaît comme un espace de liberté de création à nul autre pareil. . . . Mettre en scène des héros historiques comme le Congolais Lumumba, le Haïtien Christophe ou l'Américain Caliban, c'est exposer toutes les pieces d'un dossier historique. Elles permettront d'interroger la réalité en connaissance de cause: de comprendre le sens de l'échec du roi en Haïti, d'interroger les raisons de la chute du Premier ministre du Congo, de réfléchir à la défaite de Caliban. . . . Ce théâtre est "politique" en ce qu'il permet, en un seul lieu, d'avoir accès à l'empathie et à la critique, de comprendre et d'interroger les personnages historiques et leurs actions, de soutenir les points de vue, intérieur et extérieur, sur les faits. (Fonkoua 341–44)

Césaire's theater thus forms the ground for working through political ideas like emancipation and solidarité. Fonkoua adds further, "Le mot littéraire forge une conviction, trace un chemin, construit un objectif ou pallie un manque" (359). I will show that Césaire's plays express his solidary convictions, trace possible ways of constructing or reaching for solidarity, and alleviate the lack of linguistic articulations of solidarity.

The plays attempt to anchor francophone solidarity solidly in the Caribbean and Africa, a racialized territorialization with which Césaire came face to face when he presented his 1972 lectures at Laval University and was forced to grapple with Quebec's appropriations of *négritude*. The texts examined in this chapter represent a sequence of conceptual and rhetorical experiments that demonstrates a progression of thought for Césaire; trying on concepts of race and solidarity in his plays led up to and prepared him for the challenges of the lectures.

The performativity of Césaire's plays and the Laval lectures connects these intraracial and interracial forms of solidarity: the (sometimes potential, sometimes actual) live connection of performance makes possible audience identification with characters' diegetic aspirations, elaborating a tentative geography of French-language solidarity that attempts to bridge race and class difference. At the same time, in both plays and lectures, metaphors problematize solidarity's interracial and interclass aspirations in the context of global capitalism; aspects of performance such as ironic distance or implied accusations of the audience's complicity further emphasize this problematization. Césaire's four plays thus simultaneously construct and deconstruct solidarity, their tropes critiquing solidarity's flaws and impossibilities even as solidarity forms the structuring hope of the plays' central characters. As the plays' tropes and narrative threads dismantle interracial solidarity in the face of capitalism, colonialism, and the violence of slavery, performances of the plays—and even the textually embedded *potential* for those performances—can create the space for reflection on a poetics of contingent solidarity.

From the perspective of performance, Césaire's Quebec City lectures, given in 1972, at about the time when he was finishing the last set of significant revisions to *Une saison au Congo,* shore up the plays' progressive emphasis on textual solidarity as a basis for performative solidarity. Specifically, the extant (published and videotaped) Quebec City presentations define a similar form of contingent solidarity, a solidarity in which connection via text manifests with Césaire's presence and his response to the audience's political desire. This chapter analyzes Césaire's plays and Quebec City lectures first as texts and second as performances, deciphering the geographies and histories of the solidarities that these works tentatively construct and investigating which solidarities their performances can and cannot deliver.

### Can't See the Forest for the (Dead) Trees: Impossible Solidarity in *Et les chiens se taisaient*

The development of Césaire's dramatic works indexes the evolution of solidarity as an asymptote, an ethics that is impossible but devoutly desired. Let us begin with *Et les chiens se taisaient: Tragédie,* Césaire's first play, in which a vision of solidarity forms the crux, the central hope of the text. *Et les chiens se taisaient* evolved out of a lyrical oratorio on which Césaire started working as early as 1943.[3] The original text told the story of the Haitian Revolution,[4] with Toussaint Louverture as its martyrical-heroic central character. After thirteen years of intense manipulation and reworking, during which Césaire published sections of the lyrical drama as shorter poems and as a radio play, *Et les chiens se taisaient* was published in 1956 in the form in which it is now known. It presents the story of the anonymous Rebel, an enslaved revolutionary condemned to execution for the murder of his master and unable to persuade his mother and his lover of the purposeful, sacrificial nature of his impending death. At the heart of the play lies the problem—expressed through arboreal metaphors—of what the Rebel's sacrifice represents: he imagines his suffering as the blooming of a metaphorical forest from which solidarity will grow, while his jailers see his body as an isolated and insignificant piece of deadwood. The play, despite the jailers' voices, intimately links the Rebel's sacrifice with the Caribbean's emergence as a place of anticolonial resistance. Solidarity in *Et les chiens se taisaient*, Césaire's first experiment in the theatrical representation of solidarity, emerges as a vision of living matter that motivates personal sacrifice in the name of social transformation—a transformation that falls short of being fulfilled but that nevertheless defines a region at its anticolonial beginnings.

The Rebel's vision of solidarity, an abstract ideal, forms part of what he imagines as a historical dialectic, a chain of cause-and-effect events that necessitates violence and the sacrifice of his own life in order to achieve a future characterized by transcendent equality for all—an equality Césaire links, metaphorically, to the territory of the Caribbean. Within this envisioned dialectic, solidarity exists for the Rebel as an earthy metaphor that gives meaning and direction to his isolation and his impending death while at the same time localizing him and his vision of antislavery unity in the soil and flora of the Caribbean island where he has rebelled. For the Rebel, solidarity is the ethos of an idealized Caribbean future, which he imagines will come once the vengeance of the slaves is appeased.

The Rebel's dialectic of social change begins with the violence of slavery, which calls for a violent rebellion. The faraway cries of "Mort aux Blancs!" (55) that he hears in the distance emblematize that violent reaction to violent oppression, echoing the Rebel's own earlier violence—the murder of his white master—and defining the racial nature of power in the Caribbean (and the francophone world). The physical distance separating the jailed Rebel from these faraway cries spatializes the temporal distance, the dialectical phase that differentiates him from the still-violent crowds of rebellious slaves; in the present of the play, the Rebel, leader of rebels, has rejected the cry, recognizing that "Haïr c'est encore dépendre"

(56). Violence for the Rebel is structured by an internal, dialectical need to be surpassed, which he expresses as organic growth:

> Pour moi,
> je ne l'accepte ce cri que comme la chimie de l'engrais
> qui ne vaut que s'il meurt
> à faire renaître une terre sans pestilence, riche, délectable, fleurant non l'engrais mais l'herbe toujours nouvelle. (57)

Vengeance against the white owners is necessary to end enslavement, the Rebel acknowledges, but it is a catalyst (fertilizer) for change, not the change itself, which he metaphorically grounds in the Caribbean soil as the growth of forever-new grass. For himself, the Rebel has transcended violence and its raw cry in a dialectical movement that sees his imprisonment as self-sacrifice and equates it with imminent growth. His present suffering represents for him the connection between the violent revolutionary tactics he has renounced (without denying their past usefulness) and the revolution of the social order into an idealized future, which he can imagine only through images of local rootedness. This local rootedness, for the Rebel, is figured *as* solidarity; the landscape itself becomes a conceptual equivalent of the social bonds he yearns for. The envisioned solidary Caribbean forms the "interior geography" of his desired peace.

The rich lawn of revolution ("l'herbe toujours nouvelle"), the ultimate transformative objective of the Rebel's rebellion and the teleological end of his dialectic, morphs into a metaphorically interracial forest. Once again, this new image roots the prospect of unity in an abstract vision of the soil the Rebel stands on:

> Je suppose que le monde soit une forêt. Bon!
> Il y a des baobabs, du chêne vif, des sapins noirs, du noyer blanc;
> je veux qu'ils poussent tous, bien fermes et drus,
> différents de bois, de port, de couleur,
> mais pareillement pleins de sève et sans que l'un empiète sur l'autre,
> différents à leur base
> mais oh!
>    *(extatique)*
> que leur tête se rejoigne oui très haut dans l'éther égal à ne former pour tous
>   qu'un seul toit
>     je dis l'unique toit tutélaire! (57)

At the teleological end of his dialectic of violence and reconciliation, the Rebel metaphorically envisions future solidarity as a densely unified forest canopy composed of trees representing the French-speaking hemisphere (African baobab and American live oak) growing without impinging on one another and joining to make a protective roof. This imagined solidarity is metaphorically transracial (black fir tree and white walnut tree) and provides a way of transcending racism by focusing on the common sap that makes the trees intensely alive. But the Rebel's metaphor demonstrates an instability indicative of solidarity's slippery nature. If trees are at first metaphorized as peoples cohabiting peacefully, they soon become the structure *under which* people will find shelter. The metaphor slips from one frame to another.[5] Although he sacrifices his life for it, the Rebel cannot imagine interracial solidarity as a single, coherent metaphorical mechanism; his dialectic of violence, sacrifice, and reconciliation evolves toward a teleological end that is structurally unstable. Interracial solidarity, the disjointed metaphor suggests, cannot be imagined from within the context of colonial capitalism and the system of plantation slavery in which the Rebel's dialectic is rooted.

Before we look more closely at how the play critiques colonial capitalism, let us investigate further the mechanism of sacrifice that corresponds to the second moment of the Rebel's dialectic. The Rebel's understanding of this sacrificial moment is steeped in imagery linked to the Caribbean territory where his struggles are taking place:

> Je démêle avec mes mains mes pensées qui sont des lianes sans contracture, et je salue ma fraternité totale.
> Les fleuves enfoncent dans ma chair leur museau de sagouin
> des forêts poussent aux mangles de mes muscles
> les vagues de mon sang chantent aux cayes
> je ferme les yeux
> toutes mes richesses sous mes mains
> tous mes marécages
> tous mes volcans
> mes rivières pendent à mon cou comme des serpents et des chaînes précieuses. (84)

The Rebel imagines absolute solidarity ("je salue ma fraternité totale"—note the Rebel's gendered, masculine imagination of solidarity) as emerging from a sacrificial conjoining of himself with a specifically Caribbean American landscape, including Caribbean-specific sagoin monkeys and cays along with lianas, swamps, and volcanoes. As the Rebel discursively *becomes* Caribbean topography, flora, and fauna, what emerges is the image of a tortured body into whose flesh rivers thrust, whose muscles harden into trees and feed forests. As rivers hang snake-like and jewel-like around his neck, the intimate connection between man and land hovers on the cusp of venomous peril and exquisite bondage. The Rebel's painful identification with the Caribbean landscape—or, perhaps, the metaphorization of his pain as the Caribbean—performs the sacrifice that he hopes will ultimately bring about his vision of community as a solidary canopy. For him, the nature of human solidarity is deeply linked to the specificities of the land; the "total fraternity" he dreams of must work, however painfully, through the material conditions of the Caribbean, including the abundance of the natural world and the violence of human relationships that developed to exploit this abundance.

The play, however, makes it clear that the Rebel's desire to expiate the violence of the past is unfeasible and that his metaphorical understanding of his role is flawed. His lover (l'Amante), who tries to dissuade him, accuses him of playing "à te sculpter une belle mort . . . mais au fond de toi-même tu sais bien que les choses ne changeront pas" (60). Her ultimate challenge, "Est-ce que l'homme sera jamais plus proche que l'arbre du paysage?" (60–61), seeks to assert man's distance from the land, to unmetaphorize and unravel the Rebel's hopes for transformation through sacrificial identification with the landscape. L'Amante's insistence on the Rebel's humanness and on the value of his life rather than the value of his death represents another form of resistance against colonial capitalism, which values enslaved persons as laboring property. "Déclarons les esclaves être meubles," Louis XIV made clear in Article 44 of the Code Noir, conjuring images of sculpted and polished wood—nothing like the Rebel's living forest. L'Amante's rejoinder seems to declare that sacrificial metaphorization of the slave as inanimate object, and also as an element of the very landscape the settler colonizers exploit, plays too easily into French slavers' hands.

Colonial forces represented in the play manifest the Code Noir's method of valuing the slave as nonhuman. Furthermore, they renew the tree imagery that l'Amante dismisses when she tries to assert the Rebel's personhood. The colonial forces are represented most concretely by the Rebel's jailers: a couple, a man and a woman, whose beatings, which he takes in stoic silence, cause the Rebel's death. The colonial setting here preempts any communication that might occur between the Rebel and his jailers; the latter cannot understand the former as a human, and thus the Rebel's courageous silence is taken as proof of his nonhumanness. Meanwhile, the jailers' informal violence descends to infantile diction ("Dis c'est marrant le sang rouge sur la peau noire" [110]), further ruling out the possibility of any significant verbal exchange. The jailers' casual viciousness extends to the tropes they use to express their relation to the Rebel. Specifically, they articulate their easy dismissal of the Rebel's suffering by comparing him to "une bûche," a log, a piece of dead tree, which simultaneously dehumanizes him, nixing the Rebel's exalted vision of his suffering as sacrifice, and forestalls his hope for transcendence by transforming his image of a living, solidary forest into one of felled trees. Starting a sentence with a lowercase letter—which, in a play where typography varies fluidly, can signify intensified disdain—the Geôlière exclaims, "bûche; quelle bûche. C'est une bûche te dis-je . . . une drôle de race ces nègres . . . crois-tu que nos coups lui fassent mal? en tout cas ça ne marque pas (*elle frappe*)" (109–10, ellipses in original). The Rebel's stoic refusal to cry out is interpreted as inanimateness, and his yearning for community, his desire to become solidary forest through sacrifice, becomes a truncated lifelessness in the eyes of the jailers.

Even as the Rebel claims to have reached a level of transcendent communication through self-sacrifice—"et j'ai bu de l'urine, piétiné, trahi, vendu/et j'ai mangé des excréments/et j'ai acquis la force de parler/plus haut que les fleuves/plus fort que les désastres" (109)—the jailers refuse to hear his speech as a signifying system with communicative power; they are deaf to his vision of an interracial solidary language. In fact, the Geôlier responds to the existence rather than the content of the words: "Dis donc il se fout de nous le moricaud . . . bien sûr qu'il fait le fou./plus fort, encore plus fort" (109, ellipsis in original). For the jailers, the Rebel is defined only by his blackness ("moricaud"), which renders him incapable of having any message beyond mad antics ("faire le fou"). By focusing on his subjection and by considering him a nonperson, the jailers render impossible the admixture of rebellion and sacrifice the Rebel had imagined would facilitate transcendent, unificatory communication. His sacrifice cannot be transformative; it cannot bring about his fusion with an imagined forest of united human interests because the jailers already see him, even alive, as a different part of the forest—as deadwood. His magical transformation through suffering into a shiny, slithery, sparkling new landscape is for them a matte, colorless, lifeless one. They forestall his metaphor, assigning him to the forest floor before his death can elevate him to a visionary forest canopy. Notice that in this play Césaire gives a metaphorical structure into the hands of both the Rebel and the jailers. This experiment in what a common language can accomplish, however, reaches a rather grim conclusion; sharing French does not lead to understanding or overcoming the colonial and capitalist barriers to solidarity.

The jailers' reduction of the sacrificial living tree of man to a log metaphorizes a typified European capitalist mode of interaction with the Caribbean world. European colonizers, the play's metaphorical structure suggests, approached the Caribbean with an eye to what could be extracted from it (trees grow; logs can be sold). This reductive, for-profit vision represents an attitude entirely different from the Rebel's dream of merging with the landscape. And in fact, barely hidden behind the jailers' murder of the Rebel are the very real vested interests of European planters. The Rebel's death is necessary precisely because his vision of unity, of the "equal ether" of his solidary canopy, runs counter to the interests of the landowners who need slaves as property, not as equals, to maximize their profits. The vested capitalist interests that define the Caribbean and that form the backdrop to the Rebel's death subtend the play, providing insight into a world system that requires the free labor of enslaved people defined as nonhumans, or, in other words, of slaves whose labor is hidden by their nonhumanness even as it reaps profit for their owners.

Sublimated labor, and the exorbitant profits it enables colonialists to collect, furnishes the play's context; in turn, the play explicitly lays out the transoceanic capitalist network that sustains these profits. A group of colonial bishops, representing the Catholic mission associated with capitalism's intrusion into the American continent,[6] personifies this exploitative relationship. As the bishops totter briefly onto the stage, they utter a series of bizarre non sequiturs. The first bishop exclaims, "Quelle époque: mes enfants vous avez fait là une belle boucherie" (17). With detachment and irony ("une belle boucherie"), he evaluates colonialism and deems it to have been carnage. Continuing this series of unrelated clerical affirmations, a second bishop exclaims, "Une époque étonnante mes frères: la morue terreneuvienne se jette d'elle-même sur les lignes" (17). Here, the second bishop comments on European capitalism's surprisingly easy revenue. For him, the nature of European profits is miraculous, magical: the fish jump on the line to be caught. The magic comes, however, simply from the fact that the labor that produces the profits is mystified through the brutal dehumanization of the workforce. Furthermore, the second bishop's comment also reveals the land and ocean territory covered by capitalism: the early capitalist French Atlantic.[7] The carnage taking place in the Antilles is intrinsically related to the cod fishing in the North Atlantic; they feed each other, monetarily and also literally, since slaves were fed salt cod, supplied by the northwest corner of the Atlantic quadrangle. The jumping cod symbolizes the maw of capitalism, its power to press on toward profit, to mystify into nonexistence the suffering of those whose labor produces capital. In a way, the fourth bishop's abstruse conclusion, following the previous statements, summarizes the state of capitalism as it links the New World to Africa and Europe: "Une époque phallique et fertile en miracles" (18), he declaims, as the other bishops gesture to the audience to suggest that he has lost his mind. But in his madness, the fourth bishop echoes the discourse of exploration and colonialism in the sixteenth through the eighteenth century, which allegorized the encounter with the New World by gendering European invasion as masculine and new territory as feminine, as Anne McClintock shows in the paradigm-shifting monograph *Imperial Leather*.

Within the context of Atlantic capitalism, the Rebel's imagined interracial solidarity is utterly unattainable. Any vision of equality threatens capitalism's necessary mystification because it unsettles the system's reliance on an invisible labor force, invisible specifically because its humanity is denied in the context of an edict-enforced inequality. The play portrays rebellion and hope for change as chimeras inhabiting bodies that are paradoxically denied the possibility of thought and communication, all within a rapid and global flow of capital. The dominant metaphors of the bishops' passage onstage (butchery, cod, male fertility) complement the wood and forest metaphors discussed thus far, fashioning the symbolic order of the play along the lines of colonial capitalist tropes and renewing the "deadwood" metaphor's dehumanization of slaves. The absurd bishop scene concludes Césaire's experiment, which had identified solidarity with the communicative transcendence of a living forest, by grimly reasserting the total impossibility of communication between the colonizers and the beings they consider inanimate cogs in a capital-producing system.

The play's overall movement, however, is to freeze the flow of capital and to allow the Caribbean to emerge as more than an appendage to Europe's tentacular system of wealth extraction. If the Rebel's death can lead to anything, the play suggests (or if the Haitian Revolution represents anything, we understand), it is the hoped-for possibility of existence in a mode other than capitalist exploitation. The play ends with the Rebel lying face down, his arms spread out, as the two narrators (le Récitant et la Récitante) call out to the forests, the rivers, and the plants of the Caribbean islands, eventually merging with them in the light of a brilliant sunrise: "Je suis une de vous, Iles!/(*Le Récitant et la Récitante vacillent sur leurs jambes puis s'effondrent, le choeur sort à reculons./Vision de la Caraïbe bleue semée d'îles d'or et d'argent dans la scintillation de l'aube*)" (124). The narrators' role throughout has been to relate and comment on the Rebel's journey to death and the sun's revolution over the island, marking the passage of time over the suffering of the land and its people. Now, as the Rebel's body lies on the forest floor in the shape of a cross, an image of martyrdom, the play itself fuses with nature. The tragedy of the Rebel's death becomes a coronation, the precious metals shining as a diadem over his prostrate body, jarringly recalling the chorus's thrice-repeated chant, "O roi debout" (35, 75, 114). The Rebel cannot become the upright king desired by the chorus precisely because his vision of interracial solidarity would make impossible the fabulous profits realized by European colonizing capitalists. Instead of a king, however, what does emerge in this final scene is a glimpse of the Caribbean islands as a self-contained whole, separate from the rest of the world. The shimmering diadem of islands into which the characters melt arises from the words of the narrators, quite distinct from the European map of the Atlantic world as an interrelated system with its component parts cannibalistically feasting on one another, all relying on the invisible labor of slaves. The Rebel's death metaphorically takes the Caribbean out of this devouring cycle, just as it physically removes his body from the labor force, crystallizing the islands as an entity in and of themselves, awaiting the beginning of a new day.

In spite of the transformative potential of the Caribbean landscape, however, an element of unease remains. The play's title, "And the dogs were silent," hovers over the entire play, unexplained by the events onstage. The dogs of the title certainly help establish the Caribbean plantation world as the setting: dogs formed an intermediary link between owners and slaves, occupying a position paradoxically parallel to that of the slaves (as property of the master, although there was some debate about whether dogs could be owned) but inimical to them (as watchdogs and trackers of runaways).[8] Within the context of the plantation world, the existence of dogs problematizes the dehumanization of slaves and the brutal treatment of those deemed nonhuman. "For Césaire," writes Jane Hiddleston in *Decolonising the Intellectual,* "the reappraisal of the borders between the human and the inhuman is not part of a project to assert the superiority of man over the non-human animal, since precisely, humans are frequently in his work compared with or associated with animals, and this association is part of his call for a mode of living within the natural world and not with a desire to master it" (255). Dogs, then, test the limits of what is considered "human," suggesting that the distinction is entirely wrongheaded. For Hiddleston, the Rebel of *Et les chiens se taisaient* "is himself linked with the dogs of the title—both the dogs of the slave masters and the dog-headed deity of the Egyptian God

Anubis" (255). In this light, the dogs of the title represent the Rebel's role as a go-between, a position he assumes in multiple ways: by approaching the slave masters first in violence and then in hopes of reconciliation, by balancing on the verge of life and death (here the reference to Anubis, the guide of souls, works particularly well), and by facilitating the emergence of a newly conceived Caribbean.

But Hiddleston's reading, while it explains the dogs' presence, does not explain their silence—*Et les chiens se taisaient*. The trope of silent dogs, silent for the unspecified sweep of time implied by the imperfect tense, suggests that the dogs, in their mediating position, are watching, lying in wait, not crying out.[9] The dogs remain spectators to the unfolding violence, and their silence implicates the real spectators of the play—the audience. The title constitutes a veiled accusation, a protest against an audience that can watch and understand the historical injustices represented in the play and yet not necessarily take a position and speak out against them and against the contemporary injustices that devolve from or that resemble the conditions of colonial capitalism. In this sense, *Et les chiens se taisaient* shows the futility of rebellious hopes for interracial solidarity, staging the audience as observers who identify with these hopes and are invited to invest emotionally in anticolonial disruption but who ultimately watch motionless as retaliatory violence is mobilized to prevent change. Césaire uses the traditional theatrical format suggested by the play's form to stir up feelings of solidarity even while calling out spectators who will not act on those feelings. The Caribbean, the title suggests, remains a test ground for solidarity for contemporary audiences; it is still the central node of interracial, interclass francophone interactions, and these interactions continue to be unbalanced and unequal. *Et les chiens se taisaient* offers a solidarity that is structured as out of reach, an asymptote for which we are ever grasping.

## Rope versus Trope: Solidarity between Abstractions of Labor in *La tragédie du roi Christophe*

Césaire's interest in the Haitian Revolution as a foundational moment for possible francophone solidarities does not end with the death of Toussaint (*Et les chiens se taisaient*) or with the declaration of independence.[10] His second play, *La tragédie du roi Christophe*, shows a preoccupation with the aftermath of revolution, with the unfolding of self-determination in the context of global capitalism. Christophe's tragedy is shaped by his position within a racialized capitalism that prevents him from forging coherent solidarities either with the European abolitionists who theoretically support him or with his own Haitian subject-workers. This section outlines Christophe's quest for a system of metaphors that would enable him to understand the human relations characterizing Caribbean capitalism, an inquiry doubled by Césaire's own quest as he experiments with metaphors that can accommodate the colonial complications of interracial solidarity.

Césaire's interest in Haiti (he spent eight months there in 1944)[11] and its revolution as a model or paradigm for independence attests to the revolution's importance in establishing the parameters of possibility for francophone political imaginaries. Haiti's struggle for independence, by extending the French Revolution's ideals of equality to include slaves, by allying itself with France at its most progressive moment, and then by breaking this alliance when reactionary forces reinstated slavery under Napoleon,[12] created the notion that solidarity could be related to the French language but not necessarily to the French nation. Nick Nesbitt names this thing that exists in French but that is not French a "universal principle" (*Caribbean Critique* 16). To establish the concept of a "Caribbean critique," for example, he explains, "Louverture does not at all identify . . . with France as a white, European seat of power. Rather, he identifies directly, without Fanonian alienation, with a universal *principle*, one that contingently happened to be articulated and defended in a revolution in France in 1789" (16). France itself does not represent the eternal embodiment of the principle, and the French tongue merely emerges as the contingent language in which this universal principle is elaborated and in which critique is articulated; it is a tool among others, privileged only by its renewed use to articulate, from the French Revolution onward, abstract universal concepts of justice and human rights.[13]

Francophone solidarity in this, its Haitian revolutionary root, is in essence a transnational revolutionary drive for the recognition of ex-slaves as human. And this is precisely the solidarity that king Christophe finds challenging to uphold in *La tragédie du roi Christophe*, faced with a kingdom caught between grand abstractions such as "humanity" and the concretely dehumanizing experiences of slavery. What emerges as a central problem is the varying degrees of abstraction that qualify solidarity, making it unstable, and the ways that race crystallizes this problem of particularity versus abstraction and makes it unavoidable, pitting the rope (of work, of labor) against the trope (of unity, of solidarity).

*La tragédie du roi Christophe*, published in 1963, explores the rise, reign, and death of Henri Christophe in the newly independent kingdom of Haiti, spanning roughly the years 1806–20. The play shows Christophe attempting to protect his people's hard-earned freedom. Paradoxically, the play suggests, in the early capitalist context of the imperial Caribbean, protecting his people's freedom means forcing them to work—in conditions that resemble slavery—on the construction of an enormous defensive stronghold, the Citadelle. *La tragédie du roi Christophe* is an investigation not only into capitalism but also into the way capitalism is intrinsically racialized, bringing to light the problem of capitalism as solidarity's ultimate horizon.

Nick Nesbitt's fine-tuned definition of capitalism is remarkably apt for understanding the (post)colonial political economy active in *La tragédie du roi Christophe*: "Capitalism . . . should be understood not primarily as a mode of (free-market) *exchange*, for which the question of *ownership* of the various forms of wealth is central (private versus state, capitalist versus proletarian), but as a *mode of production* devoted to the production of surplus value and for which the question of *labor*, as the source of that value in capitalism, is the key" ("From Louverture to Lenin" 137). Christophe's flaw, if it can be considered his flaw and not the system's, is that he sees no alternative but to join (or continue in) the course of capitalism: capitalism is his only framework. "Je réclame pour ce peuple/son droit!/sa part de chance!," he exclaims (131), oblivious to the fact that rights and luck in the context of early nineteenth-century empire are prepositionally defined as rights *over* and luck *in* monopolizing surplus value. Nesbitt, analyzing Césaire's political writings, suggests that the flaw of seeing no horizon beyond capitalism also defines Césaire's perspective. He argues that twentieth-century postcolonial (and state communist) ideology was unable to imagine a horizon beyond that of (industrial) production of surplus value; equality was (and is) understood in terms of the social distribution of wealth, without any fundamental transformation of the "telos of global capital" (139).[14] Indeed, the play's dysfunctional solidarities are firmly grounded in Césaire's interpretation of the capitalist global economy as an exhaustive structure; this structure becomes the play's truth, with rifts between characters originating in their different understandings of and positions within this truth.

The play formulates its incisive criticisms of racialized capitalism abstractly through a network of water metaphors that relate intimately to the particular mechanisms of capitalism on the island. The overarching structural metaphor in the *Tragédie* represents King Christophe's project of statehood, a capitalistic experiment, as a raft hurtling down the Artibonite River. Like a raft, the play suggests, the fledgling nation can either catch the mooring rope (the rope of this section's title, also the rope representing labor and continued participation in exploitative capitalism) or be swept out to sea. With this metaphor, Césaire critiques models of solidarity that ignore racial difference; the metaphor functions by highlighting the disadvantaged position of the Haitian ex-slaves within global capitalism.

The Artibonite appears in the *Tragédie* as simultaneously a literal river, a figurative worker, and a carrier of the symbol of the state. It is described by the Présentateur during an *intermède* between acts 1 and 2 as "le papa-fleuve de Haïti . . . Et il porte, comme pas un, le gaillard! Fragments d'épopée, . . . l'espoir et le désespoir d'un peuple" (65). The abstract binary of hope and despair inexorably carried down the river is concretized in the objects, the immense rafts, that travel from the mountains to the coast. The Artibonite facilitates the transportation "d'énormes troncs de bois liés en radeaux: c'est du campêche. . . . Cinquante mètres carrés de superficie, dix tonnes de poids, le tout flottant à moitié immergé . . . , ces kontikis[15] ne sont pas commodes à diriger. Point de voile. Point de gouvernail" (66). This ungainly, awkward, unmanageable craft represents the state Christophe must learn to maneuver.

As such a raft appears onstage in the same *intermède,* the Captain makes explicit how a people's hope and despair relate to the river, explaining to an apprentice that at the mouth of the river "on te lance une corde. Si tu la prends, ça va, tu abordes terre et tu amarres! Si tu la manques, à-Dieu-vat! il ne reste plus qu'à te jeter dans les bras de Maman D'Leau. . . . Il faut dire: adieu radeau! Les campêches, c'est pour la mer. La mer les avale et les crache. De l'autre côté, chez les Blancs d'Amérique, qu'on dit, j'ai pas été y voir" (68). The dangerous gamble the raftsmen face at the mouth of the river parallels the situation of the new nation, which navigates capitalism as the raft navigates the Artibonite. Mirroring the inexorable movement of capitalism, the river's swift current presses on and orients all interactions in the direction of profit for the powerful. The mouth of the river can symbolize any moment—because this is a system in which risk is inherent to any hope of profit—but especially the moment of independence, when the nation either finds mooring, enters the system of exchange, and stands to profit or else does not "catch the rope." If the young nation is not strong enough or skilled enough to gain a foothold in a swift and merciless capitalist system, the metaphor suggests, its profits will be lost.[16] The Captain's final assertion, "C'est pas le métier. C'est la vie," by its very inequation affirms the supremacy of work in the lives of the Haitian ex-slaves and establishes a parallel between the risks of his river work and the life of the nation. The raftsmen's work as allegory for the nation's life encapsulates the necessity and urgency of Christophe's state-building project. It also symbolizes the drastically isolating nature of the capitalist system, as each raft must find its way, alone, through the current. And while the current might force a unity among the raftsmen who discuss their dangerous craft, and while this solidarity may metaphorically unite the nation represented by the craft, this is not a solidarity in which Christophe can share. He remains isolated from his subjects (himself a force of repression that unites them against him) as well as from the world.

The image of spitting (*cracher, crachat*) is closely associated with the metaphor of capitalism as river but also extends beyond it to Chrisophe's understanding of slavery as a radical setback for his people. *La tragédie du roi Christophe* anthropomorphizes the principal mechanism of capitalism as the action of spitting: the sea swallows and *spits out* the raft's logs if the raftsmen fail to catch the mooring rope. In addition, Christophe refers to the stain of slavery as an "all-denying *gob of spit*" (Césaire's neologistic "omni-niant *crachat*" [59, emphasis added]) dehumanizing slaves as well as marking ex-slaves. Christophe further insists on the dehumanization-as-spit motif. In act 3, ill and dying, he speaks with the court jester, Hugonin, recalling his old hopes: "Parce qu'ils ont connu rapt et crachat, le crachat, le crachat à la face, j'ai voulu leur donner figure dans le monde, leur apprendre à bâtir leur demeure, leur enseigner à faire face" (139). In a running pun on *face*, Christophe here expresses his aspiration for his subjects as an overcoming of slavery's spit in the face; the metaphor of "building their dwelling" is aligned with the images of facing up to ("faire face") and making a name for oneself in the world (in French, *donner figure*, with *figure* a synonym for *face*). In this passage, it becomes clear that overcoming slavery's spit in the face is Christophe's central preoccupation, the main task he sets himself.

Within the larger context of the play, where spit metaphorically represents the operation of capitalism, Christophe's formulation of slavery as spit articulates capitalism's intrinsic racialization. Capitalism, the play suggests, carries everyone swiftly on its unavoidable current, but black people are predeterminately structured as victims of its dehumanizing mechanisms ("la victime parfaite," states the Rebel in *Et les chiens se taisaient* [46]). Christophe denounces capitalism—a capitalism that is always already racialized—as the structuring feature that sets different limits for his people than for white Europeans. Addressing his wife and his courtiers, he exclaims,

> Je demande trop aux hommes! Mais pas assez aux nègres, Madame! S'il y a une chose qui, autant que les propos des esclavagistes, m'irrite, c'est d'entendre nos philanthropes clamer, dans le meilleur esprit sans doute, que tous les hommes sont des hommes et qu'il n'y a ni Blancs ni Noirs. C'est penser à son aise, et hors du monde, Madame. Tous les hommes ont mêmes droits. J'y souscris. Mais du commun lot, il en est qui ont plus de devoirs que d'autres. Là est l'inégalité. Une inégalité de sommations, comprenez-vous? À qui fera-t-on croire que tous les hommes, je dis tous, sans privilège, sans particulière exonération, ont connu la déportation, la traite, l'esclavage, le collectif ravalement à la bête, le total outrage, la vaste insulte, que tous, ils ont reçu, plaqué sur le corps, au visage, l'omni-niant crachat! Nous seuls, Madame, vous m'entendez, nous seuls, les nègres! Alors au fond de la fosse. C'est bien ainsi que je l'entends. Au plus bas de la fosse. C'est là que nous crions; de là que nous aspirons à l'air, à la lumière, au soleil. Et si nous voulons remonter, voyez comme s'imposent à nous, le pied qui s'arcboute, le muscle qui se tend, les dents qui se serrent, la tête, oh! La tête, large et froide! Et voilà pourquoi il faut en demander aux nègres plus qu'aux autres: plus de travail, plus de foi, plus d'enthousiasme, un pas, un autre pas, encore un pas et tenir gagné chaque pas! C'est d'une remontée jamais vue que je parle, Messieurs, et malheur à celui dont le pied flanche! (59)

As Fonkoua summarizes, Christophe "doit conduire un pays, assurer son indépendance économique, avec des moyens rudimentaires forgés par trois siècles d'esclavage et de colonisation, autant dire avec rien" (335). There can be no equality when some people (black) start at the bottom of a pit and others (white) stand at the top; for this reason, Christophe must ask more of his subjects than is asked of others. For him, this is capitalism: the curse of the worker, but racially defined, a proletariat marked intergenerationally (because of the inheritance of racial traits and social station) and defined by exploitation that is validated by an imposed racial difference.

Christophe's critique of capitalism extends also to the faraway abolitionists and revolutionaries who technically support the ex-slaves' right to liberty, the "philanthropes de tous les pays, vous étrangers aux préjugés, qui reconnaissez en nous le type de l'auteur commun" (116).[17] *La tragédie* refers to these *philanthropes*[18] on two occasions without presenting them on stage, suggesting that they form the horizon of Haitian independence—distant but ideologically indicative of the new state's global position, both because they are the state's external exponents and because their universalizing idealism cannot conceive of the injustices faced by the former slaves. In a scathing critique, the play condemns a philanthropy that wants to extend the European concept of equality to the newly independent territory without considering that the concept as it exists cannot account for the evolutionary process of ex-slaves who achieved their liberty suddenly, in violence, and who must advance their interests "à grands coups d'années, à grands ahans d'années" rather than "à petits coups de siècles" (139), little by little, as the Europeans did. In the speech quoted above, Christophe decries the *philanthropes'* flawed claim that slaves, and black people more generally, are identical to white people. Christophe accuses the *philanthropes* of being armchair philosophers ("penser à son aise"), able to make such sweeping statements because they have known nothing but comfort. Christophe says the equality *philanthropes* dream of lies outside the world ("hors du monde"), outside the capitalist system that structures the circumstances of the ex-slaves' lives. The *philanthropes* love the human in the (ex-)slave abstractly, but they do not understand the particulars of that being's condition or context; the solidarity that supposedly defines their nature as *philanthropes* remains a theoretical construct, an abstraction that cannot found concrete action. The *Tragédie* reveals the capitalist bases of the inequities that make solidarity between the white *philanthropes* and the black ex-slaves an asymptotic relation, where the perspectives of the two groups fail to reach each other.

Beyond the critique of the *philanthropes'* relation to the former slaves, Christophe's speech also shows how capitalism defines the relations among Haitians. Christophe delivers this speech in reaction to his wife, who wants to protect her "children" (the Haitian people); Christophe sees his subjects not as children but as *nègres* and as workers, *his* workers. Christophe's response crystallizes his choice of the construction metaphor over the family metaphor. The Haitian people cannot be conceived of as a family precisely because of the affronts they have borne. The dehumanization that slavery constituted makes the family metaphor ill-fitting, first because this metaphor elides the fact that families cannot exist when children and adults are saleable property and second because it does not take into account the figurative *fosse*, the pit from which the former slaves must hoist themselves. The family metaphor is shown to be a "universal" European one whose universality slavery contradicts.

The process of ascension out of the metaphorical pit is *labor*, not a family affair; Christophe is thus unable to conceive of his people as anything other than workers.

This is, not coincidentally, exactly how the slavers conceived of them. Here is the flaw in Christophe's understanding of the world, a flaw caused by the capitalist system from which he sees no escape and by his resulting need to hoist his people out of the pit through the capitalist path of profit as defense. He literalizes this ascension by forcing his subjects up a mountain, carrying stones to build a fortress—the Citadelle—that will protect independence and provide a guarantee against further foreign exploitation. Christophe, then, replaces the abstract metaphor of the family, inappropriate to his reality, with a metaphor of labor that transcends figurativeness and correlates with the work he forces his subjects to accomplish. Familial allegiance based on love is thus supplanted by a connection enacted in communal work, a workers' solidarity in which Christophe, as leader forcing his subjects to labor, cannot share. Whereas he considers himself equally stained by the *crachat* of plantation slavery, the solidary "nous, les nègres" cannot withstand an independence governed by the same capitalist fundamentals as colonialism.

Part of Christophe's problem is that liberty, an abstraction, has to have several practical articulations because it is neither direct, self-evident, nor self-contained. Christophe himself (or his iron will) is the guarantor of the Citadelle, as fortress and vision of protection; the Citadelle and its cannons, then, are military guarantors of the nascent state as independent territory; and the independent state is the guarantor of the people's liberty. Liberty, which is no more than nonslavery or ex-slavery, is thus articulated over three independent hinges: a person, an edifice, and an institution. Of course, *all* liberty is articulated this way; there is nothing natural about liberty, which is always an achievement that needs to be protected. For Christophe's Haiti, however, these articulations are all yet to be. Unlike his European contemporaries, Christophe starts his rule with the opposite of inherited institutions protecting civil and personal liberties. He starts from slavery, which had articulated the status of slaves as not free—personally, through ownership by slavers; physically, through the chains and barracoons that restrained slaves' movements; and institutionally, through edicts such as the Code Noir.

Although Christophe understands his subjects' abject condition as ex-slaves, he also is separated from them by the triple articulation of their liberty, which he sees himself as responsible for realizing. He deeply distrusts his subjects, perceiving them as dangerously indolent and frivolous: "Quelque part dans la nuit, le tam-tam bat ... Quelque part dans la nuit, mon peuple danse ... Et c'est tous les jours comme ça ... Tous les soirs ... le chasseur d'hommes à l'affût, avec son fusil, son filet, sa muselière; le piège est prêt, le crime de nos persécuteurs nous cerne les talons, et mon peuple danse!" (60, ellipses in original). Christophe fears that the *chasseur d'hommes* represents the very real menace of reenslavement threatening his people. In spite of the king's clear grasp of the dehumanizing effect of slave labor on his subjects, he cannot sympathize with their resulting resistance to hard labor because his position in the articulation of his people's freedom requires him to force them to work to defend their liberty. And what the *Tragédie* points out is that despite Christophe's earnest desire to defend his subjects, the multiple articulations of liberty he undertakes—personal, physical, and institutional—are all mechanisms of capitalism. They contribute, always, to the production of surplus value, which alone is presented as able to defend Haiti. This necessity to accumulate capital from the perspective of having been themselves capital (having been enslaved persons, the property of slave-owners) is what Christophe means by starting "au fond de la fosse," with the mark of the "omni-niant crachat."

The imagery of the *crachat* forms part of the figurative network of rivers and other fluids that metaphorizes Christophe's arduous task of sustaining freedom within global capitalism. His reference to the white, European *philanthropes*, who imagine themselves in solidarity with (ex-)slaves, reminds us that they are unwitting voyagers on the same river. What the *philanthropes* fail to understand, however, is that if they do not feel the all-denying spit on themselves, they necessarily are (or their position is one of) spitting. All are participants in this global system, the play suggests: the current carries everyone in its perpetual flow of merchandise and exchange. For some, however, these exchanges entail a viscous, dehumanizing affront, while for others they represent an unrecognized right to comfort, to ease ("C'est penser à son aise," as Christophe describes the *philanthropes*). In this context, interracial solidarity remains unattainable because any solidary relation would be based on selective blindness, the *philanthropes*' failure to see and acknowledge their privileged implication in the system they theoretically oppose.

The "all-denying gob of spit" that plagues the fledgling nation is also coded into Christophe's metaphorization of the state as a boat navigating a river, which he invokes as he urges the peasants to work ever more assiduously: "Une *raque*. Vous savez ce que l'on appelle une *raque*? l'énorme fondrière, l'interminable passage de boue ... cette boue compacte, infinie . . . et ce siècle c'est la pluie, la longue marche sous la longue pluie. Oui, dans la *raque,* nous sommes dans la *raque* de l'histoire./En sortir, pour les nègres, c'est cela la liberté" (98, emphasis in original). Christophe envisions the nation's current status on the river of capitalism as going through a swamp (*raque,* emphasized with italics at his every use), the most arduous section of a ship's journey, where it must be pulled or pushed. If the rain falling on the ex-slaves as they traverse the swamp echoes the image of spit plastered on their faces, Césaire's use of the word *raque* further conjoins the parallel running metaphors of the river as capitalism and spit as its dehumanizing mechanism. The French *raque* (swamp), some have surmised, derived from the German *raus*.[19] But there is also the verb *raquer;* derived in the late thirteenth century from the onomatopoeic root *rakk-*,[20] it literally means "to spit," although nowadays it is more commonly employed metaphorically to mean "to pay up" (again an interconnection of profit and spit). Because of this lexical link, the metaphorical swamp through which Christophe wants to lead his subjects toward liberty connects neatly with the spit of capitalism he imagines staining their faces. These various images of viscid obstacles metaphorize for Christophe the suction-like resistance he feels as he tries to place his people in a position to profit in a global capitalist system. It is a struggle both for and against his subjects, *for* them in its aim to achieve and protect their liberty and *against* them in that he must pit his will against theirs as he forces them to work.

When the *philanthropes* think "outside the world," it is precisely the refraction of liberty through capitalism that they fail to grasp; the particular articulations of capitalism as it structures human life disappear behind the abstraction of "liberty." Christophe inherits a territory that was the highest-functioning (that is, the highest wealth-producing) region in the European imperial capitalistic enterprise; as such, this territory remains extremely desirable for European imperial powers. The French lawyer and chronicler Médéric-Louis-Elie Moreau de St. Méry, for example, wrote an immediately postindependence "history" of Saint-Domingue in order to have a clear record of how the French ran the plantation system. As the historian Laurent Dubois makes clear, "It was worth telling the story of Saint-Domingue, Moreau insisted. If there was to be a reconstruction of the colony, as he firmly hoped, it would have to be based on knowledge of what the ruined plantations and towns had once been, and an understanding of how the colony had functioned. . . . It was possible, Moreau believed, to make the colony once again 'a source of riches and power for France'" (Dubois 10–11). Moreau's chronicle would be ready for the moment, which he conceived as imminent, when France would recapture and resettle its colony, reenslaving black people in the process.

Christophe's sense of manic urgency is thus legitimate. When he hallucinates the Citadelle, when he names it into being, he equates it with liberty precisely because it can defend against recolonizers: "Je dis la Citadelle, la liberté de tout un peuple" (62–63). The promontory of the Citadelle becomes a crucial point on the map of the *Tragédie*'s political and geographical imaginary, at once a symbolic and an actual defender of the ex-slave's liberty. Moreover, Christophe imagines the Citadelle's functions using the metaphorical mechanism associated with capitalism: "Voyez, . . . ses bouches *crachent* la mitraille jusqu'au large des mers" (63, emphasis added). The fortress will defend against (French) naval attack, but it can only do so if it gains a foothold in a system of wealth accumulation whose metaphorical mechanism is spitting. Only from the vantage point of capitalistic profit, Christophe's words suggest, can his people's "liberty" be defended—or even imagined. And within this closed system, the (capitalist) defense of liberty for the nation paradoxically takes precedence over the construction of solidarity with the nation.

Christophe's tragedy can be summarized as an impasse: there are for him no alternatives to capitalism, which alone can preserve his people's liberty, but this liberty is no more than a de facto reenslavement for the vast majority of his subjects, their labor forming the basis of the nation's capitalist value. But Christophe's tragic impasse can also be understood in terms of levels of abstraction. For the *philanthropes*, Christophe's would-be supporters abroad, liberty exists as a total abstraction, devoid of the strictures of capitalist victimization and its rigid racial markers. Similarly, Christophe's abstract, metaphorical understanding of his nation's position within a global capitalist network cannot be communicated to his subjects, to the workers and peasants who people the play's *intermèdes* and the margins of many of the play's scenes. In reaction to Christophe's metaphor of the *raque* as the necessary obstacle his kingdom faces, a peasant grumbles, "La raque, drôle d'idée d'aller se piéter dans la raque. Une raque, ça se longe. C'est bien connu. La raque, c'est le piège" (99). Notice that whereas in Christophe's speech *raque* remains italicized with every use, the peasant de-italicizes it; the word is integrated in his language, a commonplace for him. The *raque* is an abstraction for Christophe much as *liberty* is for the *philanthropes;* he uses the metaphor *raque* to express unavoidable toil, just as they use *liberty* to express the kind of freedom to which they are accustomed, without considering the practical implications or implementation of the terms. The peasant criticizes Christophe: "Faudrait, n'oncle, savoir les fleuves" (99). Diverging from the expected phrase *connaître les fleuves,* the verb *savoir* entails a different kind of knowledge: *savoir* (as in *savoir son métier*) implies competency, experience, mastery over something. *Connaître quelque chose,* by contrast, suggests "avoir présente à l'esprit l'idée plus ou moins précise ou complète d'un objet abstrait ou concret, existant ou non" (CNRTL), implying a much more abstract knowledge. The old man is complaining that Christophe's knowledge of fluvial travel and work is learned, abstract, whereas a worker's relation to that same river is practical and born of experience. There can be no more reconciliation between Christophe and his subjects in their understanding of their plight than there can be between Christophe and the *philanthrophes;* both are structured as asymptotic relationships, where the abstraction of language promises yet fails to bridge a gap. In fact, the metaphorical gridlock surrounding the *raque* suggests that Christophe's quest for a system of metaphors that would enable him to understand, once and for all, the human relations characterizing Caribbean capitalism is doomed to failure. Linguistic abstraction cannot account for his experience nor for his position as participant, leader, guarantor of ex-slaves' liberty, and builder of a black nation.

The gap between the peasant's and the king's types of knowledge, and between the king's and the *philanthropes'*, represents the fundamental impediment to solidarity in *La tragédie du roi Christophe*. Christophe is isolated both from his subjects and from the abolitionists who theoretically support his realm, unable to forge productive solidarities with either group. As the various actors supporting independence try to bring it into being, they face one another across a chasm separating the abstract from the particular, into which the terms of their struggle for independence slip as soon as they are uttered. The play suggests that racialized capitalism, more than simply a factor that can be understood or misunderstood, is the cause of the structural problem that makes understanding and solidarity impossible. What I mean by this is that if the *philanthropes* cannot grasp the racism and the pressure of capitalism faced by Christophe and his people, and Christophe cannot grasp the material needs and working conditions of his people, it is in fact racialized capitalism that makes their comprehension impossible because it structures their positions of blindness. Racialized capitalism determines the actors' situation in the world; even if some of them try to take racialized capitalism into account as they redress its wrongs, they are always caught in its machine of abstraction from the particular. Christophe's quest for the right metaphor to express liberty is always a doomed quest because, by looking into the realm of abstract language, he is already in the realm of capitalist abstraction. Global capitalism in the age of Europe's empires, the *Tragédie* shows us, first creates blackness as a labor category to be exploited and then abstracts the blackness of labor in its creation of exchange value. Any solidarity must somehow account for this abstraction of racialized labor in its discursive and political existence, or it will have no material effect. The *Tragédie* explores solidarity's inability to escape the fundamental racism of capitalism.

Solidarity emerges from *La tragédie du roi Christophe* as a fragile, asymptotic ideal. The play accuses those who attempt it of relying on the same abstractions of life, labor, and race as capitalism; solidarity can be imagined, the *Tragédie* suggests, only when it elides the concrete differences that exist in the global system of capitalist exploitation and profit, including, especially, the suffering of black laborers. Any solidarity with these black laborers that originates from people in another position within the hierarchy is determined by racialized capitalism; even if it is presented as solidarity with the suffering of these laborers, it is in fact complicit in their suffering, since there is no standing outside the system of profit/exploitation and comfort/suffering.

## Abstractions of Difference: Intellectual and Worker Unite in Une tempête

*Une tempête,* Césaire's 1969 transposition of Shakespeare's *The Tempest,* performs, in a sense, the opposite motion from *La tragédie du roi Christophe.* Whereas the *Tragédie* constructs a richly detailed, highly particular vision of a specific moment in the Caribbean past, delving into the ways capitalism abstracts these particulars, *Une tempête* is itself a sort of abstraction, an exploration of the broad strokes of colonialism. Its geographical and temporal setting remains equivocal: Prospero is paradoxically banished to the New World by the Inquisition for surmising its existence, but characters speak with distinctly twentieth-century diction, and the actual location of Caliban's island is nebulous. *Une tempête* has been read as an allegory for African American liberation politics—Caliban demands to be called "X," and Césaire had hinted that he would write a play about African Americans—and its vagueness in terms of time and place makes it a perfect starting point from which to build allegories. In fact, unlike the *Tragédie, Une tempête* does not represent any specific event from the historical record; instead, it imagines the forces at play in the colonial relation in almost impressionistic strokes, disjointedly representing these figural forces with the precise vocabulary of twentieth-century French colonial rule (e.g., Prospero has "un arsenal anti-émeutes" [77]). The play thus tries to imagine the potential shapes of solidarity within a generalized colonial situation and outlines three archetypal figures who characterize this situation: Prospero, a malevolent white master whose cupidity is hardly hidden behind a veneer of magnanimity; Ariel, a mixed-race slave amenable to the master because he is treated reasonably well; and Caliban, an indomitably rebellious black slave (these racial gradations are specified in the *dramatis personae* as "précisions supplémentaires"). Césaire's title, *A Tempest* instead of *The Tempest*,[21] indeed, suggests that the events of the play do not represent a single fanciful story but are in fact part of a series—one among many colonial tempests that follow a similar pattern. If Césaire's other plays map the solidary potential of francophone historical moments geographically, *Une tempête* hovers over both geography and history to investigate the generic mechanics of solidarity in an abstract representation of the colonial encounter, and it does so using abstract language.

Within *Une tempête*'s theatrical investigation of the colonial relation, multiple archetypes of possible solidarities arise. The play offers, besides a reprise of an impracticable vision of total solidarity (such as the Rebel had imagined in *Et les chiens se taisaient*), a concept of unity in destruction. Specifically, Ariel envisions, in idealistic terms, a solidarity with both Prospero and Caliban. But the play bears out something similar to Caliban's vision instead: one of destructive unity through inescapable violence, a vision that is transformed in Prospero's madness at the end of the play into a delirious discursive union. Tropologically, the play constructs these various dysfunctional models of solidarity through metaphors of business, of explosion, and of impalement. *Une tempête* also offers a more functional, though limited metaphorical representation of solidarity as fraternity presenting an idealized but workable solidarity between the play's two slaves, the mixed-race (*mulâtre*) Ariel and the black Caliban.

Let us examine first the two slaves' differing visions of unity. Ariel, the island's educated slave (Prospero at one point dismisses Ariel as an intellectual: "C'est toujours comme ça avec les intellectuels" [23], he says when Ariel flinches at the suffering he is instructed to inflict), imagines himself as a potential mediating link between the antipodes represented by Prospero and Caliban: "J'ai fait souvent le rêve exaltant qu'un jour, Prospero, toi et moi, nous entreprendrions, frères associés, de bâtir un monde merveilleux, chacun apportant en contribution ses qualités propres: patience, vitalité, amour, volonté, aussi, et rigueur, sans compter les quelques bouffées de rêve sans quoi l'humanité périrait d'asphyxie" (38). An unstable hybrid between the family and the business metaphor, the "frères associés" of Ariel's imagination in fact gets telescoped further and further into unreality; his vision is a dream, a "rêve exaltant," "un monde merveilleux," but structurally it necessitates yet more dreaming: the "bouffées de rêve sans quoi l'humanité périrait d'asphyxie." Ariel's dream eats its own tail, in a sense, caught in circular, groundless hope; the businesslike brotherhood that opened the vision is unsustainable.

Caliban, by contrast, envisions an entirely different unification with Prospero: "Cette île, mon bien, mon œuvre, . . . tu la verras sauter dans les airs avec, je l'espère, Prospero et moi dans les débris" (38). His interface with Prospero is a struggle to the death, and if he cannot kill the master-magician, he wills their combined destruction, metaphorically imagined as an explosion.[22] In Caliban's vision, Ariel participates as a spectator "du haut de l'empyrée où tu aimes planer" (38); the explosion obliterating master and slave is elevated to significance in the gaze of this third consciousness, which understands Caliban's orchestration of the murder-suicide. Part of what Ariel is called on to witness is Caliban's ownership of the island ("mon bien, mon œuvre"); his work on the island and his inheritance of the land from his mother, Sycorax, make it his to dispose of.

Neither of these visions is materially achieved in *Une tempête*. After he is finally freed, Ariel disappears, never to return; for him, dreams of solidarity accompanied his condition as slave but lose significance once he is free. The vanishing of the freed slave, and of the vision of solidarity he had imagined while in captivity, resolves, in a way, the tensions brought to theatrical life in the previous two plays. The total freedom of Ariel's immaterial condition—as is typical of this abstract play, his enslavement and release are defined within a magical rather than a capitalist context—represents the horizon of solidarity's utility and possibility. Whereas the Rebel and Christophe struggle to achieve or maintain liberty in the context of a geographically defined racialized capitalism where solidarity remains vitally important yet unattainable, the freed Ariel represents a model of detached plenitude. Solidarity, *Une tempête* suggests, exhausts its purpose in the vacuum of abstraction represented by Ariel's idealized (and impossible, outside the context of abstraction and magic) freedom.

For the other two characters, however, *Une tempête* offers a different experimentation with solidary abstraction: Caliban's conception of solidarity as mutual destruction finds an echo in Prospero's mad imaginings at the play's conclusion. In the final scene, Caliban is out of sight; still enslaved by virtue of Prospero's decision to remain on the island (Césaire's major deviation from Shakespeare), he becomes Prospero's hunted enemy as the struggle to the death materializes on an islandwide battleground ("Et maintenant, Caliban, à nous deux!" [91]). Caliban's destruction, which Prospero perceives as the victory of civilization, becomes Prospero's only purpose. The "à nous deux" of Prospero's threat, however, is psychologically literalized as his obsession progresses. Indeed, Caliban's vision of destructive unity with Prospero becomes realized in the mad delirium of Prospero, who shudders alone, in a grotto, surrounded by the increasingly invasive natural world: "plus que toi et moi. Toi et moi! Toi-Moi! Moi-Toi!" (92). Prospero loses his sense of self in the hunt for Caliban, fusing with his slave in a hallucinatory reciprocity without hierarchy ("Toi-Moi! Moi-toi!"). Meanwhile, snippets of Caliban's song "LA LIBERTÉ OHÉ, LA LIBERTÉ!" drift in from offstage; Caliban has become the third-person, outside observer that he had imagined Ariel being, freed by Prospero's internalization of their struggle. Caliban's singsong mantra gives a glimpse into the other side of Prospero's hunt: Caliban, though still technically a slave, has freed himself, his reinstated power over the island symbolized by the reemergence of the animals that Prospero frenetically attempts to shoo away, screaming, "Des pécaris, des cochons sauvages, toute cette sale nature! . . . On jurerait que la jungle veut investir la grotte" (92). The visual absence of the black slave emphasizes Prospero's isolation, recalling Caliban's earlier threat: "Je t'aurai," he had told Prospero, "Empalé! Au pieu que tu auras toi-même aiguisé! Empalé à toi-même!" (88). The identitarian cul-de-sac of impalement to oneself, a gruesome trope, constitutes the other side of the coin of the master's delirium: madness engulfs Prospero, the only character of the trio who had not envisioned solidarity of any kind with his slaves, and engulfs him in a torturing bond with the despised Caliban, as Caliban himself remains nominally enslaved but escapes beyond the reach of his master.

In opposition to Ariel's ineffective dream of fraternity, to Caliban's uniting murder-suicide, and to Prospero's delirious discursive unity with Caliban, the play represents solidarity in the form of a strong, loyal bond between the two slaves; this is the play's realized solidarity. "Je sais que tu ne m'estimes guère," Ariel admits to Caliban, "mais après tout nous sommes frères, frères dans la souffrance et l'esclavage, frères aussi dans l'espérance. Tous deux nous voulons la liberté, seules nos méthodes diffèrent" (35). The brotherhood Ariel articulates with Caliban is unqualified, unlike his imagined "association" with Prospero, and Caliban, for all his disdain and rebellion, ultimately accepts and reciprocates Ariel's proffered alliance: "Je te souhaite bonne chance, mon frère" (38), he tells Ariel, voicing a desire for the success of Ariel's vision of solidarity even while he plots his own and Prospero's death. *Frère,* as in Aquin's *Trou de mémoire* (discussed in chapter 2), is the gendered metaphor chosen to stand in for the absent vocable for *solidary agent;* its affirmation of biological proximity closes a gap between people who are considered biologically different, their different "races" clearly demarcated in the *dramatis personae,* which defines and separates the characters by race.

As with the putative solidarity linking Christophe to the *philanthropes,* the alliance between Caliban and Ariel can be arrived at only through an abstraction of their realities: "la souffrance de l'esclavage" is materially different for Ariel and Caliban, as are their hopes, their visions for unity. But unlike the *Tragédie, Une tempête* presents this abstraction of difference in a positive light. The conjoining of Ariel and Caliban's irreconcilable visions represents an idealized alliance between intellectuals and workers, a solidarity Césaire never ceased trying to articulate. As Nesbitt writes, "The problematic exploration of the subject's distantiation from an objectified mass . . . recur[s] throughout Césaire's aesthetic practice. . . . Césaire's constant exploration of the problematic relation between the individual artist and his audience bears witness to his refusal to accept the alienation implied by the space he occupied within the intellectual field" ("History and Nation-Building" 142). Indeed, in a 1972 press conference in Quebec City, Césaire protested, "Je ne me suis jamais conçu comme séparé de mon peuple" (*Conférence de presse*); a reelection poster plastered across Martinique in 1976 read simply, "Aimé Césaire l'homme du peuple."[23] Whereas *Une tempête* suggests clear limits to solidarity—alliances that imagine solidarity between master and slave, for example, can never be more than dreams—it also very hopefully gives body to a solidarity between classes (workers and intellectuals) who share a condition of dispossession. This particular solidarity effects a contingent solidarity that exists only during the moment of shared dispossession (Ariel disappears after he is freed) but that is symptomatic of a desire for interclass unity among colonized peoples. *Une tempête*'s abstract experimentation with the colonial context provides the freedom from historical circumstance necessary to imagine a working solidarity between characters who represent widely differing interests, the almost mythical quality of the play's events allowing Césaire to articulate the essence of a solidarity he sought to embody in his own political and aesthetic position. The play also highlights a defining trait of Césaire's *négritude:* that it applied to all of the African diaspora, regardless of racial admixture. *Négritude* in this light becomes a way to overcome intra-black interracial divisions; it expresses the essential quality of blackness not in terms of degree of color but rather as a sociopolitical construction overlapping with a wide range of colors. In making *négritude* a category more capacious than a single self-identical race—and thus opening it up for appropriation by Quebecois intellectuals—Césaire is trying to guard against the splitting up of anticolonial solidarity that coincides with the end of colonization. *Une tempête,* in its absolute abstraction of the colonial setting, allows for the imagination of an interclass, inter-black alliance.

## Myths of Solidarity against Historical Neutrality in *Une saison au Congo*

Césaire's third play, *Une saison au Congo,* was published in 1966 and first performed in Paris in 1967, before *Une tempête* was written. I analyze it last because Césaire made significant revisions to the play until 1973, when the definitive version was published, and these revisions alter the play in such a way as to carry it beyond *Une tempête* in its deliberations on solidarity. The play tells the story of the last few years of Patrice Lumumba, the first prime minister of the free Democratic Republic of Congo, from his campaign for his country's independence to his assassination[24] at the hands of conspiring Congolese and international players. *Une saison au Congo,* part verse, part prose, stages the historical events of the Congo Crisis and simultaneously mythifies the solidary possibilities they could have represented. While the play presents Lumumba's demise as a result of a lack of solidarity, it also nostalgically imagines alternative solidarities within the tight frame of the play's tragic limits and history's deadly record.

Lack of solidarity and the elaboration of alternative solidarities are woven together as recurrent themes, sometimes doing justice to and at other times fictionalizing the historical record. Unlike *Une tempête,* this play is clearly historical; it evokes historical events, actors (although the villains' names are modified slightly), and a very specific period and place. The possibility for solidarity enters in the margins of a double mode of historicity, namely, the historicization of personal will and the personification of historical forces. What I mean by this is that the play's method for representing history is twofold. On the one hand, the discursive desires and opinions of individual characters—Lumumba, (Dag) Hammarskjöld, or the thinly veiled Kala-Lubu (altered from Joseph Kasa-Vubu), Mokutu (from Joseph-Désiré Mobutu), and Tzumbi (from Moïse Tshombe)—are elevated to the status of history and presented as symbolic of their entire historical persons. The character Lumumba becomes the sum of his words, and his words become the (partly fictional) history of the Congo. On the other hand, the play reverses this first function of historicizing personal will by personifying the various forces, groups, and communities that participated in the Congo Crisis, creating unnamed, category-type characters that represent them. The play thus constructs abstract historical forces as actors, placing them in a nuanced historical field of complex enmities and alliances through symbolic references to cultural phenomena. For example, the Bankers (First, Second, Third, Fourth, and Fifth, representing an overtly greedy version of the numbered bishops in *Et les chiens* or the *Tragédie*'s abstract *philanthropes*) personify Western financial interests, synecdochically representing *all* the bankers, financiers, corporations, and powerful political lobbies that played a determinative role in the development of events. They speak in stilted, sometimes rhyming verse reminiscent of (though perverting) classical alexandrines, parodying Western interests' hypocritical formality: "DEUXIÈME BANQUIER: Ainsi, de l'Indépendance ils ont fixé la date!/TROISIÈME BANQUIER: Hélas! ils ont de ce macaque, accepté le diktat!" (23). Similarly, the Grand Ambassadeur Occidental, with his anglicistic "colt facile" and his "politique du rocking-chair," who speaks for his "Nation" in the plural and claims that "on n'est pas seulement les gendarmes, on est aussi les pompiers du monde . . . [contre] la pyromanie communiste!" (52), clearly constitutes a personification of the United States. More amorphous characters such as "La Mama Makosi (ou femme puissante)" or simply "Une femme," "Un partisan," "Un Mungala" represent segments of the population of the Congo, each individual actor voicing a different community's position. Characters can slip in and out of the amorphous anonymity of the representative group: "Le bonimenteur," who opens the play peddling Polar beer, for example, is soon revealed (by anonymous Belgian policemen) to be Patrice Lumumba. Lumumba's oscillation between anonymous type (personified historical force) and specific historical personage (historicized personal will) prefigures his role as a single being whose desire is to merge with the whole, with the entire and diverse community of the Congo. In this way the play's tendency to personify historical forces tropifies the theme of unification, which remains the character Lumumba's elusive dream. In other words, Césaire metaphorizes Lumumba's wish to represent the nation as a unified political whole through this character who symbolizes an entire group.

The solidarity of a hypothetical and highly desirable Congolese political unity thus remains the play's asymptotic guiding vision. In *Une saison au Congo,* this always potential solidarity is the visionary contrast to equally abstract forms of neutrality; solidarity becomes the ideological opposite not of isolation but of impartiality in its various, manipulable forms. Solidarity thus emerges as a model of engagement rather than of parallel beliefs or common goals. The play's central proponent of neutrality is Hammarskjöld, a character representing the real-life UN Secretary-General (1953–61) Dag Hammarskjöld, who proclaims himself the "neutral man" needed to solve the Congo's problems: "Je suis un homme neutre. On s'est parfois demandé si cela peut exister, un homme neutre. Eh bien, j'existe! Dieu merci! j'existe! et je suis un homme neutre" (51). For Hammarskjöld, neutrality means justice: "Qu'est-ce qu'être des hommes neutres sinon des hommes justes?" (51). *Une saison au Congo* belies this belief wholesale, however, as various parties (Belgium, the United States) end up exploiting Hammarskjöld's noninterventionist stance to further their own interests.

The play questions Hammarskjöld's neutrality, even before it becomes clear that it will be taken advantage of, by hinting at his partiality in poetic matters. The distance from the poetic to the political is minimal, the play suggests, and Hammarskjöld's bias in one field implies the impossibility of his impartiality in the other. The play codes Hammarskjöld's nonneutrality as a flight of solemn fervor, during which he quotes a poem:

> Messieurs [he tells his experts], si en ce moment solennel je voulais essayer... de synthétiser l'esprit dans lequel je souhaite que vous entrepreniez votre tâche ici, au Congo, c'est aux vers du poète que je croirais devoir avoir recours:
>
> > "Je t'ignore litige, et mon avis est que l'on vive!
> > Avec la torche dans le vent, avec la flamme dans le vent,
> > Et que tous hommes, en nous, si bien s'y mêlent et s'y consument
> > qu'à telle torche grandissante s'allume en nous plus de clarté..."
> >         (50, poetry ellipsis in original)

Roger Little has identified the cited poem as the opening of section 3, canto 5, of *Vents,* a poem by Saint-John Perse (pseudonym of the Guadeloupean French poet and diplomat Alexis Léger). For Little, the poem, inserted in the context of *Une saison au Congo,* "represents a visionary witness to human values beyond contention or reason" ("Césaire, Hammarskjöld" 14), and the remoteness of the passage's high rhetoric from political machination mirrors Hammarskjöld's own exalted vision of his role (15). This poetic citation, however, does more than parallel Hammarskjöld's well-meant unrealism; by inserting it Césaire was also, perhaps bitterly or perhaps with a high-minded sense of irony, suggesting that neutrality is impossible.[25] I refer to Hammarskjöld's determined partiality toward Perse in the realm of poetry. Perse's poem in Hammarskjöld's mouth proves the impossibility of neutrality by drawing into the context of the play another aspect of Hammarskjöld's multifaceted career: as a member of the Nobel selection committee, he staunchly supported Saint-John Perse's candidacy for the Nobel Prize in Literature, which Perse won in 1960. So as Hammarskjöld was proclaiming neutrality as a tenet of his personhood ("Je suis un homme neutre. . . . Dieu merci! j'existe!"), he was simultaneously bringing to successful conclusion a battle of persuasion over his fellow Nobel selection-committee members, a battle that he had begun in 1955 and that included the publication, in 1960, of Hammarskjöld's own translation of Perse's poetry into Swedish (Little, "Césaire, Hammarskjöld" 17). Little expresses some surprise at Césaire's being aware of the link between Alexis Léger and Hammarskjöld, but it is certain that in 1966, when Césaire was writing *Une saison au Congo*, Perse's laureateship would still have been fresh in Césaire's mind, especially considering that Perse's victory assured that he, Césaire, another French Caribbean poet, would be effectively disqualified from consideration for the Nobel for the foreseeable future. It is thus not wholly remarkable that Césaire followed the 1960 Nobel celebrations carefully enough to cite, in a speech he gave in 1966 in Dakar, Alexandre Léger's Nobel acceptance speech (see "Discours prononcé par Aimé Césaire" 209). Césaire was fully aware that the character he imagined proclaiming himself "un homme neutre" was, in other arenas, not neutral at all; the citation of the poem ironically gives the lie to Hammarskjöld's affirmation and establishes the impossibility of complete neutrality even as he affirms it.

Hammarskjöld's ethereal "neutrality" stands in impotent contrast to Mokutu's parallel but very concrete "neutralization" of Lumumba. In this season in the Congo, the play suggests, neutrality means enforced powerlessness. "Guerre civile, guerre étrangère, anarchie, j'estimais que tu coûtais trop cher au Congo, Patrice," Mokutu tells Lumumba. "Alors, je t'écarte! J'ai décidé de neutraliser le pouvoir!" (88–89). Mokutu describes his coup as a "neutralization" of the warring factions of the government, putting Lumumba under house arrest and forbidding his recourse to the radio to galvanize supporters. Essentially, if for Hammarskjöld "neutrality" was a position of power from which to facilitate communication, for Mokutu it represents a reduction to powerlessness with and through the silencing of communication. Hammarskjöld seems to imagine that his "neutral" presence will allow solidarities to flourish; Mokutu's "neutralization" shows, however, that solidarity needs a secure place of enunciation from which to stem. These two deployments of neutrality, so different from each other, indicate the tropological nature of these uses of language; the term *neutrality* serves as a vehicle for the various meanings characters have the power to point it toward. Lumumba's attempts at cultivating solidarity and his elevated vision of Congolese unity flounder within this figurative double field of neutrality.

Lumumba's vision of solidarity is given voice in the play through the mythical figure of the Sanza Player—the poet, songster, and trickster. As *Une saison au Congo* brings to theatrical life the historical forces and figures that animated the Congo Crisis, solidarity itself is personified in this ahistorical, mythical figure who haunts the margins of most of the play's scenes. For Roger Little, the Sanza Player simply represents "the African soul" ("Césaire, Hammarskjöld" 15). Because of his sometimes exterior, atemporal perspective (he is both a diegetic character in the play and a metadiegetic commentator), however, the Sanza Player can also be thought of as representing Césaire and his retrospective hopes for the solidary developments that he knows would not (did not) take place. The Sanza Player's voice is the voice of the solidarity that could have been, a nostalgic mode of solidary possibility.

It is deeply revealing that the repressive forces within the play do not take the Sanza Player's influence seriously. As sometime court jester, sometime sorcerer, the Sanza Player expresses himself in parables and songs and for this reason is considered harmless by the Belgian police, even as he sings hymns urging independence (14) or recounts fables that allegorize the obtuse but highly destructive violence of Belgian colonization (18–19). The play insists on the omnipresence of potential solidarity through the figure of the Sanza Player; his frequent but misunderstood interruptions suggest the enormous importance of the Congo's failure to become a solidary unit. Lumumba, in contrast to the other characters, takes the Sanza Player seriously, understanding his cutting insults as representing his people's deep alienation (58) and heeding the Sanza Player's warnings about the disintegration of solidarity even as he, the prime minister, tries to establish the human and institutional links that would simultaneously save him and his newborn country.[26] This intimate understanding between the two characters helps put solidarity at the very heart of the play.

Indeed, the understanding between Lumumba and the Sanza Player provides an allegory to explain the moment when Lumumba's fate is sealed by a lack of solidarity—the moment when Africa refuses to cooperate with him in the face of UN inaction and Western involvement, when the character of Ghana (a personification of a historical force representing both an individual UN soldier and the country) refuses to help him communicate over the radio while he is under house arrest and has no other means of reaching the masses of his supporters. The Sanza Player magnifies this moment by rendering it as a mythical "African fable." A shrewd analysis of the dysfunctional solidarities that will ultimately bring Lumumba closer and closer to death, the fable imagines a scene in which salutary communication *could* be possible:

> Africains, c'est ça le drame! Le chasseur découvre la grue couronnée en haut de l'arbre. Par bonheur la tortue a aperçu le chasseur. La grue est sauvée direz-vous! Et de fait, la tortue avertit la grande feuille, qui doit avertir la liane, qui doit avertir l'oiseau! Mais je t'en fous! Chacun pour soi! Résultat: Le chasseur tue l'oiseau; prend la grande feuille pour envelopper l'oiseau; coupe la liane pour envelopper la grande feuille . . . Ah! J'oubliais! Il emporte la tortue par-dessus le marché! Africains mes frères, quand donc comprendrez-vous? (88, ellipsis in original)

African solidarity falls apart; it cannot save Lumumba and the fragile unity with which he is trying to weave the Congo's national fabric. Diegetic solidarity fails to establish the genuinely independent state of Lumumba's vision.

But this moment of intimate copresence between Lumumba and the Sanza Player—the Sanza Player addresses his fable to the play's audience but also to Lumumba, who remains onstage after Ghana deserts him and who explicitly participates in the imagined dream of solidary communication—suggests another, extradiegetic solidarity. The Sanza Player's confidential copresence with Lumumba represents the closeness Césaire structures between himself and Lumumba in *Une saison au Congo*. Mediating the historicization of Lumumba's personal will and the personification of Ghana's refusal, Césaire inserts a mythical solidary vision—and, of course, his own knowledgeable hindsight[27]—in the person of the Sanza Player, the voice of the future looking back, a nostalgic future that sees, retrospectively, what went wrong. Placing the Sanza Player (and through this character, himself) in a privileged relation with Lumumba means that Césaire's understanding of the Congo's failed solidarities becomes Lumumba's as well, shoring up a conclusion in which solidarity becomes the character Lumumba's dying vision.

The various solidarities existing and lacking in *Une saison au Congo* are tied up in the play's theatrical nature. Thus a character like the Sanza Player (Césaire) can directly interpellate the audience, forcing it to conform to the structures set by the play; the audience becomes, uncomfortably, the personification of the historical forces that did nothing to stop the murder of Lumumba. And yet the audience is also the repository of the play's visions of solidarity, a participant in the continued hope presented by Lumumba's dying vision (more so than in the other plays because of the directness of Lumumba's address). At the end of the play, as he dies, the character Lumumba imagines a paradoxically autarkic solidarity, a radical dispersion of the self as dew covering the territory of the Congo and uniting its people. When M'siri presses his bayonet into Lumumba's chest (simply, and ominously dehumanizingly, "il enfonce la lame"), Lumumba conceives of his death as an embryonic solidarity uniting the Congo. He portrays this solidarity through the dissolution of his body into the Congo, another instantiation of the metaphor of the body becoming land:

> Je serai du champ; je serai du pacage
> Je serai avec le pêcheur Wagenia
> Je serai avec le bouvier du Kivu
> Je serai sur le mont, je serai dans le ravin. (125)

The anaphoric repetition of *je serai* affirms presence and presentness to Lumumba's vision of the future scattering of his self. His dissolution into nourishment for his people (fields, livestock, fish) recalls the fable of the hunter and his prey; if he is to be killed, if he has been betrayed, he will now feed those whose solidarity might have saved him, becoming one with them as they unite with one another across the vast territory.

Lumumba's vision of his future omnipresence echoes Mokutu's worries: "Mort, il sera plus redoutable encore" (117). And indeed, Lumumba projects himself beyond his own being: "Oh! cette rosée sur l'Afrique! Je regarde, je vois, camarades, l'arbre flamboyant,[28] des pygmées, de la hache, s'affairent autour du tronc précaire, mais la tête qui grandit, cite au ciel qui chavire, le rudiment d'écume d'une aurore" (125). Lumumba sees the redness of his blood settling dewlike across Africa, echoing the redness of the flamboyant tree, which he imagines, even as he/it falls, summoning to the sky the beginnings of dawn. This triple metaphorical articulation of his tearing apart (blood, flamboyant, dawn) as a redness spreading over the continent harks back exactly to the "communist pyromania" that the American Grand Ambassadeur Occidental feared. The color of Lumumba's solidary martyrdom constitutes a quiet reminder that Césaire himself is not politically neutral, that he holds and defends a specific position as leader of the Parti progressiste martiniquais (PPM), the socialist party he created in 1958, two years after defecting from and roundly denouncing the French Communist Party. *Une saison au Congo* suggests that solidarity requires a supporting leftist politics, "a non-aligned or generic form of communism" (Nesbitt, *Caribbean Critique* 110), an evolution beyond the problem exposed in the *Tragédie du roi Christophe,* where capitalism was the horizon, for even imagining solidarity. Lumumba's "red" solidarity soaking up the Congolese land suggests an envisioned new order inspired by leftist, anticapitalist tenets.

The solidarity extends beyond the Congo, however, since the radical dispersion of Lumumba's discursive being as poetics in the reiterative stagings and readings of *Une saison au Congo* transplants his vision to audiences (addressed directly as "camarades") in a manner that is both time-bound in its fixedness and timeless in its repetition. Lumumba's final speech makes his death very different from the Rebel's in *Et les chiens se taisaient* or Christophe's in *La tragédie du roi Christophe;* his dying words enact a promise of solidarity, spluttering beyond the play's characters to sustain the imagination of progressive change. With Lumumba's death as solidary dispersion of the martyr, the francophone world is promised the possibility of a nonaligned communist future.

The metaphor of the body becoming land emerges as a master trope in Césaire's articulations of solidarity. *Et les chiens* imagined the Rebel's martyrdom as the painful fusion of his body with the island in the process of becoming a solidary canopy. Caliban metaphorized his desired murder-suicide of himself and Prospero as an explosion destroying the entire island, imagining unity with his master as a mutual obliteration that also engulfs the territory. Lumumba envisions his blood staining the land, forming the basis of a socialist-inspired national solidarity. Material geography therefore is central to the elaboration of solidary imaginaries for Césaire, the land serving as a kind of medium phantasmically linking individual bodies if they will figuratively merge with it. The landscape holds the promise of solidarity—an exterior geography propping up the "interior geography" of the solidary affect.

*Une saison au Congo,* however, does not end with this transcendent promise of body solidarily becoming land. Two short scenes follow the disappearance of Lumumba, taking the last word away from him, dampening his vision of unity and his hope with regard to his sacrifice. The final scene, added to the play in 1973, seven years after its original publication, indicates a radically pessimistic shift on the part of Césaire. In this scene, which postdates the character Lumumba's death by several years, Mokutu has ascended to the role of supreme leader; he appears before the Congolese people in the leopard skin Lumumba had earlier declined to wear, and among cries of "Vive Mokutu!" and suppressed cries of "Lumumba uhuru!" (131), Mokutu announces that Patrice Lumumba will henceforth be considered a martyr for the nation. When the jubilant crowd reacts with too much enthusiasm, however, screaming "Gloire immortelle à Lumumba! À bas le néo-colonialisme!" (132), Mokutu orders his guard to fire on the masses. "Il faut que ce peuple sache qu'il y a des limites que je ne tolérerai pas qu'il dépasse," he tells one of his ministers (133), the demonstrative adjective *ce* (*this* people) establishing the distance between himself and those he rules—a far cry from Lumumba's own conception of his connection to the people. And as the stage directions specify, the Sanza Player lies dead among the bodies after the massacre. If the Sanza Player had represented Césaire, the optimistic voice of 1966 nostalgically looking back at the changes Lumumba could have wrought and hoping that Lumumba's emblematic death might yet transform the Congo, the Sanza Player's death represents the 1973 recognition that those 1966 hopes will not be realized. With the coming to violent power of the anticommunist Mokutu, the mythical spirit of solidarity, which the Sanza Player represented and which Lumumba had tried to embody as he was disembodied, no longer has any hope of actualization; it must perish. In the 1973 edition of *Une saison au Congo,* Césaire thus eclipses himself, the possibility of solidarity symbolized by the Sanza Player, and the "red" hopes of Lumumba's dying scene. In this version, "le texte définitif," as the edition's endnote specifies, solidarity does not rescue Lumumba's hope and will not transform the Congo, which is represented as too far ensconced in the authoritarian violence of Mokutu's regime.

*Une saison au Congo* extends Césaire's geographical and historical experimentations with solidary francophone possibilities to the African independences, which, as reviewers and scholars have pointed out, his plays structure as parallel to the Haitian Revolution and Haitian independence.[29] What emerges is an insistent search for solidarities in the context of French imperial encroachment. Solidarity is a central aspiration, an ambitious objective that Césaire territorializes in those crucial moments of colonial dissolution when change is possible. Solidarity structures the imaginary of each play, of each hero's visions for change, and each of the spaces (or nonspaces, in the case of *Une tempête*) where Césaire sets his plays affords new possibilities but also new limits to solidarity. Solidarity emerges as a desire that can only be expressed tropologically—metaphorically and parabolically; the territories of francophone solidarity imagined in the plays are therefore attempts to ground, geographically and historically, asymptotic solidarities that are always only discursive. Each play attempts to ground solidarity in a landscape precisely because it remains always part of an imaginary and is bound by the limits of that imaginary.

Solidarity is thus at the center of Césaire's four plays, thematically because it recurs as a hope in many of his heroes' visions of a better future and structurally because it always has the potential to implicate the audience, either to reproach them or to give them hope. Although Césaire is wary of the big narratives that can carry or co-opt solidarity—national narratives, party narratives—he returns to solidarity's possibilities in each play. Césaire focuses on the foundational moments of francophone worldedness, on the becoming global of French (the colonial encounter, the Haitian Revolution, the independences), precisely because he is haunted by the conundrum of solidarity in a world where the language of French is shared, but shared across such an unequal power differential. As we have seen, the racial nature of this power differential orients Césaire's choice of theatrical heroes and settings. His focus on Toussaint, Christophe, the deposed king Caliban, and Lumumba appears itself to be a form of solidary identification: he identifies with the plight of these rulers of colonized spaces and with the tragic constrictions imposed on them by the history of empire. In this metatextual sense, the poetics of solidarity defines the shape of Césaire's oeuvre and locates his Caribbean space and time, his post-1945 Martinique as department, at the nexus of a particular French-language solidarity.[30] Even plays that highlight solidarity's impossibility become touchpoints for thinking further about and potentially establishing solidarity. This solidarity for Césaire is characterized by the racial features that shaped the French-speaking world, with its history of enslavement of Africans. The (post)colonial leaders with whom Césaire identifies are black; though his plays repeatedly represent failed solidarities among black people, when he spoke of Africa structuring his "interior geography," he did mean it as something of an essentialist gesture. The solidary imaginary of anticolonial struggles as it emerges in Césaire's plays is a racialized one, generally opposing black colonial subjects to white Europeans.

## Césaire in Quebec, Quebec in Césaire: Facing Francophone Solidarity's Northern Realizations

The response to Césaire in Quebecois literature problematizes the blackness of a *négritude*-based solidarity as well as the placelessness of solidarity's imaginary nature. White Quebecois writers venerated Césaire as an emblem of an anticolonial solidarity that could be territorialized in Quebec and that included them, in spite of their whiteness. They were eager to try to root francophone solidarity in their own land and in their own political context in order to justify positioning themselves as colonial victims of the British and of English Canadians. This section analyzes Césaire's response to Quebec's appropriation of Caribbean and African anticolonial discourses in order to explore how his use of tropes shifted to accommodate and challenge this projection of francophone solidarity beyond the bounds of *négritude*.

White Quebec, for Césaire, echoes the conundrum that haunts his plays: here are French-speaking intellectuals who have appropriated the discourse with which he carved out the space for a black Caribbean people to understand its own cultural and political being in the world. In a sense, Quebec, a white settler colony, represents a reprise of Christophe's *philanthropes,* with the difference that Quebecois intellectuals somehow recognized themselves in and modeled their struggle on that of the colonized, rather than trying to assimilate the colonized to a "universal" mode of progress. The issue of Quebecois francophone solidarity entered Césaire's world in 1972, when he was invited for ten days as a guest of the Département des études françaises at Quebec City's Laval University in the context of a series of visits by African and Caribbean writers (*écrivains négro-africains,* a category at once geographical and racial). These lectures represent a crucial moment in Césaire's oeuvre because they called on him to position himself with respect to those for whom he had been such an inspiration. The encounter brought to a head Césaire's concerns with solidarity, and with solidarity's simultaneous necessity and impossibility, because he came face to face with an eager audience for whom solidarity was not only a distinct possibility but also a defining feature of their sense of francophone belonging.

There is no question that Césaire's work was extremely influential in shaping francophone Quebecois anticolonial solidarity in the 1960s.[31] Among Quebecois sovereigntist intellectuals, Césaire ranked with Albert Memmi, Frantz Fanon, and Jacques Berque as a leading anticolonial thinker. Ching Selao labels Césaire's influence in Quebec, particularly on the writers associated with the sovereigntist journal *Parti pris,* an "engouement," an infatuation (37). Max Dorsinville, longtime professor at Montreal's McGill University, in his article "L'influence d'Aimé Césaire au Québec" meticulously outlines the historical conditions that led to the appropriation of Césaire in Quebec and the main modes of that appropriation: the Quebecois writers "subordonnent la spécificité de la condition coloniale antillaise à un vocabulaire, un ton et un style susceptibles d'appropriation" (118).[32] Indeed, Quebecois intellectuals affirmed their political and cultural alignment with Césaire in spite of the immense differences that separated their historical context from Martinique's. Césaire was co-opted unambiguously as a symbolic father by proindependence Quebecois intellectuals who recognized in his works a yearning for equality and self-determination similar to theirs—and who ignored, in a way Martinican independentists could not, his championing first of departmentalization and later of political autonomy within France.[33] Their mode of appropriation was textual solidarity, a poetics of cultural alliance. They incorporated various Césairian tropes and concepts into their literary imaginaries: "les poètes des années soixante au Québec se sont reconnu des affinités avec Césaire qu'ils manifestent dans leur conception de la fonction et de la pratique poétique" (Dorsinville, *Pays natal* 44). Hubert Aquin's paradigmatic essay "La fatigue culturelle des Canadiens français," for example, draws its term *fatigue culturelle* from Césaire's "Culture et colonisation";[34] Aquin understands the particularity of his own situation through an abstract similarity, aligning and allying himself with Césaire by finding a common ground in the thick of difference. The Quebecois intellectuals' intertextual borrowings and references constitute a poet(h)ics of solidarity, a moral or ethical engagement on a political front they imagined to be aligned with the Martinican situation.

Césaire, however, seems to have been unaware of this influence until his 1972 visit to Quebec, when he famously noticed Pierre Vallières's *Nègres blancs d'Amérique* in a bookstore display and was faced with the northern derivations of his concept of *négritude*. In fact, his trip to Quebec City tested the limits of the solidarity with which Césaire had been experimenting in his plays, limits imposed by race and class differences; the term *nègres blancs* simultaneously highlights and violates the horizon of *négritude*. Here is the context in which Césaire acknowledged the term and claimed an appreciation for it. In his *Discours sur la négritude* (1989), originally given as a speech in 1987 in Miami, Césaire quipped, "Je me souviens encore de mon ahurissement lorsque, pour la première fois au Québec, j'ai vu à une vitrine de librairie un livre dont le titre m'a paru sur le coup ahurissant. Le titre, c'était: 'Nous autres nègres blancs d'Amérique.' Bien entendu, j'ai souri de l'exagération, mais je me suis dit: 'Eh bien, cet auteur, même s'il exagère, a du moins compris la Négritude'" (*Discours . . . suivi de Discours sur la négritude* 81). Césaire's sympathy for Vallières's exaggerated title echoes his "affirmation that a universal, non-identitarian Négritude is not a biological fatality or essence, but is to be measured 'au compas de la souffrance'" (Nesbitt, *Caribbean Critique* 12). Césaire himself acquiesced in an interview when Jacqueline Leiner asked him, "Vous ne [croyez] pas, au fond, à la biologie, à la race, mais à la culture" (Leiner 124). Césaire's nonidentitarian enlargement of *négritude* is performed as an indulgence characterizing the general tone of the extant texts that preserve the Laval visit: a published essay, originally given as a lecture; a filmed presentation of a second essay (included in *Conférence de presse . . . [suite]*); a press conference (*Conférence de presse*); and a filmed interview with the Laval professors Michel Tétu and Fernando Lambert and guest scholar Lilyan Kesteloot (*Conférence de presse . . . [suite]*). Césaire's 1972 presentations and interviews at Laval suggest that the visit represented for him a revelation of the extent of his influence in Quebec and that it constituted a turning point in his understanding of the uses and misuses to which his words and persona had been put.

Césaire's plays, all composed before the 1972 visit, had staged various explorations of solidary possibilities but had consistently found white-black interracial solidarities impossible. The imaginary structuring of his theatrical works precluded the possibility of a *nègre blanc,* of a nation defining itself as white and solidary in oppression. The texts that immortalize Césaire's confrontation with the reality of his influence in Quebec, however, exhibit a graciousness that manipulates discourse in order to grant the existence of Quebecois interracial solidarity, if only through the slippery tropes of figurative language.[35] Césaire's presentations and interviews exercise a tropological expression of similarity with Quebec that finds solidary parallels in poetics rather than in material conditions and lived experience.

The recordings (both textual and audiovisual) of Césaire's performances in Quebec City chronicle his coming to terms with his hosts' expectations of solidarity; in fact, it is precisely in *performing*—a performing marked by indulgence, politeness, and generosity—that Césaire is able to reconcile their idealistic view of interracial solidarity and his own skepticism. Lectures and interviews of course demand different things of their audiences than theatrical performances do; for our purposes, let us agree that plays act on their audiences via abstraction, while lectures hold the speaker more accountable to a particular room of people and for his particular opinions. Given this distinction, however, Césaire's use of poetic abstraction in his lectures constitutes a mode of *theatricalizing* the lecture form. Césaire's performance of affability as he concedes a certain poetic solidarity to his audience (without relinquishing all reservations) suggests that his lectures were designed to "play" to his audience's desire for reciprocity.

During the Laval interviews, the issue of Césaire's position regarding Quebec came to a head when the Africanist and Caribbeanist scholar Lilyan Kesteloot, who was also a guest at Laval University at the time, questioned Césaire about Quebec.[36] At the press conference, she asked point blank, "Vous êtes venu ici au Canada, vous êtes venu ici au Québec . . . ce n'est pas seulement parce que l'Université Laval vous invite. Est-ce que ce pays vous intéresse? Et pourquoi?" (*Conférence de presse*). Césaire paused before answering. Ultimately, though, the position he decided to take with respect to Quebec endorsed the solidary appropriations of his work for the furthering of Quebec's independence: "Ce pays m'intéresse profondément parce que je pense, j'ai le sentiment qu'il s'y passe des choses importantes et qui . . . qui en un certain sens me concernent et qui peuvent avoir une certaine conséquence pour l'avenir—excusez-moi de parler presque égoïstement—un petit peu pour tout le continent. [Silence; Césaire taps hands on desk.] Faut-il en dire plus?" (*Conférence de presse*). At which the audience laughs knowingly, appreciatively, and then questions return to the Martinican economy. Césaire's indirect yet quite clear reference to Quebec's drive for independence and to its continental importance were doubtless welcome to sovereigntist listeners. The significance of a Césairian mark of approval to members of a movement inspired by Césaire's writings cannot be underestimated, and Césaire, with his pregnant pauses, his small but emphatic hand taps, was quite conscious of the momentousness of his words. With these performative tools, he articulated a discursive solidarity with Quebecois sovereigntists, responding to their expectations of support and heightening their sense of the importance of Quebec's movement for independence. And yet, even as he performs solidarity, he simultaneously (and diplomatically) keeps his distance by not delivering an overt blessing for Quebec's independence.

This position of solidary but incompletely articulated support and recognition extends through all of Césaire's extant presentations at Laval

University in 1972, taking on a variety of nuances. The lecture "Société et littérature dans les Antilles," originally given at Laval the evening of April 11, 1972,[37] and published a year later in the Laval University journal *Études littéraires,* introduces the problem of culture in a colonial situation. Césaire describes the Caribbean (specifically Martinique) as culturally dispossessed, a situation he reads as devolving from colonialism and neocolonialism. The colonized people's culture, he explains, is replaced by a "subculture," which does not belong to the people but rather is imposed from the metropole through institutional processes such as education (14). In this lecture, Césaire grants his audience's desire for recognition of their own "colonial status" by borrowing the words of Quebecois poets to express Caribbean alienation.

Césaire first quotes Quebecois poetry in the process of defining colonialism as an estrangement from the self, a cultural phenomenon. Before reaching the Quebecois analogy, he explains, "Là où l'homme est piétiné, écrasé, bâillonné, là où il est défiguré, et à la limite nié, il n'y a pas de place pour la culture dans le sens où nous l'avons définie, c'est-à-dire comme expression originale du mode de vie du peuple. Or, c'est précisément le cas pour le monde colonial, c'est le cas pour le monde antillais" (11). Césaire here asserts the colonial status of the Caribbean world as the basis for a cultural alienation that he metaphorizes violently as a trampling, a crushing, a gagging, a disfigurement, and a denial—violent imagery warranted by the brutality of Martinique's slaving past, to which he is clearly referring. What is unexpected is that he chooses to illustrate Martinican alienation through the words of the sovereigntist Quebecois poet Gaston Miron:

> Aliéné, l'homme martiniquais l'est puisque diverti de lui-même, devenu marginal par rapport à lui-même et pour employer les mots de Gaston Miron, le grand poète québécois:
>
> > Dépoétisé dans ma langue
> > et mon appartenance
> > déphasé
> > et décentré
> > dans ma coïncidence
>
> Dépossédé aussi l'homme antillais l'est puisque privé de son héritage. (11–12)

Dropping the imagery of violence, Césaire now metaphorizes the alienation of colonialism as a "marginalization with respect to the self," counterposing the geographical isolation of Martinique to the sentiment of distance from one's own being. Césaire graciously allies this feeling of radical colonial dispossession with Miron's image of being "depoeticized" in his own tongue, which suggests the double discomfort of being unable to express himself poetically in French and of being stripped of the title "poet." Miron's lines refer to the perennial French Canadian insecurity of losing the French language, of not being "French" enough—the threat of losing French to an English continent. Miron's dizzying image of being "déphasé/et décentré/dans ma coïncidence" recalls Césaire's feeling of orbiting his identity from afar, which he describes as a "marginalization from the self." For both Césaire and Miron, the feeling of being wrenched apart constitutes the structure of alienation; this is the similarity with which Césaire gratifies his Quebecois public. It is a far cry, however, from man being trampled, crushed, and disfigured; ultimately, Miron's problem in this verse is with language, not with violent oppression. Césaire, however, is willing to abstract a common feeling of disempowerment from the two experiences. Césaire's post-quote linking sentence ("Dépossédé aussi l'homme antillais l'est puisque privé de son héritage") reads as an enormous concession to Quebec's claims of cultural dispossession, the topsy-turvy syntax placing emphasis on commonality by moving up *aussi* in the sentence's word order.

Césaire's identification with Miron's goal of preserving French as a foundational part of his identity, however, poses a difficulty for Césaire. In the same speech Césaire argues, with an irony he does not acknowledge, "Il y a une discordance profonde entre la langue officielle qui est le français et la langue vraie, la langue du peuple qui est le créole, on ne peut pas le nier" (17). So whereas Miron finds refuge in and wants to strengthen his ties to French, Césaire's people must reject French to find their own, "true" language: Creole. The independence era, and sixties and seventies Césaire as emblematic of that era, however, glossed over this contradiction, using French as a tool to affirm the right to self-assertion and to establish connections between widely different colonized peoples. The period of transition that led from (French) colonialism to the various postcolonial options that developed from it was facilitated through the use of French, its new clefts and solidarities articulated in the former colonial language. This was precisely what made Quebec's participation in the literary solidarity of the era conceivable: a continued (if, for some regions, temporary) reliance on French, even as the language's preeminent status came to be contested. Césaire's lavish citation of Miron, then, represents a "tongue tie," a connection made possible by and yet also constrained by the use of French, constrained to ignore or downplay its own contradictions.

Another contradiction Césaire finds himself obliquely avoiding in his construction of a textual solidarity with Quebecois intellectuals has to do with the question of race. The second time he cites Miron, Césaire again creates an explicit link between Quebec and Martinique, but he feels the need to add, seemingly as a non sequitur, a clarification about race:

> Excusez-moi de citer un poète québécois (depuis deux jours je suis à Québec):
>
> > Poésie mon bivouac (*dit Gaston Miron*)
> > Ma douce et fraîche révélation
> > de l'être.
>
> Eh bien, c'est vrai aussi pour les Antillais et sans doute pour les mêmes raisons qui ne sont pas des raisons raciales, on le devine, mais des raisons sociologiques. (18)

Nothing in the Miron citation explicitly suggested race, and yet Césaire specifies that the parallel reasons for which both Antillean and Quebecois people require and relate to poetry are *sociological* rather than racial. Poetry transpires as a connection borne of social discontents. Césaire, in this comparison of the Caribbean with Quebec, insists on the Martinican as a social rather than a racial being; this is the only time he mentions race in this speech, furthering his point that Martinican alienation is cultural. However, race is a double-edged tool in the context of Quebec's postcolonial associations. Césaire's diversion away from race here forms simultaneously an inclusive gesture, suggesting that Antillean and Quebecois problems are similar because they are sociological, and an exclusive one, denying Quebec's claims to (metaphorical) blackness.

It is curious that this denial of race is the subject that prompts Césaire both to apologize ("forgive me for citing a Quebecois poet") and to mark himself geographically and temporally ("I've been in Quebec City for two days"). It is as though his presence in Quebec has heightened his awareness of the racial difference that separates the northern province from the Caribbean, even as Quebec's social problems and the poetic reactions they have inspired strike him as similar to his homeland's. Distancing himself from the *négritude* that had so inspired his Quebecois readers throughout the 1950s and 1960s, Césaire instead maintains with Quebecois intellectuals a *poetic* connection, useful precisely because he can manipulate the referents of its metaphors as he sees fit.

"Interior Geographies" 69

Césaire's solidarity also skirts the problematic issue of land-ownership and governance. Again he cites a Quebecois sovereigntist poet's verses to broach the question, while leaving it ultimately unresolved, as Quebec's 1972 struggle for independence differed significantly from Césaire's own federalist goals for Martinique. Citing Jean-Guy Pilon, Césaire writes,

> Pour un peu
> On te dirait avec des mots
> Qui ne sont pas les tiens
> Que tu n'es pas d'ici
> Que tu n'as pas droit
> Au paysage
>
> Eh bien, c'est valable pour l'Antillais! (19)

If Pilon begins again with the problem of language (the language of property in Quebec was English, as the poem hints: "des mots/Qui ne sont pas les tiens"), Césaire focuses instead on the two last lines of the quoted stanza, "Que tu n'as pas droit/Au paysage," to construct a complex argument regarding the right to land. Pilon's *paysage* is already metaphorical. A landscape is captured with paint, with words; it is the *territory* on which the landscape is anchored that is an object to be legally owned. Césaire uses Pilon's oblique reference as a launching pad to speak, also obliquely, about possession and ownership: "La littérature antillaise n'est pas seulement récupération de l'être; elle est aussi récupération de l'avoir, rapatriement de l'essentiel et remise en possession d'un héritage contesté ou tombé en désirance" (19). This fascinating passage combines concrete vocabulary for the physical transfer of goods and people with abstract concepts; thus the "récupération de l'être," which Césaire had discussed earlier as redressing alienation, becomes the "récupération de l'avoir," the recovery not just of one's state of being but also of one's state of *having*, what one owns or is owed. *Rapatriement* suggests a very concrete repatriation, but "rapatriement de l'essentiel" immediately metaphorizes the physical and legal action into the reclamation of a cultural essence. Similarly, the "remise en possession d'un héritage contesté" clearly suggests a redistribution of land and wealth that Césaire's pun "tombé en désirance" mitigates. Indeed, the expected phrase *tomber en déshérence* would suggest the absence of legal heirs for a very real inheritance, but the near homonym *désirance* instead operates in the phantasmic realm of nostalgia, transforming *héritage* into an abstract legacy. Over and over, Césaire flirts with the vocabulary of concrete land demands—which could amount to reparations, sovereignty, self-determination, independence—but each time he bifurcates into culture, memory, identity. The juxtaposition of the concrete vocabulary of ownership to the abstract vocabulary of culture implies, without affirming, that a recovered culture, a people's essence, has a chance of leading to the concrete goal of self-determination.

In terms just as veiled, Césaire goes on to describe the role of literature in this process of concretizing abstract self-possession: literature will be "le rétablissement de l'homme dans ses appartenances et ses relations fondamentales avec sa terre, avec son pays et avec son peuple" (20). *Appartenances* here functions simultaneously on the concrete and the abstract levels, evoking both a sense of belonging and the belonging, to him, of the objects of the following clause: his land, his country, his people. By broaching the question of possession in these terms at once abstract and concrete, Césaire bridges the gap between Quebec's burgeoning aspirations to independence and his own federalist policy for Martinique. He made this policy quite clear in the press conference he gave at Laval University; several questions from journalists prodded him to express more and more precisely the governmental relationship he wanted to institute between Martinique and France, and in reply, Césaire elaborated on the idea of "Martinican autonomy" under a French federal umbrella, an autonomy that would allow Martinique the opportunity to develop "d'autres solidarités que celles à sens unique qui nous sont imposées" (*Conférence de presse*). Here as well, Césaire hints that although his political goal for Martinique (autonomy) differs from Quebecois sovereigntists' for Quebec (independence), the flourishing of both visions would only strengthen francophone American ties.

Césaire concludes his lecture "Société et littérature dans les Antilles" by citing yet another Quebecois, the anthropologist Jean Benoist, who had just published *L'archipel inachevé, culture et société aux Antilles françaises* (1972). Césaire finds himself in the delicate position of forming part of the community studied in the book, the community on which Benoist was considered an eminent specialist. Benoist's gift of his book to Césaire emphasizes Césaire's dichotomous belonging both to the Martinican people and to a transnational network of French-speaking intellectuals, but it still leaves Césaire in a space where he is confronted with his people's studiable nature, with their anthropological otherness with respect to Quebec. Césaire responds to the situation by situating the anthropologist in his national context in turn, and by heightening his public's awareness of Benoist's Quebecois origins:

> J'ai trouvé cela admirable, *l'Archipel inachevé* . . . [Benoist] conclut son livre de la manière suivante:
>
>> D'une façon générale, les sociétés et les cultures antillaises originales qui ont la chance (et le malheur) d'avoir un passé si brouillé que leur avenir doit être inventé ont besoin d'abord de mieux se connaître.
>
> Eh bien, j'accepte cet appel à l'imaginaire et à l'invention:
>
>> Inventer le pays!
>> Inventer l'homme!
>
> On ne saura mieux dire. Et il est hautement significatif que ce soit un Québécois qui ait écrit cela à propos des Antilles. En tout cas, tout y est. C'est bien cela la charte de la littérature antillaise: prendre en charge le passé, éclairer le présent, débusquer l'avenir, bref, aider à achever et à conduire à sa vraie naissance *l'Archipel inachevé* . . . (20, ellipses in original)

In these highly suggestive yet open-ended concluding words, Césaire suggests that Quebec is well placed to talk about inventing a country, inventing humankind; in Quebec's moment of effervescent transformation, of hope for sovereignty and self-determination, Benoist's interest in self-knowledge as the basis for future creation is an implied reflection of Quebec's own need. Césaire turns the anthropological lens back on Quebec and incorporates the northern province into the "unfinished archipelago," requiring introspection and imagination for its further development, for its coming-to-itself. Solidarity here lies paradoxically in Césaire's insistence on Benoist's nationality. While on the one hand the phrase seems to drive a wedge between the anthropologist-subject and his objects of study ("un Québécois qui ait écrit cela à propos des Antilles"), on the other hand it magnifies the link by giving it an unspecified significance ("il est hautement significatif"). Césaire's leaving the significance open ended allows his public to infer that the reference is to Quebec's struggle for self-definition and sovereignty as a parallel to Martinique's colonial situation, and yet Césaire does not affirm that connection in so many words. The poetics of solidarity, in the context of Césaire's speech, means letting the bond form in his audience's imagination without having to explicitly grant the Quebec-Martinique analogy.

This analogy is not, in fact, one of equivalences.[38] For Césaire, solidarity means reciprocating the impact his poetics has had on his hosts without conceding the specificity of Martinique's colonial, racial, territorial, and linguistic predicaments. Unspoken in Césaire's lecture is a hierarchy of solidarities in which allegiance first to Martinique and second to *négritude* tacitly takes precedence over allegiance to Quebec. Césaire could have had little doubt that his audience would appreciate the solidary analogy he was suggesting and would not be overly concerned with his tacit reservations; after all, as the portrayal of the *philanthropes* in the *Tragédie du roi Christophe* has shown (their blindness to their position within racialized capitalism: "if you're not spat on, you're spitting"), the privileges associated with being white condition and limit imagination. And yet his performative position with regard to Quebec is much gentler than Christophe's trenchant accusation of the *philanthropes;* Césaire grants what solidarity he can graciously, forming a practical alliance with his hosts even as his discourse delineates the limits of mutual understanding.

Another lecture, titled "La situation du poète antillais et les caractéristiques poétiques de l'Antillais," shows one of the ways that Césaire's solidarity with Quebec differs from his Martinican ties by bringing up the question of class. The talk has not been published but remains available for viewing on video at the Laval University archives. In it, Césaire analyzes the effects of colonization on poetry in Martinique, which he calls the "laboratoire de la colonisation—l'endroit privilégié pour qui voudrait étudier les effets de la colonisation" (*Conférence de presse . . . [suite]*). Césaire describes the alienation and monadization of the Caribbean people and then focuses on poetry's role in returning their sense of identity and their "communication vitale" with the collectivity. For Césaire, poetry represents an ideal mode in which to search for the self because it grants "accès à l'être par les soins du langage," access to what he calls "l'être nu, natal," which exists beyond the alienation of colonial life. Césaire adds, "J'ai l'impression que cette attitude ne vous est pas étrangère au Canada si j'en juge d'après le vers de Gaston Miron dans *La vie agonique*, 'je retrouverai ma nue propriété.' Eh bien, c'est un vers qu'un poète antillais pourrait contresigner" (*Conférence de presse . . . [suite]*). Miron's verse thus emblematizes the desire for a reconnection with the essence of the self, an essence characterized by the same nakedness or bareness that Césaire had employed to describe the Antillean being obscured by three centuries of mystifying colonization. This signatory overlap of two poets (the Quebecois Miron and a hypothetical Caribbean poet) creates an alignment of French-speaking intellectuals across geographical distance. This alliance stands in sharp contrast to the alignment of worker and intellectual temporarily effected in *Une tempête*. Transnational solidarity, in "La situation du poète antillais," emerges as a bond between writers, suggesting an esoteric stratum of cosmopolitan exchange quite distant from the peoples whom the writers imagine themselves representing. If, for Césaire, there exists a hierarchy of imagined solidarities, these solidarities differ in their class structure: solidarity within Martinique strives to be interclass, while solidarity with Quebec is based on intraclass (intellectual) affinities.

Despite this class definition of Césaire's solidarity with Quebec, "La situation du poète antillais" goes further than other Laval talks in identifying Quebec with the Caribbean: while affirming a philosophical division between France as colonizer and the Caribbean as colonized, Césaire associates Quebec with the Caribbean, not with France. Specifically, he describes French poetry as a relation to language that is enumerative ("il y a . . . il y a . . . il y a . . ."), whereas the relation of Caribbean poetry to language is "vitale, participante, ontique" ("ce que j'ai, c'est . . . ce qui m'appartient, c'est . . ."). Césaire insists that Caribbean poetry is "non seulement recherche de l'être mais aussi recension de l'avoir," explaining that "en recensant son avoir" the Antillean poet "définit son être." To illustrate this relation between language, ownership, and identity, Césaire quotes "le vers, le très beau vers du poète canadien Gratien Lapointe, 'j'épelle dans ma main le nom de chaque chose'" (*Conférence de presse . . . [suite]*). The Canadian[39] image of closing one's fingers over words symbolizes for Césaire Caribbean poetry's need to assert ownership of language in order to forge a distinct Caribbean identity. Césaire slices the French-speaking world in a novel way that accounts for anticolonial solidarities: Quebec, because of its desire to own language, belongs to the category of colonized peoples, in spite of its perceived whiteness and its first-worldness.[40]

Césaire never acknowledges that the striking resonances he finds in Miron and other Quebecois poets are due in significant part to his own influence on their work. Miron's poetry from the early 1960s is filled with verses echoing Césaire's, precisely because Miron had devoured Césaire's works and been transformed by them (see Miron's correspondence with Claude Haeffely, quoted in Selao 44). Martinique's three centuries of colonization had thus affected Quebecois writers like Miron indirectly, through the vector of poetry. Reading Césaire's texts, they discovered their own alienated selves in his alienation, and they struggled to express their "naked being" by modeling their poetic search on his. Césaire's naturalizing of these sentiments as essentially Quebecois rather than recognizing them as appropriated from the writings of other colonized peoples constitutes in itself a gesture of solidarity. His speeches at Laval accept the adoption and territorialization of colonial victimhood in Quebec, and if he nuances the modality of his acceptance, he does so in a spirit of solidarity: Césaire shows a willingness to express solidarity in spite of difference, in spite of the racial hierarchies that continue to structure the French-speaking world.

In sum, throughout his Quebec City talks Césaire complicates the various themes through which Quebecois intellectuals may have found solidarity with him, with Martinique, and with the (post)colonial world more generally—colonialism, race, language, self-determination. Césaire shows that Martinique is a colonial space and suggests that Quebec is similar to it, but without affirming Quebec's colonized status. He affirms that Creole (not French) is Martinique's "true language," and yet he draws parallels, *in French,* with Quebecois writers' desire for a more assertive belonging to (and recognition of) the French language. He remarks on race, but merely to profess its irrelevance to cultural alienation as he asserts that alienation's sociological similarity to Quebec's. He adroitly skirts the question of land-ownership and independence by metaphorizing its objects. And yet he nevertheless offers his audience an appreciation of the metaphors of alienation as a common ground for understanding, a common expression of alienation *as* solidarity; in short, he offers a *poetics of solidarity.* Césaire's reliance on borrowed poetry to do the work of solidarity allows him to prevaricate on the central issues that might have separated him from Quebecois intellectuals. The overarching metaphorical structure of his solidarity functions thanks to the abstract nature of metaphors, whose structure points to or represents something other than themselves. Césaire uses this abstraction to construct a solidary reciprocity with Quebec's poets, using their metaphors to build his own edifice of sympathies and parallels without reducing Martinique's past and present suffering to a universal. His poetics of solidarity offers the manipulation and transformation of a shared language as tools for transnational political agency.

Césaire's plays experiment with solidarity across locations in francophone history and geography, mapping the possibilities of solidarity in the French-speaking world. Overall, the plays are quite grim in the solidarities they construct; these solidarities are most often flawed, impossible, unreachable, or unrealized. Visions of solidarity consistently haunt the plays' characters; these visions shape their actions and expectations but nevertheless do not transform the world in the ways the characters hope they will. In other words, the characters' worlds do not mirror or bring to life their visions of solidarity, which remain highly desirable but always imaginary. The only vision of solidarity that is realized is the intra-black, interclass solidarity between slaves in *Une tempête,* which harks back to Césaire's concept of *négritude*, the idea of a black cultural movement unifying Africa with its diaspora in a colonial moment characterized by racialized dispossession.

The very real solidary response to his writings and persona in Quebecois literature, then, jars Césaire's plays' bleak view of solidary possibilities. Confronting this white identification with colonial blackness means reassessing the limits of the solidarities his plays had imagined and staged; it means practicing a form of solidarity that does not at all resemble the abstract perfection of the Rebel's dream. But abstraction does *structure* solidarity for Césaire, both in the plays and in the Quebec City lectures. The plays suggest that solidarity can fail in the tug between abstraction and particularity because the abstraction of one group's reality allows the differences that define their relation to other groups to be downplayed. This same technique, however, alternating abstraction and particularity, can also enable solidarity to exist. Césaire practices it when approaching Quebecois literary solidarity by creating abstract categories (such as "colonized people" or "alienation") that allow him to place Quebec in the same category as Martinique or the Caribbean. What enables him to skim over the very real differences that exist between Quebec and Martinique is his use of a poetics to define and articulate the limits of these categories; he grants Quebec Martinican solidarity through the two regions' shared metaphorical representation of colonial victimhood. In Césaire's plays and lectures, poetics is what allows solidarity to exist at all.

## 2 Interlace, Interrace

### Anticolonialism and White Babies in Hubert Aquin's *Trou de mémoire*

THE NOVELIST and essayist Hubert Aquin (1929–1977) was one of the Quebecois intellectuals deeply influenced by Aimé Césaire. I have mentioned already the titular term in Aquin's famous essay "La fatigue culturelle" as a borrowing from Césaire. His novel *Trou de mémoire* is reminiscent of Césaire as well, producing a spiraling, fictional echo chamber in which aspects of Césaire's work and biography resonate faintly. Aquin's image of the ailing nation, for instance, echoes the *Cahier*'s extended metaphor of colonialism as infectious disease. *Trou de mémoire* also gestures to Césaire's familial biography; Césaire had a brother who, in structural parallel with an Ivoirian pharmacist in *Trou de mémoire*, lived and worked as a pharmacist in Guinea.[1] These seeming coincidences give elements of *Trou de mémoire* something like the shape of Césaire's world—a game of introducing nonfiction into fiction that attempts to establish a connection with Césaire by referring to both his lived experience and his writing. This chapter examines *Trou de mémoire*'s unstable metaphorizations of interracial solidarity as experiments in articulating a desire for connection that remains always potential or asymptotic.

Criticism on Hubert Aquin has tended to evince a racial logic that forestalls a consideration of race, even in a novel such as *Trou de mémoire* (1968), which explicitly thematizes race. To date, scholarship on *Trou de mémoire,* the second of Aquin's five novels, focuses mainly on narrative strategies (the novel's extremely complex form or the use of anamorphic imagery as structural feature), on the borrowed paradigm of decolonization as part of a larger project linking Aquin's oeuvre, or on gender. The tacit classification of Quebec as a white space, which has situated Aquin as a white writer, just as it has singularized Quebec within studies of francophone literature and anticolonialism, tends to sideline or preclude the study of race in Aquin. Notable exceptions to the study of Quebec as a white space include monographs by the historians David Austin and Sean Mills and the index of biographies of Haitian Quebecois edited by the engineer Samuel Pierre. These works problematize the conception of Quebec as a homogeneously or even principally white space, and they rightfully bring attention to the nonwhite Quebecois, who not only are struggling for recognition as a considerable presence but also participated significantly in the imagination and construction of contemporary Quebec. These scholars' work is indispensable to understanding Quebec as a social and political space, and it should also inform our readings of Quebecois literary texts. After all, authors like Aquin were living in the very Montreal Mills and Austin describe, rubbing shoulders with the professionals whose biographies Pierre collected; they witnessed and were marked by events such as the 1968 Montreal Congress of Black Writers, the 1974 antideportation protests, and, later, the 1983 taxi drivers' strikes. These writers' Montreal, their Quebec, was not homogeneously white. In contrast to the majority of Aquinian criticism, my reading of *Trou de mémoire* develops the possibility that the novel endeavors to debunk the myth of a white Quebec. Specifically, why, in a novel abounding with uncertainties and suspicions of all types, is the one thing that goes unquestioned (both within the text and by critics) the ambiguous paternity of the unborn baby, and therefore its whiteness?

*Trou de mémoire*, this chapter argues, deploys metaphorical structures to establish an interracial and intercontinental masculine francophone solidarity that satirically critiques the metaphor of revolutionary violence as rape by literalizing it. This masculine solidarity, triangulated through the assaulted woman's body, then produces a baby of unknown race that destabilizes the myth of a white Quebec by figuring its ambiguously raced future social body. In *Trou de mémoire*, poetics makes it possible to see abstract hope for an interracially solidary future through the violent particulars of a damaging solidary "brotherhood." Ultimately, this chapter seeks, by examining *Trou de mémoire*'s tropological transracial and transnational solidarity, to understand the eccentric position of Quebec within francophone studies and within empire.

*Trou de mémoire*, a complex thriller-like novel featuring multiple fictional editors, types of texts (a letter, a journal, competing editors' notes), and cities (Montreal, Grand-Bassam, Lagos, Lausanne), structures itself around the concurrent solidarity and opposition pairing two revolutionary pharmacists, a white Quebecois and a black Ivoirian—Pierre X. Magnant and Olympe Ghezzo-Quenum. Both are struggling for the liberation of their nations from colonial or neocolonial oppression;[2] their solidarity arises precisely out of their parallel anticolonial activities. But what emerges as an anticolonial connection based on shared political goals is figured throughout *Trou de mémoire* as an increasingly interpersonal identification. The solidary dyad articulates itself first as a professional (pharmacistic) association: in its mock-serious tone, the narrative affirms that revolution necessitates pharmacists, ostensibly to help cure the ailing state—"Mon activité politique," writes the Quebecois pharmacist, "me prouve que j'incarne une image archétypale de pharmacien, car je rêve de provoquer des réactions dans un pays malade" (69). The novel's second articulation of solidarity emerges from a conjoined (solidary) possession of women's bodies. In a novel that literalizes the metaphor of revolutionary violence as a struggle over the feminine body of the nation, the trope of pharmaceutical intervention devolves into the actual drugging of women's bodies, leading to their murder (Joan Ruskin) and rape (Joan's sister, Rachel Ruskin). The third, inexplicit articulation of solidarity takes the form of the soon-to-be-born child that either Magnant or Ghezzo-Quenum could have conceived during the rapes they perpetrated in a (problematically satirical) defiguralization of the figurative language of decolonization. But the unequivocally transracial nature of the alliance between the two revolutionary pharmacists should bring into question the race of the child and also lead us to probe the topic of the social outcomes of anticolonial transracial solidarity.

This chapter examines the novel's three central tropes for solidarity (literary ventriloquism, a metaphoric pun on the word *entrelacs,* and anticolonial revolution as counter-rape) and then analyzes their effects: questionable authorship and paternity resulting from a double rape and the problem of the "white baby." The investigation into the unborn baby's race is additionally supported by an analysis of an absurdist (anti)racist play titled "White Baby" found in the Aquin archives. The play, never published and dated only "196?," makes a strong case for Aquin's thinking about race during the very period when he was composing *Trou de mémoire.* By investigating the nature of the black-white binary solidarity on which the novel is constructed, detangling its satirical overlays and language games, and comparing it with the deadpan non sequiturs of "White Baby," this chapter analyzes the ways in which *Trou de mémoire* simultaneously perpetuates and troubles the exclusion of blackness in understandings of Quebec and the violence against women inherent in discourses of decolonization.

## A Brief History of Modern Quebec

Ironically, historians refer to the period immediately predating the Quiet Revolution[3] as the Grande Noirceur (Great Darkness), the era during the late thirties and then from 1944 to 1959 when the Union nationale premier, Maurice Duplessis, instituted conservative policies, chiefly anti-communist and anti-unionist, that were backed by the Catholic Church. The irony is rooted in Duplessis's emphasis on rural rather than urban development, which helped reinforce the myth of Quebec as a great white expanse, both meteorologically in terms of the long snowy winters and demographically since most of Quebec's black population has historically tended to live in cities, principally Montreal. With the election of the Parti libéral premier Jean Lesage in 1960, Quebec began its transformation into a secular welfare state, and ownership of the modes of production started to shift away from US- or English Canadian–owned corporations to local francophone-owned companies. Language entered politics to a new degree, with struggles for French to overtake English in business and trade. Of course, this Quiet Revolution did not unfold in isolation from the rest of the world; it participated in the global social upheaval of the sixties, and specifically, it was inspired by solidarity with francophone anticolonial movements. This solidarity was so intellectually productive that it developed into an imagined correlation: Quebecois intellectuals reversed the flow of colonial power in their territory, becoming not French colonizers of First Nations territory but rather French victims of English colonization.[4] The solidarity imagined in Aquin's *Trou de mémoire* between the white and the black revolutionary pharmacists fictionalizes a very real imagined connection.

Reading *Trou de mémoire* almost fifty years after its publication, revisiting this Quebecois classic with an eye to the racial profiles it inscribes on Quebecois society, participates in a still loaded debate that continues to trouble Quebec over its definition of itself. When the sovereigntist Parti québécois (PQ) closely lost (50.58% to 49.42%) the 1995 referendum on national sovereignty, the then leader Jacques Parizeau exposed the exclusionary vision of some influential PQ members; in his concession speech, Parizeau suggested that the referendum had been lost owing to "money and the ethnic vote," a hardly veiled reference to immigrant and Jewish communities. Parizeau's portrayal of Quebec as an essentially white, Christian space threatened by difference has haunted the PQ's subsequent efforts at greater inclusion and inspired some trenchant reflections on the state of race and place in the province. In her paradigmatic short story

"Pur polyester" (1998), for example, Lori Saint-Martin responds to this divisive denunciation of *otherness,* imagining the double dashing of an immigrant girl's sovereigntist hopes, first by the loss of the 1995 referendum and almost immediately afterward by the PQ leader's denying the possibility of people like her harboring sovereigntist hopes at all. The PQ's 2013 attempt to pass the Charte des valeurs québécoises and its 2019 successful passing of law 21 (La loi sur la laïcité de l'État), a law that makes it illegal for public servants to wear prominent religious symbols, has been interpreted as a hypocritically ethnocentric piece of legislature, especially because it does not ban the wearing of small symbols (rings, pendants) or the presence of crucifixes in schools or hospitals. Opponents of the law read it as unfairly affecting non-Christians specifically and immigrants, both white and nonwhite, more generally, and opposition to the project contributed to the ousting of the Parti québécois from power in 2014. The heated protests following the announcement of the 2013 bill and the 2019 law show clearly that questions of religious, ethnic, and racial identity continue to polarize the Quebecois population and to affect regional and national politics.

That is what has happened in recent years "on the ground" in Quebec in terms of debates regarding perceptions of the province's identity, debates that reveal a society rife with internal deliberations about race. But from the outside perspective of a wider francophone world, Quebec is still largely perceived as overwhelmingly white; this has contributed to its ambiguous status within francophone studies, a field that is racially marked, as I outline in this book's introduction (see Lionnet and Shih, *Creolization of Theory* 13). Some independence-era Quebecois intellectuals, however, sought to express, before francophone studies became an academic discipline, the heterogeneous porousness of race in French-speaking regions, including Quebec. Far from the "dogma of racelessness" to which the scholar Fatima El-Tayeb ascribes Europe's whitewashed self-image (El-Tayeb 230), some Quebecois thinkers, out of a sense of solidarity with anticolonial movements, in the sixties and seventies were eager to see themselves as *not white*. This affective interracialization developed, in the case of some, into an awareness not only of the racial heterogeneity found in Quebec (especially in its urban centers, Montreal particularly) but also of the social pressures that made this state of racial copresence and mixing a contested fact. For Hubert Aquin, in his complicated novel *Trou de mémoire,* global francophone solidarities are articulated over complex metaphorical networks that illustrate the affective impulses making an awareness of racial and intellectual mixing in Quebec possible.

## *Trou de mémoire* as Solidary Ventriloquism

Aquin's novel *Trou de mémoire* opens with a letter from Olympe Ghezzo-Quenum,[5] a self-described revolutionary pharmacist from Grand-Bassam, Côte d'Ivoire, to a fellow revolutionary pharmacist in Montreal, Quebec, named Pierre X. Magnant. The two have never met, but Ghezzo-Quenum writes that he has read one of Magnant's anticolonial revolutionary speeches in a newspaper and that from this speech developed a feeling of great affinity with the Quebecois insurgent: "J'ai le sentiment que nous sommes, vous et moi, incroyablement frères!" (5). The coincidences that link them, Ghezzo-Quenum explains, are too great to leave him indifferent: the two men share an analogous career, similar anticolonial political aspirations and practices (e.g., giving speeches from the roofs of cars), and the same favorite authors; in addition, they have a mutual acquaintance in the person of yet another pharmacist, Ghezzo-Quenum's lover, a young English Canadian woman named Rachel Ruskin living in Lagos, Nigeria.

Ghezzo-Quenum follows his assertion of brotherhood with a long aside, a caveat riffing on the intercontinental power relations and attending racial characterizations that would normally divide him from his fellow revolutionary pharmacist:

> (J'allais écrire: jumeaux! Mais, une fois de plus, je me suis contraint à exprimer moins que je ressens, ce qui veut dire que je m'applique à psalmodier selon le Discours de la Méthode et à taire le chant barbare de mes intuitions. Je n'ai jamais dit à un Européen qu'il était mon ami, à plus forte raison un "frère." . . . Vous mesurez, dès lors, la qualité de mon trouble . . . quand je vous pressens comme un frère, alors même que la pigmentation de ma peau me conditionne d'emblée à vous désigner comme un Blanc fils d'Européen, comme un sale Blanc! Et Dieu sait que les Blancs sont de sales Blancs, pour nous du moins . . .) (5, parentheses in original)

The ambiguous racial antagonism apparent in this passage structures the novel, taking as its base a hostile face-off across a colonial line that coincides with a color line. In this parenthetical aside, the racial dichotomy takes shape as a series of allusive stereotypes—first, the ironic and amplificatory reference to Senghor's "L'émotion est nègre, comme la raison est hellène" (295), identifying Europe with Descartes's *Discourse on Method* and contrasting its codified chant ("psalmodier") to the "barbaric singing" of intuition; second, the spirited reversal ("sale Blanc" for "sale nègre") of the insult by which Fanon construes black subjecthood as an objectifying interpellation in *Black Skin, White Masks*.[6] Ghezzo-Quenum stages this racial antagonism as a corporeal reflex that has conditioned him to see first and foremost skin color and to interpret it geographically. But in suggesting that Magnant is both a European and a "son of Europeans," Ghezzo-Quenum oscillates, revealing his own ambivalence with regard to Magnant's racial and geographical status as a Quebecois. Moreover, by extending the original family metaphor of brotherhood and twinning it with the image of Magnant as a "son of Europeans," Ghezzo-Quenum draws a tenuous familial connection between himself and Europe, further undoing the racial binary he erects, undermining his own blackness and rootedness in Africa at the same time that he seeks to affirm these through a performance of racial hatred. The ambivalence of Ghezzo-Quenum's expression of solidarity with Magnant, together with the unbelievability of his original assertion ("incroyablement frères"—the adverb's common hyperbolic use leads us to forget its denotation), points to the asymptotic nature of the solidary relation; Ghezzo-Quenum tries to articulate his desire for solidarity linguistically but repeatedly balks at the impossibility of the task.

In addition, although I use this passage to establish the (asymptotic) *solidarity* between the two protagonists, solidarity has no agent noun. The word that Ghezzo-Quenum uses repeatedly is actually *frère*: in the absence of an accurate vocable for contingent solidarities articulated across regionally constituted power differentials, he imagines between himself and Magnant a link of fraternity. This metaphorical brotherhood lies on the same spectrum as solidarity, but it differs from the latter in significant ways. First of all, it limits the scope of solidarity by inescapably gendering its participants. Indeed, it is no coincidence that the two revolutionary pharmacists are men. As Katherine A. Roberts has argued in her article "Making Women Pay," the goal of decolonization that unites them plays itself out violently on the bodies of women (the murder of Joan Ruskin by Magnant in the first half of the novel and the rape of her sister Rachel by both Magnant and Ghezzo-Quenum in the second half). And Ghezzo-Quenum's insistence on *frère* points to a lacuna in the vocabulary and concept of solidarity: there exists no substantive to label the agent of solidarity. This void doubtless stems, at least in part, from the fact that in comparison with terms of kinship (e.g., *brother* for the relation of *brotherhood*), the vocabulary of solidarity is relatively recent, dating back only four hundred years or so. But the absence marked by the nonexistent vocable for *solidary person* does structure the ways that the concept of solidarity can be used and applied, forcing speakers who want to interpellate such a person in French (or English, for that matter) to resort to other, related terms that are, incidentally, weighed down by their own connotations, associations, and restrictions (e.g., gender). Ghezzo-Quenum's solidarity with Magnant must take the channels available to it, and these channels coincide with and reinforce the violent gendering inherent in the context of colonization and decolonization.

The interracial brotherhood proclaimed by Ghezzo-Quenum, the metaphoric kinship of solidarity that is his striving for unity with Magnant, can be read as an instance of wish fulfillment on the part of Hubert Aquin. The novel's act of locating professions of interracial kinship in the writing body of the fictional character Olympe Ghezzo-Quenum, the self-proclaimed revolutionary black man, intimates a persistent need for an ever closer identification with the racial other on the part of Aquin. Attesting to Aquin's fascination with colonization, Albert Memmi, in his postface to the 1972 Quebec edition of *Portrait du colonisé*, writes,

> Je ne songeais évidemment pas aux Canadiens français en écrivant mon livre. . . . J'ai reçu une lettre d'un jeune Canadien, qui devait devenir l'un des écrivains de la nouvelle école de Montréal: Hubert Aquin. Il me demandait de parler de mon expérience de la colonisation devant la Télévision Canadienne Française. J'ai dit oui, bien sûr, tout en m'étonnant que les Canadiens puissent s'intéresser tant à la colonisation. . . . J'ai compris pourquoi lorsque j'ai constaté que Hubert Aquin me suggérait constamment des comparaisons entre ma description et ce qu'il sentait et pensait lui-même comme Canadien. Ce fut le début d'un dialogue et d'une correspondance. (137)

Aquin's assiduous interest in the experience and theory of (de)colonization manifests a desire to hear the colonized other acknowledge Quebec's colonial status.[7] In his postface Memmi obliged, abstracting colonialism to its purest power relation ("the colonial relation is relative" [139]), making the concept pliable enough to adapt to Quebec—a solidary willingness symbolized by the Quebecois reedition of the *Portrait*. The specific mode of *Trou de mémoire*'s articulation of decolonial solidarity, the validation of Quebec's colonial victimhood by Ghezzo-Quenum, performs a similar gesture to Memmi's but does so (in the realm of fiction) unprompted, spontaneously. Ghezzo-Quenum's freely assigned fictional fraternity can be seen as representing the asymptotic solidary ideal for which Aquin yearned.

We must ask ourselves what patterns of domination this particular mode of fictionalization represents. Aquin, the white Quebecois author, gives voice to the acknowledgment he desires from the colonized, racially different other in an act of literary ventriloquism. Although every fictional character can be understood as a nodal point for the author's voice and every author could therefore be considered a ventriloquist, *Trou de mémoire* stands out in several ways. First, the anticolonial solidarity that Ghezzo-Quenum articulates is of recurring interest to Aquin, documented in his essays[8] as well as in Memmi's friendly narrative of his meeting with him. Second, Aquin as an authorial figure insists on his own presence in *Trou de mémoire,* populating its margins with coded references to himself; Aquin the author haunts the novel's nebulous frontiers between fiction and a historical "reality," bringing into play his own political and literary personhood. Third, as we will see, the novel pointedly thematizes writerly impersonation when it broaches questions of authenticity and counterfeiting. These features, negotiating the ontological gap between the white author Aquin, his "biolectographical"[9] novel *Trou de mémoire,* and its black protagonist, shore up the argument for conceptualizing Aquin as ventriloquizing his fantasy of transracial confraternity through Ghezzo-Quenum.

But more important, and in spite of Aquin's affirmed interest in the discourse of decolonization, this ventriloquism inscribes itself in a long history of (white) Western representations of (nonwhite) others, a discourse imbued and entangled with histories of imperialism and domination. *Trou de mémoire* shares some of orientalism's fascination with scientific (anthropological and geographical) knowledge: descriptions of Grand-Bassam, for example, and an emphasis on Ghezzo-Quenum's ethnicity and the blackness of his skin, bring to fictional life an overly determined Fon Ivoirian writing subject. This enumeration of information as an attempt to determine and pin down the other compounds a problematic projection of desire. To make a black character articulate an alliance that he—Aquin—covets, to inscribe onto that character his own fantasies, Aquin must inhabit a position of relative power, even on the most literal and practical level of his ability to be published (Montreal, Paris). And as David Kazanjian argues in the context of early American depictions of indigenous peoples, biloquism (a doubling projection of the voice or, Kazanjian suggests, a modern version of "Gothic" ventriloquism) rests on the "incorporation and mastery" of the other (Kazanjian, "Biloquial Nation" 484). The biloquist (or, similarly, the ventriloquist) assimilates otherness and tames difference—and in the case of *Trou de mémoire* compels difference to profess affinity.

## Interlace and Inter-lakes: On the Dual Nature of Solidarity in *Trou de mémoire*

*Trou de mémoire* visibly labors to mitigate the imperialism inherent in Aquin's speaking through and for Ghezzo-Quenum. The narrative introduces a doubling in the metaphorical network that redefines the solidarity between Magnant and Ghezzo-Quenum as a fluid and potentially productive exchange through the creation of a pun on the oft-repeated word *entrelacs* and its verbal relative *entrelacer*. Since, as I show in the next section, solidarity in *Trou de mémoire* happens (satirically) through the violent treatment of women, the punning redefinition of productive solidarity finds expression specifically at the moment when the narrative recounts (or elides) the dying moments of Joan Ruskin. This passage, arguably a nodal point connecting *Trou de mémoire*'s complicatedly interrelated sections (a letter, diary and journal entries, editors' notes and counternotes), connects Joan's final moments to the solidarity linking Magnant and Ghezzo-Quenum. The first step in establishing this link is to metaphorically displace the suffering of Joan onto the littoral of Lagos, the geographical and linguistic connection between the two men:

> Elle est partie de honte pour fuir vers le sud mon échec et aussi, sait-on jamais? parce que je n'ai pas voulu fuir à Lagos quand elle me suppliait de partir et qu'elle énumérait, dans sa lassitude finale, les beautés humides de Lagos et du littoral *entrelacé* de la Côte des Esclaves qui se love interminablement en une noire écharpe déprimée à travers laquelle l'eau lente se couche sur son lit sableux. Il me semble soudain que ma tristesse me déporte trop tard sur la côte basse, ennoyée, d'où soudain j'aperçois Lagos, ville funéraire, que je ne sais trop comment rejoindre, tellement je ne m'y comprends pas dans le secret des lagunes et des deltas innombrables qui me séparent de la femme que j'ai perdue. (*Trou de mémoire* 109–10, emphasis added)

Coming at the end of Magnant's drug-addled anticonfession to having murdered Joan Ruskin, this passage culminates a process of narrative subterfuge. As Magnant announces from the onset, he is writing this narrative in order *not* to confess—one of the *trous de mémoire*, or memory losses/blackouts, of the title.[10] In a manner typical of his solipsistic style, Magnant's extravagant prose here distorts regular usage to elide Joan's dying: the standard idiom should read "elle est *morte* de honte" (already a figurative phrase that means embarrassment rather than death), but he substitutes the euphemistic "*partie* de honte," avoiding any direct reference to death. Moreover, abusing the verbal governance of *partir*, he completes the image of Joan's parting with not one but two prepositional phrases ("pour fuir vers le sud mon échec"), the first of which detaches the second from its object, obscuring Joan's movement *away* (from him, from life) with the suggestion of her purposeful movement *toward* a geographical destination. Through this multiplication of phrases, he continues to digress and distract from the original turn of phrase, from the eclipsed past participle *morte*, putting the physical, geographical phrase "vers le sud" *in the way* of an already more figurative allusion to murder, superimposing land over body. The imagery of this superimposition is erotic and mystifying, overlaying the purportedly unknowable geography of Lagos on the opaque body of Joan, whose disappearance, in death, eradicates the tantalizing but impossible prospect of a full revelation of her mind and ideas to Magnant.

By thematizing the Slave Coast in this Montreal murder plot, Aquin also reactivates the African-Quebecois solidarity of the prefatory letter, this time in the voice of his white, Quebecois character. To reinforce this link, Magnant's narrative refers directly to "Grand-Bassam," the memorable opening word of *Trou de mémoire* (the city is Ghezzo-Quenum's place of residence and thus the origin of the prefatory letter he sends to Quebec); Magnant specifies that the Slave Coast "goes from Grand-Bassam, in the Ivory Coast, to the innumerable mouths of the Niger." In this way, an evocation of the Slave Coast is used to highlight a link between francophone insurgents and spaces: "Grand-Bassam" connects Magnant's narration to Ghezzo-Quenum's letter.

In association with the reprise of the solidarity between Grand-Bassam and Montreal, the narrative emphasizes the word *entrelacé*, repeating both its adjectival and its substantive form (*entrelacs*) several times. *Entrelacs* can be read as the central pattern governing *Trou de mémoire*, first with regard to the novel's structure, with its narratives crossing and overlapping,[11] and also with regard to the relationship quadrangle structuring the novel—Magnant and Joan on the one hand, Ghezzo-Quenum and Joan's sister, Rachel, on the other, intersected by the intercouple rape of Rachel by Magnant. This passage's insistence on the geography of the Slave Coast and its clear allusion to Ghezzo-Quenum's letter suggest that another of these *entrelacs*, the masculine interlinking of Magnant and Ghezzo-Quenum, provides a way to read Joan's disappearance into topographic and liquid metaphors as central to the novel's imagining of solidarity.

I will return to the central problem of the violence done to women in *Trou de mémoire*, but first let us examine the nature of the solidarity suggested by this passage. *Entrelacs* forms part of an elaborate pun typical of Aquin's almost academic wordplay. Etymologically related to the Latin *laqueus* (noose—related to the English *lace* and *lasso*),[12] *entrelacs* refers to ornamental patterns created by interweaving strands. But Aquin plays with the homonymics of *lacs* (strings, nooses) and *lacs* (lakes, derived from the Latin *lacus*), superimposing riparian imagery onto the weaving imagery: *entrelacs* in the context of *Trou de mémoire*'s punning thus means both "interlace" and "between-lakes." This homonymic game represents two alternate or simultaneous forms of solidarity, or rather, two different sets of metaphors through which solidarity can be understood. If solidarity is an interlacing of different perspectives, or in this case different continental revolutionary purposes, we are left, on the one hand, with a kind of braid of distinct racial threads: though woven together into a complex strand, these threads maintain the black/white dichotomies established by Ghezzo-Quenum in his prefatory letter. If, on the other hand, we read solidarity through the riparian imagery, figured as a flowing between lakes, then any conception of distinctness or discrete perspectives must fade away: intercontinental solidarity becomes a transracial solidarity, one that implies, welcomes, reveals, or makes necessary racial mixing. Reading solidarity as waterway allows us to conceive of Quebec and Africa not as irrevocably distant but rather as intimately linked—as the Atlantic Ocean linked the Slave Coast to the New World, the waterway playing the tragic role with which we are familiar. Aquin's wordplay, far from being trivial, brings these historical flows to the fore and suggests a form of solidarity that takes them into account. In contrast to Aquin's ventriloquial mode of imposing solidary discourse on his black character, a mode that mimics or perpetuates empire, solidarity as waterway acknowledges the imperial structures that endure and configure human relations. At the same time, obscuring Joan's murder with the watery metaphor *entrelacs* emphasizes the erasure of women from a solidary anticolonial discourse that frequently metaphorized revolution as a violent reclaiming of feminized territory.

The name of the city of Lagos (Portuguese for "lake") adds to the network of littoral lexemes. Lagos catalyzes the plot of the novel by providing a triangulated meeting point between the two male characters: it is in Lagos that Ghezzo-Quenum meets Rachel Ruskin and obtains Magnant's address, which makes possible the prefatory letter. In the context of Aquin's playing with *entrelacs* as "between-lakes," Lagos becomes a paradoxical composite space, both a body of water and a metropolis, at once the setting for sinuous rivers and the cosmopolitan capital (at the time) where a black man dating a white woman might go unnoticed, as Ghezzo-Quenum appreciates. This doubling of Lagos parallels the double metaphorical edifice structuring solidarity as either fluid amalgamation or interweaving of discrete perspectives. As my subsequent analysis shows, *Trou de mémoire,* which begins by favoring the interwoven model of solidarity in Ghezzo-Quenum's letter, relies increasingly on the fluidity model, which comes to predominate at the end of the novel. Moreover, framing solidarity through these abstract structures of meaning (interlace and interlake) prepares the reader to understand the novel's concerns with past and future francophone transracialisms and with Quebec's solidary place within these relations.

### Satire and the Occlusion of Violence against Women

The fact that this imagery illustrative of solidarity enters the narrative at the moment of Joan's death is significant: it points to the link, which Katherine A. Roberts has brilliantly exposed, between gender, violence, and revolution. As Roberts writes, "Aquin's liberation process as expressed here in Magnant's narrative involves the act of reducing the English-Canadian/oppressor's woman to the status of defeated entity and thus forcing her to share in the humiliation that has dominated the French-Canadian psyche since 1760. Magnant is thus brought into being, 'régénéré' by the extermination of a woman who symbolizes the enemy; but also, more importantly, her death symbolizes the annihilation of his own metaphorical femininity as a member of a colonized people" (23). Roberts traces the gendered violence in Aquin's text to anticolonial thinkers like Fanon, whose *Black Skin, White Masks* includes chapters titled "The Woman of Color and the White Man" and "The Man of Color and the White Woman." Her argument provides an authoritative reading of gender and anticolonial relations in the twentieth century: she shows how "Aquin's victimization of women stems from the sexual tropology that invariably accompanies the adoption of the (de)colonization paradigm. Borrowing heavily from such thinkers as Frantz Fanon, Albert Memmi, and Aimé Césaire, Aquin has adopted a pre-existing master narrative of sexual relationships in which the submissive position is already marked as female" (17). Indeed, earlier imperialist and colonialist discourse against which Fanon, Memmi, and Césaire were reacting also armed itself with the metaphorical tools of feminization, virginity, and sexual conquest to characterize and justify Europe's exploitative relation to the lands and peoples it annexed. As Anne McClintock argues, "Enlightenment metaphysics presented knowledge as a relation of power between two gendered spaces, articulated by a journey and a technology of conversion: the male penetration and exposure of a veiled, female interior; and the aggressive conversion of its 'secrets' into a visible, male science of the surface.... In [Enlightenment] fantasies, the world is feminized and spatially spread for male exploration, then reassembled and deployed in the interests of massive imperial power" (23). Or as Sylvia Söderlind contends in her analysis of the formal problems presented by *Trou de mémoire,* "Rape [is] . . . symbolic of the colonizer's appropriation of the colony's history" (71).[13] The master texts of decolonization reply to Enlightenment gendered visions of empire in terms of hypermacho desire because these visions have established the pattern of territorial possession as a masculine, (hetero)sexual gesture. If Fanon, Césaire, and Memmi assert a colonized black masculinity, it is only after generations of colonial power emasculated black colonial subjects; their anti-imperialism may represent an antiwoman stance, but it is part of a larger structure of metaphorical (and real) aggression dating back generations.

*Trou de mémoire* inscribes itself in the antiwoman discourse of imperialism and anti-imperialism by problematizing it with satire. The novel makes explicit and carries to extremes the relationship between gendered violence and decolonization. In a section entitled "Cahier noir," which, as the fictional editor explains, was written before the main events of the novel take place, the character Magnant narrates his transformation into a revolutionary, a transformation triggered specifically by reading *La femme frigide* (a treatise written by the psychoanalyst Wilhelm Stekel in 1937):

> Joan, cette nuit-là, s'est endormie avant moi pendant que je lisais ce livre éminemment excitant: je voyais toutes sortes de femmes à violer, toute une succession de nobles et respectables inconnues que j'aurais volontiers pénétrées sans avertissement, sans égard, mais non sans plaisir. . . . En fin de livre, j'étais tellement excité que je me suis mis à harceler cette femme endormie à mes côtés; mail il n'y avait rien à faire. Joan, inerte de par l'effet de son barbiturique, ne bronchait pas: sa gélatine ne lui servirait pas, de toute évidence. Quel non-sens! C'est alors que . . . * et je suis resté les yeux grands ouverts jusqu'à l'aube morbide. À mon réveil, je suis devenu révolutionnaire, faute d'avoir possédé ce soleil aux yeux cernés.
>
> *Passage vraiment indécent que je me suis permis de supprimer. *Note de l'éditeur.* (*Trou de mémoire* 130–31)

A gesture of transference structures this paragraph, repeated with variations that make the actions described oscillate between reprehensibility and humor. The vocabulary and syntax used to describe Magnant's phantasms of rape, drawn from polite conversation ("volontiers" and "sans avertissement, sans égard, mais non sans plaisir"), ludicrously transfer the social respectability of the "noble women" onto Magnant's radically asocial, violent desires. The narrative also transfers the sexual excitement inspired by Magnant's reading of the scholarly tome on frigidity, already an implausible conceit, onto his unconscious lover's body in what becomes an offensively inappropriate, if preposterous, act. The absurdity of Magnant's meticulous, almost scientific language as he describes Joan's body ("inerte de par l'effet de son barbiturique") dangerously minimizes the seriousness of the offense, which the narrator does not shy away from naming as harassment; his casualness with respect to the contraceptive ("gélatine") that he plans not to use is at once horrific and hilarious. The editor's note announcing the omission of a "passage vraiment indécent" finally resolves the tonal ambiguity and clinches the paragraph's nature as satirical: the spectacle of squeamish censure is ironic, especially coming from an editor who at another point in the novel does not hesitate to narrate the public cunnilingus rumored to have been performed by Magnant on a drunken Joan in a restaurant.

But this passage's culminating satirical transference, and the one that interests me most, is Magnant's awakening from sexual frustration to revolutionary zeal, which at once explicitly reveals the trope linking decolonization to violence against women and exposes its absurdity, a pivotal moment in *Trou de mémoire*'s representations of violent sexual relations. To be sure, a spotty narration, combined with dense overlaying of imagery, mystifies the ironic relationship between sexual violence and anticolonial revolution; or rather, the layering of obfuscating details constitutes part of the irony that marks this relationship. Such a profusion of narrative tricks points to a purposely deceptive narration. First, after the elided supposedly "indecent" events, Magnant writes, he both stayed awake until dawn with his eyes wide open and woke up with the firm intent of becoming a revolutionary. In Magnant's otherwise chronological and precise narration (too precise, according to the straitlaced editor), the omission of his falling asleep comes as a contrivance, a distracting element. Moreover, his ascribing to the dawn his own morbid attraction to Joan's inert body and his association of the sun rising during the bleak dawn with Joan's own fatigued mien further detract from and even mask the statement whose direct causality is otherwise clear: "je suis devenu révolutionnaire, faute d'avoir possédé ce soleil aux yeux cernés." In fact, this narration of transference (eliding Joan by transferring her traits onto the sun) masks the basic causality of the trope linking sexual violence to Magnant's transformation into a revolutionary.

*Trou de mémoire*'s satirical linking of decolonialism with violence against women goes beyond this transference of sexual frustration into revolutionary zeal; it also structures and defines the solidary link between the two male protagonists. Indeed, if Ghezzo-Quenum's solidarity with Magnant is imagined as a kinship, a brotherhood, this kinship is made flesh through the bodies of the Ruskin sisters, who are the two men's lovers: through these women they are, in a way, brothers-in-law. And when Magnant rapes Rachel, Ghezzo-Quenum's lover, and Ghezzo-Quenum then repeatedly reenacts the rape in an effort to know its narrative, the two men become sexual alternates for each other; through a kind of sexual transubstantiation, they become each other's phantasmic double.[14] This multifaceted instrumentalization of women's bodies to serve as stepping stones between the main (male) characters is abhorrent, but it typifies, if exaggeratedly, the uses to which the trope has been put: in Fanon's *Black Skin, White Masks,* for example, possessing a white woman means, among other things, possessing the white man's property and object of desire and thus taking the white man's place. The white woman is incidental to this revolutionary transformation of social relations. *Trou de mémoire* literalizes what Fanon leaves as metaphorical: the woman, no longer merely a symbol of status (although Joan *is* anglophone, the Montreal equivalent of Fanon's desired whiteness),[15] is the precondition for Magnant's entering the world of revolution (and thence entering a relation of solidarity with Ghezzo-Quenum) with the goal of overthrowing an anglophone "colonial" rule.

As Roberts's problematization of the rape and murder featured in the novel shows, the satirical tone of *Trou de mémoire* does not annul the violence of the text;[16] in fact, in a sense irony gives license to exaggerating violence, to carrying it to extremes, at the same time that it allows for a casualness in its description that remains extremely alarming, satire or no satire. And yet *Trou de mémoire*'s satirical revival of the trope drawing a parallel between decolonial discourse and violence against women constitutes the text's way of exposing and problematizing that trope; the novel shows that this type of revolutionary novel, this type of anticolonial imaginary, is structured on the suffering and erasure (or the erasure of the suffering) of women. Reading irony into Magnant's (and Ghezzo-Quenum's, with Rachel) casually, caressingly gruesome relationships with

Joan and Rachel Ruskin becomes key in understanding the ways bodies and texts are similarly used and misused in the novel.

Extending the satirical critique, the novel suggests a connection between sexual and revolutionary violence and interracial solidarity. The paragraph quoted above is the opening of a longer section that develops the leitmotif explicitly linking sexual violence to decolonial revolution. The section ends with an apparent non sequitur, a brief mention of Gilles Legault, the real-life Quebecois revolutionary:

> En amour, je me tiens près du degré zéro et je ne suis bon qu'à m'acharner à profiter (sans profit réel!) de Joan et des autres femmes. . . . Gilles Legault vient de se suicider dans sa cellule de prison\*\*; et c'était un jour de Pâques: Jacques était un patriote, un frère. . . . Soudain, je n'ai plus de goût à rien: jamais on n'avait fêté un jour de Pâques de façon aussi tragique. Mais j'ai le cœur fendu: j'en perds mes moyens.
>
> \*\*Le dimanche de Pâques 1965, Gilles Legault, prisonnier politique, s'est suicidé dans sa cellule à la Prison de Montréal. Ce passage du cahier noir m'a appris que P. X. Magnant et Gilles Legault se connaissaient; je l'ignorais tout à fait. . . . Il se peut donc que les deux patriotes aient eu des relations de type opératoire; sait-on jamais? *Note de l'éditeur.* (134)

Thematically, this passage introduces suicide as the fate of revolutionaries, foreshadowing the doppelganger suicides of Magnant and his alter ego, the editor (more on which later), as well as the separate but parallel suicide of Ghezzo-Quenum.[17] But it does more. Although this is the novel's only mention of Gilles Legault, the fact that he really existed (1934–1965)[18] changes the significance of this brief and cryptic passage. Specifically, the nature of the crime that put Gilles Legault in the prison where he committed suicide codes interracial solidarity into this section of *Trou de mémoire*. Legault was arrested in February 1965 for colluding in the plot to blow up the Statue of Liberty, the anecdote with which the introduction to this book opens; he allegedly provided dynamite to Michèle Duclos, the twenty-six-year-old white TV announcer and member of the Front de libération du Quebec, who drove it across the Canadian border with the purpose of delivering it to members of the Harlem-based Black Liberation Front. The conspirators had been infiltrated from the beginning by the FBI and the Gendarmerie royale du Canada and were arrested well before any attack was carried out. And yet the unlikely alliance remains, an interracial solidarity structured around Quebecois activists' identification with colonized and oppressed people with whom they felt they shared a cause. In *Trou de mémoire,* the collocation of the seemingly unrelated topics of Magnant's revolutionary violence against women and the Legault incident stresses the link between revolution, the suffering of women, and interracial solidarity, a link that the rest of the novel bears out. Indeed, by literalizing decolonial discourse's violence against women in the double rape of Rachel Ruskin and concluding the novel with the announcement of her pregnancy, the novel broaches the question of paternity, of filiation, and of inheritance: within an interlaced network of solidarity, who, literally and figuratively, is the father of the revolutionary future?

## Questioning Authorship: Text and Child

*Trou de mémoire* repeatedly makes explicit its concern with the ambiguity of the authorship of texts, and the novel implicitly connects this ambiguity to biological paternity and racial identity. Let us start with the equivocal nature of authorship. The novel's fictional editor, whose name is later revealed to be Charles-Édouard Mullahy, produces a chapter immediately following the extended passage about the Lagosian littoral that questions the authorship of the Lagos passage: "Et voici que j'interviens maintenant dans ce livre pour mettre en question les pages qui précèdent" (113). There follows a mock-erudite passage laying out Mullahy's many reasons for doubting Magnant's authorship of the passage concerning Africa: First, the passage is not delirious enough (Magnant was supposedly drugged while writing it). Second, the passage is too "étudié," an adjective meaning both learned and mannered—inconsistent, for Mullahy, with Magnant's profession and his drugged state. Third, the passage shows a type of local knowledge that should be available only to natives, for example, in its mention of Grand-Bassam as the westernmost point of the Slave Coast, when Grand-Bassam is not the official boundary of the region but the unofficial one, rooted in the (historical) reality of the slave trade. Fourth, the passage's vocabulary ("les failles du littoral," "les limans," "les redents," "les isthmes décrochés"), drawn from the fields of geography and geology, shows a type of erudition that is incompatible with a pharmacist's knowledge base, on the one hand, and with Magnant's presumed thirdhand familiarity with the region (through Joan's retelling of the letters received from her sister Rachel), on the other. Mullahy even goes so far as to consult an ostensibly objective psychiatric doctor—the editor emphasizes his objectivity—who diagnoses, from a reading of the text, the writer of this supposedly inauthentic passage as someone suffering from "confusional psychosis."

These various reasons for doubting are variously preposterous; the editor's claims about the types of knowledge that Magnant as a Quebecois pharmacist cannot have are patently false and refer obliquely to Hubert Aquin's own famous erudition and love for reading esoteric texts on all sorts of topics.[19] In addition, every objection presented by Mullahy becomes moot when the novel reveals, at its conclusion, that Mullahy himself is none other than Magnant, who faked his own death in order to escape financial and legal difficulties.[20] Mullahy's doubts about the text's authenticity disingenuously perform distrust; his emphasis on the doctor's objectivity is ludicrous when compared with his own duplicitous pretense at detachment. Mullahy's questioning of the authenticity of Magnant's Slave Coast imagery thus both thematizes doubt about authorship and masks, unobtrusively, his own supplanting of Magnant. This particular moment of suspicious authorship does not resurface and is never resolved in *Trou de mémoire*, but it inscribes itself in a larger pattern of deceptive textual production, an elaborate game of identity masking in which all the narrators (save Ghezzo-Quenum) engage.

Other passages are not only doubted but also revealed as false. Mullahy, for example, reacts with anger and repugnance to a passage introduced into the manuscript by Rachel Ruskin, calling it false and apocryphal. In this passage, Rachel herself plays with the veil of anonymity that conceals a writer's identity: "On pourrait me reprocher de ne pas m'être identifiée plus tôt (eh oui! par un 'e' muet . . .)" (139, parentheses and ellipsis in original). In the equivalent of a textual striptease, Rachel brings attention to the grammatical obligation that reveals her gender. Part of a struggle over the role of final editor (a struggle to the death, we later find out, which will end only with Mullahy's suicide), this "middle passage" by Rachel has been identified as a key to the text: "Rachel Ruskin's section constitutes the central mirror in which the surrounding narratives, as well as the editorial commentary, are reflected" (Söderlind 77). It does function this way, but it is also significant in its intentional, flagrant untruth with regard to the (fictional) events it recounts. Specifically, Rachel, after revealing her identity, claims to have been the real author of the entire Magnant manuscript; then, she affirms herself as Joan's lesbian lover (rather than her sister) and avers that Joan was not a primatologist as Magnant maintains but a stage designer. Unlike Magnant's passage about the Lagosian littoral, however, Rachel's central section is later revealed to be a fabrication, and Rachel herself explains the narrative subterfuge in great detail, ludicrous in its sleuthing realism (she managed to enter Mullahy's Montreal office at night to read and doctor his files). The revelation of Rachel's elaborate falsehood destabilizes the truth value of the text and reinforces the doubts about authorship and truth repeatedly expressed by Mullahy, who, like his alter ego Magnant, harbors fantasies of absolute control over the text as well as over the bodies of women.

But *Trou de mémoire* evades any absolute pinning down. Its narrative, full of self-corrections, contradictions, and errors (accidental or deliberate), functions like something of a quantum text: the more precisely the authorship of a section can be determined, the less precisely its truthfulness is known, and vice versa. The novel is alive with ambiguity; it teems with highly technical, precious, and pseudoscientific language that gives the illusion of exactness and verifiability to identities, events, and descriptions that ultimately refuse to be tethered.

In fact, the text delights in and problematizes the paradoxical relationship between writer and written word: the writer is necessary for the creation of the text, but the written artifact itself contains no certifiable trace of the writer's identity. Similar to Plato's *pharmakon,* which simultaneously serves as an aid to memory and weakens the muscles of memory by putting them out of practice, the written word both affirms a writer's existence and effaces the writer's identity.[21] It is the nature of writing to be dislocated from the bodily presence of its writer, and any attempt to secure an identity, to certify a text's authenticity, or to attach a proof of authorship invites falsification; the signature in all its forms guarantees concurrently the identity of the author and the possibility of forgery.

*Trou de mémoire* features the paradox of the signature as stamp of authenticity and imitable trope and complicates it by contextualizing the concept in geographical and racial terms, centering on the term *griffe*. In his elaborate description of the counterfeited nature of Magnant's description of the Lagosian littoral, the editor Mullahy writes, "Je ne puis plus douter que le manuscrit de Pierre X. Magnant a été retouché pour tout ce qui regarde sa description de l'Afrique, du système ébrié (tout près de Grand-Bassam) jusqu'aux bouches argileuses du Niger. Sans vouloir faire un mauvais jeu de mots, cela sent la 'griffe' comme on dit aux Antilles de certains métissages" (120). As Chris Bongie notes in his chapter on Haiti in *Islands and Exiles,* "In Larousse's *Grand dictionnaire universel du XIXe siècle* (1872) we are told that the word 'griffe' is used to refer to the 'characteristic signs through which one recognizes that a work is by a particular writer or a particular artist,' as well as to a 'stamp imitating a person's signature' (8.1525): the word thus has a double meaning, one that sign(al)s both the authentic and the inauthentic, the original and the copy" (260). Bongie also cites the eighteenth- and nineteenth-century texts that define *griffe* as a racial category in the Caribbean context: Bongie details how, basing his information on Moreau de Saint-Méry's 1797 *Description de la partie française de l'Isle de Saint-Domingue*, Victor Hugo in his first novel, *Bug-Jargal*, defined a *griffe* as an "'espèce générique' between the *noirs* and the *blancs*" that "can have between twenty four and thirty two parts white [blood] and ninety six or one hundred and four parts black" (Bongie, *Islands and Exiles* 237). So the "bad pun" that the editor in *Trou de mémoire* so obtrusively wants his readers to notice draws on the cultural record of French colonial racial and racist taxonomy, and it adds a pseudobiological dimension to questions of authenticity. Thus if *Trou de mémoire* dissolves certainties regarding authorship and textual authenticity, it also associates this dissolution with anxiety derived from a history of uneasiness about racial purity.[22] These two domains concern the uncertainty of knowledge, with the *griffe* in both cases constituting a nodal point that signals this uncertainty and on which anxieties are therefore focused.

The juxtaposed questioning of textual authenticity and biological lineage, as well as Magnant's introduction of the concept of *métissage*, raises doubts about "authorship" both literal and figurative. If some of the narratives of *Trou de mémoire* appear not to have been written by their ostensible author, parentage—paternity more specifically—should also be interrogated. In addition, the indeterminate lineage and fluid intermingling that characterize texts and bodies recall the novel's defining wordplay on *entrelacs*, which imagines solidarity as waterway. The text's geographical models for transatlantic and interracial solidary imbrication suggest that the paternity of the unborn child, whose imminent birth closes the novel, should be reconsidered: the text's investment in affirming the white paternity of this child, the symbol of francophone Quebec's revolutionary future (as the text spells out), becomes suspicious, and suspicion is necessary with a text that has trained us to be skeptical of it, that has developed writing as an exercise in concealment and thematized reading as a "suspicionary" practice.

The transposition of the unborn baby into a symbol for Quebec's future is triangulated through a reference to Rachel's sister, Joan. Rachel writes, "Comme [Joan] l'a fait, j'ai *moi aussi* changé de langue et je suis devenue Canadienne française—Québécoise pure laine!" (236, emphasis added). Indeed, Joan had told Magnant, in Magnant's narration of her death (which Rachel, as final editor, has read), "j'absorberai tous les médicaments possibles, so that I become a genuine French Canadian sauveuse de race—like you!" (101). Rachel's child, because of the parallel that Rachel herself established, can thus be understood to represent the future of French Canada, of a possible decolonized Quebec. The phrase "sauveuse de race," in the context of Joan's delirious last moments, is deeply ironic: if French Canadian–ness is considered a biological racial entity that can be rescued, it cannot be attained by identity transformation, either pharmaceutical (the type Joan envisions) or cultural (the type Rachel envisions). Rachel's similarly ironic distortion of the racial and racist term *pure laine* (a Quebecois taxonomical label meaning of unadulterated French—and white—descent) to include herself, and by extension her child, raises questions about genetic inheritance more generally.

The unborn child's origin and nature thus remain perpetually ambiguous, both in the literal sense of who its father is and in the figurative sense of what this ambiguous paternity represents for the future of Quebec, which the child symbolizes. The misuse of texts (as objects whose control permits concealment rather than revelation) parallels the misuse of racialized bodies (also as objects to control and manipulate). The white body of Rachel Ruskin, misused—raped—by the white Magnant and the black Ghezzo-Quenum, becomes pregnant, both literally, with child, and also figuratively, with concealed meaning. She can be understood as *Trou de mémoire*'s ultimate concealing "package" demanding decryption, and on this decryption hinges the imagination of a future for postrevolutionary Quebec.

Scholars have generally skirted the question of the child's paternity and thus of race in *Trou de mémoire*'s imagining of Quebec's future social body.[23] For example, Anthony Wall shows brilliantly how the text draws its reader into its search for truth and accuracy, what he calls the *régime du doute* (306), forcing the reader to perform the kind of fact-checking that each fictional editor (and then, as the "real" editor Marilyn Randall has, not coincidentally, pointed out, each "real" editor as well [Randall 124]) purports to perform. And yet he limits his fact-checking to the scholarly and scientific references on which the narrators rely, even though he does mention in passing more "narrative" inconsistencies such as the irreconcilable dates of Ghezzo-Quenum's diary (more on this below). The literary critic Jacques Cardinal constitutes the beginning of an exception in terms of addressing race in *Trou de mémoire*. He refers to race once, although without naming it: in discussing Ghezzo-Quenum's final suicide, which Ghezzo-Quenum commits after assuming the name of Magnant, Cardinal writes, "il ne fait aucun doute, par ailleurs, que la police, découvrant le cadavre de Ghezzo-Quenum sous le nom de P. X. Magnant, ne sera pas dupe de la substitution" (161). For Cardinal, the bodies of Ghezzo-Quenum and Magnant are not interchangeable precisely because they *look* so different that even the police (an institution that is particularly inept in this part murder mystery) would detect the discrepancy. Notice that Cardinal leaves race unspoken even as he refers to it. Cardinal then goes on to say that the act of borrowing Magnant's identity makes sense only "s'il a pour but l'inscription symbolique du sujet" (161). So after evoking race, Cardinal transcends the racialized bodies and reads them as symbols, metaphorizing and distilling to a Lacanian search for subject identity an aspect of *Trou de mémoire* that clearly constitutes a deferential nod to racial difference.

Construing the always unstable "facts" of *Trou de mémoire* to take into account the novel's play with race and racism produces other metaphorical readings than those so far proposed by critics. Serious consideration of race as a structuring element of the novel reveals a concern not only with the "symbolic inscription" of the (implicitly white) subject but also with the inscription of a racialized (white or otherwise) subject in community as solidary construction. Aquin, as a good reader of Fanon, writes a crime novel in which the final mystery remains a reading of race.

## Double Rape: Conceiving (of) Quebec's Revolutionary Future

If the baby on whose imminent birth the novel closes represents the future of revolutionary Quebec, the race of the father is significant in determining how the novel imagines this neoteric nation. Two narrators—Ghezzo-Quenum and Rachel Ruskin—affirm that the unborn baby was conceived during Magnant's rape of Rachel, implying without overtly stating that the baby would be white. Whiteness remains the unspoken, silent race of the majority in *Trou de mémoire* and also in readings of the novel, as critical whiteness studies would condemn.[24] The novel's final assertions regarding the whiteness of Rachel's baby contribute to a dominant critical assumption making of Quebec a white space. The characters' assumption about the baby's whiteness dovetails nicely, for example, with Pierre Vallières's vision of Quebec as the homeland of the "nègres blancs d'Amérique," representing French Canadians' powerlessness in anglophone North America through the metaphor of race while at the same time asserting French Canada's whiteness. And yet Quebec was never the space of whiteness that *nègres blancs* implies, and *Trou de mémoire* in fact complicates this concept of a white province.

It is of the utmost significance that the race of the baby, who, within the frame of *Trou de mémoire,* remains in a permanent state of imminent birth, is undetermined. The final assertions of certainty about the baby's paternity should not be trusted; as the novel has repeatedly trained its readers to doubt it by providing examples of both suspicious reading and unreliable writing, its final assertion of total knowledge, expertise, and control comes across as another in a series of bogus claims. Thus when Rachel writes "Je sais tout (car j'ai lu tout ce qui a précédé)" (236) or "ce roman secret est désormais sans secrets pour moi" (234), it should be clear that she does *not* know everything: her footnotes throughout the text, for example, are filled with errors, and this in spite of their apparent erudition. And indeed, she *cannot* know everything from reading the preceding text because it is flawed, a disparate collection of documents marked by inaccuracies, discrepancies, outright lies, and unclear chronologies. Moreover, Rachel draws attention away from her pregnancy through a diverting subterfuge, which, in the context of *Trou de mémoire*'s suspicionary reading practices, makes it all the more important. Indeed, her remarks about her pregnancy appear in the context of her account of her major personal transformation, which unfurls a futurity that simultaneously demands a radical shift in perspective and distracts from the interracial potentialities the pregnancy represents. Rachel writes, "Comme l'a fait l'assassin de ma sœur et le père de mon enfant, je vais moi aussi changer de nom [Magnant changed his name to Mullahy]. Déjà, j'ai déclaré au médecin, l'autre jour, que je m'appelle Anne-Lise Jamieson (Jamieson: car mon père était irlandais: cela explique tout, même l'accent que j'ai quand je parle français). Bien sûr, je n'ai pas encore dit que le père était Pierre X. Magnant . . . Si c'est un garçon, il portera le nom de son père; si c'est une fille, je l'appellerai Joan—oui, Joan X. Magnant" (236). The text presents Rachel's public renaming, her affirmation of her new hybrid French Irish *pure laine* self, simultaneously with her naming of her unborn child's father and of the child itself. But renamings in this novel are not innocent; they mask more than they transform (as Magnant's mutation into Mullahy has shown). And namings are no less problematic. As Jacques Cardinal writes, "Si le nom est, d'entrée de jeu, la marque oblitérée par où s'institue la coupure avec l'origine, il est aussi l'instance à partir de laquelle s'ordonne une logique de l'identification et de l'appartenance à la communauté" (12–13). Thus naming at once fills a void, an irreparable fissure separating the subject from its father (like the signature affixed to a written text with respect to its author), and also inscribes the subject in a community determined by named paternal descent. Cardinal insists that Rachel, by naming her child Magnant, "obéit . . . , en définitive, à la loi du nom et au désir de paternité fondatrice mise en œuvre par Magnant" (160), linking the posthumous baby to Magnant's sociopathic fixation on and search for francophone identitarian stability in the context of anglophone Canada.

But the novel's final words do protest too much, drawing attention to the baby's conception and to name changes in a way that demands closer attention: "J'ai changé de nom," writes Rachel, "je porte un enfant qui s'appellera Magnant—et jusqu'au bout, je l'espère, et sans avoir peur de son nom. Et je veux que mon enfant soit plus heureux que son père et qu'il n'apprenne jamais comment il a été conçu, ni mon ancien nom" (237). This double insistence first on masking the past and second on grounding a firm, fearless identity in the name Magnant is preempted by Rachel's plan to publish the entire text that is the novel: "Je m'apprête à le quitter [*le* here being the collective text formed by Olympe's letter and 'le récit strictement affreux de Pierre-X. Magnant et tout ce qui s'ensuit'] pour le confier aux presses et à ce public qui n'attend que l'instant de le dévorer" (234). Hence her desire to hide the truth from her child, who will bear the same name as the character of this presumed bestseller (Magnant was, in *Trou de mémoire*'s fictional world, a well-known revolutionary), is ludicrous. The final paragraph and the repeated intent to name the unborn child after Magnant signal the text's desire to pin down and resolve something that the novel configures as indeterminate: the dyad formed by Magnant and Ghezzo-Quenum, initiated as an anticolonial revolutionary solidarity, develops, disturbingly, into a sexual doubling, and the product of this merging of the two male characters remains, within the confines of the novel, an unborn promise—a fetus.

And the fetus's paternity remains indeterminate. Structured in such a way that Ghezzo-Quenum could just as well be the father as Magnant (Rachel's assertions notwithstanding), the novel ends with the imminent birth of a child that could be not white but mixed-race, changing the nature of the novel's concluding launch into Quebec's revolutionary future. Racial ambiguity rather than an unspoken certainty of whiteness results from the fluid solidary interlacing of Magnant and Ghezzo-Quenum over the brutalized body of Rachel. The *trou de mémoire* of the title becomes, for Magnant and Ghezzo-Quenum, not the matrix in which racial difference disappears but, misogynistically, the body of the woman, the vagina, which swallows up men's identity and erases all memory of them, or rather forces them to relinquish control over their memory, the memory that the future will have of them. This is exactly what Magnant and Ghezzo-Quenum fear, what the "continents sombres" (95) of womanhood mean for Magnant, the fact that out of this *trou de mémoire* will emerge something new, a new being that will take the future out of their control; this fear drives both Magnant and Ghezzo-Quenum to suicide. They are terrified that the violence of their own character, their own actions, which they had sought to bury deep inside Rachel, will resurface, that they will be faced with its revolutionary power, a power that it derives from them but that is put out of their reach inside the woman's body. The violence they inflicted on the mother, thinking it would end there (especially with their precautions to control her body), threatens to resurface with the birth of the child. The racial ambiguity of the unborn child is symbolic of what they stand to lose, of the unstable and unknowable identity of a future over which they must relinquish control.

This unknowability is marked in the text by an overdetermined yet imprecise emphasis on the days surrounding the conception of the child. The text has trained its readers to be suspicious of it and to participate in its game of *dépistage*—not simply of decoding its symbolic significances but also of fact-checking and cross-checking that happens on the ever-expanding horizon of the novel's reality (see Wall). Keeping in mind this imperative of doubt, reading *Trou de mémoire* becomes the same kind of exercise in calendar calculation that Ghezzo-Quenum tries to perform to determine whether Rachel Ruskin is pregnant after being raped by Magnant, inscribing readers in Ghezzo-Quenum's sinister process of attempting to understand (and control) Rachel's reproductive cycle. The novel is at once painstakingly precise and ambiguous on the chronology of Rachel's pregnancy. The events surrounding her rape are recounted in the diary kept by Ghezzo-Quenum, which means that this section of the text, unlike the others, includes dates and days of the week. But these dates confound as much as they illuminate, even bringing into question the year of Rachel's rape in Lausanne. Ultimately, the narrative is settled somewhat firmly in 1967, but the inexactitudes of Ghezzo-Quenum's journal, as the only source of information on Rachel's incipient pregnancy, nevertheless unsettle any certainty about which rape produced the pregnancy.

Magnant raped Rachel first. Ghezzo-Quenum's journal then traces his own jealous desire to achieve complete knowledge of Rachel's rape by Magnant in all its physical circumstances. According to the diary, the rape by Magnant occurs during the night between May 17 and 18. The period following this event is marked by Ghezzo-Quenum's growing control of Rachel's body: immediately following the rape, "Rachel Ruskin était dans un tel état de trouble que je l'ai confinée d'autorité dans notre chambre" (194), the expression *d'autorité* taking on here the disturbing tone of masculine control over a powerless female body. Rachel's semiconscious captivity turns into a gradually more permanent and severe drugging, as Ghezzo-Quenum regularly administers overdoses of sodium amytal in the hope of "narcoanalyzing" Rachel and hearing the full narrative of her rape by Magnant.

This growing authority and control over Rachel extends to a pseudo-medical knowledge of her reproductive cycle. Ghezzo-Quenum writes,

> Est-elle enceinte? . . . Non, je ne crois pas; je crois me rappeler qu'elle était alors [during the rape] en période infécondable. Il me semble avoir vu la petite enveloppe de plastique dans laquelle elle remet son diaphragme. Et, en général, quand elle le remet dans sa sacoche antiseptique, c'est que les jours dangereux sont passés. Mais je me suis peut-être trompé, sait-on jamais? Puis, de toute façon, il peut toujours se produire une seconde ovulation après un orgasme. Cela est déjà arrivé à F. T.* et, si mon souvenir est bon, à la femme de Raoul Agboton**. Enfin, je ferais mieux de ne pas me braquer là-dessus. Dans huit ou neuf jours, Rachel Ruskin devrait avoir ses règles. Je serai fixé alors.
>
> *J'ignore à quelle femme ces initiales se rapportent. Note de l'éditeur.
>
> **Raoul Agboton est aussi pharmacien à Grand-Bassam. *Note de Rachel Ruskin.* (203)

Ghezzo-Quenum's almost voyeuristic parsing of the signs through which Rachel's ovulation cycle is legible to him is redolent of a sinister intimacy, especially since he takes upon himself this silent calculation and voids any kind of autonomy Rachel might have with regard to knowing and understanding her body. He speaks of his *own* certainty ("Je serai fixé alors") as though Rachel were an entirely passive object, and the masculine exchanges about wives becoming pregnant because of a second ovulation due to orgasm reeks of boastful machismo, clever feminine dupery, or both. Besides, the entire paragraph performs a soft annihilation of certainty. All the affirmations are shaded by modal doubt: "je ne crois pas," "je crois," "il me semble," "en général," "Mais je me suis peut-être trompé, que sais-je?," culminating in the scientifically dubious assertion that "il peut toujours se produire une seconde ovulation après un orgasme," which implies that a woman's body is hypothetically always fertile, especially because, in Ghezzo-Quenum's understanding, a woman necessarily experiences orgasm when penetrated by a man: "Rachel Ruskin est une femme et, sans doute, a-t-elle joui d'être pénétrée par un homme—et cela, même si c'était sous contrainte" (197). These revolting declarations about rape and women's experience of sex contribute to the satirical misogyny of *Trou de mémoire,* but they also begin to cast doubt on the paternity of Rachel Ruskin's baby.

The dates of Ghezzo-Quenum's erratic diary become important because Ghezzo-Quenum's methods for drawing out Rachel's memories of the rape involve his repeated (unprotected) reenactment of the event, making him, potentially, the father of Rachel's unborn child. Ghezzo-Quenum narrates his own rapes of Rachel retrospectively, of course, and with tremendous ambiguity: because of the fudged dates and the accordioning of the narrative on those days following the initial rape with flashbacks and other forms of narrative padding, Ghezzo-Quenum's diary misleads us into thinking that there is a considerable lapse of time between the rape and his enactments of it. Concretely, the narrative intersperses precise dates (some of which must be inaccurate, if only because they are repeated in reference to different days) with vaguer references to the passage of time. The narrative also provides sometimes radically detailed, bulging descriptions spanning a relatively short interval and at other times sparse, terse information covering several days.

Let us examine how the narration of the chronology unduly distances the rapes by Magnant and Ghezzo-Quenum. The diary begins at midnight on May 14, 1966,[25] in Sion, Switzerland, where the lovers have fled from Magnant, who was following them in Lagos. The following entry is simply and ambiguously labeled "Lendemain. . . . Il sera bientôt onze heures du matin" (170), which could mean either May 14 (if he means the next morning) or May 15 (if he means the next calendar day). For the next entry, on the crucial day of the rape, Ghezzo-Quenum gives a precise place—Ouchy, in Lausanne—although he admits that "j'allais écrire: Lagos!," indicating an alarming confusion in his conception of spatiotemporal location that makes his diary even less reliable. But he is less precise about the time: "Nous avons quitté la colline enchantée de Sion sans trop savoir exactement où nous allions échoir. En tout, cela a pris deux jours avant de nous rendre ici, face aux Rochers de Mélise et au Massif de la Meillerie" (174). The entry on this uncertain day, which could be as early as May 16 but could also be several days later, comprises detailed descriptions of Ghezzo-Quenum's *état d'âme,* of his search for Rachel, of his arrest by the racist Lausanne police—the last two elements necessarily narrated on the following day, May 17 at the earliest, after his night in jail and after he finds Rachel sleeping in their hotel room following her rape by Magnant. Then, "Deux jours se sont passés depuis que j'ai retrouvé Rachel Ruskin endormie dans notre chambre de l'hôtel La Résidence" (194). So Rachel and Ghezzo-Quenum spend another two days at least in Lausanne. The next entry, which marks their departure—"Puis ce fut la même chose dans le TEE-Cisalpin Lausanne-Paris. . . . Nous avions quitté Lausanne à 16h25" (195)—provides a precise time but no indication as to the date. The end of the entry, however, clarifies that two days elapsed between the rape by Magnant and the couple's arrival in Paris (198–99).

Once Ghezzo-Quenum and Rachel arrive in Paris, the city where Ghezzo-Quenum repeatedly rapes her, the passage of time hinges on changing hotels: they settle first in the expensive Hôtel des Arromanches, but Ghezzo-Quenum specifies, "Il va falloir changer d'hôtel demain ou après-demain au plus tard" (201). Arriving in Paris in the evening two days after Ghezzo-Quenum found Rachel asleep in their hotel room after the rape, thus May 19 at the earliest, Rachel Ruskin (who has been "hypotonic" during the entire journey [195]) falls asleep immediately. While Ghezzo-Quenum watches her sleep, he writes, "Je ne peux pas m'empêcher de la désirer; je ne peux pas non plus m'empêcher de penser à P. X. Magnant en train de la violer! . . . Je suis surexcité et d'ailleurs trop éveillé . . . je ne pense à me coucher que dans le but de violer le sommeil profond de Rachel Ruskin. Ce soir justement, il ne faut pas; il ne faut absolument pas. Je dois la laisser tranquille encore cette nuit" (202–3). The next entry is located in both time and space: "Hôtel La Bourdonnais, mardi le 30 mai" (204). That date, however, is necessarily erroneous because May 30 returns later (after two entries marked "Lendemain"), followed by entries dated May 31 and June 1. So the events in the entry marked "Hôtel La Bourdonnais" must in fact have taken place earlier than May 30. All this to say that in this entry Ghezzo-Quenum writes,

> L'autre nuit, à l'hôtel des Arromanches [thus immediately after their arrival in Paris, since Ghezzo-Quenum planned to leave the hotel the following day or the day after that, namely, as early as May 19], Rachel Ruskin s'est comportée de façon pour le moins bouleversante: je m'étais endormi paisiblement près d'elle, puis, au milieu de la nuit, je me suis senti divinement réveillé, soulevé par un plaisir intense. . . . Puis j'ai ouvert les yeux: Rachel Ruskin était sur moi, assise presque. . . . Elle avait les yeux mi-clos et un visage extasié. J'étais moi-même au sommet de l'excitation; je n'eus presque rien à faire pour entrer en elle. (204)

Here begin Ghezzo-Quenum's nightly reenactments of rape. During these sexual acts, Rachel is either drugged or in a somnambulistic state, so that although Ghezzo-Quenum records that she initiates each incident, his avowed desire to rape her and her lack of consciousness ("J'avais une envie folle de me glisser en elle pendant que l'amytal la rendait si passive . . . j'ai réalisé, instantanément, que le projet qui venait de me traverser l'esprit ressemblait singulièrement à un viol" [211]) problematize the concept of consensual sex.[26] Ghezzo-Quenum himself describes their "indecent" intercourse (so loud it gets them kicked out of a hotel) as a "recapitulation of the rape" (209). All in all, the inaccurate dates, elongated narration (on the day of Magnant's rape, notably), and blurring of Ghezzo-Quenum's desire to rape and actual rape make it appear that the initial violation by Magnant took place long before the start of its recapitulations by Ghezzo-Quenum, but in fact there could have been as few as two days between those events. Any calculation of the date of conception of the child, therefore, proves to be difficult, especially given Rachel's traumatized (later drugged) state and our ultimate ignorance with regard to her reproductive cycle.

In addition, Ghezzo-Quenum's punning on vocables and imagery related to pregnancy as he narrates his and Rachel's sexual activity perpetuates the possibility that the child can have been conceived with him. Ghezzo-Quenum, as a narrator, is abnormally fond of puns: he describes the "sol soluble d'Ouchy" and the "Massifs massifs" of the Lausannois landscape, constructing a striking opposition between the yielding lake edge and the hardness of the mountains opposite. And yet he remains apparently unaware of his wordplay as he writes, "[Rachel] criait sans cesse, en se balançant sur moi . . . elle voguait sur une mer tumultueuse dont chaque vague la faisait chavirer dans un *dérèglement* incalculable de plaisir" (205, emphasis added). Together with the alarming ascription of pleasure to Rachel as she somnambulistically relives her own rape, this sentence stages an equally troubling (because unconscious on her part) disruption of her menstrual cycle: the "dérèglement incalculable de plaisir" alludes to an interference with her *règles,* her period. Similarly, describing Rachel's fit of asthenia on June 8 Ghezzo-Quenum writes, "Une tempête de noirceur vient de s'abattre sur elle, provoquant un torrent tumultueux et soudain comme le sang menstruel, souillant le blanc de ses yeux et le tréfonds de son âme" (223). Menstruation here occurs figuratively rather than literally.

The callous use of this intimate physiological metaphor concurs with Ghezzo-Quenum's encroaching power over Rachel's body and with his utter lack of compunction regarding the part he has played in causing the bout of weakness: "C'est peut-être entièrement de ma faute: je ne l'ai plongée dans le sommeil que pour l'en tirer prématurément afin de la faire parler; et j'ai dû la forcer sans tenir compte de son état d'épuisement et sans même remarquer les signes annonciateurs de sa dépression" (223–24). Here, a pun that is seemingly unconscious (on Ghezzo-Quenum's part) makes a palimpsest of his "narcoanalyse" and rape: *forcer* is a euphemism for *violer*. Voicing Ghezzo-Quenum's desire to know and control Rachel's body through all these puns that accentuate her distress and reproductive powerlessness contributes to the novel's satirical treatment of violence against women. These actual rapes also give the novel's overarching metaphor of interlace/inter-lakes a physical referent in the intermingling of Magnant's and Ghezzo-Quenum's semen within Rachel's body, literalizing the model of solidarity as fluid exchange while at the same time metaphorizing the two men as lakes of spermatozoa—emphasizing, again, the hypermasculinity of anticolonial discourse.

For Ghezzo-Quenum, Rachel Ruskin's corporeal presence is a vessel containing the memory of her rape by Magnant—the colonized subject (Ghezzo-Quenum) desiring and replicating, in the violated body of the woman, the power of the colonizer (Magnant). But in this narrative that portrays colonization as rape and revolution as counter-rape, Magnant's and Ghezzo-Quenum's relative positions are unstable. Indeed, both men to some extent imagine their rape of Rachel to be a counter-rape. Magnant imagines himself as a colonized victim, and his rape of Rachel amounts to a counter-rape against the (English) colonizer's woman; Ghezzo-Quenum identifies with Rachel in his imagination of her rape, which reflects his position as colonial subject and explains (within the framework of the novel) his desire to rape her in turn.[27] And yet a fundamental inequality emerges between Magnant and Ghezzo-Quenum as the white man's rape of Ghezzo-Quenum's girlfriend reproduces tropes of colonialism rather than anticolonialism. Their revolutionary brotherhood, proclaimed in the prefatory letter, appears to disintegrate as Ghezzo-Quenum's obsession with Rachel's rape by Magnant (simultaneously a revolutionary counter-rape and a rape representing colonization) drives him to a second-degree counter-rape aimed ultimately against Magnant. Anticolonial political goals, while they may be obscured by interpersonal violence and jealousy, continue to structure Magnant's and Ghezzo-Quenum's perspectives and imaginaries; violence and jealousy in fact devolve directly from their striving (together and separately, that is, solidarily) for distinct political outcomes, each in his own country.

Indeed, the return of Ghezzo-Quenum's narrative to the image of *entrelacs* reasserts the two men's solidarity and watery confluence.

Glancing outside from his Lausanne hotel, Ghezzo-Quenum borrows from Italian the term *lungolago*—"qui longe le lac"—to leap into a juxtaposition of Ouchy and Lagos: "Ce n'est pas devant le lac Léman que je me tiens, mais face au golfe de Guinée, dans cette Marina éblouissante qui le retient d'envahir Lagos et qui le repousse mais sans trop d'énergie, si bien que l'eau sombre circule partout dans une vasolabilité continuelle qui fait de Lagos tout entière, un véritable angiose nodulaire et rameux, fait de canaux, d'écluses, de *lacets* fluides, d'entrecôtes vaseuses et floues" (175, emphasis added). *Lacet* as a metaphor to describe a stream integrates both meanings introduced by Magnant's pun on *entrelacs*: interlacing and between-the-lakes. The recurrent image (*lacet* is etymologically related to *laqueus* and *entrelacs*) links together the two masculine narratives of revolutionary rape, which seem to ignore even as they mirror each other. Written at the time of the initial rape, as Ghezzo-Quenum awaits Rachel's return, this passage confirms the masculine solidarity that flows together, or that is represented as a porous fluidity, through the body of a woman—Rachel Ruskin, the "white" (meaning both white and English) man's woman. Indeed, the representation of woman as liquid is explicit in Magnant's narrative: "On ne se baigne jamais deux fois dans la même rivière. Il en va de même de l'acte sexuel: on ne couche jamais deux fois dans le même lit, on ne se baigne jamais deux fois dans la même partenaire héraclitienne" (62). Magnant and Ghezzo-Quenum's solidarity remains asymptotic: Ghezzo-Quenum's desire for revolutionary solidarity with Magnant is ultimately mediated through Rachel's body, which is itself not a fixed object but an ever-changing element.

Overall, the interlaced solidarity of Magnant and Ghezzo-Quenum only reinforces the diary's obfuscatory temporal descriptions and also its recurring puns suggestive of impregnation. All of these elements reflect the impossibility of arriving at any absolute determination regarding a point of origin—here, the inception (conception) of Quebec's revolutionary future in the form of Rachel's child. But the diary's insistence on dates (the uneven and erratic flow of time) and its unrelenting puns also highlight the importance of this uncertainty: the novel is structured around a search for an unknowable truth. Similarly, Quebec, the novel implies, as a nation that has never known self-determination, remains unmoored from any single foundational narrative on which to base its national myths; its future is thus much freer of ties to the past than Rachel imagines as she ascribes Magnant's name to her child. The novel therefore closes on the imminent birth of a child that could be either white or mixed-race.

This open-ended conclusion in fact brings a form of closure to the racial tensions that are very present in the text but are never resolved. The incident of Ghezzo-Quenum's arrest in Lausanne, for example, a rather unambiguous example of discrimination on the part of the Swiss police (see Roberts 24), closes anticlimactically with Ghezzo-Quenum's reflection "Bien sûr, me suis-je dit, je n'ai qu'à reconnaître que je n'ai pas été emprisonné et, du coup, je suis libéré" (191) without further elaborating on the racist structures that inform the logic of this catch-22. More perniciously, Magnant's anticolonial revolutionary stance is not by any means antiracist, so that when Ghezzo-Quenum confronts Magnant/Mullahy in Mullahy's last narrative segment, Magnant/Mullahy fulminates, "Ce *sale* petit pharmacien est en train de me désarçonner! . . . 'Allons donc,' continua le *nègre* insidieusement" (230–31). This passage clearly echoes the Fanonian archetypal encounter between a black subject and the stereotypical racist he encounters in a predominantly white society ("'Sale nègre!' Ou simplement, 'Tiens, un nègre!'" [Fanon 88]). Nothing in the novel explicitly corrects this bias or resolves the unspoken racial tension. But the novel's coded questioning of the baby's race does pose an alternative to Magnant/Mullahy's performance of a (white) racist Quebec—and to the (white) future of revolutionary Quebec.

### White Baby—or Not?

It is time to do away with all parentheses. Aquin, his papers suggest,[28] was thinking explicitly about race during the sixties, when he was writing *Trou de mémoire*. An English-language play titled "White Baby," dated "196?" and located amid Aquin's notes, drafts, and projects for novels and articles, some published and others unpublished, reveals a sharp concern with race and racism as they structure identity and culture. Whether Aquin wrote the play himself (unlikely given that he hardly ever wrote in English, apart from his correspondence) or whether he considered translating it, there is little doubt that he had some knowledge of its contents. And this play, as the title unequivocally and almost oversimplistically suggests, deals with race head on, specifically with the "invisibility" of whiteness and with the cultural and racial identity of babies with respect to their parents, biological or adoptive.

Much can be said about "White Baby," which was never published and whose place in the Aquin archives remains mysterious (as Aquin's partner Andrée Yanacopoulo said wistfully in a phone interview, "La vie d'Hubert est pleine de mystères"). A satirical meditation on racism as a foundational bias of Western civilization, the play would be difficult to stage because of its blatant and insensitive satire of racial relations. For example, it prescribes that nonwhite characters be played by white actors wearing makeup—essentially, in blackface; it gives voice to extremely problematic racist statements; and it stages the racially motivated murder of a Jewish character. In a way, the portrayal of race relations in "White Baby" resembles *Trou de mémoire*'s portrayal of misogynist violence. But the parallel constituted by unsettling satirical stances is not the only feature to link the two works; "White Baby" also illustrates the types of racial reefs on which the narrators of *Trou de mémoire* founder.[29]

Interestingly, early drafts of the novel (dated 1962, a date confirmed by entries in Aquin's published diaries)[30] did not include the figure of the black revolutionary and the racial ambiguities that ensue from his relationship with Rachel.[31] The thematic and tonal similarities linking "White Baby" and *Trou de mémoire* suggest that the component of the novel dealing with race was introduced into later drafts as a result of Aquin's reading of the play. While the solidarity between the Ivoirian revolutionary and his Quebecois counterpart constitutes an obvious nod to the anticolonial discourse that inspired Quebec's Quiet Revolution, it also represents a less obvious reflection on the limits of that discourse's influence on a fundamentally racist world order. In other words, Aquin's addition of elements from "White Baby" to *Trou de mémoire* suggests that he was conscious of Quebecois intellectuals' tendency to imagine Quebec as white in spite of the usefulness of the metaphor of blackness and asks that we take this consciousness into account in interpreting the novel's concluding gestures about race.

This progressive perspective on the part of Aquin fits with the kinds of problems he encountered on reading "White Baby," a(n) (un)broken conversation about the anxieties a white patriarchy experiences in terms of reproducing itself in a world where constantly increasing mobility and intercultural contact make controlling women's bodies more and more problematic. Specifically, "White Baby" stages asylum inmates who, abandoned by doctors drafted into service during a "universal war," leave the separate hospital wings where heretofore they have been kept segregated by skin color: "non-Caucasians" together in the North Wing and another group (Caucasian by silent default) in the South Wing. The play opens with the arrival of a young white woman (the Girl), the only young woman in the play, in the South Wing. Being new to the asylum, she has not adopted the other patients' fears and habits: she opens the supposedly forbidden wardrobe and finds bathrobes, which the naked patients don and through which they gain identities. The Girl, for example, choosing white and thus becoming "the Princess to be married," comes to embody the essence of nubility—and the object of obsessive concern for the white male (and one elderly white female) South Wing patients. The Princess's fertile body represents the possibility, even the threat, of (re)producing a nonwhite baby, as the inmates are left to ordain reproductive regulations for themselves.

"White Baby" traces the anxieties of the white men when the only fertile woman present, the Princess, chooses to marry the "handsome negro" from the North Wing. So doing, she triggers the white inmates' apprehensions regarding identity, its boundaries, and the limits of their control over it. Giving voice to these fears, the play scatters into endless circular syllogisms and compulsive non sequiturs about religious, linguistic, and cultural belonging—all of which, in the inmates' mad attempts at coherence, are ultimately problematized by race. Marking the white inmates' concern with identity is the unexamined premise that different identities are necessarily and permanently mutually exclusive. The mainstays of their philosophy of identity center on two parables, the only two passages that narrate events that took place in the world outside the asylum: the stories (the inmates call them "lies," further destabilizing their status) of how Otto Fikkermann/the Rabbi and the Little Man/the Judge went insane and were sent to the asylum. These parables assert the parallel maxims that "everyone wants to be certain with a certainty that is absolute and exclusive" ("WB" 10) and that "everybody wants to be loved with a love that is absolute and exclusive" ("WB" 54). As the characters grapple with these axioms, they cannot quite acknowledge that if everyone wants to be certain/loved with a certainty/love that is absolute and exclusive, then everyone wants to be alone in being certain and loved: certainty and love satisfy and provide a sense of security only when they trump all other possible certainties and loves. This paradigm is applied to religious groups (the Rabbi and the Cardinal each understand their relationship to God to be true, in contrast to all other possible relationships to God), but it extends to identity more generally: each way of being in the world (religious, cultural, linguistic) is expressed as a desire to touch or be attuned to a truth that transcends religious, cultural, and linguistic difference. Conversion, translation, and immigration—any form of encounter, in fact—are presented as points of struggle, antagonisms that precipitate a confrontation with the incommensurability of difference.

And while certain aspects of identity can mutate, others are presented as unalterable. This is the case even for the hypothetical babies that inexorably crop up when the characters try to define the origins and horizons of identity: where or how does identity (religious, linguistic, cultural) begin and end? For example, Patients 1, 2, and 3, narrow-minded know-it-alls, investigate the origin of religious belief with the more thoughtful Idiot:

> Idiot: Where does religion come from? . . .
> Patient 2: People absorb it when they're babies.
> Idiot: Is it in the milk?
> The Three: Oh God! (ETC.)
> Patient 1: They inherit it from their parents.
> Idiot: If Hindu parents adopted a Christian baby, would the baby be a Hindu?
> Patient 2: (SHARPLY) How old a baby?
> Idiot: Two weeks.
> Patient 3: Nobody adopts a baby two weeks old.
> Patient 1: It would be a Hindu.
> Patient 2: Not if it was baptized.
> Patient 3: If it didn't know it was baptized it would be a Hindu.
> Patient 1: How could a baby know it was baptized?
> Patient 3: It couldn't. It would be a Hindu.
> Patient 2: But it would be a Christian because it was baptized.
> Patient 1: It would know because of the colour.
> Patient 2: When it was older, yes.
> Patient 3: Yes, it might suspect something because of the colour. ("WB" 34–35)

At issue here is the difference between culture (religion as cultural construction) and transcendental truth. Is baptism a cultural event inscribing a baby into a community, an event that needs frequent follow-ups in order to be a significant part of the baby's life—religious ceremonies, rituals and rites of passage—or is it a "true," essential transformation of that baby's being? The answer depends entirely on one's perspective, and the play does not resolve the conundrum. The asylum patients abandon it and pass on instead to skin color, which is, for them, absolute and essential, and absolutely and essentially linked to religion. In other words, for them each religious community is united and defined by its appearance, its "colour." In this view, each (homogeneously colored) community practices its own religion; each culture is constructed by a racially defined people. And for these inmates who understand identity as absolute and exclusive, the boundaries between these different racial and religious communities ought to be clear-cut. The Idiot's question about geography reflects this belief:

> Idiot: Cardinal, why do Hindus live in India?
> Patient 2: That's not a religious question. That's geography.
> Patient 3: It's not his field. ("WB" 33–34)

But as even the insane patients must acknowledge, the boundaries between communities are *not* clear:

> Patient 1: Besides, any idiot knows the answer.
> Patient 2: It's like asking why Moslems live in the desert.
> Patient 3: Or why Buddhists live in China.
> Patient 1: Any idiot knows the answer.
> Idiot: Cardinal, is religion the same as geography?
> Patient 2: If it were he'd have answered the first question. Besides, there are Hindus in England. ("WB" 34)

This dialogue about the "transport" of religion (the Idiot asks, "Did they take it in ships?") complicates the association of religion, or more broadly culture, with geography. But when the Idiot wants to know of the Cardinal, "What colour is a Christian?" ("WB" 34, 35), he is getting to the heart of the problem. The Cardinal, presented as eager for converts and always hungry for new souls and the tithes they pay, *would,* if he were allowed to get a word in edgewise, repeat the answer made by the missionaries aiding and abetting the European imperialist project since the sixteenth century: "All colors." And yet the patients insist that skin color still defines something essential about the Hindu-adopted Christian baby.

For all their madness, these patients' opinions are symptomatic (and provide a trenchant satirical critique) of very real conditions. Indeed, in spite of Christianity's theoretical uniformity of souls, and as European imperial domination demonstrated in practice, the development of what the philosopher Étienne Balibar terms the *économie-monde* was and is still structured along racially discriminatory lines:

> Il nous faut convenir que la multiplicité des stratégies et des modes d'exploitation recoupe . . . une grande division mondiale entre *deux modes de reproduction* de la force du travail. L'un est intégré au mode de production capitaliste, il passe par la consommation de masse, la scolarisation généralisée, les diverses formes de salaire indirect. . . . L'autre laisse tout ou partie de la reproduction . . . à la charge des modes de production précapitalistes . . . ; il communique immédiatement avec les phénomènes . . . d'exploitation *destructive* de la force de travail et de discrimination raciale. (Balibar 238, emphasis in original)

And, Balibar argues, this racial division of the proletariat into salaried and destructively exploited workers exists both *within* nations and *among* nations, structuring racial inequality both locally and globally on a worldwide scale. So the racist perspectives of the patients in "White Baby," who insist on race as a fundamental essential difference, relate to real and seemingly absolute modes of racial discrimination structuring the global economy that "White Baby" critiques.

But not all characters see race as immutable. The actions of the "non-Caucasians" in "White Baby," only three of whom have speaking roles (the others are merely listed as "Four assorted non-Caucasians"), reveal that for them, power relations define race, and not vice versa. In one instance, the Fiji Islander–Real Estate Salesman "tries to act as the missionaries taught him to do" ("WB" 1), refusing to sell the Rabbi a house in a "good" Christian neighborhood, eventually luring him into the bushes and beating him to death. The murder triggers a trial that runs amok as the characters get more and more mired in questions of race and identity. Another "non-Caucasian" who believes in the variable nature of race, "The Colonel: A large, handsome Negro who thinks he's a Kentucky colonel" ("WB" 1), who becomes the Princess's love interest, has so thoroughly assimilated the manners of a Kentucky plantation owner that he terrifies the Old (white) Man into behaving like a (black) former slave:

> Old Man: (AFRAID OF HIS LIFE, BUT HUMOURING THE COLONEL) Mawnin', Colonel, suh! . . .
> Colonel: Good Mawnin', Tom. Were you grateful for bein' freed, Tom you old rascal?
> Old Man: Suttinly was, Colonel, suh!
> Colonel: Very well, Tom. Git along, you old rascal.
> Old Man: Suttinly will, Colonel, suh!
> Colonel: Mawnin', Tom. (HE THROWS UP HIS ARMS AND MAKES A SUDDEN FORWARD STAMPING MOTION WITH ONE FOOT SUCH AS ONE MAKES TO SHOO AN ANIMAL, OR IN FENCING.) ("WB" 23)

For the Colonel, race is an epidermal phenomenon that is not necessarily associated with a person's essential being. In fact, when the Princess asks the Colonel about the (white) Old Man and Old Lady, "What colour would they be?," the Colonel answers, "White, ma'am, but it's only skin deep. Come here, Tom, you old black rascal!" ("WB" 22–23). Blackness here is not epidermal but metaphorical, an expression of the Old Man's fear, which renders him powerless; blackness and whiteness constitute positions in a power relation that is quite distinct from actual skin color—at least for the Colonel. In the social void represented by the asylum, the inmates manipulate the racial dimension of the power dynamics customary to American plantation slavery.

But the Colonel's fantasy of plantation power only functions because the Old Man has quite a different understanding of race. For him, color is *not* skin deep. When the Old Man and the Old Lady first see the Colonel, they are genuinely terrified:

> Old Man: (HE SEES THE PRINCESS EMERGE ALONG A PATHWAY, ON THE COLONEL'S ARM) Oh God! What's that!
> Old Lady: The princess!
> Old Man: With a black man!
> Old Lady: Don't notice. Keep walking.... (THEY ARE BOTH TERRIFIED AND DEADLY SERIOUS.) ("WB" 22)

The Old Man's fear of the black Colonel makes him play along in the charade in which he performs servitude, so that his terror, characteristic of and caused by racism, ironically takes on the appearance of a black slave's fear of the white master. At stake for the Old Man is his life (he is "terrified and deadly serious"); he fears death at the hands of the black Colonel. And through the mismatched mirror of the transracial role playing, the Colonel justifies that fear by including in his performance of white power the right to violence ("as in fencing") that a plantation owner historically exercised over his enslaved laborers.

This interracial fear, combined with a view of race as absolute, marks the horizon of the "Caucasian" characters' absurdist investigations into identity. In the course of trying to define the forgotten crime for which they mount a trial, the white inmates attempt to parse the cultural belonging of "a German baby that deserted from the French army" and fled to Greece ("WB" 77). The World War II resonance of these nationalities, especially given the military context, is reinforced by the fact that the actual forgotten crime for which the trial was called was the beating to death of the Rabbi. But that repressed backdrop of European genocide fades before the inmates' most deep-seated fears: "What if it had been Africa . . . instead of Greece" ("WB" 77) into which the hypothetical baby had been adopted? In the context of Africa, the baby's national and cultural identity vanishes, and he becomes simply a "white baby"—the white baby of the play's title. The inmates' free play with linguistic, cultural, and religious identity comes to a sudden halt when they consider skin color. "He could change it in the sun," says one inmate. "But he couldn't keep it dark," answers another. "Everybody would know" ("WB" 78). No amount of linguistic adaptation ("Not if he spoke the language? Accent-free?") will enable the white baby to blend in with the black Africans, and "the Africans would never believe he was African" ("WB" 77–78). This certainty regarding the absoluteness of skin color is accompanied on the part of the inmates by hyperbolically racist comments:

> Patient 1: He wouldn't be safe for a second.
> Patient 2: Blacks are extremely intolerant.
> Patient 3: Show them a white baby, they go hog-wild.
> Patient 1: Put him on a long spit.
> Patient 2: Roast him alive. ("WB" 79)

The free play of identities stops with skin color because for the white inmates black skin calls up an entire history of terror, the terror of the imperial encounter in which European violence established an always insecure domination.

Imputing cannibalism to Africans is of course not a new offense;[32] it symbolizes the fear of racial dissolution, of disappearance—the swallowing of whiteness. In the context of the play, the narrative of Africans eating white babies responds parabolically to the white inmates' anxieties about the Princess's sexuality and reproductive potential. Their fear regarding their inability to control her body and to ensure that her offspring will resemble them and will reproduce them as they see themselves (absolutely separate and essentially different from the "non-Caucasian" characters) gets extrapolated in this parable, in which the hypothetical white baby is simultaneously the Princess (lost to them because "consumed" by the Colonel, with impalement as symbol of sexual penetration) and the white child she will never have, whose very possibility is evaporating as she disappears into the North Wing with her lover.

"White Baby" enriches readings of *Trou de mémoire* because it highlights the racial instabilities introduced in the novel. The play peoples the margins of *Trou de mémoire* with hyperboles of the racism that in fact structures the novel, if in a more nuanced way. Ghezzo-Quenum's detainment in Lausanne, Magnant's fear of and disdain for Ghezzo-Quenum, and Ghezzo-Quenum's representation of human relations as a struggle between black and white people refer to a racist context that "White Baby" makes explicit through satirical exaggeration. And as an underlying influence, the play seeps its preoccupation with the reproduction of race into the novel, providing a parallel for problematizing an unborn baby's skin color. Both works end with a *vision* of a white child, a revelation of the white characters' parochially imagined geopolitical future. Indeed, the play and the novel warn against the dangers of remaining trapped in the hatreds and misunderstandings that shaped the twentieth century, as represented by references to World War II, the Holocaust, and colonialism. In the end, both texts satirically sublimate an anxiety about the reproduction of whiteness into digressive tirades that define the authorial personae, silently writing prejudiced narrators and characters into existence, as radical thinkers about the nature of systematic race- and gender-based structures of privilege.

Despite these parallels, *Trou de mémoire* differs from "White Baby" in many ways. For one thing, it gives voice extensively to Ghezzo-Quenum, whereas the "non-Caucasian" characters of "White Baby" remain silent, save for three who articulate their assorted conversions to white prejudice. More significantly, however, the novel sustains an interracial solidarity that goes beyond the narrators' various racisms. The equivocal opposition between white and black in the context of Quebec, as exposed by Ghezzo-Quenum in his prefatory letter and as metaphorized in the *entrelacs* imagery, comes to fruition or reaches fulfillment with the undetermined skin color of Rachel Ruskin's baby. Ultimately, the novel positions a potentially mixed-race Quebec as the inevitable development following from Quebecois intellectuals' fascination with and borrowings from anticolonial thought. The solidarity that was articulated at the outset of the novel as a revolutionary masculine (not to say chauvinistic) solidarity transforms itself through the dirty work of satire and hyperbole. Rape shatters the structure of its use as a metaphor for anticolonial revolutionary propaganda (Magnant writes, "Je me souviens . . . de cette foule compacte qui me demandait, ni plus ni moins, de la violer" [45]) when it results in a pregnancy; the flesh-and-blood offspring of the rapist and his victim does not map onto the same metaphorical plane as the projection of rape as retaliation or displacement. In *Trou de mémoire*, the pregnancy gives agency to the woman, as both male characters commit suicide rather than be faced with the child resulting from a sexual act they can only conceive of as the conquest of the white (English) woman. Ultimately, the solidarity between Magnant and Ghezzo-Quenum is valorized in spite of the satirical extremes that characterize it; it survives in the form of a child who could be either man's but who will be raised *in the absence of men* to "save" a new "race," to borrow Joan's delirious words. This new revolution offers the hope of overtaking the sexual and racial rancors bequeathed by colonialism.

If the baby (Rachel's with Magnant or Ghezzo-Quenum) constitutes a metaphor for the interracial solidarity that Quebec intellectuals feel with (formerly) colonized subjects, it is also the fictional literalization of that metaphor. Aquin, it seems, imagined the archetypal *nègre blanc* not as white but as necessarily potentially mixed-race. The ambiguous paternity of the baby, which is so far from being imaginable to Rachel that she affixes Magnant's name to it before birth, exists in the narrative as a redemption beyond the characters' bigoted purview: the ultimate literary solidarity of the novel corrects for the narrators' racism, both Magnant's outright disdain for or fear of Ghezzo-Quenum and Rachel's white expectations.

*Trou de mémoire* articulates its solidarities at the conjuncture of literary satire and political earnestness. Aquin's ventriloquizing "black power" moments communicate simultaneously on multiple levels, teasing out a very serious consideration of anticolonial thought from a much lighter play with anticolonial rhetoric. Similarly, the novel's (ill-)treatment of women revolts in both senses of the word, at once perturbing us and urging revolution. *Trou de mémoire*'s new Quebec, with its ambiguously coded racial possibilities, helps to define the connections that formed a networked poetics of solidarity during the independence era. In fact, the solidarity that structures the novel is indicative of the kind of work that a poetics of solidarity can accomplish by envisioning social and political imaginaries. The oscillation between concrete and abstract in the novel—rape is both physical and symbolic; the baby is both a flesh-and-blood fetus and a metaphor for the future; Lagos is both a city and an allegory for solidarity—suggests the complexity of intercontinental French-language connections. At the same time, the tropological dimension of *Trou de mémoire* implies, by the very slippage between abstract and concrete that defines it, a way to return to the realm of the concrete. Ultimately, by understanding solidarity as inter-lake (porous fluidity) rather than interlace (interwoven discreteness), the novel breaks down Quebec's isolation from the rest of the francophone world; if bodies of water—oceans—are perceived as connectors rather than dividers, Quebec becomes accessible and indeed has always been accessible, from the slave trade onward. And understanding this accessibility means abandoning myths of purity—the concept of a *Québec pure-laine*, white and French at its origin. For Aquin, the anticolonial metaphor of blackness revealed beyond the term *French Canadian* a reality that did not match the "whiteness" it generally implied historically and in Aquin's present.

## 3 Publishable Offense

Simile, Solidarity, and Mongo Beti's Quebecois *Main basse sur le Cameroun*

IF CHAPTER 1 examined Césaire's iterative experimentations with performing literary solidarity and chapter 2 analyzed the possibilities for transracial textual solidarity in Hubert Aquin's *Trou de mémoire*, this chapter turns to publicatory solidarity—the solidarity that was articulated to explain the republication of a proscribed text. In 1972, Mongo Beti (nom de plume of Alexandre Biyidi-Alama) published *Main basse sur le Cameroun: Autopsie d'une décolonisation* with Éditions Maspero, a radical leftist press in Paris. The essay was immediately banned and removed from circulation. This censorship was based on a nineteenth-century law restricting the distribution of "foreign" texts in France and relied on questioning the validity of Beti's French citizenship.[1] But for a man who had been born in the French protectorate of Cameroon, who had lived mostly in France since 1951 (before Cameroon's independence), who had been educated in Aix-en-Provence and at the Sorbonne, and who had spent most of his adult years serving the French educational system as an *instituteur* in Rouen,[2] the question of origin was merely a pretext. The censorship in fact came at the request of Cameroon's postcolonial dictatorial regime—the government of President Ahmadou Ahidjo—to France, its ally and former colonial protector. Ironically, the request was made through the intermediary of another Cameroonian author, Ferdinand Oyono (*Une vie de boy*, 1956), who was at that time serving as Cameroon's ambassador to France.

Beti and his editor, François Maspero, initiated legal proceedings against the French government, eventually winning in 1976. In the intervening four years, however, a small publishing house in Montreal jumped to the banned book's defense and republished it in 1974.[3] Montreal at the time was the vortex of the Quebecois Quiet Revolution, which had begun in the 1960s. The publishing world participated in this social upheaval, developing a network of progressive organs and mechanisms that supported one another in the publication of militant materials and analyses. Beti's *Main basse sur le Cameroun* entered Quebec during this period of turmoil; it was attractive to Quebecois intellectuals because it participated in the radical transformation of the province as part of a growing global awareness and sense of international solidarity and responsibility.

The Montreal edition of *Main basse*, however, also represents a crucial turning point in Beti's career. First, "les tournées de conférences qu'il [Beti] effectue au Canada remontent son moral et réactivent ses ardeurs qui auraient pu être refroidies par tant de détermination à supprimer sa voix" (Kemedjio 190). Second, and more importantly, the profits he made selling the Montreal edition in Europe allowed him and his wife, Odile Tobner, to launch *Peuples noirs—Peuples africains*,[4] a journal that was published from 1978 to 1991. The journal, which quickly became an important subversive periodical, launched Beti and Tobner on their way to becoming an essential node of distribution of French-language black radical texts, leading eventually to the 1994 founding of their bookstore in Yaoundé, the Librairie des Peuples Noirs. The Montreal edition of *Main basse* must thus be seen as an integral part of Beti's professional trajectory, as must the act of censorship that brought about the Montreal edition. Censorship thus played a paradoxical role in the *déroulement* of Beti's career. As the first Quebecois preface affirms without irony, some readers were attracted to *Main basse* specifically because it was censored: censorship brought notoriety, and this helped the book sell both in Canada and in France, where Beti and his wife smuggled books across the border from Belgium.[5]

This chapter situates the 1974 Montreal publication of *Main basse sur le Cameroun* within the complicated context of French-language solidarity by analyzing its unusually weighty paratextual support structure, which even includes a documentary. The fact that *Main basse sur le Cameroun* was banned in France immediately after publication underlined its challenge to the status quo and simultaneously made it eminently, urgently publishable. Quebec arises as an indispensable third way for Beti, who was in the awkward position of needing to affirm his French nationality in order to restore the distribution of his virulently anti-neocolonial essay, which attacked France for its collusion in the repressions and atrocities of Ahmadou Ahidjo's regime. The outsider position of Quebec with respect to France *and* Cameroon was also ethically necessary to pointing out the ironic participation of the French government in the repressive act of censoring a book whose central theme is French neocolonial repression.

Here, I analyze how Beti and his various publishers negotiated spaces of solidarity and resistance for *Main basse,* relying particularly on the trope of the simile to draw comparisons between distant places and also to define the difficult-to-articulate concept of solidarity.

The interest between Quebec and Beti was mutual—a reciprocal opportunism of sorts. Where Beti found a publisher, Quebecois intellectuals found a means to express their solidarity and a vehicle for suggesting parallels between Quebec and African (post)colonies. The book's subtitle facilitates such allegorical readings. *Main basse* calls itself an "autopsy" of decolonization. In the strictest sense, this subtitle incisively affirms the death of decolonization or the failure of independence. Autopsies, however, provide two different kinds of information: they provide, first, forensic information related to the death of the specific body that is being examined and, second, scientific information related to the function of bodies, illnesses, and injuries in general. Beti's *Main basse sur le Cameroun: Autopsie d'une décolonisation* parses the specific incidents that contributed to the end of decolonization in Cameroon, leaving the nation in neocolonial limbo; in this respect, it is *une autopsie,* a specific, unique investigation into the death of anticolonialism in Cameroon. For Quebecois readers, however, *Main basse* also represents a more general examination of attempts to repress anticolonialism. In fact, the new paratexts to *Main basse*'s Quebecois edition position Cameroon's anti-neocolonial movement in parallel with Quebecois resistance to Canadian federalism and American economic encroachment. The autopsy of Cameroon's deceased decolonial hopes thus becomes a model through which other colonial situations can be understood, revealing and analyzing symptoms more generally attributable to the colonial disease.

The writers who participated in the making of *Main basse*'s Quebecois edition express the solidary parallel between Quebec and Cameroon through *simile,* or an explicit comparison of similar yet different things. Simile, in the edition's paratexts (and in *Main basse* itself), evolves as an ideal avenue for expressing solidarity, which is itself the privileging of a common quality over infinite difference. The act of comparing, of finding a similarity, is an essential gesture of solidarity, even if perfect correspondence is an unreachable asymptote. The authors' reliance on simile to express the solidary links they imagine, however, reveals more than connections: it also reveals the approximative nature of language, the abstracting and waffling tendencies that give the lie to its attempts at precision and accuracy.

The similes contribute to placing the Quebecois edition of *Main basse sur le Cameroun* under the sign of solidarity. This solidarity is explicit. As Cilas Kemedjio, an intellectual biographer of Mongo Beti, writes, "L'activité éditoriale et cinématique autour du livre de Mongo Beti tisse la trame d'une internationale des peuples en lutte pour la revendication de leur part d'humanité" (187). What makes the Quebecois publication valuable in this study of solidarity is that the Montreal publishers saw their own solidarity as worthy of publication and publicity: they documented the *déroulement* of their solidarity not only in the prefatory texts but also in a documentary film. The film, produced in Quebec two years after the Montreal publication,[6] investigates *Main basse*'s claims regarding Ahidjo's repressive neocolonial dictatorship, the censorship the book faced in France and Cameroon, and the Quebecois republication of the text. Tellingly, the film was titled *Contre-censure;* the Quebecois intellectuals who made the film clearly saw their own work, and the work of the publishers of the Quebecois edition of *Main basse,* as acts of resistance against the censorship faced by Mongo Beti. Thus, first, *Main basse* was made urgently publishable because of the offense imputed to it by French censorship; second, the fact of neocolonial censorship triggered a series of publishing processes, and the solidary mechanisms driving those processes are intimately narrated in the paratexts to the Quebecois edition. This chapter analyzes the similes that populate the margins of *Main basse*'s Quebecois publication (the multiple prefaces produced to locate the text and the documentary film that describes the multiple stages of *Main basse*'s early publication saga), examining how these similes erect a structure of desire for solidarity and identity among different francophone independence movements.

### *Main basse:* Solidarity in (Spite of) French

Ambroise Kom has called *Main basse sur le Cameroun: Autopsie d'une décolonisation* "the most legendary of Beti's texts" ("Introduction" 14). Its censorship and seizure amplified Beti's stature by initiating a global current of sympathy, indeed of solidarity. The French Marxist historian Jean Suret-Canale, for example, describes the campaign of the Association française d'amitié et de solidarité avec les peuples d'Afrique, of which he was copresident, in support of Beti's book and in defense of his right to French nationality (201–3). Cilas Kemedjio calls the support for Beti a mass-produced brand: *Main basse,* he claims, became a "véritable usine de production de la résistance. . . . 'Main basse Incorporated' désigne cette extraordinaire marque déposée engendrée par l'essai" (181). In this section, I link the book's international mobilization of militants to *Main basse*'s own construction of solidarity, which happens in French, or rather, *in spite of* French. French, Beti's essay suggests, is inadequate to express the solidarity that defines Cameroonian anti-neocolonial revolutionary efforts; the language's best approximations are merely *similes,* simulacra of the "true" feelings and actions of Cameroon's revolutionaries.

I argue that undergirding *Main basse* is an anti-neocolonial solidary relationship that forms the long essay's *point de capiton*. *Main basse* has been described as "a virulent book-length pamphlet which purports to expose the horrifying inside story of the relationship between Gaullist France and the Ahidjo government, the sinister manipulations which behind the façade of democracy destroyed the UPC [Union des populations du Cameroun], the corruption, repression, torture, and concentration camps—all in the service of the Cameroonian bourgeoisie bleeding the population so that they can in turn be ripped off by the French-based big business: and all with French government connivance" (Sherrington 397).[7] Beti himself summarized it, caustically, as a description of "le climat dans une ancienne colonie française redevenue colonie française" (quoted in Diop 88).[8] All of this is true, but the central topic of *Main basse sur le Cameroun* is none of these things in itself. In his essay, Beti sets out to analyze a very precise set of events, namely, those culminating in the so-called "procès camerounais," the Cameroonian political trials of 1970–71, whose most prominent accused were the UPC leader Ernest Ouandié and the bishop of Nkongsamba, Albert Ndongmo. The essay is structured as a series of vignettes about the main characters and events. And at the heart of *Main basse sur le Cameroun* lies a central question that the book raises, answers partially, and raises again: what was the relationship between the two central accused figures, the Catholic prelate and the UPC maquisard, and can it be considered one of solidarity?

Beti's detailed essay addresses the nature of the relationship between Ouandié and Ndongmo in several ways. The Ahidjo regime had amalgamated the two trials in spite of their seemingly unrelated charges. Beti proposes that this combining gesture was not only convenient but necessary for Ouandié's and Ndongmo's persecutors. Ouandié was accused of leading revolutionary actions, including violent actions (assassinations, arson, pillage); Ndongmo, by contrast, was accused only of having plotted a "mystical" assassination attempt on Ahidjo, an accusation that was shown to be groundless during the trial but for which Ndongmo was nevertheless sentenced to death (the sentence was commuted to life imprisonment). The necessary but cynical reason why these two trials were conjoined, Beti writes, was the following: "Le régime s'acharne . . . à créer artificiellement des liens entre ces deux affaires . . . parce que l'une, qui n'existe pas, ne prendra quelque consistance que si elle est, peu ou prou, contaminée par l'autre, qui, elle, existe tellement . . . qu'elle n'a jamais été un mystère pour les dirigeants camerounais" (178). Beti is categorical: "Ce qui est patent, . . . c'est que faute de pouvoir se débarrasser autrement d'un homme [Ndongmo] qui était une gêne et même une menace pour son régime, Ahmadou Ahidjo a décidé de le faire comparaître aux côtés d'un chef révolutionnaire dont la présence sur le banc d'infamie n'étonnait point" (178). For Beti, the cases were amalgamated and the trials made to coincide in order to facilitate the otherwise difficult condemnation of Ndongmo, whose business actions, although technically legal, interfered with the economic mechanisms of Ahidjo's autocratic state. Beti explains that Ndongmo had recently begun to invest energy and funds in enterprises aimed at generating local wealth, fulfilling regional needs, and funding diocesan public projects. According to Beti, these enterprises, not the implausible mystical-political assassination plot of which Ndongmo was accused, were the true reason for the prelate's arrest and sentence.[9] As Beti exposes in *Main basse*, the Ahidjo government's entire system of rule was based on foreign ownership of all economic assets. Ndongmo's rapidly successful Mungo-Plastique initiative, producing plastic and leather goods, represented a local challenge to foreign investment, a challenge that threatened the status quo through its potential for emulation by other local enterprises. Because there was nothing technically illegal in Ndongmo's business practices, however, the only way to get the bishop of Nkongsamba permanently out of the way was to link him to Ouandié, whose guilt was so certain that he had spent his last few years expecting execution and was ready for the verdict.[10]

Besides providing his own analysis of the government's probable reason for amalgamating the two trials, Beti dismisses the legal reason given by Ahidjo's investigators: a taped confession that the Cameroonian authorities had presented as evidence of Ndongmo's guilt. In this confession, during which Beti surmises Ndongmo was either drugged or enduring some other form of abuse, Ndongmo admitted to the "mystical" plot and to being linked with the UPC. Beti's essay, however, is structured so as to suggest that this confession, while most probably false, nevertheless revealed something important about the connection between Ndongmo and Ouandié. What the taped confession simultaneously reveals and masks, the essay implies, is an actual link between Ndongmo and Ouandié, not the ludicrous one fabricated discursively and recorded under duress, but a real solidarity. While *Main basse* explains at length the fabrication of legal links between the two trials, however, it merely hints suggestively at this human connection. *Main basse*'s emphatic refusal to name the exact nature of this most important relationship structures that relationship as the essay's enigmatic narrative center, a kernel of solidarity that *Main basse,* in French and in essay form, cannot express. At the heart of *Main basse,* in other words, is an unnamed solidarity that the text asymptotically points to but does not articulate fully, and the text cannot articulate it fully because French offers only *similes* that approximate the actual relation linking Ndongmo and Ouandié.

Let us unravel the essay's exposition of this human relationship. Beti recounts that the connection between Ndongmo and Ouandié was originally encouraged by the Cameroonian state for purposes of espionage and conversion.[11] The relationship began as espionage but failed to deliver the fruit the government desired: the arrest or deradicalization of Ouandié. During his trial, Ndongmo defended himself for not outright facilitating Ouandié's arrest, explaining rationally why he had offered some material support to the maquisards of his diocese: "pour être en position d'influencer le mouvement révolutionnaire et le détourner de la pratique de la violence" (183). Even as it reproduces Ndongmo's logical and humane claims, Beti's *Main basse* also expresses a hopeful belief that Ndongmo and Ouandié were linked by more than a reasoned approach to state-sponsored espionage. The relationship between the revolutionary and the priest, argues Beti, developed secretly in spite of (although always within) the state-mandated structure of espionage. Their relationship was not clandestine *in fact* (it continued to be sponsored by the state, and Ndongmo held his *laissez-passer* until his arrest), but Beti suggests that it grew to be clandestine *in nature*. From an espionage assignment, the relationship developed into something like a solidarity, although the text does not use the word. Ultimately, what provided the basis for the amalgamation of the two trials was this problematic relationship whose state-sponsored cover no longer covered the extent of the affinities between Ndongmo and Ouandié.

When it comes to actually articulating the nature of the affinities between Ndongmo and Ouandié, *Main basse* falters, not out of a lack of articulateness on the author's part but rather because of a kind of impossibility structuring the text itself. Beti approaches the problematic description in this way: "Quand une félonie interrompt sa carrière révolutionnaire, on a dit qu'Ernest Ouandié est sans doute en route pour rencontrer un émissaire de Mgr Ndongmo, ou peut-être l'évêque [de] Nkongsamba lui-même, avec lequel le chef de maquis entretient de longue date des relations qu'il est bien difficile de caractériser avec les termes de la langue française, mais auxquelles on peut, à la rigueur, attribuer le qualificatif de fraternelles" (116). The relationship between the two men developed, as Beti describes it, in a way that the French language is not equipped to characterize, and the nature of the relations that cannot be characterized in French is precisely *solidary,* something like fraternal relations. The very syntax of the sentence informs this problem in communication: the syntax is complex, in the grand tradition of French clausal subordination and parenthetical explication. Beginning with a subordinate clause, "Quand une félonie interrompt sa carrière révolutionnaire" (the "félonie" Beti refers to here is the betrayal that resulted in Ouandié's arrest), the sentence then anchors itself on its impersonal and vague main grammatical subject, "on." In fact, the sentence's main clause is retelling hearsay ("on a dit"). The uncertainty of this central clause is reinforced by the modifier "sans doute" and by the equivocating "ou peut-être l'évêque . . . lui-même."

After thus illustrating the doubtful and contested circumstances of Ouandié's arrest, Beti finally enters a terrain of grammatical certainty: the concluding half of the sentence, which describes the relationship between Ndongmo and Ouandié, does not equivocate. What the sentence does, however, is heighten the suspense surrounding the actual nature of the relationship until the sentence's very conclusion. Beti here proves himself a master rhetorician, introducing parenthetical clauses ("à la rigueur") and parallel structures ("relations *qu'il* est bien difficile de caractériser . . . mais *auxquelles* . . .") that postpone the arrival of the last word, "fraternelles," which finally qualifies Ndongmo and Ouandié's relation. Using this technique of clausal accumulation, Beti builds tension and focuses attention on "fraternelles," which closes not only the sentence but also the paragraph and the chapter. The convoluted (although precise and elegant) prose leading to the final word simultaneously buries and highlights "fraternelles," the exactness and "scientificity" of the interlocking parenthetical clauses pushing back the enigmatic truth of the sentence and intensifying the absence of the precise word, the perfect expression, which is lacking in French. The syntax of the sentence *performs* the stiltedness of French, the fumbling imprecision of its best syntactical practices, which Beti puts on learned display. Here, syntax mirrors meaning. The structure of Beti's sentence is an example of what it describes; it shows the precise imprecision of the French language, illustrating how the French language adapts rhetorically to its limits, to the narrowness of its expressive possibilities.

At the heart of this linguistic problem is the concept of solidarity. Fraternity, or a form of asymptotic solidarity that is not expressible in French (nor, presumably, in English), is the sticking point in the French-language narration of the Cameroonian trials. The simile Beti develops (expressing that these warm feelings are *like,* but *not entirely like,* brotherhood) demonstrates the limitations of French and implies, by contrast, the wealth, complexity, and variety of modes of connecting that are available outside the imperial(ist) cultural context. Solidarity (or something similar to it) emerges as a shimmering reality beyond the French language, something that connects people resisting French neocolonial encroachment in ways that the French language cannot encompass. Ahidjo himself had hoped to exploit the fact that both Ndongmo and Ouandié were ethnic Bamilékés when he asked one to spy on the other: one of the things that links them is the kinship of a shared ethnic group. But there is another dimension to the closeness of their connection, one more akin to politics and ideology: the two men cared deeply about the well-being of the poor. Supporting this idea of a solidarity more ideological than ethnic, Beti himself claimed in a public speech in 1991 that "the only blood relationships I recognize are those of the battles we have fought together" (quoted in Kom, "Mongo Beti Returns" 418). *Main basse* suggests, similarly, that the prelate's link with the revolutionary lies in their political opposition to the ruling party. The essay furthermore argues not that this relation of solidarity is inexpressible but rather that it is *new to French,* inexpressible in the colonial language.

French is the language of communication of Beti's book: it is the language of global exposure and international denunciation, and yet it cannot express the complex relations that subtend the situation. French is also the tongue of neocolonial power.[12] Beti establishes the link between French and power when he delves into the role of Maître Louis Pettiti, a French jurist sent as international observer to the trials of Ndongmo and Ouandié. Beti has no difficulty establishing that Pettiti's characterization of the trials as "réguliers" flew in the face of flagrant irregularities (e.g., declarations by the accused that they had been tortured). Beti concludes, "Si les mots doivent conserver leur sens, comment qualifier tout cela [the various irregularities Beti documents] de régulier?" (175). The problem for Beti is really one of semantics in the face of power: he is pointing out the flawed flexibility of language. Pettiti can qualify the trials as "réguliers," voiding the word of its meaning, because of his position as an unchecked adjudicator. Pettiti's uncontested power in defining the trials to the world, in "translating" the proceedings into evaluative French for an absent and uninformed international public, has the force to bend language. Pettiti, in his barely veiled partisan support of Adhijo's military justice, plays a small part in the neocolonial theater of French support for Cameroon's authoritative regime, but his part makes clear that the French language is another normalizing tool in the service of neocolonial power. French thus emerges as infinitely flexible in the hands of power, a tool to misrepresent morally suspect positions. French bends to power, untrustworthy and vague—another flaw of the language in the neocolonial context of 1970s Cameroon. No wonder Beti was wary of the French language's terms for *solidarity.*

Solidarity as it exists in *Main basse* links, beyond the French language, the various members of society who oppose Ahidjo's government. Solidarity does not, in Beti's essay, go beyond these local connections; Beti regards French leftist "philanthropic" instincts with the same cynicism as Aimé Césaire's Christophe. Regarding the insufficient investigation of Maître Louis Pettiti, the French jurist brought in as an international observer, Beti writes, sarcastically, "Bien qu'ils [i.e., the accused] fussent détenus depuis quatre mois, dans des conditions sur lesquelles il [Pettiti] n'avait ni recueilli, ni d'ailleurs sollicité aucune garantie, il ne leur a pas fait montrer les dents pour s'assurer de leur bonne nutrition; non, Me Louis Pettiti est un philanthrope, et non un maquignon" (176). Only a cattle seller would examine the physical condition of the accused, Beti implies sarcastically. Pettiti is a *philanthrope,* a lover of mankind, a do-gooder who does not delve into the indignities of physical examinations of prisoners. The dripping sarcasm indicates that Pettiti *should,* in fact, have looked into the prisoners' mouths to see whether they had been malnourished. But the parallel between the sarcastically suggested act and the slave trade's humiliating and dehumanizing procedures of physical assessment destabilizes the text, implying that the entire setting of Cameroon's military-justice system can only function justly if it functions as a slave-trading post. The prisoners' condition is the condition of slaves, the text suggests, and Pettiti's squeamish attitude is out of place in this context. Thus the impartiality of the outside observer, who was internationally charged with vouching for the trials' regularity and on whose solidarity the prisoners might have relied if the jurist had been otherwise inclined or if he had relinquished what Beti clearly considers his partisan position, is impossible in the context of France's neocolonial interests in Cameroon, with which Pettiti is complicit.

Beti's sarcasm undermines philanthropy also in the context of the wealthy French Left, continuing to show power's semantic distortions of language. In a chapter scathingly titled "À gauche comme Chez Maxim's?" Beti describes a dinner he once attended in a fashionable Saint-Germain-des-Prés apartment, elegantly muted in spite of its location at the center of the metropole. "Left-leaning like Maxim's" forms something of an oxymoron: Chez Maxim's is, and has been since the thirties, one of Paris's chicest restaurants, attracting the rich and famous—cinema stars, barons of industry, and wealthy tourists. The Saint-Germain-des-Prés apartment is described as similarly chic, offering the nuanced comforts that only wealth can offer ("La salle à manger, étroite et discrète, comme feutrée, était un univers ouaté où parvenaient à peine les rumeurs de la grande ville" [193]). Beti's hosts, thinking to please him, had invited a French "intellectuel de gauche" who had just returned from Cameroon. Far from being pleased, Beti found the man's humoristic travel tales macabre. The eminent intellectual bragged over an "excellent Bordeaux" about his meetings with Ahidjo and other Cameroonian leaders, including Jean Fochivé, the head of the Cameroonian political police, whom Beti later calls the torturer of Ouandié. Beti disdainfully classifies this would-be leftist—"l'homme qui, sans doute, allait signer des pétitions en faveur d'Angela Davis" (193)—as a hypocrite, comparing him to "ses ancêtres, 'membres de l'Institut, savants et gens de lettres, philosophes, philanthropes, théophilanthropes' qu'évoque Chateaubriand et qui, pendant l'occupation alliée en 1814, 'passaient leur vie chez l'autocrate Alexandre, chez ce brutal Tartare, et en revenaient comblés, chargés d'éloges et de tabatières'" (193).[13] The use of *philanthropes* in this context is strikingly similar to Césaire's use of the word in *La tragédie du roi Christophe*: the term implies a position that purports to be supportive and respectful of the lives and rights of the people of color under French power but that is in fact unwilling to admit complicity in the injustice these same people experience. *Aimer son prochain,* Césaire and Beti suggest by using the word *philanthrope,* is not enough. Love is not a political position, even though these *philanthropes* imagine that their position is political. A political position would entail taking specific steps to allow slaves, former colonial subjects, and current neocolonial subjects to raise themselves out of their pauperized state,[14] even at the cost of relinquishing comfort and advantages—a wealth both abstract and material that results from the exploitation of the African continent and its diasporic populations. "Loving mankind," or "philanthroping," implies Beti, remains a sentimental position rather than a political one, and a falsely sentimental one to boot, in that it is hypocritically and unevenly applied (petitions for Angela Davis but indifference toward Cameroonian political prisoners).[15]

*Main basse* thus unsettles the French linguistic and cultural basis it so fluently appropriates to denounce France's neocolonial involvement in Cameroon. Beti shows on the one hand the language's lacunae, the cultural and linguistic difficulty of expressing anticolonial solidarity in a historically imperial language, suggesting that Ouandié and Ndongmo's relations were inexpressibly (in French) more than fraternal. On the other hand, he demonstrates the flexibility of language as a tool of neocolonialism. French's history makes it particularly pliable to imperialist uses, Beti suggests, showing Pettiti's easy alteration of semiotic relations and accentuating the weakness of a term like *philanthrope*. Thus brotherhood and love of man as French humanistic models—because French in language of expression and in historical practice—are unsuited to Beti's needs for Cameroon. It is ironic, in the face of this articulated suspicion regarding solidarity in French, that the publication and censorship of Beti's book sparked such a fervent solidary reaction from francophone readers. The text, while it denied the French language the ability and nuance to express anti(neo)colonial solidarity, undisputedly *transmitted* this very solidarity, in French, throughout the francophone world.

## *Main basse* in Quebec: Between Philanthropy and Solidarity

Beti's *Main basse* problematizes white, supposedly leftist European sympathy (*philanthropes*) by showing the unreliability of language in a postcolonial context. Of course, Beti would not include Maspero, his French editor, in this same category; for Beti the term *philanthrope* is not a blanket term covering the entire French Left, only its sentimental but apolitical members. Essentially, Beti accuses of hypocrisy those "white liberals" who protect their assets while proclaiming their indignation in the face of global injustice and their solidarity with those who suffer from this injustice. Though the question of how the (white) Quebecois Left would receive his book would not emerge for a couple of years, Beti's essay already indicated his awareness of the dangers of how white leftists might react to the situation in Cameroon—"philanthropically" rather than in solidarity. Quebecois intellectuals assert their solidarity based on what they argue is their own status as colonized, but the status is obviously debatable (Memmi, for instance, had to adjust his definition of *colonization* for Quebec, stating that "the colonial relation is relative"; see chapter 2 above). Here is the problem represented by Quebecois solidarity for anticolonial causes: it resembles "philanthropy," the dogmatic stance articulated from a position of relative comfort and accompanied by proclamations of affinity and other empty rhetoric but void of actual political commitment. Are Quebecois intellectuals "à gauche comme Chez Maxim's," or do they represent actual allies for Beti and the anti-neocolonial movement? If the latter, what can they do to make effectual political commitments?

The Quebecois intellectuals who picked up *Main basse* for publication saw their edition of the banned book and the making of the documentary *Contre-censure* as examples of such a political commitment. To enact this commitment, they strove to match specific models of solidarity offered by Beti's text. For example, they offered Beti (and the reading public) the type of explication countering a legal decision that Beti himself had written about Ndongmo and Ouandié. In addition, the Quebecois publishers tried to replicate the connection between the revolutionary, the bishop, and then the exiled writer by crossing unaccustomed arenas of difference in order to establish likenesses (similes) between Cameroon and Quebec. In their reading of *Main basse,* the Quebecois editors sense the rapprochement between Beti and his subjects (the prelate and the revolutionary), the inexpressible "fraternity" in the solidary stance of the book, and they latch onto it. And Beti, conversely, matches this opportunism with his own interest in seeing the book republished.

I am not suggesting that the French language in Quebec was somehow better able to define or characterize the solidarity linking Ndongmo and Ouandié. No, the French tongue remains the French tongue, with its same limits: Quebecois French speakers are no more able to understand the specificity of that solidarity than French colonials. But Quebecois intellectuals see and sympathize with this unintelligible (for them) solidarity allying a Marxist revolutionary with a Catholic bishop against French neocolonial oppression, and they try to understand how to graft their own solidarity onto the anti-neocolonial "brotherhood" (for lack of a better term) of Ndongmo and Ouandié. It is a kind of secondary solidarity, or rather a tertiary solidarity, which cannot fully grasp the original solidarity at the heart of *Main basse* but inscribes itself in its wake by siding with Beti. Beti himself represents a kind of scholarly insider intellectually participating in or supporting Ndongmo and Ouandié's "relations fraternelles": as an exiled intellectual with a thorough knowledge of Cameroon's cultural and social norms, the text suggests, Beti *does* grasp the solidarity between the prelate and the revolutionary, and by broadcasting this solidarity through the publication of his denunciatory essay—by pointing to its existence beyond the bounds of the French language—he participates in the solidarity secondhand. For the writers, editors, and journalists in Montreal who published and reviewed *Main basse,* the book itself, the banned text, constitutes a kind of fetish of solidarity, an object they can brandish and revere and through which they can channel the solidarity inscribed in it (first, between Ndongmo and Ouandié, and second, between Beti and these martyrized revolutionaries). The fetish then legitimizes their own position.

The French language of course enables this fetishism; it is the language in which Beti writes and in which the Quebecois publishers read and write in turn. The Montreal *Main basse* as an object thus brings to a head the very problems its content explores, namely, the symbolically difficult status of French as an anti(neo)colonial language. The book as French-language fetish for anti-French solidarity crystallizes the paradox of Beti's and the Quebecois editors' positions.

The Quebecois intellectuals draw on *Main basse*'s method of expressing solidarity through simile to express their own fetishistic extension of this solidarity. Let us look back at Beti's work-around for the French-language lacuna he emphasizes so pointedly, which brought out the central, enigmatic solidarity structuring the trials and the text analyzing them. Linking Ouandié and Ndongmo, Beti writes, are "relations . . . auxquelles on peut, à la rigueur, attribuer le qualificatif de fraternelles." Beti's work-around functions like a simile, a trope that suggests similarity. The actual relations between Ndongmo and Ouandié, insists Beti, are *like* fraternal relations. The use of the simile structures *comparison* as the necessary paradigm for understanding and communicating across cultural difference. Similes are necessary to the intercultural expression of solidarities; in other words, as a wobbling remedy for French's linguistic inadequacy, simile becomes a viable tool with which to structure and express solidarities.

### Paratexts: Locating *Main basse* in Quebec

The Quebecois edition of *Main basse* is surrounded by a robust paratextual structure that situates the text for its readers.[16] Why does this particular text necessitate such a robust paratext? It is the result of the book's (post)colonial transplantations: a book about Cameroon needs to be contextualized for its non-Cameroonian reading publics. If *Main basse* had been published first and only in Cameroon, it probably would not have needed a preface; local news reports would have made the events and characters discussed in the essay familiar to an alert readership. But the very structure of repression and the revelatory nature of the text made publication in Cameroon impossible, and beyond Cameroon, context needed to be provided for readers, especially in the face of the international press's inadequate coverage of the situation, which the essay attacks specifically. I discuss each preface in detail below, but first I want to give an overview of the structural work they accomplish as a collection of texts in three different contexts: global anti-imperialism, local politics, and methods for establishing solidarity.

First, the prefaces structurally locate the publication within a global context by making clear the current of international solidarity in which the publication participates. The Quebecois edition integrates itself into what the critic Cilas Kemedjio calls the "*Main basse* trademark": "L'interdiction de l'essai a pour effet de mobiliser autour de l'écrivain une 'réserve révolutionnaire' qui va des dissidences intellectuelles africaines aux militants québécois en passant par les réseaux tiers-mondistes français" (181). Paradoxically, pointing to this abstract current of solidarity means focusing on the concrete events of the text's publication. The Quebecois edition calls attention to its own apparatus of publication, multiplying prefatory texts, to show that it is invested in doing more than simply reproducing Beti's banned essay. It wants to bring attention to the essay's censorship, accentuating and accompanying the accusations made in *Main basse* by explaining the authorities' wish to silence them, imitating, in a way, Beti's own method of explicating the Cameroonian trials. The edition makes very clear both its denunciation of French and Cameroonian neocolonial repression and Quebec's solidary links with dissidents in an overabundance of paratextual materials: a pre-pre-preface, titled "Présentation," and a "Préface à l'édition québécoise" precede the "Note de l'éditeur" by the original Paris editor, François Maspero, and the "Avertissement" by Beti. The need for the "Présentation" in addition to the "Préface à l'édition québécoise" suggests the extraordinary nature of the material object the reader has in hand. The physical presence of the book in its North American version demands a quadruple explanation: two layers of clarificatory Quebecois voices, followed by the French editor's note and a warning by the author—paratextual folds that position the fabric of the "main text" within a very specific and complex political and ethical transnational francophone context.

Second, the essay's Quebecois edition articulates its role within local networks and personalities of publication, pointing out its affiliations with Montreal leftist political concerns. The Quebecois *Main basse sur le Cameroun* was published by Léandre Bergeron, an unconventional Quebecois professor, activist, playwright, historian, and publisher with sovereigntist and anticapitalist inclinations. Bergeron the personality represents a signifying point in the ecosystem that produced *Main basse*. Representative of this signifying personality, the epigraph to Bergeron's (auto)biography (*Léandre Bergeron, né en exil*) symbolizes his iconoclasm:

Du
Regard
De
L'autre
Je
Me
Contresaintciboirise . . .

This categorical statement (ellipsis in original), characteristic of Bergeron's radical positions, improvises on Quebecois *sacres,* or religious swearwords, a range of culturally subversive terms based on accessories of the Catholic Church (here the *saint ciboire,* the wafer box). By transforming the *ciboire* into the verb "je me contresaintciboirise," he is saying *je me fous*—"I don't give a damn"—in a way that is quite aggressively directed at the established cultural order and that at the same time remains humorous for those who see beyond the sacrilegious nature of the act. Bergeron's aphoristic epigraph proclaims his independence from social norms and expectations. In a similar spirit, Bergeron had created the publishing company Les Éditions Québécoises in 1970, as a countercultural gesture, in order to produce his revolutionary *Petit manuel de l'histoire du Québec* without the interference of an external editor or press.[17] Subsequently approached by fellow militants who hoped to have their own texts published, Bergeron then built a repertory of political texts, including *Main basse* in 1974 (Rivière 79). Before moving to rural Abiti and integrating a subsistence-farming community, Bergeron was actively involved in various Montreal popular networks—unions, popular clinics, history classes for union workers—and political groups, including the sovereigntist Mouvement de libération populaire founded in 1965 by Pierre Vallières, author of *Nègres blancs d'Amérique*. These were the networks on which Bergeron relied for the material production of the texts his Éditions Québécoises published.

The publishing apparatus that produced *Main basse* in Quebec, then, is solidly inscribed on the left of Quebec's political landscape, associated with workers' rights, the sovereignty struggle, and transnational cooperation. The copyright page reads simply, in small print, "Février 1974/Lithographié par Journal Offset Inc./254 Benjamin-Hudon, Ville St-Laurent [a borough now integrated into Montreal]," followed by the logo of the Confédération des Syndicats Nationaux: this was a unionized press. Among the other materials printed by the printer, Journal Offset, were union newspapers (as well as other types of newspapers), Parti québécois projects, and works edited by the left-leaning sovereigntist press Éditions Parti pris.[18] Thus the editing and printing team that took on the project of publishing *Main basse* in Quebec did so from an ethical and social position associated with the radical Left in Quebecois politics. The physical mechanisms of the publication were solidary, working through union channels and bringing together nationalism (Quebecois sovereignty) and internationalism (global anticolonial thought).

In establishing *Main basse*'s role so firmly within local political structures, the Quebecois prefaces also played an important role in the distribution of the book: by emphasizing censorship, they complicated importation to France. Ambroise Kom's biography-like *Mongo Beti parle* implies Beti's gentle frustration with the Quebecois first prefacer's decision to advertise censorship in his first line of text;[19] it is as though Beti were decrying the lack of awareness of Quebecois readers, for whom things must be spelled out and even sensationalized. But of course the problem was Quebec's isolation; the prefacers needed to emphasize the French censorship of *Main basse* because the general Quebecois readership would not have known about it, and censorship *is* one of the book's central selling points, as well as the reason for its republication in Montreal. For these reasons, the first Quebecois preface states the importance of censorship overtly: "Lu de certains par goût de défier la censure, *Main basse sur le Cameroun* fera découvrir un pays divers et attachant à l'histoire tourmentée, un livre passionnant sur des événements tragiques dont l'écho s'est répercuté jusqu'à l'Europe et l'Amérique, et enfin le style musclé d'un écrivain de grande classe" (ii).[20] The preface in this statement emphasizes censorship to entice a Quebecois generation that defined itself by its resistance to authority. The North American province's isolation from the French news cycle, and from the neocolonial games enmeshing France in the political and cultural life of its former colonies, required this sensationalist preface; otherwise readers would not have understood the edition's raison d'être.

This need to educate readers and contextualize the essay—first for French and then for Quebecois and international readers—led to a third commonality among the four prefaces: they all function in the mode of the *simile*, establishing comparisons in order to explain both the text's international importance and its local applicability. The Quebecois prefaces strive to place Quebec in parallel with Cameroon, and the French prefaces strive to construct parallels between Cameroon and other French neo-colonies. All these prefaces suggest that Cameroon is not unique, even as *Main basse* itself expands on the specifics of the singular situation surrounding the Cameroonian trials. The prefaces contextualize *Main basse* by putting these trials in the perspective of similar (neo)colonial situations. The solidarity at the heart of *Main basse*, articulated through similes and fulfilled by Beti's solidary essayistic analysis, thus becomes part of a series of parallel experiences. The half-articulated non-French solidarity is made transposable by its own simile structure, which suggests that working approximations are possible and that the original revolutionary solidarity can be "similed" across space and time. In the iterative process of creating similes, the French language is anchored at the center of the mechanism, playing the role of both medium and point of critique. French allows solidarity to travel and be transposed; the mechanism of creating anti(neo)colonial similes reclaims solidarity from French. French permits the creation of similes, which then disarticulate French's (neo)imperial dominance.

Postindependence Cameroon presented particularly apt parallels for intellectuals intent on relating it to the Quebecois anticolonial schema. The fact that Cameroon was already independent in 1974 (since 1960) may seem to place Bergeron's publication of *Main basse* beyond the "independence era"; in *Main basse,* after all, Beti is writing about postindependence Cameroon, not the struggle for independence. And yet the plight of Ndongmo, outlined in *Main basse*, and of others like him can be considered the aftermath of Cameroonian independence. It represents the betrayal of the hopes of independence, namely, the severe and violent repression of the union-led liberation party Union des populations du Cameroun both before and after independence. For Quebecois intellectuals who were, in the early to late 1970s, debating the possibility of Quebec becoming a sovereign nation, Cameroon's struggle against a neocolonialist dictator represented a continuation of the very same anticolonial struggles (in Africa) through which Quebecois writers had defined their own colonized position. Anti-neocolonial dissidence in Cameroon was thus adopted as a cousin to shore up the argument that the struggle in

Quebec was indeed of an anticolonial nature. Bergeron's publishing company embraced its role as champion of the oppressed writer, maneuvering its privileged position (it was free to publish) to benefit those it wanted to position as its anticolonial allies. In turn, the presence of anti(neo)colonial allies demonstrated Quebec's colonized status by highlighting the parallels among multiple colonized and postcolonial spaces, a demonstration the prefaces to *Main basse* carry out through the use of similes.

### Presenting *Main basse sur le Cameroun* in Quebec

The accumulation of prefaces, each framing the remainder of the book, creates an effect of repeated *mise en abyme*, each preface influencing how readers encounter the following paratexts and the main text. The fact that the Quebecois prefaces appear first, postponing the two original French prefaces, places Maspero's and Beti's introductions within a particular structure of similes determined by the Quebecois prefaces, which emphasize the value of *Main basse* as a support for Quebec's own decolonizing efforts. In addition, the four prefaces' similes accrue, constructing a cumulative effect of similarity over and above vast difference and distance, producing a multipronged articulation of solidarity around the Montreal publication of *Main basse*.

The first preface a reader of the Quebecois edition of *Main basse* encounters is Gérard Le Chêne's "Présentation," which sketches out the French-language geographical triangle of solidary exchange that produced the book. Gérard Le Chêne, a Canadian journalist of French origin specializing in coverage of Africa for the Agence de Presse Tiers-Monde, would later direct the 1976 film *Contre-censure* defending *Main basse* (on which more later). This first preface opens by forcefully attacking French censorship, orienting Quebec immediately as a "third space," geographically and ethically separate from both France and Cameroon, that becomes the locus of criticism of censorship and of championing *Main basse*. In fact, the entire short text (the "Présentation" runs less than two pages) functions according to a series of telescoping triangles that structure comparative connections between Cameroon, France, and Quebec. The "Présentation" opens, for example, with the declaration that "Les Éditions Québécoises rééditent le livre d'un écrivain africain saisi par le gouvernement français à la demande des dirigeants du Cameroun" (i). In taking this very clear position against France and neocolonial Cameroon, Le Chêne actually schematizes the situation somewhat naïvely. Calling Beti simply "un écrivain africain" erases the entire problem of Beti's nationality and citizenship, which had triggered and provided a legal rationale for the censorship of *Main basse*. It appears that what Le Chêne may have been trying to articulate by writing *africain* is in fact Beti's race, his blackness, which would have appealed to a range of Quebecois militants interested in interracial solidarity. Le Chêne thus asserts the text's racial location at the same time that he insists on new politico-ethical imperatives that can reshape the nature of colonial space's triangulation (Cameroon–France–Quebec). These new imperatives include not only freedom of expression and full self-determination but also antiracism. Le Chêne expresses these politico-moral imperatives by overlaying the triangular geography with a series of binary opposites that manicheistically delineate the good from the bad. Within this charged political field, Le Chêne then defines alliances based on suggested comparisons, using similes to establish parallels.

The "Présentation" identifies the key transcontinental alliances that define *Main basse*'s Quebecois edition and that unite author, French publisher, and Quebecois publisher against the censorship of French and Cameroonian authorities. To describe this triangular solidarity of revolutionary publication, Le Chêne writes that Léandre Bergeron's combative attitude toward censorship is an "attitude vigoureusement partagée par Maspéro [sic] et Mongo Béti [sic]" (i). Le Chêne imagines this "vigorously" united countercensorship triumvirate as the origin of the Quebecois reedition: he creates an imaginary solidary bond connecting Mongo Beti, the dissident Franco-Cameroonian author, François Maspero, the French publisher and major figure of the Parisian internationalist Left, and the revolutionary historian and nationalist publisher Léandre Bergeron in Montreal. In so doing, Le Chêne elevates the lesser-known Bergeron. In addition, by erecting this triadic structure of *grands personnages,* each connected to a revolutionary cause, Le Chêne brings the plight of sovereigntist Quebec into the realm of international causes dear to the radical Left. The triangular solidarity thus begins to structure sovereigntist Quebec as a parallel for anti-neocolonial Cameroon and the French radical Left.

The erection of this triangular solidarity necessitates a clear distinction between the French radical Left and the French government's neocolonial policies. Le Chêne opens:

> Juillet 1972. En vertu de l'article 14 de la loi sur la Presse qui permet d'interdire tout ouvrage "de provenance étrangère" sans avoir à en donner les motifs, la police française fait irruption chez l'éditeur François Maspéro [sic] connu pour son obstination courageuse à publier des ouvrages politiques

"non-orthodoxes" qui, souvent, n'ont pas l'heur de plaire aux "autorités." . . . Dans le cas de Mongo Béti [sic], agrégé de l'Université française, professeur dans un lycée de Normandie, "provenance étrangère" se transforme en alibi grotesque.

Ainsi donc les auteurs africains francophones interdits dans leur pays se voient-ils muselés aussi en France. C'est pourquoi le geste de Léandre Bergeron revêt une importance considérable. (i)

Le Chêne sets himself and the Quebec republication of *Main basse* clearly outside France, judging the French government's actions with the scornful detachment of scare quotes. In this way, he overlays the triangular solidarity with a moralistic binary opposition between France and Quebec, which he further accentuates by aligning Quebec, and Bergeron, with an illustrious genealogy of publishers of texts banned in France, the "éditeurs hollandais qui, aux XVIIème et XVIIIème siècles, publiaient les ouvrages jugés subversifs en France, pour causes religieuses ou politiques, de Descartes, Pascal ou Voltaire" (i). Placing Quebec in a grand genealogy of countercensorship further isolates neocolonial France and its censoring powers on the immoral side of a Manichean schema that aligns Beti, by contrast, with Descartes, Pascal, and Voltaire—icons of French reason. On one level, Le Chêne's gesture does something similar to Beti's use of the French language: it relies on a common reference with cultural clout within France and French culture, even on icons of French rationalism as symbols of an older and more "progressive" France, as means to decry the contemporary French government's actions. This appeal to a French-language cultural history shared among educated francophones the world over unearths some of the countercurrents of French thought that animate independence-era solidarities: French was always more than an imperial language.[21] Le Chêne's gesture, his drawing on this common francophone experience of a French education, represents yet another way in which he aligns himself with Beti.

Le Chêne justifies the moral obligation of republication by highlighting a parallel between Quebec and Cameroon. Le Chêne, who favored sovereignty in Quebec, uses his "Présentation" as an occasion to make an oblique reference to Quebec's struggle for independence. As he reproaches the Ahidjo regime with the transformation of the Federal Republic of Cameroon into a unitary state, he asks, rhetorically, "Destin du fédéralisme dans les sociétés politiques dites biculturelles?" (ii). Le Chêne clearly alludes to the Canadian federal government and to some Quebecois' fears that the federal government would try to curtail provincial self-governance, with consequences they considered particularly dire for French-majority Quebec. The "Présentation," then, the first paratextual fold introducing *Main basse,* locates the text's subversive power first in Cameroon's need to censor it both at home and in France, and second in its potential as an allegory for francophone Quebec's situation with regard to Canada. The text's elaboration of a triangular solidarity among French-speaking leftist political movements, flattened in the context of a larger binary opposition that marks Quebec—not France—as the better custodian for and authority on radical reasoning, finally evolves into a simile that sees Quebec as Cameroon's structural double. The Quebec-Cameroon simile, by establishing a blanket parallel between Quebec and Cameroon, brings to light the anticolonial discourse animating both regions' efforts to ensure self-governance, but it forecloses consideration of the modalities of this comparison.[22] More precisely, the text's solidarity (triangulated through France by virtue of the Maspero edition of *Main basse*), once it has been flattened into a simile that focuses primarily on Quebec and Cameroon, has become something slightly different: a discursive solidarity that has to pass by way of France (by way of the French language, historical French rationalists, and contemporary French radical thinkers) but that ultimately paints Quebec as more like Cameroon than like the radical Left in France.

## Prefacing Quebec in *Main basse*

Le Chêne's allusions to Quebec remain subtle compared with the explicit, Quebec-centric comparisons structuring the "Préface à l'édition québécoise" penned by Jacques Benjamin, professor of political science at the University of Montreal. Benjamin takes advantage of his significant platform (the solidary republication of a banned book) to air local grievances and to establish parallels between these grievances and the authoritarian situation in Cameroon. The "Préface à l'édition québécoise," the Quebecois publication's second preface, openly uses Mongo Beti and the neocolonial situation in Cameroon as a frame for discussing economic and cultural inequities in Quebec; the structural simile is taken for granted. Benjamin brings Cameroon up specifically at the beginning and at the end of his preface and uses those references to bracket and structure the implicit simile—Quebec—at the center.

Benjamin's "Préface" performs several tasks that unite his seeming tangents detailing local, transitory news events. In part the preface's purpose is to establish Quebec as a colonized space similar to Cameroon. But the preface also works to garner Quebecois interest for the book; making local readers understand the local relevance of a book that plunges into the nitty-gritty of Cameroonian corruption requires a clear exposition of the parallels between the two territories. The preface therefore attempts to sell the book to local activists and to arouse their interest by referring to their own local causes célèbres. A third purpose of the preface is to find a wider audience outside Quebec and to expose to these potentially solidary outsiders the colonial relations that structure Quebecois society. As the preface's local anecdotes make clear, the Quebecois edition is a vehicle for Quebecois intellectuals to show their solidarity for anti(neo)colonial causes and to canvas non-Quebecois anticolonial French speakers for recognition and support of the Quebecois nationalist cause, seeking additional solidarity across even broader francophone geographies.

Benjamin begins his preface with a brief biography of Mongo Beti and outlines the twentieth-century history of Cameroon, focusing on the neocolonial networks of exploitation characterized by the continued overall flow of capital *out of* Cameroon toward France. Benjamin emphasizes the psychological and cultural links between the former protectorate and the metropole that facilitate continued French economic dominance. But Cameroon's neocolonial situation serves mostly as a sort of preamble to Benjamin's main concerns, which center on economics and education in Quebec. Benjamin segues deliberately from Cameroon to Quebec: "Ce que décrit Mongo Béti [sic] dans *Main basse sur le Cameroun* ce sont des situations que les Québécois connaissent bien" (iv). The statement seems ludicrous: the arrest and public execution of Ernest Ouandié and the fabricated evidence against Monseigneur Albert Ndongmo, which Beti is at pains to deconstruct in *Main basse,* are by any standard vastly more repressive than the situation in Quebec. Even if Quebecois members of the Front de libération du Quebec (FLQ—inspired by Algeria's Front de libération nationale) might wish to liken their struggle to the UPC's 1970s guerrilla warfare, the two situations were significantly different. But just as Benjamin, in his description of neocolonial Cameroon, favors economic arguments over a critique of dictatorship, here he avoids the flagrant differences between Quebec and Cameroon in order to focus on economic parallels between them, using the Quebecois scholar André d'Allemagne's 1966 book on Quebec as a colonial space to establish a loose connection. "André d'Allemagne, dans *Le colonialisme au Québec,* avait souligné le lien entre l'économique et le culturel, entre la présence de capitaux étrangers et l'influence qu'ils exercent sur la vie politique et culturelle au Québec" (iv). Benjamin's concern here is thus with the impact of economics on culture, which he reads as a central concern of *Main basse;* this focus allows him to address several key issues for Quebecois sovereigntists in Montreal.

Having mentioned foreign investment as a major problem in Cameroon, Benjamin elaborates a simile between Cameroon and Quebec by criticizing foreign investment in Quebec, giving very precise numbers: "$47 milliards d'investissements étrangers au Canada, soit le tiers de l'activité commerciale et industrielle, dont 75% aux Américains" (iv). Benjamin lists this information in the form of a sentence fragment, suggesting the complete transparency of the facts by omitting to frame them syntactically. At the same time, he jumps back and forth between the provincial and national scales, moving in one sentence fragment from the context of Quebec to that of Canada and returning to Quebec in the next: "$5 milliards d'investissements totaux au Quebec." His position is a Quebecois nationalist position—ultimately the "cultural" ramifications he describes represent the linguistic and educational interests of Quebecois nationalism—but in the economic part of his argument it is statistically difficult to separate Quebec from Canada or to calculate, for example, how much of the nonforeign investment in Quebec might be considered Canadian rather than Quebecois (or how such a distinction might be arrived at). The foreign investment figures that Benjamin clearly wants to portray as astronomical thus muddy the waters of distinctive Quebecois nationalism as an economic and cultural aspiration, further complicating the structural parallel he is trying to establish between Cameroon and Quebec since Quebec remained attached to Canada economically in a way that had no exact parallel for Cameroon. His desire for comparison-based solidarity is asymptotic; the many differences between Cameroon and Quebec prevent his articulation from matching his desire.

In spite of these difficulties imagining an exact parallel (owing to different levels of violence and repression and the difficulty of determining the nature of foreign investments in Quebec), Benjamin continues to structure his preface asymptotically, as though the parallel between Quebec and Cameroon were self-evident. The political situation in Quebec, tangential to the events described in *Main basse,* only makes sense as a central topic of the preface if Quebec functions as a simile for Cameroon. Instead of returning to the subject of Cameroon or of Beti's banned book, Benjamin zeroes in even more on Quebecois provincial matters, bringing up several specific issues that constituted local controversies at the time but that would have been largely unknown outside Quebec. Benjamin's local emphasis brings to light the types of things Beti considers in *Main basse;* that is, Benjamin models his method on Beti by focusing on the hyperlocal. First, Benjamin delves into a 1972 interview with then Quebec Liberal premier Robert Bourassa, quoting both the interviewer and the interviewee:

> (Quebec-Presse)—Est-ce que le capitalisme, qui s'applique de façon sauvage au Quebec, prenons le cas d'ITT [American-based International Telephone and Telegraph, which was active in the forestry industry in Quebec], subventionnée très largement par les deux gouvernements, vous satisfait comme premier ministre?
>
> (Bourassa)—Je ne vois pas d'organismes, publics ou privés, au Québec et au Canada, qui soient capables comme ITT de faire pareil investissement, $500 millions, dans un secteur en déclin. . . . ITT a les marchés, le *know-how,* le capital. (iv, quoted from *Québec-Presse,* January 23, 1972, ellipsis in original)[23]

Benjamin reproduces this interview snippet to make an anticapitalist, anti-Liberal (pro–Parti québécois) statement, relishing *Québec-Presse*'s criticism of capitalism in Quebec as "savage" and Bourassa's own repetition of the word *capital* as he lists ITT's assets. The anticapitalist bias for which *Québec-Presse* was known is used to demonstrate the political leanings of *Main basse*'s Quebecois publishers. In addition, Bourassa's use of the English term *know-how* to refer to ITT's business savvy, a term protestingly italicized in *Québec-Presse,* shores up a larger argument that Benjamin makes in the preface: that English is the language of finance in the province. But although ITT-Rayonier's purchase of land in Quebec was "highly controversial,"[24] it did not make international news, and it is hard to find a direct, content-based link between Cameroon and the ur-Quebecois industries of logging and paper-pulp manufacture.

The link Benjamin is attempting to construct between Cameroon and Quebec is, instead, indirect, a loose parallel between the ruling mechanism that defines "native" elites in both French-speaking regions. In the Cameroonian frame to his preface, Benjamin mentions the "élites africaines . . . disposées à continuer à participer au réseaux économiques existants" (iv), leaving to the main text of *Main basse* the task of elucidating specific instances. Part of his strategy for establishing the parallel between Quebec and Cameroon is to ascertain the existence of a similar *comprador bourgeoisie*[25] operating in Quebec. The specific example of Bourassa's crassly candid appreciation for ITT's capitalistic clout helps Benjamin construct a parallel between Quebec and Cameroon that is not entirely evident; after all, it is much harder to suggest colonial involvement on the part of ITT in Quebec than on the part of French enterprises in Cameroon. Benjamin's simile is structured following a particular type of inductive logic according to which he lists a certain number of local circumstances in Quebec that are like local circumstances in Cameroon in order to suggest that the uniting cause of those circumstances must also be the same: a type of general colonial-style repression.

In his discussion of the political implications of foreign investment, Benjamin makes explicit the parallel between Quebec and Cameroon, equating the powerful lobbies supporting logging and fossil-fuel exploration in Quebec to the French-backed building of the Tiko-Douala road, a thoroughfare that facilitates the exportation of goods produced in the interior of Cameroon (iv–1).[26] Here again, Benjamin's portrayal of Quebec as a structural parallel to Cameroon minimizes some of the most glaring differences between the situations in the two nations: the fact that logging interests have been able to sidetrack environmental reforms in Quebec pales compared with the fact that French "industrials and merchants" (1) located in Cameroon dictate infrastructural developments over and above the needs of the general population. Benjamin's parallel points asymptotically to similar structures of economic influence on government policy, but while it does this, it obscures significant differences in scale.

This is the structural problem that characterizes Quebecois intellectuals' solidarity with African anti(neo)colonialists, and yet Benjamin, unlike many other writers, does not acknowledge the problem or question its implications. Ambroise Kom in *Université des Montagnes,* for example, describes the parallel between Quebec and decolonizing African countries but also qualifies it:

> Pareille situation m'interpella parce qu'elle rappelait à s'y méprendre les luttes pour l'indépendance des pays africains à la différence près que le Canada est une démocratie et un pays industriel avancé comme dirait Marcuse. . . . Nous assistâmes au déploiement fascinant d'un projet de société longuement mûri par les militants péquistes [Parti québécois militants]. Il s'agissait là du genre de démarche qu'auraient dû adopter les pays africains au lendemain de la proclamation de leur indépendance. . . . Comparaison n'est pas raison, et le Québec comme le Canada sont évidemment très éloignés de l'Afrique. Comment ne pas me rappeler qu'en 1959, à la veille de l'avènement de l'indépendance du Cameroun, j'ai enjambé des cadavres entre Batiè et Bayangam le lendemain du jour où mon oncle fut pris en otage pour servir d'infirmier au "maquis." La prise

d'otage avait été précédée par une terrible nuit d'affrontements entre l'armée française dite de pacification et les "maquisards" dont plusieurs avaient perdu la vie. (42–47)

Kom's striking phrase "Comparaison n'est pas raison" highlights the problems with using simile as a basis for solidarity; by making explicit the violence of Cameroon's guerrilla warfare, Kom reminds readers of the inexactitude of the simile and grounds his solidarity with *péquiste* militants in a much more nuanced understanding of their similar but different circumstances. But unlike Kom (who, granted, writes retrospectively about events that had taken place decades earlier), Benjamin is most interested in setting up a structural parallel and advancing the idea of a political simile that validates sovereigntist perspectives in Quebec—producing rhetorically, by implicit simile, a form of solidarity that erases the striking differences of scale at its foundation.

The structural simile linking Quebec to Cameroon constitutes such a self-evidence for Benjamin that he even leaves it out of parts of his argument, focusing on Quebec with the understanding that an implicit comparison to Cameroon undergirds the discussion. This is the case in his discussion of the cultural ramifications of foreign economic influence. By *culture* Benjamin means specifically education, his own domain—he was a professor at the University of Montreal—and even more specifically the failure of Quebecois education to create, through a French-language education, a class of successful francophone businesspeople. Benjamin's equation of culture with education and of education with future business leaders is of course paradoxical; it makes the link between economics and culture a circular one, curtailing culture's transformative potential. Part of the paradox seems to stem from a commonplace Quebecois belief in the social importance of English at the time: the phenomenon, which Benjamin criticizes, of French-speaking parents sending their children to English schools, considering an education in English "plus 'rentable,' plus 'pratique'" than an education in French (1). For average Quebecois who think primarily of social advancement, English represents a useful tool. For a nation hoping to define itself linguistically, however, Benjamin suggests that the preservation of French should be a central concern and that current educational policy, like current economic policy (such as that dictated by Bourassa's respect for foreign companies' "know-how"), does not address the issue satisfactorily.

Throughout this entire discussion of Quebec's language politics, Cameroon remains absent, even though Benjamin's argument is rooted in an implicit comparison to the Cameroonian situation. Benjamin's preface here erases Cameroon even as it relies on it to furnish the simile that lets problems in Quebec be stated. Paradoxically, the difference in scale discussed above in fact *enables* the making implicit (or the leaving unsaid) of Cameroon, because the more extreme and taken for granted the neocolonial repression in Cameroon is, the more it can be relied on to bring to light injustices in Quebec. Benjamin's construction of solidarity is thus based on an assumed simile so rhetorically effective that it can function even with half its equation elided.

Cameroon is similarly absent from Benjamin's discussion of the politically incendiary question of a "French McGill." Benjamin bemoans the Quebecois government's decision to fuse two existing colleges into Concordia University, Montreal's second anglophone university. The decision, he declares, supports "'des intérêts qui ne sont pas ceux de la majorité des Québécois'" (1, unattributed quotation), where that majority is francophone. Benjamin here refers to the local struggle of students, professors, and workers to increase the availability of higher education in French in Quebec, a struggle that began in the 1960s and came to a head with a massive demonstration in March 1969 for a "McGill français" (McGill was and is Montreal's elite English-language university). Among other complaints, demonstrators resented the fact that anglophones were disproportionately represented in the population of university students in the province: anglophones made up 42 percent of university enrollments, although they constituted only 18 percent of Quebec's population (Warren). Such popular demonstrations opposed what the protesters considered McGill's inbred support of and by the financiers of Montreal's "English ghetto" (Warren); Benjamin, however, in attacking the creation of a second English university, laments the lack of "une politique de formation de la main-d'œuvre hautement qualifiée," judging that "les diplômés anglophones quittent . . . le Québec en grand nombre" (1). Thus for Benjamin the problem is that Quebec chooses to provide higher education for a population that then fails to contribute its skills to the province, or rather to the province's economic development. Ultimately, the paradox remains: Benjamin's preface, in spite of its purported defense of local culture, ironically limits culture to its uses in advancing local economic interests. The answer to "savage capitalism" profiting foreign companies is not an alternative to capitalism but rather a local capitalism benefiting Quebecois francophones.

In the labyrinth of Benjamin's unpacking of the "French McGill" question, Cameroon is entirely absent, although the implicit simile continues to run through this section of the argument. Benjamin is in fact following Beti's example in endorsing local capitalism; *Main basse* sanctions the kind of grassroots capitalism represented by the small manufacturing enterprise of Monseigneur Ndongmo, whose arrest, trial, and death-transmuted-to-life sentence Beti claims resulted from his local business successes. Benjamin's interpretation of the "French McGill" problem constitutes another layer of the implicit comparison with Cameroon that undergirds his larger argument.

Unacknowledged in Benjamin's endorsement of local capital as part of an implicit comparison with Cameroon is the linguistic situation that represents yet another elided difference between Quebec and Cameroon. Benjamin's argument relies on the French language to be the foundation of economic viability for Quebec. For Beti, however, French forms an ultimately inadequate tool for solidarity, and the local businesses Ndongmo founded were not only opposed to French economic interests but also aimed at improving living conditions largely unrelated to language questions. The economic projects of Bishop Ndongmo, listed by Beti in *Main basse,* shed light on a business strategy driven by need rather than by linguistic or ideological precepts: at the time of his arrest, Ndongmo's diocese owned or planned to own hotels, bookstores, butcher shops, plantations, a notebook manufacture, a sock factory, and a mutual investment fund to benefit members of the clergy (120–21). Benjamin's insistence on the importance of French in Quebec for cultural and economic survival betrays, in a way, the implicit comparison with Cameroon, since such a concern with linguistic preservation was not an integral part of the Cameroonian situation as Beti describes it in *Main basse.* Benjamin's unarticulated reliance on a comparison with Cameroon imputes to Cameroon concerns quite foreign to it.

Benjamin's assumption that a strong structural parallel exists linking Quebec to Cameroon accounts for his abrupt transition back to Cameroon in his short concluding paragraph, a transition that underscores the extent to which the comparative link between Quebec and Cameroon has been the guiding line for Benjamin's prefatory essay, even when unacknowledged. The concluding paragraph, though it reverts to the subject of Cameroon, is still focused on Quebec, bolstering Benjamin's argument that the situation in Quebec is related to that in neocolonial Africa by returning to topics he has previously covered in his discussion of Quebec. Just as he did in the context of Quebec, in the Cameroonian context Benjamin links culture and economics, again emphasizing culture's economic reaches: "Comme le soulignait un nationaliste camerounais [unnamed in

Benjamin's text], quand la culture étrangère domine le pays, c'est-à-dire qu'elle sert d'instrument de gestion à son administration et à son économie, la coopération avec l'étranger joue inévitablement en faveur d'une minorité de privilégiés au détriment de la majorité" (1–2). Here again, culture functions solely as a management tool; in Benjamin's imaginary, culture constitutes a kind of economic variable (Benjamin was a political scientist), and therefore a dominant foreign culture leads to foreign dominance in economics. The phrase "minorité de privilégiés" represents the *comprador bourgeoisie*—the true target of *Main basse*'s criticism—and, coming as it does immediately after the discussion of Quebec's politics and education, raises the issue of who (personally, linguistically, and politically) Quebec's own "privilégiés" are. For Quebecois readers who endorsed his criticisms of Quebecois politics and society, Benjamin's introduction presents *Main basse* as a less than cryptic reference to current events, a kind of *essai à clef* whose local villains' identities merely await decoding.

For *Main basse*'s nonlocal readers unfamiliar with the situation in Quebec, however, Benjamin's preface reads not as an *essai à clef* but rather as a revelation of Quebec's "colonized" status. This revelation represents the flip side of Benjamin's prefatory essay. If the structural simile linking Quebec to Cameroon's politics is obvious to his Quebecois readers, Benjamin's message could also reach a new audience of radical Left militants beyond Quebec thanks to their interest Beti's book. Benjamin's decision to construct his preface as an extended simile comparing Quebec to Cameroon thus becomes a method for parlaying the northern province into international limelight and garnering further sympathy for its plight, a plight that gains in seriousness when it is portrayed in parallel with the case of Cameroon. Drawing a parallel between Quebec's "coloniality" and Cameroon's repressive neocolonial situation accentuates Quebec's victimhood and legitimates its struggle for sovereignty.

Simile here forms a convenient avenue for expressing solidarity, the abstraction of common similarity in the midst of infinite difference. Benjamin's simile-based solidarity presents certain strengths; in the context of the Montreal publication of *Main basse,* it skillfully entices Quebecois readers by presenting the text's parallels with their local circumstances, and it also introduces the problem of Quebec to the international network of militants eager to read Beti's banned book. In this sense, it serves a worthy purpose; as a mobilization of a similarity-based solidarity in the service of sharing information and pooling together global intellectual resources, it exemplifies the current of solidarity that came to Mongo

Beti's defense when *Main basse* was censored. But Benjamin's reliance on the erasure of an implicit simile to found this solidarity also presents limitations: his implied comparison smoothes over the glaringly uneven ground of different decolonial struggles, minimizing inequalities and variations in scale and violence. The ultimate result of Benjamin's erasure of the Cameroonian side of the solidary equation amounts to a disregard for Cameroonian lives—the very lives Kom mourns in his essay.

## Maspero's "Note de l'éditeur": Recentering Similes around Cameroon

François Maspero, *Main basse*'s first publisher, in 1972, was a central figure of the Parisian radical Left. Founded in March 1959, the Maspero publishing house appeared in reaction to the French government's actions in Algeria and proceeded to publish a range of influential anticolonial texts (including, for example, Fanon's *L'an V de la révolution algérienne* [1959] and *Les damnés de la terre* [1961]). The associated bookstore above the publishing house, La Joie de Lire, located in the Latin Quarter, became an "anticolonial meeting place" (Kalter 193) and was the victim of raids by police and of brick and bomb attacks by the Far Right.[27] Maspero was the heart of the place, the core of the loose-knit radical network. Beti himself describes François Maspero as "de l'extrême-gauche, presque anarchiste, anti-néocolonialiste à mort" (*Beti parle* 95).

Maspero's "Note" was written to accompany the original 1972 edition, placed before Le Chêne and Benjamin's prefaces. As presented in the Éditions Québécoises version, however, it appears *after* the two Quebecois prefaces, so that these prefaces in effect condition how the French editor's "Note" is received by readers. Benjamin takes the Quebec-Cameroon parallel for granted, but the Quebecois edition's general prefatory structure naturalizes that connection for the reader, so that it is Maspero's "Note" that seems jarring rather than the Quebecois prefaces. For instance, the details that Maspero gives identifying Cameroon as a very specific place disturb the broad simile that had made comparison with Quebec possible—an effect created by the achronological appearance of Le Chêne and Benjamin's prefaces ahead of Maspero's, when in fact Maspero's similes had originally connected Cameroon to places other than Quebec. In addition, the similes he does choose orient Cameroon toward other parallels and activate different solidarities, and these connections appear slightly unexpected precisely because the Quebecois prefaces ignore them. Maspero writes, predictably, about French-Cameroonian relations, detailing Cameroon's protectoral background and generally inveighing against France's role and interest in maintaining Cameroon's corrupt postcolonial government. Solidarity, for him, unites radical French militants with African anti-neocolonial activists. This choice stands out as a specifically delineated strategy (rather than as it might first have appeared, that is, as a general introduction to Beti's book) because it contrasts so sharply with Benjamin's "Préface à l'édition québécoise." Maspero also gives an idea of the other texts written on neocolonialism (many published by him),[28] situating *Main basse sur le Cameroun* in a genealogy of similar texts rather than presenting it as an isolated event. Though he presents Cameroon's situation as unique, that is, Maspero situates it within an established method for developing international solidarity: the publication of anti-neocolonial writing and its distribution to French radicals.

Maspero's introduction performs different functions than do the Quebecois paratexts; since it is not trying to establish a parallel with the quite distinct situation in the French-speaking Canadian province, it instead provides specific information that differentiates Cameroon from other anticolonial settings. Maspero, rather than drawing the broad lines necessary to structure an abstract simile based on "coloniality," a comparison that would unite all colonies as the same, instead deploys similes to identify the specificities of Cameroon's situation, contrasting it to France's other African colonies. In highlighting how Cameroon is distinct from other French-colonized countries, Maspero emphasizes his own solidarity (a solidarity linking France to Cameroon) while underplaying potential solidarities among non-French francophone spaces.

> Pays placé "sous tutelle" de la France par les Nations Unies, il n'a pas été besoin d'y jouer, comme dans les autres colonies françaises, la comédie du référendum. Simplement, les forces françaises ont "déblayé" le terrain avant la fin du mandat, en intensifiant la répression contre l'Union des Populations du Cameroun, nationaliste, pour préparer la route à des hommes à leur dévotion.
>
> Elles ont purement et simplement assassiné ses leaders nationalistes: Ruben Um Nyobé a été abattu au Cameroun par les troupes coloniales, le 13 septembre 1958, et Félix Moumié par la police parallèle française à Genève, le 3 novembre 1960. (8)

The first simile set up by Maspero is a negative comparison: Cameroon, *unlike* the other French colonies, he writes with devastating irony, did not have the benefit of participating in de Gaulle's 1958 referendum, which had offered colonial territories the possibility of becoming federal republics closely linked to France—although Maspero's bitter use of the expression *jouer la comédie* makes clear how trifling the actual benefits were. Extending the negative simile, Maspero ironically repeats the adverb *simplement* to refer to French military (rather than political) involvement in Cameroon, emphatically exposing France's assassinations of Cameroonian revolutionary leaders. The precise information Maspero gives in the form of a negative simile locates Beti's essay within a specific "protectoral" context that was in fact worse than the colonial situations of France's two large African colonies (French Occidental Africa and French Equatorial Africa). The Quebecois prefaces, by contrast, gloss over this distinction, preferring, in order to structure a parallel with Quebec's own (for some, dubiously) "colonial" situation, to paint Cameroon with the broader strokes of a general colonial-versus-anticolonial discourse.

Somewhat paradoxically, given Le Chêne's and Benjamin's efforts to make *Main basse* relevant to Quebec, Maspero also presents the stakes of Beti's intervention much more globally than the Quebecois paratexts do. Maspero, for example, introduces an imperial United States opposed to France's exclusive economic relations with its former colonies and territories, and he places this competition in the context of the Cold War by tying it to the US engagement in Vietnam. In Maspero's preface, the Cameroonian situation is *factually* linked to North America, instead of being held up as an abstract structural simile for Quebec. Writing in France, for a French public, a few years before Le Chêne and Benjamin, Maspero of course faced the need for a different kind of framing of colonized places. Maspero approaches Cameroonian neocolonialism from the perspective of global politics; Le Chêne and Benjamin, by contrast, approach it from the point of view of a francophone solidary geography. Both perspectives tell stories that link global spaces, but with different interests and methods.

Maspero does not avoid positive parallels altogether; on the contrary, he builds several comparative parallels to highlight the violence of repression in independent Cameroon. First, he labels Ahidjo's government "un régime de type nazi" (8) and qualifies its method as "nazisme à la petite semaine" (12), inserting the Cameroonian situation into a European moral schema in which Nazism represents the ultimate evil.[29] Second, he compares Cameroon to the Basque Country: "À la fin de 1970, les progressistes français se réjouissaient de la grâce des condamnés à mort de Burgos. Au même moment, Ernest Ouandié, leader de l'Union des Populations du Cameroun, était exécuté après un simulacre de procès à Yaoundé, dans une quasi-indifférence, sur l'ordre du président Ahmadou Ahidjo et avec l'aval du gouvernement français" (9). This comparison places neocolonial Cameroon in the same arena as European struggles for independence. Third, Maspero constructs a parallel between Cameroon and what was then named Zaire (Maspero writes "the Congo"), likening Ahidjo to Mobutu and comparing murdered Cameroonian UPC leaders (Ruben Um Nyobé, Félix Moumié, Osendé Afana, and Ernest Ouandié) to Patrice Lumumba. This simile orients *Main basse* toward parallel situations on the African continent, structuring that continent as a basis for anticolonial comparisons with Cameroon. But the Congo simile also erects a distinction between "France," which Maspero roundly incriminates for its corrupt participation in a vast network of "cooperation" and military "aid" on the continent (scare quotes are Maspero's), and the French radical Left. The simile thus delimits both sides of the equation: on the neocolonial victims' side, Cameroon is in a parallel situation with "the Congo," but on the neocolonial perpetrators' side, "France" is not a homogeneous entity, and France's government must be understood as separate from its leftist intelligentsia. Maspero's types of similes, more overtly articulated than Le Chêne's and Benjamin's, delineate specific guilts and animate precise solidarities; they demarcate variants among French positions, rallying a certain category of readers (pro-Resistance, antiracist) and allowing them the room to differentiate themselves from the positions of the French government.

Fourth, Maspero compares the resistance to neocolonialism in Cameroon to the conflict in Chad: "Dans cette guerre civile [the conflict between the Ahidjo regime and the UPC], bien plus longue et bien plus sanglante que celle du Tchad, les Français sont impliqués, soit directement, soit par fantoches interposés" (10). The Chad simile allows Maspero to transfer the term *civil war* from the Chadian context to that of Cameroon, where the UPC's resistance was not universally recognized as a civil war. Parallels such as the ones Maspero constructs between Ahidjo and Hitler and between Cameroon and the Basque Country, the Congo, and Chad provide a moral commentary on France's significant official neocolonial involvement as well as on the failure of the French progressive Left (or at least *a* French progressive Left) to contend with its government's collusion with African corruption. In addition, these parallels beam outward to illuminate the vastness of the collusion between big business and government—or the capitalist backing of political governance. Unlike Benjamin's preface, which zooms in on the situation in Quebec as a single parallel to the situation in Cameroon, Maspero's introduction zooms out to offer a fuller perspective of France's tentacular neocolonial reach. These techniques imply calls to action to the radical Left both in the

Hexagon and across the French-speaking world, creating links between different anti-neocolonial causes.

Maspero's aim in writing his introduction differs significantly from Benjamin's, which explains their different choices of simile structures. Whereas Benjamin's 1974 preface strives to establish a parallel between Cameroon and Quebec and to interest local North American readers in a book about a seemingly faraway structure of neocolonial violation, Maspero's 1972 preface seeks to mobilize the French Left to change the neocolonial structure linking French to Africa, first through a war of information. "C'est le devoir des révolutionnaires français," writes Maspero, "d'être aux côtés des révolutionnaires africains *dans ce combat comme dans les autres;* sinon, à quoi servirait de parler d'internationalisme?" (13, emphasis in original). More than simply introducing *Main basse,* Maspero's text outlines a new French-based revolutionary internationalist readership necessary for the reception of Beti's essay. "Mongo Beti le rappelle: le combat contre l'oppression commence ici même, en France, et d'abord par *l'information* sur les guerres coloniales que mène en secret, honteusement mais avec constance, (ou encourage ouvertement par ses fournitures d'armes), la Ve République, au Tchad, au Cameroun et ailleurs" (13, emphasis in original). The armature of similes that structures Maspero's preface works specifically to motivate a European audience: by comparing Ahidjo to Hitler, it triggers memories of the not-too-distant Nazi occupation of France. Comparing Cameroon to Chad and to then Zaire likewise intensifies European culpability by expanding the theater of its destructive neocolonial presence. If Maspero's aim is to arouse solidarity for Beti's cause, for Monseigneur Ndongmo, and for the UPC, the similes he selects effectively corner French readers into taking sides, in support of either anti-neocolonial solidarity or neocolonial (and Naziistic) complicity.

With the 1974 edition, this function of Maspero's preface serves to locate the text in its original European context and to make present for North American and international francophone audiences the echoes of fascism that haunt the text for French readers. Of course, the achronological ordering of the French and Quebecois prefaces naturalizes for readers Benjamin's Quebec-centric perspective, bizarrely provincializing Maspero's focus on France.

### The Simile as Accusation in Beti's "Avertissement"

Presciently (it was published with the first edition, in 1972), Beti's prefatory "Avertissement" seems to warn of *Main basse*'s impending censorship. This particular paratextual support addresses the French press's silence[30] with regard to the recent trials in Cameroon specifically and postcolonial Africa's anti-neocolonial struggles more generally. At the center of Beti's preface is a meditation on the silencing of these topics in French public opinion. He structures this meditation through a series of organizational similes, comparing coverage of Cameroon with coverage of other foreign crises addressed in the French press. Cameroon is both like and unlike these foreign locations, Beti shows: the four situations are similar in that they *should* all garner the support of leftist press organizations for their causes (various types of resistance against oppression), but Cameroon is dissimilar from the others in that it did *not* receive the same lavish treatment in the French press.

Beti focuses on French press coverage of three crises: civil unrest in Santo Domingo, a youth uprising in Ceylon, and US interference in Guatemalan politics.[31] Beti insists that the exposé of each of these crises represented a political *prise de position* for the French press, implying, then, that the nonexposure of the situation in Cameroon also represented an ideological stance: "Pleurer sur le pauvre Guatemala, n'était-ce pas dénoncer une politique de force déterminée à étouffer l'originalité et le libre arbitre des peuples d'Amérique latine? Braquer les projecteurs de l'actualité sur Saint-Domingue, n'était-ce pas mettre en lumière la vigueur du courant castriste et l'embarras éléphantesque dans lequel il plongeait les Américains? Inviter le lecteur à méditer sur l'insurrection de la jeunesse de Ceylan, n'est-ce pas vouloir signaler les dangers à longue échéance d'une décolonisation à courte vue—à la manière britannique, bien sûr?" (17). Corollarily, Beti affirms, the press's "forgetting" of the Cameroonian trials also reveals the papers' political position: "Si l'omission d'une affaire grave n'est pas moins révélatrice d'une intention politique, 'oublier' les récents procès du Cameroun après avoir constamment 'oublié' depuis dix ans, la guerre civile camerounaise, c'est trahir que le problème gêne. . . . On ne peut se proposer d'examiner de près ces procès sur lesquels la presse française parut si préoccupée de se taire, sans être amené en même temps à se demander qui ce sujet aurait pu incommoder et pour quelles raisons" (17–18). The similes that Beti introduces (Santo Domingo, Ceylon, Guatemala), so different from those selected by Maspero, Benjamin, and Le Chêne, erect entirely new horizons for comparison.

Chronologically, Beti's "Avertissement" was written first, but in the 1974 Montreal edition, framed by the three other prefaces, the similes he employs represent novel and unexpected parallels. The target of Beti's similes is not the actual situation in Cameroon but rather the treatment of this situation in the press. Focusing on these similar but different situations allows Beti to overtly accuse the French press of collusion with the French government's neocolonial interests: he taunts, in his preface, those who would have been "inconvenienced" by full press coverage of the Cameroon trials, revealing the ideological motivation of the French press in its reluctance to admit French participation in and support for a repressive neocolonial regime in its former protectorate. Structuring this taunt according to a framework of negative similes gives Beti's oblique reproach the rhetorical force of logic. Beti's cumulative simile has the effect of providing evidence of the French press's unequal treatment of a situation concerning France's imperial power, and it gives proof of the political motivations for the effective erasure of Cameroon's neocolonial regime from public knowledge in France.

In fact, what the multipronged simile really highlights is a missing solidarity, or even the lack of a political bent that might determine solidarity. Beti ironically points out that he can recount the Guatemala crisis "de mémoire, sans avoir besoin de consulter aucune fiche, tant la lecture de la presse me familiarisa avec les hommes du Guatemala, ses mœurs politiques, les rapports sociaux de ses habitants" (16)—and much more. As a casual reader of newspapers, Beti argues, he knows *everything* about Guatemala. What he implies is that the press's intimate interest in Guatemala is, in its political motivation, a *solidary* interest: the press positions itself in solidarity with the resistance to American influence in Guatemala. Solidary, as well, is the coverage of Ceylon and Santo Domingo. Solidary coverage of Cameroon, however, is absent. Beti's similes thus constitute an appeal for a solidarity whose absence has resulted in silence with respect to the situation in Cameroon. And to bring home the link between solidarity and expression, it is precisely by breaking the silence that he hopes to arouse solidarity. The "Avertissement," then, is addressed simultaneously to readers, warning them of their impending responsibility to solidarity, and to the authorities, those "inconvenienced" by Cameroon's truth. As *Main basse*'s history shows, the text succeeded on both counts, on the one hand suffering censorship and on the other giving rise to a wave of solidarity.

For readers of the Quebecois edition, immersed in a North American media environment, Beti's reproaches to French public opinion likely mattered less than his call to solidarity. Coming after two Quebecois prefaces that lumped French governmental censorship together with France more generally, the similes Beti arrayed against the French press lost some of the element of surprise they might have held for French readers. Indeed, Le Chêne's "Présentation" inserts into the context underlying Beti's critique Quebecois intellectual interest as the solidary answer to the French press's silence with respect to Cameroon.

### The Simile as Structural Element: *Contre-censure* and Solidarity

Beti uses cumulative similes in his "Avertissement" to show that Cameroon is a distinct case, a neglected opportunity for much-needed solidarity in the French press. The Quebecois film that protested *Main basse*'s censorship likewise took up the tool of successive, cumulative comparisons in order to drive home the fact of Cameroon's particular state of repression and violence. The production of the documentary *Contre-censure* contributed to the structure of fetishization; it was a way for the Quebecois militants who supported the text's republication to put their solidarity on display while they continued the work of *Main basse* by further exposing the repressive nature of Ahidjo's dictatorial neocolonial regime. Indeed, the projects of republication and documentary production were logistically linked: the Canadian journalists who made the film were the instigators of the republication project. Gérard Le Chêne, the journalist who also wrote the first preface to the Quebec edition of *Main basse sur le Cameroun,* constituted the linchpin of the coordination effort. Learning of the book's seizure during a stay in Paris, Le Chêne (together with another journalist) went to Rouen to interview Beti, began imagining the production of a documentary on the *Main basse* question, and then put Beti in contact with Léandre Bergeron at Éditions Québécoises.[32] As Cilas Kemedjio, the main scholar to have written at length about the documentary, explains, "Le film *Contre-censure* . . . trame la toile d'une logistique de ce que Françoise Lionnet et Shuh-mei Shih désignent par l'expression de transnationalisme mineur. Le concept suggéré par Lionnet et Shih a l'avantage de dépasser l'orientation étroitement culturaliste des mouvements transnationaux. . . . Le concept permet de saisir les motivations politiques qui structurent les réseaux de solidarité qui se placent sous la bannière de la gauche internationaliste" (190). "Minor transnationalism," or the set of connections among margins theorized by Lionnet and Shih, thus provides for Kemedjio a useful lens through which to understand the solidarity linking Quebecois intellectuals with Beti, a solidarity subtended by a leftist humanist politics. (Kemedjio writes also about the "croyance en l'humanisation de notre planète" that defines the period [186].) Clearly, a feeling of solidarity inspired the making of *Contre-censure,* contributing to the documentary's unabashed *prise de position* and to its one-sidedness. Like many other documentaries that expose a subject from a predetermined ideological and political position, *Contre-censure* is structured according to a predictable pattern of interviews given by people who have similar perspectives. What emerges from this structure, then, is an implicit comparison based on expected similarity. Given that all interviewees share a more or less similar, anti-neocolonial viewpoint, each interviewee introduces to the film specific points that together form a unified body of information. In this way, the structure of the documentary can be understood as a series of cumulative similes that support one another through the common (abstract) perspective from which they all arise but that also invite comparison among the (particular) specificities each contributes to that perspective. I begin by analyzing the documentary's smaller, individual moments of comparison—including similes that appear in the documentary as early as the opening credits—in order to show how the film paves the way for the cumulative effect of the serial interviews, which behave as a series of larger-scale similes.

The small-scale similes expressing solidarity that open the film emerge in the form of wordplay and montage. The first figure, wordplay, forms the guiding principle that articulates the documentary's solidary positions even before any live footage begins, because the title and pseudonyms invented by the film producers and displayed in the opening credits are puns—"sound similes" based on homonymic play. This particular form of figurative language accentuates both the ironies of the censorship plaguing *Main basse* and the militant stance of the banned book's Quebecois supporters, but it does so by introducing ambiguity. The pun is "a subversive agent," affording the reader or listener "the fundamental poetic pleasure of apprehending *likeness in difference.* . . . Puns supply 'the gift of gap,' the opportunity to feel ourselves making connections between apparently unrelated and impertinent contexts and meanings. Such connections provide us with the temporary experience of comprehension and control, an illusion immediately subverted by the effect of further instability" (McDonald 141–42, emphasis added). Wordplay around *Contre-censure* creates exactly this impression of simultaneous insight and doubt, demanding that viewers affirm participation as they disentangle multiple semantic possibilities. Like the similes discussed in previous sections, which accentuate both similarity and difference, homonyms combine similar sounds with different meanings. Homonyms thus function outside language's prescriptive signifying practices; they subvert those practices and show their flaws, just as similes fill a semantic gap in the language as literary figures (think of Beti's use of similes to imagine a non-French model of solidarity, for example). Wordplay in *Contre-censure* (puns specifically) draws attention to the abstraction of language, to its perpetual removal from any reality.

The title constitutes the first pun. *Contre-censure* is the term the Quebecois militants devised to express their own position, to label the energies that animated their support of Beti, his book, and the UPC. Implicit in their support of Beti is a parallel support for the rights of all peoples, including the Quebecois people, to full self-determination. *Contre-censure* is the documentary's first pun, hovering between two meanings: it is both a statement of position "against censorship" and an *action* of "counter-censorship" (in parallel with such compound nouns as *contre-attaque*). *Contre-censure*, functioning on the ambivalence of these two related meanings that sound exactly the same, allows room for the implicit solidarity to be both a feeling and an act. On the one hand, the feeling inspired the production and inflects the political position of the film; on the other hand, the documentary, beyond the "performances" it includes (interviews, voiceover narration), *performs* solidarity.

The pseudonyms adopted by the film's director and producer—Gérard Le Chêne and Nathalie Barton—also use wordplay to reflect a political position.[33] Le Chêne takes the pseudonym Alain d'Aix, which, while it is a fully plausible French name, also constitutes a pun on the phrase *à l'index*,[34] which means, literally, "on the index," that is, on the list of books banned by the pope. The pun here refers to the Inquisition: the Index was instituted in Europe in the sixteenth century in order to censor books deemed threatening to the Catholic Church (Michon 1:197). Thus, Le Chêne's pseudonym anticipates the documentary's opening sequence, which draws a parallel between the Inquisition (and other historically significant book burnings) and the censorship of *Main basse*. The pseudonym also begins to do the work, which the documentary later takes up, of amalgamating church censorship with secular (state) censorship, and in its action of counter-censorship, *Contre-censure* addresses both secular and church oppression by exposing not only French collaboration with Ahidjo's repressive regime but also the collusion of the Catholic Church with the Cameroonian neocolonial project.

Le Chêne's collaborator, Nathalie Barton, took the pseudonym Morgane Laliberté, a nonironic revendication of liberty. The name Morgane also holds wordplaying potential, suggesting a project of organizing (for) liberty. These three puns form the paratext of the documentary and set it up as a multivalent text, as an object that both takes a position and acts on it; at the same time, they suggest the ethical content and breadth of the action they propose. Wordplay thus emerges as a technique of counter-censorship. First, the legal names of the film's producers (Gérard Le Chêne and Nathalie Barton) remain protected through a form of self-censorship (hidden identity) that presents an obstruction to the state's power of knowledge. Ironically, director Gérard Le Chêne (Alain d'Aix), essentially puts his own name *à l'index,* masking his identity or hiding it from the public to avoid another exercise of state power: the revocation of travel rights. Moreover, the wit of a punning pseudonym like Alain d'Aix, the productive humor of its power of suggestion, represents a form of resistance to state power as control. Humor evades regulation. Although the documentary itself is not at all humorous, the flippant pseudonym is an expression of defiance toward the censoring organs of the French and Cameroonian states. Wordplay becomes, then, part of the act of contestation: it subverts cultural norms through the sound similes (homonyms) that subvert linguistic expectations.

The second type of small-scale simile structuring the opening of *Contre-censure* takes the form of a montage that juxtaposes combinations of image and inscription representing parallel instances of book bannings throughout history. The documentary opens by drafting a series of historical and visual parallels that establish *Main basse* as one casualty in a history of banning texts: the burning of Protagoras's works, which put into question the existence of god; the Inquisition's destruction of mountains of books, as well as its execution of 350,000 writers between 1450 and 1808; the Nazis' burning of texts in 1933; the repression of Wilhelm Reich and his books in the United States in 1956; and finally the banning of *Main basse sur le Cameroun* in France in 1972. The sequence ends with an image of the French edition of *Main basse* superimposed with images of flames licking its margins. The recurring image of flames sustains a simile built of images linking banned books and authors through the ages in spite of the vastly different contexts that characterized acts of censorship. Creating unexpected rapprochements between France's Fifth Republic and Nazi Germany or the Inquisition is precisely the goal of the documentary. The figure of the simile constitutes an ideal tool for suggesting the similarity between France and earlier repressive groups without needing to address the details of circumstantial differences; the similarity remains asymptotic, an abstract commonality. In a way, the simile-montage opening *Contre-censure* structurally resembles the similes that define the Quebecois prefaces to the 1974 edition of *Main basse:* they create broad similarities by ignoring circumstantial differences.

The large-scale form of simile that structures *Contre-censure* is parallel interviews, which are common to ideologically determined documentaries. The series of parallel interviews given by Beti, as well as by Europeans and Canadians who lived in Cameroon, build the narrative tension of the film precisely by reinforcing interviewees' similar information and perspective while introducing new (and gradually more atrocious) information about the Ahidjo regime. The film reinforces this structure of cumulative parallels by introducing periodic news clips and newspaper photos accompanied by the voice of the narrator[35] summarizing the important political developments at the time in Cameroon. These periodic interruptions expose a progressing history even as the interviews perform a much more static revelatory function, describing an ongoing situation of repression and torture. The interviews constitute structural similes because they are all *like* one another, and cumulatively, by adding enough "like" things, the documentary amasses proof. These parallel interviews recall the function of Maspero's cumulative similes in his preface, when he compares Ahidjo's regime to Nazism and repression in the Basque Country, or Cameroon to Chad and Zaire. The documentary's similes, however, rather than comparing the overall situation in Cameroon to other neocolonial situations, compare similar interviewee perspectives. By structuring the interviews as narrative similes and choosing not to interview anyone siding with Ahidjo, the documentarians develop an iterative position of solidarity supporting the project of countercensorship, Beti, and Cameroonian militancy more generally.

These cumulative similes result in a steady teleological progression advancing inexorably to the denunciation of the extreme violence being perpetrated in Cameroon by the government's Brigade mobile mixte (the political police). Beti, white journalists, and white missionaries lead the documentary into increasingly specific descriptions of torture.[36] Interviews with Beti tend to appear toward the beginning of the documentary; he is the main thinker featured in the film, the one who gives the background for and establishes anti-neocolonialism as a distinct political position. Continuing the motif of *Main basse* as fetish, *Contre-censure* in a certain sense fetishizes Beti's presence as a martyr of censorship. While Beti traveled to Canada twice in 1974, the Cameroonian government made it impossible for him to attend the 1975 conference of the Association canadienne d'études africaines.[37] This interdiction helps explain somewhat the emphasis on Beti's simply being there: he was a man under surveillance, which entailed a possibility of restriction that seems to have intensified his physical presence for those around him.

One particular moment stands out as emblematic of the relationships structuring the Montreal encounter of Bergeron and Beti: Bergeron removes a piece of dust from Beti's shoulder as Beti sits next to him during a press conference. This happens on stage, on camera, and the footage is included in *Contre-censure*. Bergeron focuses in on the shoulder of Beti's suit, concentrating, frowning slightly, and picks at something invisible with his thumb and forefinger. The gesture suggests a desire for (intellectual) intimacy. Beti simply ignores him, unaware. The micro-scene is unsettling because it points to the very inequalities that the Quebecois editors and documentarians want to both account for and evade in their expressions of solidarity. Beti, for all his brilliance, is present in Quebec thanks to the editorial intercession of Bergeron, who seems to expect in exchange a display of solidary intimacy with which Beti may or may not feel comfortable. This particular articulation of solidarity emphasizes its relational nature, as Bergeron and Beti have entered into a mutual exchange that presents benefits and opportunities for each of them—a kind of "opportunistic solidarity." But the fact that Beti is not aware of Bergeron's gesture of friendly intimacy highlights the asymptoticity of solidarity; it is impossible to know exactly the extent of the solidary relation or to pinpoint its range.

For all the documentary's emphasis on Beti's physical presence and spoken word, Beti could not attest personally to the recent atrocities *Main basse* documents, because he had been in exile since 1951. The documentary instead interviews witnesses who lived in Cameroon in the 1960s and early 1970s. Beti's dominant presence in the opening scenes, however, means that the other interviews function as similes: they are always structured as being "like Beti," as advancing his agenda—and the agenda of *Contre-censure*.

The testimony of journalists and white missionaries (both religious and secular) in Cameroon thus bolsters Beti's claims, gradually establishing the existence of concentration camps, torture, and complicit knowledge of these atrocities as the norm in Cameroon. Another effect of the similarities between the interviews is to portray the situation as static; neither the emergence nor any foreseeable end of violent repression is documented in the film, and the similar interviews emphasize the repetitive continuation of violence. Layers of positionally paralleled interviews describe as part of an ongoing process the destruction of villages caused by the civil war (in which the UPC opposed first the colonial and then the Ahidjo regime), the extradition of Ndongmo's white European business associates, the illegal and unacknowledged detention of innumerable prisoners in camps and jails, the display of the heads of UPC militants on village squares, the extreme torture endured by detainees, and the insanity of the prisoners who are occasionally released. An interviewed nurse, Lina Domazon, heard the screams of tortured prisoners and knew of concentration camps; a teacher, Claude-Guy Pilon, lived near a detention camp and worked in a school where the science department was regularly called on to repair the police force's electrodes ("Tout le monde savait, au moins dans le monde de la colonie blanche française-canadienne, que ces électrodes servaient pour un travail policier"). Pilon also recounts being invited by local dignitaries in Bafoussam to the execution of Ernest Ouandié, an invitation he refused. Successive interviews thus gradually accumulate to give an increasingly full picture of the repressive situation in Cameroon.

Since the film builds up gradually to these revelations of rampant torture and public executions, and since their atrocity is extreme, it seems that these abuses should form the climax of *Contre-censure*. The structural similes provided by parallel interviews all point in the direction of revelations of torture; with this structuring technique, the documentary seems to be oriented toward the exposure of these violent acts of political repression. The film veers from this trajectory in its conclusion, however. The final revelation, whose structural location at the end of the film closes the loop begun by the opening credits' Alain d'Aix/*à l'index* pun, turns out to be the involvement of the Canadian Catholic Church in the scandal, specifically the complicity of the Canadian cardinal Paul-Émile Léger with the Ahidjo government.[38] This complicity, the documentary's climaxing structure suggests, is the ultimate crime, or at least it is so for the local Quebecois public. Quebec's own latent participation, its link to the affair, its clergy's abetting of torture and execution—these constitute the documentary's ultimate revelations. In a forceful footnote to a 1978 article in the first issue of the journal he edited, *Peuples noirs—Peuples africains,* Beti himself accuses the Canadian Catholic Church of being party to neocolonial interests it shares with Canada's federal government:

> Mgr Albert Ndongmo . . . réside aujourd'hui au Canada, sous la protection suspecte de l'Église catholique de ce pays. L'ancien bagnard du chouchou de Paris, Ahmadou Ahidjo, est, apparemment, astreint à de telles conditions de discrétion et de dénuement matériel et moral qu'on est fondé à se demander si la faction la plus réactionnaire du clergé catholique canadien, celle par exemple

de l'ex-cardinal Léger, ami d'Ahidjo et aussi de Mgr Lefèbvre, n'a pas accepté, à la demande du dictateur camerounais, très bien en cour auprès de Pierre-Elliott Trudeau, qui lorgne les matières premières camerounaises, et avec le consentement des autorités politiques canadiennes, de retenir en otage le malheureux prélat bamiléké. (6n3)

Indeed, as the historian David Webster demonstrates, the Canadian government's self-image as innocent of colonial outrages contrasts sharply with its actual record: Webster notes "the gaps between the Canadian diplomatic self-image and the less altruistic practice of Canadian diplomacy" (157), a practice that consistently considered Canadian interests above all others even as it sometimes denounced international abuses with "strong words," if not with actions (173). While Webster does not specifically mention Trudeau's interest in Cameroonian natural resources, or Cameroon at all, for that matter, still Beti's suspicion of the Canadian government with regard to the so-called third world is consistent with Webster's findings.

This Canadian neocolonial involvement is precisely what the *Contrecensure* documentarians want to differentiate themselves from. Their solidarity with Beti constitutes a *prise de position* against Canada as a doubly colonizing agent—a neocolonial power in Africa and, they argue, a colonial power in Quebec; they are thus opposed to the Canadian government in two parallel, similar but distinct ways. The documentary firmly establishes its own distance from Canadian interests in its concluding scene, which departs from the film's previous reliance on structural similes. While all previous interviews are oriented according to a similar perspective (i.e., supporting Beti's argument and decrying the Ahidjo regime's violent repression) and are consistently edited so that the image of the interviewee coincides with the words she or he says (i.e., viewers see the interviewees speaking), the concluding moments of the documentary function very differently. First, the documentary lets viewers hear the words of Cardinal Léger, who denies any knowledge of torture or violence in Cameroon; second, the documentary does not show Léger being interviewed but rather accompanies his words with grainy video footage of him formally shaking the hand of Ahidjo. The image of Léger shaking Ahidjo's hand, the film's structure suggests, undermines Léger's words of disavowal with respect to his knowledge of violence. This last "interview" breaks with the pattern of structural similes that had defined previous interviews, offering as the film's conclusion a contrasting position (that belonging to an ally of Ahidjo) and simultaneously suggesting its hypocrisy. In addition, the focus on the handshake between the two men suggests how loaded that moment is. For Catholics, who believe the priest's hand performs the transubstantiation of bread and wine into Christ's flesh and blood, this kind of direct tactile contact between Léger's hand and the hand of Ahidjo, which has been shown to be metaphorically covered with the blood of his regime's victims, must be particularly disturbing. A tainted hand shaking a sacred hand dedicated to serving Christ—the documentary suggests that this is the ultimate sacrilege. Of course, by 1974 the Catholic Church in Quebec had been seriously discredited, decoupled from its formerly profound involvement in politics, education, and culture. The Church, then, becomes symbolic of the *old* Quebec's involvement in Cameroon's structures of oppression. In contrast, *Contre-censure* positions a *new* Quebec (made up of secular intellectuals such as Bergeron and the documentarians themselves) against the complicit old Quebec. The new, secular, anticolonial Quebec aligns itself against the Catholic Church and its (not very) occult support of the exploitative English Canadian federal political system, which, the documentary ultimately suggests, not only had oppressed the Quebecois people but continued to oppress populations in Africa. This gesture constitutes the documentary's final simile, creating a rapprochement between Quebec and Cameroon.

*Contre-censure*'s closing simile, which carries the implicit comparison of Quebec and Cameroon oppressed by the Canadian Catholic Church and federal government, recalls the far-reaching similes of Le Chêne's and Benjamin's prefaces to *Main basse*. And yet it differs from these in that the documentary makes explicit the link between the two situations through the physical contact between Léger and Ahidjo. The simile rests on documented connections, and the Quebec-UPC solidarities it animates take root in opposition to this historical collusion between officials in Canada and Cameroon. This represents the main difference between the documentary's and the Quebecois prefaces' articulations of solidarity. The latter two harness simile as an abstracting gesture in order to justify the solidary position of Quebec with anti-neocolonial resistance, whereas the documentary takes the articulation a step further, arguing for the existence of a specific connection that warrants the abstract comparison between the two regions.

### The Simile in Solidarity

The Quebecois prefaces work on the margins of *Main basse* as engines of desire for solidarity, attempting to relate the Quebecois independence struggle to Cameroon's anti-neocolonial struggle. Ultimately, the Montreal edition is structured like a matryoshka: surrounding the kernel of solidarity linking Ndongmo and Ouandié, which cannot be expressed in French, solidarity spreads outward to include Beti, who documents the solidarity; Maspero, who publishes it; and the Quebecois editors and documentarians, who rescue it from censorship. Similes work well to express the solidarities of *Main basse*'s Quebecois edition because the structure of the simile implies the possibility of infinite parallels and infinite comparisons. On the one hand, the abstracted similarity between the two compared elements can be applied to innumerable other elements; on the other hand, different similarities can be imagined linking each of these elements to other elements. Similes thus offer the shimmering possibility of infinite articulations. Saying that Chad is like Cameroon, for instance, abstracts both situations, temporarily reduces them to a conceptual similarity in spite of their differences, and then opens the door to imagining other similar links—like the one to Quebec, for example. As each new articulating layer is added to the matryoshka, it broadens the reach of the solidarity, which extends from one layer into the next.

This chapter shows that simile is in the service of solidarity, but the opposite is also true: solidarity inspired Quebecois intellectuals to compare themselves to Beti, to compare Quebec to Cameroon. The two concepts are mutually imbricated in the resemblance of their abstracting function. Comparison, which is at the heart of simile, is the basis of these feelings or expressions of solidarity: in order to find something "in common" around which to structure or mold solidarity, situations must be compared, sometimes across immense difference. Comparisons allow for the appearance of parallels, which can then foster solidarity. In a way, simile is the ur-trope of solidarity. Solidarity thus becomes the art of simile; it emerges as a sort of trope in itself, a way of working with language, simultaneously expressed *through* tropes (a poetics of solidarity) and expressing *a* trope (solidarity as poetics). Solidarity as a form of relation therefore functions like a poetics—"Tout réseau de solidarité est en ce sens une vraie Poétique de la Relation" (Glissant, *Traité* 249).

Or perhaps simile is the trope of nonfictional textual solidarity; the explicit nature of the comparison (as opposed to, say, metaphor) makes the simile a useful rhetorical tool for persuasive writing. Fiction, on the other hand, is freer to make metaphorical leaps and looser connections to suggest solidary imaginings, as I discuss in the following chapter.

# 4 As through a Canadian Fog

*Mort au Canada* and
Other Moroccan Mysteries

THE WORK of metaphor is to linguistically conciliate objects or concepts that are sometimes wildly different. Metaphorical articulations bridge gaps—in parallel with textual articulations of solidarity, which communicate across difference to imagine relation. This chapter examines how Quebecois political effervescence inspired the Canadian novels of Driss Chraïbi (1926–2007), the Moroccan French novelist, in spite of his own scorn for nationalism. Metaphorical articulations of relation in these novels suggest that a shared interest in the French language nurtured the foundations of an unlikely solidarity between Chraïbi and the Quebec sovereignty struggle.

Driss Chraïbi searched perpetually for an outside—for *Le monde à côté*, as he titled his 2001 memoir—or at least for a way to express or describe his own outsider position. In this search he drew inspiration, and his memoir's title, from *The World Next Door,* a 1949 semiautobiographical novel by the American novelist Fritz Peters that Chraïbi and Peters hoped to adapt into a film.[1] In the context of Peters's novel, the "world next door" is the world of madness, an isolating condition that Chraïbi reads as potentially freeing: the patient's personality "s'était épanouie, intégrée et même enrichie" ("Je suis d'une génération perdue" 41). In *Le monde à côté,* Chraïbi seeks an otherworldly perspective that, like madness, might enable him to define himself. His solution is to present himself as "in-between": between Morocco and France, between Arabic and French. "Ma pensée est flottante, entre ici et là-bas, entre la langue de Voltaire et celle des médias [Moroccan media]" (24). Writing becomes his way of navigating between these two worlds and of maintaining his distance from both of them: "J'écrivais pour me situer dans le monde, dans mon monde d'origine et dans celui vers lequel je me dirigeais à l'aveuglette. Tous deux me semblaient dérisoires en regard de ma soif de vivre et d'aimer"

(30). This floating, intermediate self remains distinct from both potential landing places, although the colonial-versus-colonized in-betweenness is just as precarious and socially disparaged as Peters's madness.

Chraïbi was born in El Jadida, Morocco, and moved to Paris at the age of twenty to study chemistry, a field he abandoned to turn to writing and journalism. Chraïbi remained in France for the majority of his life, in partly chosen exile (the controversy raised among Moroccan militants by his first novel, *Le passé simple,* contributed to his decision to stay in France), and struggled to affirm his right to speak for only himself and not as a representative of Moroccans either in Morocco or in France.[2] His position as a writer of Moroccan origin writing in French and in France seemed to promise a social or anthropological explanation of the Maghreb for French readers, but he refused to fulfill this expectation. Chraïbi eschewed national (Moroccan), ethnic (Maghrebi), and religious (Islamic) attachments ("J'ai toujours refusé les contraintes intellectuelles, religieuses, sociales et politiques" [*Une vie sans concession* 37]); his exile and his writings represent an aspiration to radical detachment and individual identity beyond articulations that rely on political goals, nationalist or otherwise. This chapter argues that Quebec, where Chraïbi lived for a few months in the late sixties or early seventies, functioned for him as an outside space that, radically detached from the (post)colonial binary of Maghreb/France,[3] allowed him to reimagine human connection as well as his country of origin. Although Chraïbi avoided overtly politicizing his descriptions of Quebec, his writing suggests that he found renewal and an escape from the pressures of colonial binaries in the Quiet Revolution's political solidarities.

Chraïbi's writing in French, too, is both political and presented as apolitical, or at least as avoiding the need to voice an anticolonial position as an anti-French one. His choice to publish in French evolved from his French education and his desire to "[escape] the straightjacket . . . of the traditional Arabo-muslim society" (Armitage 47). He was often called on to defend his choice to write in French by journalists who considered him to be perennially coming to French, never fully arrived to its usage. Exasperated at one journalist's insistence on his Maghrebi origin, which the journalist implied made writing in French unusual, Chraïbi remembers, he responded with annoyance, answering the journalist's essentializing expectations with bitter sarcasm:

—Driss Chraïbi, vous pensez en arabe et vous écrivez en français. N'y a-t-il pas là une sorte de dichotomie?

J'ai vu venir le journaliste. J'aurais volontiers conversé avec lui . . . le temps . . . de dénicher la petite idée qu'il avait derrière la tête et qui devait avoir la forme d'une étiquette. . . .
—*Si, msiou! Ji pense en arabe, mais ji trouvé machine à écrire qui écrit en francès tote seule.* . . .
—À question bête, réponse idiote. (*Le monde à côté* 42–43, emphasis in original)

Refusing to engage with the journalist in the fabrication of a label (*étiquette*) for himself and his writing, Chraïbi invented the preposterous division of the (Moroccan) self from the (French) typewriter, mocking the journalist's barely veiled expectation that a North African identity meant an uneducated one. But this sarcastic fabrication of the French typewriter distinct from the Maghrebi self does in fact represent how Chraïbi desired to be perceived: simply as a French-language writer.[4]

His choice to narrate this anecdote in his memoir highlights not only the French literary milieu's racist misconceptions but also his own insistence on language as a medium independent from social experience, a machine-like tool without social or political obligations. Although a critique of colonization constitutes an important theme in his oeuvre, Chraïbi sought to discover and express humanity in his literary works, and he liked to insist that his choice of language was independent of his origins, that it plumbed human depths more universal than his own condition as a colonized (or ex-colonized) subject. The problem with Chraïbi's quest for radical nonalignment, for an outside in which to find and define his authentic nature, is that all human relations happen through language and within a cultural context. His writing attempts to define independence and to *be* independent from France: it confronts France's treatment of colonial subjects (e.g., in *Les boucs*) and attacks French "propriety" and even syntactic convention (see *Le passé simple*, among others).[5] He remains, however, caught in the binary, trying vainly to articulate his in-betweenness in French, a language that constitutes a side, a position.

## Quebec: Chraïbi's "World Next Door"

Chraïbi famously spent a fall semester plus a few additional months in Quebec City, teaching francophone literature at Laval University. Most scholars describing Chraïbi's life, however succinctly, mention that he visited or taught in Canada, even if they do not describe at length his novels about Canada. The exact dates of this visit vary from source to source. The scholar Joan Monego dates it to 1970 (109), while Fernando Lambert, now professor emeritus at Laval, dates it to 1968 or 1969, before his own arrival in 1970 (email exchange with author). Somewhat inconsistently, details of *Le monde à côté* date Chraïbi's visit to both the late sixties and the early seventies, showing that Chraïbi's memoir is sometimes more fanciful than the appellation *memoir* would suggest. Fall 1970 represents the height of revolutionary tension in Quebec; after seven years of sporadic bombings of public monuments and mailboxes, the October Crisis of 1970 saw the kidnapping of two politicians by members of the Front de libération du Québec. At the request of the provincial government, the War Measures Act was declared and the Canadian army occupied Quebec.[6] It is improbable that Chraïbi's memoir would remain entirely silent about these events if he had been present during their unfolding; it is more likely that he was in Quebec in 1968 or 1969, as Lambert affirms.

Chraïbi's time in Quebec presented him with a symbolic location capable of shifting the binary that situates writers on the side of either the colonized or the colonizer according to the language in which they write. Quebec represented a constructive *dépaysement* of French: there, the French language existed beyond the Maghreb/France colonial dichotomy and could be used to explore modes of human connection without explicitly dedicating them to the French colonial or the Maghrebi anticolonial cause. Incorporating references to Canada while writing in French, that is, lets Chraïbi sidestep the question how to foster global francophone solidarity as an explicitly *political* formation, even as his novels express their "universal" ideals (e.g., personal liberty or complete interpersonal understanding) through an idea of Quebec that was, in fact, political: the Quebecois persistence in embracing French and on resisting English-language encroachment in commerce and education. While Chraïbi's literary desire for human connection and understanding differs significantly from political forms of solidarity (it is based on linking individuals rather than identity-based groups, for one thing), Quebec's solidary energy in fact created the space for the articulation of new human connections.

Let us begin by considering the linguistic and cultural context that Quebec represented for Chraïbi. In Canada, French assumed an entirely different significance from that which it had held for Chraïbi in Morocco or France. Whereas before visiting Quebec Chraïbi had claimed French as a nonethnic medium, in Canada French *is* considered ethnic, even racial, Canadian history having been told in terms of two "colonizing races,"[7] the French and the English. In Quiet Revolution Quebec, moreover,

French took on the dimension of vindication, of a precisely *anticolonial* struggle, and continues to be valued for the barricade it represents against the encroaching North American English culture. In this way, Quebec does symbolize a space beyond in Chraïbi's life and work; by adopting the local perspective that gives French an anticolonial charge, Chraïbi withdraws from the constrictions of a linguistico-colonial Maghreb/France binary. From this Quebecois perspective, French for Chraïbi can actually serve as an outside from which to try to articulate direct human connection, connection that was otherwise circumscribed by colonial histories of violence and inequity.

Of course, Chraïbi, who rejected the labels "French-language writer of Moroccan origin" and "francophone author" in favor of the simple term *writer*,[8] fits uncomfortably in the sometimes nationalist framework of independence-era solidarity. Certainly his use of French did not automatically align him with Quebecois political concerns. In *Le monde à côté*, Chraïbi admits that he cannot understand his Quebecois students' political dissatisfaction: "Je pensais aux étudiants de France—et plus encore à ceux de ma patrie, avide de connaissance, assoiffés de savoir, démunis de tout, et qui faisaient des kilomètres à pied pour se rendre à leurs universités respectives. Ceux d'ici [Laval] étaient bien nourris, bien logés, et ils se sentaient mal dans leur peau. Je ne savais qu'en conclure" (*Le monde à côté* 125). For Chraïbi, the comfortable living conditions of Quebecois students make their dissatisfaction unintelligible. He describes their aspirations in dismissive terms: "Che Guevara était l'idole de ces grands gaillards paisibles; les jeunes filles admiraient sans réserve l'épouse du premier ministre fédéral dont les frasques défrayaient la chronique" (125). The irony of Quebec's "peaceful big fellows" idolizing the militant Che Guevara and the pettiness of the young women's fascination with Margaret Trudeau's outfits[9] suggest that Chraïbi's relations with his students, which he describes as warm and friendly, were underscored, on the subject of their revolutionary aspirations, by some disdain on his part.

Chraïbi's dismissive description of his Quebecois students' revolutionary ideals reveals a cynicism that seems to reject the earnestness associated with solidary engagement. Indeed, Chraïbi's memoir suggests that he remained cold to Quebec's sovereigntist aspirations, as he holds back even from making allusions to this project, focusing his narration on idiosyncratic personal encounters and shying away from politics, aside from the cynical disdain cited above. In light of this cynicism and his refusal to take sides, it is perhaps surprising to discover that he participated in the same solidary circuits as Aimé Césaire. Indeed, Chraïbi was invited to be a visiting lecturer at Laval University in Quebec City by Michel Tétu, the same professor who a few years later organized Césaire's Quebec sojourn in 1972. The reason for these invitations lies in Tétu's vision of a strong, vibrant, independent Quebec, which for him necessarily included a tightly knit international francophone cultural network.[10] According to Chraïbi's memoir, Tétu approached him at a book signing in Paris and invited him to give classes at Laval for a semester. Chraïbi, who describes being in a difficult period of his first marriage at that time, accepted Tétu's offer and became the first of Tétu's "négro-africain" guests.

What differentiates Chraïbi from Césaire, however, is that Chraïbi refused to play the game. He refused to respond to Quebec's solidary hopes for mutual recognition along the institutional lines Césaire had accepted when he gave public lectures acknowledging Quebecois poetry as sharing a sense of alienation with Caribbean poetry. *Le monde à côté,* in addition to narrating Chraïbi's incomprehension of his privileged students' revolutionary ambitions, also structures a distance between himself and his Laval colleagues. Chraïbi's memoir describes his colleagues as unbearably stuffy and narrates with disdain the hypocritical chill of the professors' dining room: "Le doyen de la faculté des lettres était un évêque, la plupart des professeurs des hommes d'Église. Nous nous réunîmes pour un déjeuner arrosé d'un 'breuvage' au choix: thé ou café Maxwell. . . . Il y avait bien du vin, mais dans la pièce à côté. . . . Découpée en temps de parole plus ou moins minutés selon le rang social des convives, la conversation déambulait feutrée autour des lieudits littéraires" (120). Chraïbi also narrates his refusal to occupy the campus's *logement de fonction:* "J'inspectai brièvement les lieux communs, le salon surtout. Je ne m'y voyais pas assis durant les longues soirées d'hiver, à subir des assauts d'érudition, cette poussière de bibliothèque tombée dans un crâne vide. Je déclinai l'offre de l'ecclésiastique chargé de l'intendance, d'autant que l'on m'avait signalé la présence d'un médiéviste dans les parages et d'un spécialiste de l'art roman, célibataire de surcroit" (118). To this lodging, which he describes with stereotypes of cold erudition that border on hyperbole, he preferred instead room and board with a local family, a single mother who was raising a teenage daughter with the help of her occasional lover, a bon vivant priest (*Le monde à côté* 119–20). Chraïbi's memoir, written thirty years after these events, thus structures a marked contrast between, on the one hand, the solidarity (not) offered by the Faculté des lettres, emphasizing its starchiness (the Catholic bishop dean, the medievalist and the bachelor Romanesque scholar, the high-brow alcohol-free meals), and, on the other hand, the comfortable warmth of his iconoclastic host family, the close and familiar welcome of his students, and the unexpected and eccentric friendships he struck up off campus. If Chraïbi found Quebec a place of human connection through a common use of French, then, it was not necessarily through the intellectual francophone community Tétu was attempting to create at Laval.

Chraïbi's memoir differs somewhat, it needs be said, from the account of Fernando Lambert, a Laval professor who remembers Chraïbi's stay with cordiality as "opening a new period" in the literature department: "Driss Chraïbi a compris le cadre dans lequel il intervenait et il a été très apprécié et des étudiants et de ceux qui l'avaient invité" (email exchange with author). It seems, however, that Chraïbi's interest in narrating his sojourn in Quebec City was not based on the cordial departmental relations on which Lambert reports but rather on the discoveries he made outside the university. It is also worth mentioning that in contrast to Césaire's, Chraïbi's visit left no traces in Michel Tétu's archives at Laval.

It is possible to surmise that since his was the first international visit of its kind for the department, it was less administratively structured and more institutionally marginal than later visits by international francophone authors and scholars. Chraïbi's narration of his isolation from the life of the university and his focus on his independent exploration of the province, however, may also point to a difference of opinion between Tétu and his guest. Tétu was earnestly invested in Quebec's struggle for independence; Tétu and his wife, the scholar of Quebecois culture Françoise Tétu de Labsade, author of the influential textbook *Le Québec—Un pays, une culture* (Boréal 1990), were prominent Quebec City nationalists, their French origins notwithstanding. Their scholarly and social activity in Quebec City helped shape the culture of the sovereigntist movement in that region. Chraïbi, on the other hand, was suspicious of nationalisms, which he saw as linked to intolerance (Marx-Scouras 141). In a 1966 interview, for example, he said, "S'il est un mot que je déteste, c'est bien le mot 'nationalisme'" ("Je suis d'une génération perdue" 42). Even though Michel Tétu's imagined version of an independent Quebec was profoundly internationalist (his was not a "Québec du terroir" variant), it is quite probable that Chraïbi would nevertheless have remained cold to discussions of Quebecois nationalism, especially if these related Quebec to Maghrebi nationalisms, which Chraïbi deemed suspect. Indeed, as I have shown above, Chraïbi's memoir suggests that he remained indifferent to the Quebecois struggle for independence. In addition, in *Le monde à côté* Chraïbi refers to Canada and Quebec interchangeably, even though the landmarks he names are all situated in Quebec; his novel *Mort au*

*Canada* is marked by the same ambivalent naming pattern, which declines to recognize Quebec as geographically distinct. The inscription of Quebecois landmarks as part of "Canada" in Chraïbi's writing thus serves to tacitly distance Chraïbi from the globally oriented nationalist interests that had warranted his very invitation to Laval.

Chraïbi's desire to keep his distance from the Quebecois sovereignty movement comes as no surprise, as his writings demonstrate an enduring refusal to take sides in colonial conflicts. His first novel, *Le passé simple*, for example, famously created a scandal when it was published in 1954 because it refused to represent traditional Moroccans as innocent victims of colonialism. As the critic Danielle Marx-Scouras cogently summarizes, in the novel "the 'despoliation of childhood' and the concomitant loss of identity were brought about not primarily by the French, but by Islamic fathers who acquiesced to colonialism. . . . [The Islamic patriarch] and French colonial rule are thus, in Chraïbi's mind, different aspects of the same phenomenon" (135). At a moment fraught with colonial conflict, Chraïbi refuses to side with either France or Morocco, finding fault both with French colonial society and with Moroccan tradition and angering agents on both sides in the process. Furthermore, Chraïbi's Berber trilogy—*Une enquête au pays, La mère du printemps,* and *Naissance à l'aube*—destabilizes any notion of essential Berber identity, showing instead the contingently constructed nature of this identity through a succession of usually violent encounters with other nations. Chraïbi is wary of essentialisms of all stripes and rejects all calls to conform to a group or join a cause, even that of a colonized nation seeking independence; he attempts to remain, as Marx-Scouras claims, detached from all sides, aiming for an objective position.[11]

Although Chraïbi downplays the official networks of solidarity proffered by Tétu and the Laval University professorate, however, he did branch out into Quebec in other ways. Chraïbi's narration of his Quebecois sojourn in *Le monde à côté* resembles the tale of a professor gone rogue, choosing to discover the land and people quite apart from his host institution. The autobiography narrates the connections he makes with his boardinghouse family, with students (one of whom became his lover), and with various people he meets in chance encounters. For instance, he explored Montreal on his own and narrates having been picked up at the curb, literally, by an elderly woman who invited him to join her and her friends for a fancy tea and conversation. This encounter led to an introduction to the woman's nephew, Robert McConnell, whom Chraïbi misremembers as a McGill professor (McConnell was a professor at

Toronto). McConnell in turn sponsored Chraïbi in writing a novel, a short, relatively easy book that could be used as a tool for students of French as a second language. Chraïbi tells of inventing this book on the spot. It would become *La civilisation, ma mère! . . .* , which appeared in 1972 in Paris and also in Montreal, in a pedagogical format. Though they resulted in writing and publication, Chraïbi portrays the bonds he established with these Quebecois as direct connections with "the people," bonds that bypassed the institutional Laval gatekeepers.

In describing one of these bonds with the people he met in Canada, Chraïbi's memoir suggests that his engagement with Quebec was in fact political, if in unavowed ways. This occurs when he compares the Vietnam War to the welcome he and his student-turned-lover, Marie, receive from a First Nation community during a snowstorm: "Des Indiens nous donnèrent l'hospitalité tant que souffla le blizzard du Grand Nord. Ils étaient si différents de ceux de Hollywood. Ils ne possédaient rien—rien d'autre que leur élémentaire soif de la vie. Ils partagèrent avec nous de la viande de caribou, leurs gestes lents et leur économie de paroles. Ils ne nous demandèrent ni notre nom ni d'où nous venions. À l'autre bout de la terre, des G.I. effoliaient les forêts, arrosaient de napalm des villages entiers. Un certain général Giap venait de déclencher l'offensive du Têt" (*Le monde à côté* 138–39).[12] Here, Chraïbi insists on the direct contact he made with these First Nations people, an anonymous and deeply human sharing of food that unfolded with few words. Chraïbi contrasts this experience of warmth in the storm to two situations with clear geopolitical overtones: the depiction of the First Nations by Hollywood and the Vietnam War. Both broadly represent imperial incursion, and Chraïbi relies on their political significance to provide a contrast to his own friendly encounter with the Wendat, which by implication was a nonimperial experience. This is a statement of common humanity, an articulation of solidarity that Chraïbi wishes to affirm as nonpolitical.

And yet Quebec, the setting for the encounter, was a politically effervescent place in the 1960s and 1970s. The social possibilities Chraïbi discovered there and the human connections he was able to make devolved directly from the Quiet Revolution's upheavals and from its public exploration of what constituted an imperial encounter. This chapter analyzes, within the context of the Quiet Revolution, what I call Chraïbi's Canadian novels: *Mort au Canada*, the narrative of a fictional French composer's sojourn in Canada, and *La civilisation, ma mère! . . .* , the chronicle, commissioned by a Montreal publisher, of a Moroccan mother's gradual evolution from housebound servitude to intellectual and physical liberty.

These novels reveal the liberating effect of Quebec's political energies on Chraïbi's understanding of himself and his world. Both novels express a latent solidarity with Quebec's linguistic struggle that departs from Chraïbi's usual disdain for nationalisms and reveals investments in international francophone solidarity that belie Chraïbi's explicit avoidance of political declarations. His evasion of institutional connections that relied on national identities in favor of attachments structured along other lines (romantic, domestic, neighborly) maps onto Chraïbi's avoidance of "the political" in favor of "the universal," a preference that can be seen in the types of relationships that his Canadian novels depict.

## Death in Canada, Rebirth in Quebec

Chraïbi's 1975 novel *Mort au Canada* is generally read as a literary investigation into the passion of the couple or into the psychology of a lover. Published by Denoël, the novel is described in its back matter as follows: "Un tel amour est-il encore viable dans notre société? C'est donc le problème du couple qui est ici posé." Guitte Foesser, focusing on one half of the couple, scathingly reviews *Mort au Canada* as "an improbable tale about a man's purported conquest (or is it his flaunting?) of his own narcissism" (360). These represent schematic evaluations at best, but even Marx-Scouras's masterful scholarly overview of Chraïbi's oeuvre devotes little space to *Mort au Canada*, describing it as an autobiographical study of an amorous relationship. Although Marx-Scouras uses a sentence drawn from *Mort au Canada* to define her concept of Chraïbi's *literature of departure* ("Changer de pays, changer de peau . . ."), she does not return to this aspect of the novel. All she writes about *Mort au Canada* is that it marks a "return to the West to describe an amorous relationship by means of which [Chraïbi] sought, unsuccessfully, to forge a new identity for himself" (137, 140). Categorizations of *Mort au Canada* as a type of romance novel should not be used, however, to avoid further analysis. As Lydie Moudileno has shown in "The Troubling Popularity of West African Romance Novels," much can be learned by analyzing the specific ways in which romance novels structure the "double imperative" of the form. Specifically, Moudileno refers to the romance's dual grounding in "a concrete . . . quotidian easily recognizable by the readers" and in a "'parallel universe' (Radway) that by definition differentiates itself from the real" (123).[13] Whereas *Mort au Canada* gets written off as simply a romance novel, I address here the ways in which it exceeds that genre at the same time that I respect and analyze the ways in which it embraces the genre.

Chraïbi's interest in an apolitical tone dovetails conveniently with the fact that romance as a genre is often seen as apolitical. In addition, the solidarities produced through a feminized genre like romance tend to get dismissed as less serious than the masculinized, fraternal, "intellectual" francophone solidary texts and circuits discussed in other chapters. The modes or models of solidarity that Chraïbi puts forward play specifically with the perception of depoliticization frequently associated with intergender relationships, an angle in *Mort au Canada* that makes solidarity particularly slippery to define and discuss. Recall that Aquin's *Trou de mémoire* problematizes similarly gendered definitions of solidarity, showing how the two masculine characters' exclusion of women from the "brotherhood" of revolutionary pharmacists haunts and ultimately destroys their model of solidarity. In *Mort au Canada,* the setting holds the key to understanding the political elements that undergird the "romance"; Canada as simultaneously a real and an imagined locale defines the political energies that motivate the novel's modes of solidarity.

Given the importance of the romance novel's dependence on both a "concrete . . . quotidian" and a "parallel universe," as argued by Moudileno, it is surprising that no criticism or interpretation of *Mort au Canada* has sufficiently taken into account the novel's setting, half in Quebec and half on the French Atlantic island of Yeu, off the coast of France. And yet Canada is central enough to Chraïbi's conception of what the novel does that he chose to include the name of the country in his title. Indeed, Canada emerges in *Mort au Canada* with great specificity: as the concrete quotidian defined by Moudileno. Canada also emerges, however, as a romantic construction (the "parallel universe" Moudileno also describes) that in some ways dooms the love story. Indeed, the main character's faulty understanding of the country parallels his misguided hopes for an absolute and total human connection. I show that the novel is in fact structured around three distinct articulations of the idea of Canada that not only position the characters in relation to one another but also position Chraïbi in relation to the francophone world and offer contrasting models for imagining solidarity.

*Mort au Canada* is a complicated text. It recounts the story of the fictional French musician Patrik Pierson, whose chance encounter with an eleven-year-old girl named Dominique on the beach at Yeu catalyzes a reminiscence of his savagely passionate and destructively isolating eighteen-month-long relationship with the French Canadian psychiatrist Maryvonne Melvin in Quebec.[14] The plot culminates in the revelation that Patrik is the metempsychotic double of Dominique's father, William, a gifted writer whose life parallels that of Patrik's, except that William died in Canada. The narrative frames the past story of the couple in Canada with interactions between Patrik, Dominique, and her mother in the present. The love affair in Canada is narrated through third-person free indirect discourse, mostly from Patrik's perspective but occasionally also from other characters', interspersed with directly quoted dialogic flashbacks and journal entries that obfuscate the chronology of the storyline. Adding yet another layer of complexity to the remembered affair, the first half of the novel narrates a mostly euphoric version of Patrik and Maryvonne's relationship containing only occasional hints at the couple's difficulties. The second half of the novel returns to the same period of the couple's life together, narrating instead the gradually increasing destructive aspects of their interactions. The two halves of the novel thus construct two opposite yet identical ways of understanding a romantic relationship, readings of passion that are then subsumed in the story of metempsychotic connection with Dominique's father.

Tying together the narrative frame with the story of the past romance is the idea of Canada, which the title first announces as a central unifying factor in the novel. From the perspective of sales, the Canada in *Mort au Canada* probably had the advantage of lending the book an exotic appeal to metropolitan French readers. It also indicates, however, where to begin interpreting the text. As both a geographical place and an idea, Canada functions in three distinct ways in the text to set the parameters for the kinds of human connection (modes of solidarity) that can be imagined and achieved. First, Canada is misunderstood by Patrik as an immense empty space—a misunderstanding that is underscored in the free-indirect-discourse narration by inconsistent tropes and geographical and grammatical errors. Patrik's misreading of Canada parallels his unfounded hopes for a perfect union with Maryvonne. Second, Canada exists as a mystical space of metempsychotic exchange: the transmigration of William's soul into Patrik's unconscious represents the type of perfect union that can in fact take place in this mystical understanding of Canada. Third, the name Canada in the novel actually designates Quebec, the specific place revealed obliquely through the narration of Patrik's crumbling relationship with Maryvonne. This instantiation of Canada is marked linguistically and socially as an ethical French-language resistance to a capitalist-structured English-language consumerism. I refer to the novel's setting as Quebec, then, rather than Canada, because this anticapitalist, pro-French program aligns with Quebec's Quiet Revolution, and the inclusion of this political "concrete quotidian" represent a third mode of solidarity that undergirds the novel. Patrik (or, abstractly, the figure of the artist) serves as the ethical standard in the linguistic and political struggle that haunts the background of Mort au Canada. The politically charged energy of French-language resistance, which Chraïbi seems to sidestep in creating a novel ostensibly about the "great themes" of passion and art, in fact fuels the novel's explorations of these "great themes." Indeed, I argue that what inspires the novel's structuring hope for perfect passionate union, and what makes possible the imagination of a metempsychotic artistic exchange, is precisely the politically motivated energy of the French-language province. Although neither the metempsychotic artistic exchange nor the romantic relationship is presented as a political event, Chraïbi novelizes politically motivated energy into forms of connection that he considered more universal than those forged around political issues.

## Misunderstanding Canada: A Failed Romance

Let us begin by analyzing the first use of Canada as a setting that determines or illustrates the parameters of human connection, namely, the misreading of Canada as a parallel to a failed romantic relationship. This relationship illustrates a possible mode of "apolitical" solidarity, and its structural unfeasibility suggests that the overlapping blind spots with regard to Canada and to the romantic partner participate in the fragmentation of this mode of solidarity. While Chraïbi chooses to narrate the supposedly apolitical genre of romance, which aligns with his more general refusal to adopt any political position, he ultimately tells the story of the failure of this apolitical mode of connection between a French man and a Canadian woman, ultimately problematizing his own apolitical stance. In addition, his use of colonial and touristic stereotypes informing the point of view of the French character contrasts sharply with the power he gives to the Canadian character in the relationship, turning on their head certain power structures of the France/Maghreb binary, which would traditionally figure a French man in a dominating role. Romance as a genre, with Canada as setting, enables this upset as a sort of "third way" and constitutes a further latent critique of romance as apolitical genre.

Patrik misconstrues Canada and Canadians. Chraïbi constructs Patrik as a brilliantly insightful artist, yes, but he also defines him with stereotypical French understandings of the francophone world, specifically of Canada as an empty natural landscape. Patrik's touristic misreading of Canada structures the first (hopeful) half of the narrative, while glimpses of the energies of Quebec as a revolutionary site emerge later in the second (dystopian) half. In this section, I discuss Patrik's touristic misreading as symptomatic of the false hopes he holds out for romance as perfect human connection.

The first half of the narrative relies on a stereotyped hypernatural Canada, a wild place; the narrative filters the setting through the eyes of Patrik, whose expectations condition him to see this wilderness in spite of his social experiences in Quebec. The "nature" that Patrik perceives and with which he associates his relationship to Maryvonne pervades the opening of the Canadian scenes: the physical relationship begins with a passionate kiss in the wilderness of a Quebecois forest, near the clinic named, "naturally," La Pinède (the Pine Grove). Even Canadian institutions, the clinic's name implies, are marked as natural and woodsy. The symbolic premonition that not all will go well in the relationship also takes the form of an intrusion of nature into human space: a rabbit runs across the forest road and is killed (or not: Patrik is unable to find the body) by Maryvonne's car.

Patrik's conception of Canada, as Chraïbi reveals it through free indirect discourse, is superficial and stereotypical: "Il aimait ce pays, le Canada. . . . Il l'aimait pour son infini, la juvénilité de ses habitants, l'authenticité de leurs sentiments et de leurs actes. Dans deux siècles, ils resteraient encore neufs. Si l'eau prend la forme et la couleur du vase qui la contient, oui ils étaient l'expression de leur continent. Comme lui, ils étaient au seuil de la vie" (91). This amalgamation of descriptors for Canada rings false, both in the context of the narration that has preceded it and in its figurative expressions. Patrik's reliance on well-worn stereotypes to signify Canada—infinity, authenticity, and youth—particularly from the pen of an author familiar with the receiving end of tropes of typecast colonized spaces, should raise our readerly suspicions. The stereotypical images do not correlate with the narration that has preceded it, which depicts Canada as a circumscribed living space (Patrik hardly leaves the house) and the psychiatrist Maryvonne (the main Canadian with whom we see Patrik interacting) as scarred and manipulative.

In addition, the inconsistency of Patrik's metaphors suggests that he fundamentally misunderstands the place. He imagines the country as infinite, and yet he compares its continent to a vase, a decidedly finite object defined precisely by its glassy limits. Similarly, the inhabitants are simultaneously content-full and content-less: on the one hand, they are marked by youth and authenticity, suggesting energy, form, and vivacity; on the other hand, he compares them to water, tasteless and colorless, its shape determined by the vase. Patrik's description of Canada, then, does not actually correspond to the intricate and manipulative relationship that develops between him and his Canadian lover. Moreover, the description itself is tropologically incoherent, its figurative deployment internally inconsistent. In fact, Patrik relates romantically both to the country and to Maryvonne: "Il aimait . . . le Canada," the narrative states declaratively rather than substantively, founding his declaration on metaphors of filling (here the metaphor of the vase and, as we will see later with Maryvonne, the metaphor of one partner filling the other's lack) rather than on metaphors of mutuality or comprehension.

Patrik's further descriptions of Canada include grammatical cues that also signal his misunderstanding of the place. Here, in addition to stereotypical imagery, Chraïbi inserts prepositions and articles improper to Canadian province names: "Tout était à leur mesure: le Saint-Laurent géant, la multitude des lacs, les mugissements du bétail à perte d'ouïe dans l'Ontario, la vastitude du ciel à perte de vue, la glaciation des chaussées des villes paralysant toute circulation, toute 'américanisation,' l'hiver coupant comme un rasoir, l'absence de tout horizon dans le Saskatchewan, la maternelle Gaspésie, les contreforts des montagnes Rocheuses, les conifères se lançant à l'assaut du ciel de Vancouver, l'accent chantant des voix québécoises, le second souffle de chaleur de l'été indien" (91). Here again, the images totter between stereotype and jocular exaggeration: if the sky is vast "as far as the eye can see," a standard idiom, the lowing of the cattle is loud "as far as the ear can hear"—an invented phrase that brings attention to the improbability of both constructions. The images of the razor-sharp winter cold and of the absence of horizon in Saskatchewan are both pat, whereas the description of Gaspésie as maternal is unexpected and unexplained. The idea that winter slows down Canadian cities, preventing their "Americanization," in fact reverses Canadian lore, which sees the northern nation as much better prepared to face winter storms (and much more efficient at clearing them) than its southern neighbor. Moreover, Chraïbi puts in Patrik's imagination the French phrase *l'été indien* rather than the North American appellation, *l'été des Indiens*, a slippage that represents Patrik's continued perception of Canada through a French lens. In terms of expression, the passage is bizarre because of its grammatical unfamiliarity with Canada: *Saskatchewan* is a feminine word ("*la* Saskatchewan"), and both Saskatchewan and Ontario should be preceded by the preposition *en*, not by *dans le/l'*. By ascribing to Patrik these jarring descriptors and an inability to grasp basic French Canadian grammatical usage, the narration implies that Patrik knows Canada far less well than he believes or declares.

Some of these strange images (the conifers attacking the sky over Vancouver or the cows overrunning Ontario) may remind the reader of illustrated sightseeing pamphlets, likewise suggesting a limited familiarity that relies on resources meant for outsiders rather than on an experiential understanding of place. Patrik's descriptive love for Canada *could* be based on banal touristic posters, a hypothesis the second half of the narrative supports. Indeed, when Patrik lists in his journal the objects that fill his life with Maryvonne, he writes that Maryvonne has decorated the walls of his study with some "affiches de voyage. 'C'est plus gai, tu ne trouves pas?'" (161). The posters represent only a fraction of the invasive objects that Maryvonne imposes on Patrik, defining and constricting his imaginary: "Je n'ai jamais eu tant d'objets. Je ne sais qu'en faire. Ils me regardent et je n'ai pas grand-chose à leur dire" (162). Patrik, whose life before Maryvonne was much more ascetic—and inspired—finds his thoughts returning again and again to the objects he now owns and must manage. His thoughts, among them his conception of Canada, are shaped by the colorful household articles with which Maryvonne has surrounded him, and yet it does not begin to dawn on him that Maryvonne's materialism and the networks linked to it might *also* define Canada. Patrik's burgeoning resistance to Maryvonne's invasive purchases begins to suggest that his persona as artist is opposed to her avid consumerism, a theme that returns in the dystopic second half of the narrative. Patrik's resistance aligns with Quiet Revolution–era anticapitalism, indicating the influence of Quebecois sovereigntist political energy on Chraïbi's "apolitical" novel. Patrik misunderstands Canada, but the novel positions him in harmony with Quebecois sovereigntist goals.

The narrative positions Patrik's misinterpretation of Canada ("Il aimait ce pays, le Canada") at the apogee of the euphoric narration of Patrik and Maryvonne's affair and therefore at the transitional point between the two opposite yet identical narrations of the couple's story. Patrik's erroneous description of Canada accompanies his decision to be naturalized as a Canadian citizen (*Mort au Canada* 91–92), a decision that represents, in turn, his ultimate effort to fuse absolutely with Maryvonne. The idea of Canada and of being Canadian thus functions as an essential hinge defining the structure of this couple's passion, and Patrik's misunderstanding of Canada in the passage on naturalization functions as a symbolic parallel to his misguided romantic expectations for perfect amorous fusion. The narrative is structured so as to suggest that Canada as a setting is linked to this expectation that the fusion of human minds produces absolute mutual understanding; the "natural" wilderness and emptiness of the nation mirror Maryvonne's deep craving for love, represented as emotional avidity, a need to fill a void.

Within this emphatically "natural" and stereotypically "Canadian" setting, the novel constructs Patrik's imagination of perfect fusion as absolute amorous merger: "Pourquoi donc les âmes ne fusionneraient-elles pas, si les corps le faisaient déjà? Est-ce qu'il y avait un fossé entre deux êtres qu'il ne fallait jamais franchir? lequel? pourquoi?" (103). Patrik wants to bridge the gap between two persons; he imagines overcoming the opacity and separateness of human beings—an asymptotic ideal. Even though the novel constructs Patrik as particularly skilled in establishing connections with women (the narration presents Patrik as an unusually perceptive artist, his ability to understand others deriving directly from his musical artistry: "C'était comme le clavier d'un piano—et ce clavier était chacune d'elles [the women he had known] et il en faisait retentir toutes les touches, appuyait sur le *do* grave ou le *ré* mineur qui étaient précisément leurs notes secrètes et vitales" [29]),[15] Patrik's conviction that understanding is taking place between him and Maryvonne is in fact more like his newcomer's conviction that he understands Canada—a false conviction, based on superficial details. The hopeful first half of the narration represents his delusional belief that he has understood Maryvonne perfectly and fused with her being.

The paradox of Patrik's delusion declared as perfect understanding structures the first half of the narration precisely because of the linguistic nature of narration as opposed to the extralinguistic nature of his supposed understanding. In general, the narrative describes Patrik's charm rather than actually quoting him, affirming rather than showing his approach to conversation: "Il avait ce don rare entre tous: celui d'aimer. D'écouter, de percevoir l'essentiel et d'aimer" (29). Occasionally, however, a quotation gives a taste of his abrupt style, as when Patrik flirts with Maryvonne even as Sheena is cuddled up next to him:

> —Maryvonne, je vais te dire un autre secret: tu as un beau grain de beauté sur le genou gauche, je l'ai vu tout de suite. Est-ce que tu en as d'autres?
> Il était si sincère, si brut et si simple, sans aucun sens de la culpabilité, qu'elle répondit malgré elle:
> —Oui.
> —Hmm; fit-il en levant son verre. Parle-moi de toi, de ce que tu es. (28)

The bizarre intimacy of noticing and pointing out a beauty spot on a woman's knee to get her to talk about herself exemplifies Patrik's unorthodox but (so the narration tells us) charismatic charm. In a way, however, Patrik's attention to Maryvonne's beauty mark parallels how he reads Canada through touristic posters. His confident declarations about Canada's "inner nature" (that Gaspésie is "maternal," for example) serve as a model for what he wishes his romantic relationship were: a fantasy of complete understanding of being that gets expressed as knowledge of the physical—both the body and geographical space—as well as the essential. As a model of solidarity, this phantasmic relation of complete mutual comprehension even across the boundaries of physical and cultural difference, via "nature" and an unelaborated process of "naturalization," represents a fantasy that comprehension can happen without labor or even intention to assist it. Patrik's hope for perfect understanding with Maryvonne symbolizes a desire for solidarity without work, for "naturalized" unity, but Chraïbi's narration of the couple's dissolution (and its original lack of cohesion) serves as a critique of this model of solidarity.

The apparent disjunction between the words spoken and their human impact is related to a larger problem that Patrik encounters, which this dialogue in fact brings to a head: he instinctively knows the inner self of Maryvonne, whom he has just met, and yet he interacts with her by making her speak, by trying to make her reveal her being ("ce que tu es") in words. This contradiction continues to structure their relationship and to signal the impossibility of his goal of total union. For example, a month and a half into their affair, in the optimistic first half of the narration, Maryvonne thinks, "C'est formidable d'être aimée ainsi, totalement, avec mes qualités et mes défauts, mes faiblesses et mes caprices et mes moments de dépression et de joie!" The narration counterposes Patrik's thoughts: "Je voudrais tant . . . tant qu'elle reste toujours ainsi, dans cet état-là, amoureuse et ivre! . . . Dieu! que le temps jamais ne vienne de la connaissance!" (41–42). She feels completely known and understood, "totally" loved, whereas he fears knowledge. He understands that his intuitive comprehension of her inner being will be complicated by longer acquaintance, by linguistic acquaintance. Indeed, as Maryvonne's thought reveals, the linguistic self is complex, brimming with contradictory feelings and experiences; the inner self that Patrik somehow grasps intuitively is cohesive, understandable. Maryvonne enjoys being made whole, being understood as a single coherent being, but Patrik is aware that this wholeness he understands will break apart with increased conversation. In the mapping of romance novels provided by Moudileno, Patrik's intuitive understanding of Maryvonne corresponds to the "parallel universe" of romantic ideals; it mirrors his touristic fascination with Canadian nature and inscribes itself onto the phantasmic model of laborless solidarity. But the discordant (and unspoken) thought dialogue between Patrik and Maryvonne, one of the moments of premonitory doubt that creeps into the first half of the couple's narrated history, suggests that this euphoric unity is impossible to maintain and that it relies precisely on a misunderstanding.

Just as Patrik's understanding of Canada falters, so too his expectations of a totally encompassing "Canadian" relationship founder. The narrative continues to structure the relationship as a downward-spiraling oscillation between linguistic knowledge and Patrik's intuitive knowledge: "Le premier mouvement de la symphonie de Maryvonne et de Patrik avait été d'instinct et de don. Le second fut celui de la connaissance" (69)—exactly as Patrik had feared. Of course, the chronology of their relationship, which is deliberately difficult to outline, mixes precise dates (we know, for instance, that Patrik and Maryvonne met on November 17—this date is repeated as a mantra throughout the text, as the seventeenth of the month is an anniversary that is first celebrated and eventually forgotten by Maryvonne) with unlocalizable flashbacks (often italicized in the text) and unannounced retellings (as discussed above, the second half of the narrative returns to early moments in the relationship and narrates them in a completely new light). The narration itself acknowledges that "il n'y eut pas à proprement parler d'étapes chronologiques, de 'gradations' logiques dans leur découverte mutuelle. Elle fut globale et en vrac, spontanée. Si la vue et le toucher furent les sens prédominants dans l'étude de leur corps, il leur fut adjoint la parole, qui explora ce qu'ils voyaient et touchaient, remonta le cours de temps jusqu'aux souvenirs d'enfance, fit appel à l'imagination débordante. Ce qui s'exprima par les yeux et les mains se communiqua de l'un à l'autre en paroles de connaissance, acquit ainsi une vie démesurée" (69). In this description, the "connaissance" that Patrik had feared in his inner monologue takes place instantaneously, as a physical and conversational discovery that somehow happens "haphazardly" and "spontaneously." Again, the narration (the linguistic description of the relationship) cannot accommodate the apparent transcendence of the moment; the breadth implied in conversations going back in time to childhood cannot possibly have happened instantaneously. The narrative actually acknowledges that linguistic discovery gives the physical relationship a disproportionate life ("une vie démesurée"), a kind of immoderacy that becomes independent of the two lovers and that far exceeds Patrik's original instinctive attraction. Language, then, in the form of this conversational space outside time, represents a *supplement* to the relationship even as it is integral to its development; it corresponds to the bright posters that create in Patrik's mind a fixed and stereotypical idea of Canada and that are simultaneously external to this idea, independent of it, supplementary. Language's paradoxical dual function as both necessary and auxiliary structures the phantasmic model of solidarity, bringing out the inconsistency of a model that imagines solidarity as transcendently and instantly communicative without the work of communication.

This relationship based on a phantasm of complete mutual understanding relies on the same metaphor of filling an empty vessel that structures Patrik's reading of Canada; when the disturbingly unequal relation fails, this particular metaphor founders as a template to understand solidarity. Chraïbi constructs Patrik, the musician and artist, as ideally suited to understanding women, and conversely, he builds Maryvonne as the ideal woman in need of understanding. The first part of the couple's narration positions Patrik as the perfect counterpart to Maryvonne's emotional neediness; his desire for metaphysical fusion with his lover's soul (also a symptom of his artistic nature) prepares him to enter into a pact of donation of the self (*don de soi*) with Maryvonne, who is deeply troubled and alone. What attracts Patrik to Maryvonne, then, is his perception of her inner hurt, her profound need for love. During their first conversation, he guesses immediately that she is suffering:

    —Maryvonne, tu es bien? Tu vas bien?
    —Oui.
    —Menteuse. Tu souffres. C'est ça?
    Comment avait-il pu savoir ce qu'elle cachait si bien? (38)

Patrik senses immediately, and the novel reveals gradually, Maryvonne's loveless childhood, her abusive past relationships, and her loneliness among her patients and assistants. Her deep emotional need dovetails perfectly, Patrik perceives and the structure of the narrative suggests, with his deep desire to give, to become one with another soul. The first half of the couple's narrative delves into her needs and his sacrifices (in italicized asides, Patrik's thoughts read, "*Je te donnerai tout, tout, tout! . . . Je te donnerai ma peau, mon sang, ma vie*" [136]), participating in Patrik's hope for a complete union. The narrative presents their passionate give-and-take innocently (Patrik gives, Maryvonne takes), interspersing scenes of lovemaking and peaceful cohabitation with brief, unemotional descriptions of the drastic sacrifices Patrik makes within their relationship. For instance, at Maryvonne's behest, he sends his eight-months-pregnant ex-lover back to Scotland. Maryvonne asks him to give up drinking alcohol, and he does; she burns his old clothes and dresses him according to her taste; finally, she watches him as he burns letters and photographs of his wife and children.

Patrik's willingness to sacrifice himself completely, which represents the method by which he tries to achieve his desire for absolute romantic fusion, corresponds to his perception of Canada and Canadians. If they are the "young" and "authentic" people he perceives, they innocently deserve his devotion. The symbolic burning of his previous familial ties in the form of photographs represents his adoption of "Canada," or Canada's adoption of *him* as new juvenile dependent, with Maryvonne as surrogate. Patrik's imagination of Canada's infinity and refreshing blankness shapes his readiness to give himself, his entire being, to "fill" that void. The narrative, however, proves that this void is unfillable, both symbolically (Canada) and personally (Maryvonne). As a model for francophone solidarity, the structure the metaphor suggests (of the colonies as empty receivers of metropolitan generosity, or more broadly, of solidarity as a "gift" fulfilling a "need") proves to be unworkable. But the model, by suggesting the parallel between human relation and geographical relation, also suggests the importance of place as a structuring feature of solidarity, raising the double question of what Canada and Maryvonne might represent beyond the skewed perspective of Patrik's free-indirect-discourse notions.

The symbolic parallel between Patrik's misguided romantic expectations and his misconception of Canada explains why his decision to be naturalized Canadian (to belong legally to the fantasized, stereotypical version of Canada he imagines) functions as a hinge in the narrative structure of *Mort au Canada*. The naturalization, the adoption of Canada, of a supposedly empty space, completes the loss of himself and the loss of his children; in the narrative sequence, it arrives as the euphoric (and deluded) climax of his sacrificial relationship to Maryvonne. After this point, the euphoric narration is exhausted, and the novel turns to the darker side of Patrik's relationship with Maryvonne, to his most difficult sacrifices, portraying Maryvonne's demands as cruel and Patrik's losses as engendering a dangerous form of isolation. This first instantiation of Canada as a superficial and stereotypical impression, such as a tourist might garner from pamphlets, mirrors Patrik and Maryvonne's relationship as a misled effort at total romantic fusion. The flawed geographical and interpersonal relationship in turn functions as a model for solidarity, suggesting that Chraïbi was wary of attempts at solidary relations that were structured along lines essentializing charity (or giving) and need (or receiving), that strove to imagine solidarity as absolute merger or perfect identity, or that sought to erase different (colonial) pasts. But the narrative's focus on Canada as a romanticized notion in the first half of the narrative elides the "concrete quotidian" aspects that Moudileno argues characterize the romance novel—and that, in the case of *Mort of Canada*, redefine human relations within a more "political" context, as I show in the next section. Whereas this first instantiation of Canada demonstrates the failure of human and solidary connections, the second and third instantiations indicate that Chraïbi was nonetheless interested in these types of connections, though linked to a different type of geographical understanding of Canada.

### Metempsychosis and Political Energy: From "Canada" to "Quebec"

The noxious relationship with Maryvonne, as I have shown, corresponds to Patrik's misunderstanding of the signification of the space called "Canada." In spite of Patrik's mistaken interpretation, however, and the disastrous relationship that parallels it, *Mort au Canada* establishes Canada as a space of mystical possibility and of deep human connection—and ultimately, as a place of political energy.

The second instantiation of Canada, this time as a space of mystical connection, is revealed in something of a surprise ending at the close the novel. The true connection that transpires in Canada is the enigmatic metempsychosis by which Patrik becomes the vessel for the soul of the writer William.[16] Patrik never knew William while both were living in Canada, although Maryvonne inexplicably calls Patrik "Bill," suggesting an intentional narrative overlap between the two male characters. In spite of his never having heard of William, however, when Patrik meets William's daughter Dominique several years later on the island of Yeu, the sight of her triggers his memories of Canada, establishing a narrative relationship between the child in Yeu and Patrik's affair with Maryvonne.

Canada emerges as the link between Patrik and William, this time as a space privileging exchanges between artistic, creative minds. The connection happens through the medium of music. At the narrative's climax, Patrik understands that a melody inspired by the sight of Dominique was a "secret song" known only to Dominique and her father; Patrik has reinvented—or remembered metempsychotically—a song first imagined by William. In the same way that Patrik is able to understand the hidden musical notes representing women's inner selves, so too music emerges as the expression of the deep essential link between him and William. This aspect of Canada, the mystical space of connective possibility, contrasts sharply with the description of Patrik's lived experience in Canada and with his relationship with Maryvonne.

In fact, Canada as space of mystical connection exists *musically,* beyond the bounds of the novel's narrative possibilities. The novel can describe the music Patrik creates, but the narrative reaches its linguistic limit in its inability to convey the music itself. In describing the "secret song" Patrik remembers metempsychotically, the text strives to show that music functions as a kind of universal ur-language: "Depuis qu'il avait vu Dominique sur le port . . . Patrik n'avait pas cessé d'être envahi par une aria douce et nostalgique, dont il ne connaissait pas une note. . . . Il commença à fredonner doucement puis, gorge déployée, il lança à haute voix le regret de ce qui aurait pu être, l'espoir de ce qui sera toujours en ce monde, la foi" (195). The narrative metaphorizes the material sound of Patrik's voice as the abstract ideals of regret, hope, and faith. Chraïbi's metaphor insists that art functions as an expression of emotion—a banal assertion, except that in this particular moment art transcends William's death. The novel constructs this instance of textual prestidigitation with a figure of style, communicating the central mystical connection of the novel through the conveniently inexpressible medium of music. I say convenient because the text relies on the melody's absolutely nonlinguistic existence to proclaim, through a metaphoric leap, the unlikely connection between Patrik and William; the text can assert the mystical relation, but it remains asymptotic for us readers, suggested but textually inarticulable.

The textual prestidigitation also stands for the mystical power of the idea of Canada. Canada, in this second, mystical instantiation, exists in the same metaphoric leap as the connection between art and emotion. The magical aspect of Canada occupies the space of that figuratively forged association—and, conversely, the association occurs in the magical space of Canada. The novel relies somewhat clumsily on the metaphor of art as emotion to account for the mysticism of its conclusion, and Canada as the locale in which mysticism works metempsychotic miracles remains a fragile and unexplained mirage; the metempsychotic transfer takes place offscreen, in the interval between the two periods of narration (Patrik's past relationship with Maryvonne and his present friendship with Dominique). Indeed, the metempsychotic exchange serves as the link between these two narrations. It is precisely because Patrik senses the mysterious aria when he first sees Dominique ("Brusquement . . . la musique fit monter son ancienne sensibilité à la surface de sa peau. . . . Et il était incapable d'arrêter . . . cette sorte d'aria nostalgique venue peut-être de l'inconscient" [12]) that his affair with Maryvonne resurfaces, and it is also because of the aria that he becomes attached to Dominique, an attachment that effectively replaces the loss of his own Parisian children.

The link between Canada and the strength of this musical sublinguistic experience emerges intertextually in a comparison between *Mort au Canada* and Chraïbi's memoir *Le monde à côté*, in the metaphor of rebirth that Chraïbi uses to describe both Patrik's awakening as he first imagines the "nostalgic aria" linking him to William (and also to Maryvonne and Dominique) and his own, Chraïbi's, feeling of renewal as he first made love with his Quebecois lover. In the 1975 novel, the narrator writes of Patrik first "hearing" the aria as he sees Dominique, "C'était comme l'automne du monde croulant en lui et, en même temps, le printemps du monde qui renaissait en lui" (12). Similarly, in his 2001 memoir, Chraïbi uses the image of the seasons and a parallel verbal and syntactical structure to suggest his transformative experience as he first embraces Marie, during a snowstorm: "L'étreignant, j'avais la sensation intense, indicible et intense, que tous les hivers du monde croulaient autour de moi et en moi tandis que renaissaient tous les printemps" (136). The similar imagery, which in both iterations suggests a powerful feeling of rebirth, thus associates the fictional metempsychotic exchange to an experience that Chraïbi narrates as his own lived experience in a Canadian snowstorm. The rejuvenating snowy embrace becomes emblematic of a type of deep relationship possible in Canada, and this metaphorical consistency of spring-like rebirth illuminating Chraïbi's oeuvre highlights the fullness of the mystical experience that structures *Mort au Canada*.

The musical connection between Patrik and William draws a marked contrast to the connections that form via language. Patrik's linguistic communication with Maryvonne, for example, scatters and disperses their sense of connection, whereas the absence of William prevents the communicative dissolution of the relationship. As a model for solidarity, this extralinguistic musical link between two artists suggests Chraïbi's interest in exploring ephemeral and purposely incomplete relationships as bases for significant understanding; this model indicates the power, for Chraïbi, of open-ended contacts, which evoke a sense of connection but do not strive to pin down that connection with language. Art, this mystical instantiation of Canada suggests, can serve as a strong but immaterial bond between artists. This also means that Chraïbi is invested in symbolically depoliticizing the political energy that motivated his understanding of Canada as a place of immense connective potential. The magical immediacy of the relationship and the impossibility of its narration except through metaphorical leap indicate that this is yet another model for solidarity that elides labor and politics; as with the first instantiation of Canada's failed romantic relationship, there is an expectation that human connections can happen spontaneously and that the *work* of understanding others destroys this unconstrained, intuitive bond.

The third instantiation of Canada, which emerges most evidently in the second half of the narration, offers a model that diverges from the first two models of spontaneous solidarity. Indeed, the second half of the narrative shows that underlying the rather thin figurative connection that spawns Canada as mystical space are some highly specific social and cultural phenomena that describe Quebec as a linguistic and political space. These recognizable local phenomena represent what I identify as the third instantiation of Canada in *Mort au Canada*—and they correct for the other two instantiations' elision of politics and work. I will show first how the traces of Quebecois specificity enter the narrative and then how the political energy of this aspect of Quebec inspires the novel's search for human connection.

Let us examine how exactly Chraïbi structures the novel through specific allusions to Quebec as a linguistic and geopolitical entity. First of all, Quebec forms a linguistic presence in Chraïbi's text, appearing in Patrik's encounter with Dominique as well as in (chronologically earlier) dialogues with Maryvonne. When Patrik meets Dominique, for instance, his speech is marked by Quebecois vocabulary:

—Tu étais simplement en colère, tannée?
Elle éclata de rire.
—Ça veut dire quoi, 'tannée'?
—Tannée. Fatiguée, si tu préfères. J'ai longtemps habité au Canada. Il est devenu mon pays d'adoption. (21)

Dominique unabashedly inquires about the tempo of Patrik's speech, too: "Monsieur, pourquoi vous parlez comme ça? . . . avec cette voix lente et cet accent?" (20). By the time of the frame narrative (some years after his stay in Canada), Quebec's linguistic influence has shaped Patrik's being; Patrik's experience in Canada—his stay there, his relationship with Maryvonne, and perhaps his metempsychotic encounter with William—has transformed him. The Quebecism *tanné*, not quite the equivalent of *fatigué*, connotes not only tiredness but also exasperation and boredom. The past participle, which Dominique accepts as expressing her frustration, also designates Patrik's own jaded and desolate position. This instance of adopted Quebecois vocabulary, occurring as it does in the opening framing section of the encounter with Dominique, sets the stage for the linguistic Quebecization of the text, which unfolds over the course of Patrik's narrated (remembered) relationship with Maryvonne.

The sounds of the province of Quebec materialize from these regional linguistic markers of vocabulary and syntax. The local accent also forms part of the text's investment in making the North American francophone territory central to the text. Maryvonne's language features typically Quebecois syntactical structures: "C'est-il moche!," Maryvonne exclaims (100), or "Seigneur Dieu! c'est-i pas possible!" (78). The added *ti* sound (sometimes conveyed as *tu* by Quebecois writers), grammatically superfluous, intensifies the manifestation of Quebec as a signifying space. The regional accent relentlessly returns the "universal" romance narrative to the province, insisting on the importance of Quebec as a particular place, more intimately observed than the vast and empty touristic Canada of Patrik's posters.

Quebec as specific place emerges in the interstices of the second half of the narration of Patrik and Maryvonne's affair as the signifying backdrop to their drama. The predominantly French-speaking province's English-language capitalist consumer landscape comes into relief, defining the narrative's significant sociopolitical context, when Maryvonne organizes a shopping spree to Quebec City and Montreal to replace Patrik's wardrobe. Maryvonne, unhappy with the options available at the seventeen stores through which she drags Patrik in Quebec City, takes him to Montreal, to two fashionable stores to which Chraïbi gives the typically British and Scottish names Warwick and Dalmore. These undoubtedly refer to such retailers as the Maison Ogilvy in Montreal and the Maison Simons in Quebec City. Both stores, institutions in Quebecois fashion circles, were founded in the nineteenth century by Scottish immigrants, the Ogilvy and Simons families. Both stores imported Scottish and British fashions, though Simons later created its own sartorial lines.

Going beyond merely naming the stores, the narrative also personifies Warwick and Dalmore, giving them bodily presence in the text: "M. Warwick, M. Dalmore—ou l'un de leurs employés-mannequins—penchaient la tête de côté, souriaient" (102). The plastic-like figures represent the metonymical connection between commerce and English speakers, a socioeconomic structure frequently decried in Quiet Revolution–era texts. Pierre Vallières's *Nègres blancs d'Amériques* (1968), for example, in its politically incisive and cynically articulated lesson on the history of

Quebec, equates "la population canadienne-française" (a linguistically marked population) with a class, "les travailleurs du Québec," and his central argument is to demonstrate that this linguistic group–cum–class experiences a "condition de nègres, d'exploités, de citoyens de seconde classe" (26). The exploiters, in his historical narrative, are the British and American economic interests who struggled to dominate Quebecois resources and markets: "Plusieurs Américains avaient déjà entrepris la conquête économique du Québec dès le milieu du XIXe siècle, sans trop savoir encore s'ils devaient s'appuyer sur l'impérialisme britannique encore très puissant ou sur le nouvel impérialisme américain, beaucoup plus dynamique. . . . Ils n'avaient que des intérêts de classe et des soucis de fortune. . . . Leur empire était le marché mondial des capitaux et des biens produits par cette masse de 'cheap labor' anonyme pour laquelle ils n'avaient que mépris" (47). Vallières's manifesto thus outlines a social division that coincides with a linguistic difference: the owners of capital speak English, whereas the "main-d'œuvre à bon marché" (26) speak French. Claude Jutra's 1971 film *Mon oncle Antoine* illustrates and critiques this same structure: the film opens with an interaction between a mineworker and his supervisor that highlights the worker's broken English in comparison with the supervisor's fluency. This is the only interaction in English in the film, which then turns its lens on the francophone population's culture in the town, and specifically on the general store, where workers' families spend the money they earn at the mine. The opening English-language interaction indicates the linguistic power relations that undergird the social relations forming the backdrop to the coming-of-age story of the central character, a francophone boy. Jutra's film thus contextualizes French-language culture in Quebec within an English-dominated economic field, just as Chraïbi does by narrating Patrik and Maryvonne's Montreal shopping trip. This resonance indicates that Chraïbi was attuned to the anticapitalist and pro-French revendications of Quebecois sovereigntists.

Chraïbi's salesclerks' Englishness extends beyond their (or the stores') names. As they discuss Maryvonne's purchases with her, their speech mars French with English words, which the text isolates with scare quotes and sometimes translates into standard French in parentheses: "Madame a bon choix . . . C'est 'fin,' 'smart,' 'in.' Monsieur est comme il faut . . . Je vous 'charge' (compte) aussi cette douzaine de 'bas' (chaussettes)?" (102, ellipses in original). "Smart" and "in" are English words that have entered Quebecois vocabulary, specifically because they are associated with the fashionable English-language Quebecois fashion industry. And whereas the Quebecois use of *bas* to mean "sock" is a historical displacement of meaning resulting from the geographical isolation of North American francophones, the verb *charger,* a direct appropriation of the English verb *to charge* that frequently replaces the standard French *compter* in Quebec, is a linguistic encroachment that symbolizes the English base of commerce in the province.

In the context of this English-based socioeconomic structure, Patrik sets the ethical, moral standard. First, he is represented as a point of resistance against consumerist pressure, a position with implied links to his artistic nature. I have already discussed his discomfort with the objects with which Maryvonne furnishes his workspace ("Je ne sais qu'en faire. Ils me regardent et je n'ai pas grand-chose à leur dire" [162]). The swarming furnishings prevent him from creating music; the text thus implies that the creation of art must remain outside the consumerist cycle. Patrik also emerges as a model of antimaterialist detachment: as Maryvonne burns his old clothes, Patrik "était silencieux et pensif: ce n'étaient là que des objets et il y avait longtemps qu'ils avaient perdu leur âme" (100). Giving up objects accords with his general willingness to give in to Maryvonne in his effort to fuse with her. But while Patrik gives in to Maryvonne and accepts her transformation of his life, he remains unconvinced by the materialism with which she surrounds him. His radical inability to learn to drive ("Rien à faire, chérie. Ce n'est pas pour moi" [113]),[17] in the same vein, represents a resistance to the consumer society that is sustained by and that sustains car ownership and rapid travel.

Patrik also embodies resistance to consumerist pressure because he acts as a barrier against English. The text constructs him as a preserver of the French language, which he values in its Quebecois variant:

—À côté de toi, je ne sais pas grand-chose, mon âme [says Maryvonne]. Je suis "ignarde."

—*Re!* corrigeait-il. *Ignare!* Au Québec, la langue française est pure. (89)

Patrik, in correcting Maryvonne's error, performs an act of resistance in sync with the efforts of Quiet Revolution–era Quebec, which sought to value the French language as a vehicle for cultural survival and eventually an argument for independence.

The third instantiation of Canada that emerges from these moments in the narrative thus zeros in on a more precise location—Quebec—that gives the novel meaning, throwing light on the characters' sometimes cryptic motivations. Although these moments of regionally specific consumption and resistance to consumerism appear tangential to the novel's central "love story," they in fact structure it. Maryvonne's unquestioning acceptance of consumerism defines her character as insatiably needy; her ever-growing needs delimit and determine her nature. And Quebec as setting takes on vital importance in that it offers, in the revolutionary moment in which the narrative is set, a backdrop that represents a model for resistance. Politically charged Quebec constitutes the energy that animated Chraïbi's memories and imagination of Quebec. The experiences that he describes in *Le monde à côté*, even as he remains cynical about the superficiality of his students' revolutionary spirit, and that underlie his writing of *Mort of Canada* indicate a type of exchange that is possible precisely because of the Quiet Revolution's cultural rediscovery and development of Quebec as a distinct, anticapitalist French-speaking nation. The Quebecois scholar Fernando Lambert recalls the connections between sovereigntist impulses, a Quebecois search for identity, and Quebec's opening to the francophone world:

> Les répercussions de *Nègres blancs d'Amérique* (1968) de Pierre Vallières étaient bien vives et renvoyaient, cela semblait aller de soi, à la colonisation connue par l'Afrique et les Antilles. Parler de littératures négro-africaines dans ce cadre avait une résonnance forte. . . . Il y a eu, c'est certain, une grande curiosité, la découverte d'autres peuples et d'autres cultures, mais aussi pour plusieurs une forme de communauté de sentiments, une impression de comprendre et peut-être de partager une situation ayant beaucoup de points communs avec ce que les Africains et les Antillais avaient vécu. La littérature, la chanson, le théâtre du Québec qui connaissaient une croissance remarquable . . . prenaient une force et un sens très fort nourrissant la prise de conscience d'une identité à reconquérir et à affirmer avec orgueil et fierté. (email exchange with author)

Quebec's interest in African and Caribbean cultures and literatures in the late 1960s and early 1970s here emerges specifically from an ideological, political, and cultural project aimed at reinventing Quebec as an anticolonial francophone nation. Chraïbi's experience of the province, which he portrays as an apolitical affection for specific individuals rather than an ideological encounter with a nation, was in fact nourished, for the Quebecois who were meeting him, by an ideological enthusiasm and a feeling of solidarity for francophone (former) colonial subjects. The warmth with which *Mort au Canada* evokes Canada as a space of possible connection results precisely from the solidarity with which Chraïbi was greeted in Quebec.

Of course, as I have shown, Chraïbi's novel does not celebrate this solidarity in a simple or direct way. In fact, *Mort au Canada* proposes models that reveal the unfounded hopes for impossible unity that underpin solidary expression. His character Patrik fails to understand Canada, and his touristic misreadings represent just such an unfounded hope for total unity. The artistico-mystical fusion between Patrik and William offers a kind of immanent connection through artistic genius, and yet the linguistic inarticulability of this relationship derails attempts to see it as a textual form of solidarity. But the fact that Chraïbi's Canadian novel insists on proposing these models of extravagant solidarity (perfect fusion, artistic metempsychosis), combined with his attentive portrayal of Quebec's linguistic and economic struggle against North American English interests, indicates the extent to which Chraïbi was influenced by the political energies that animated Quebec in the late sixties and early seventies and that motivated the warmth of the welcome he experienced.

*Mort au Canada* on the surface appears to be, and has been read as being, about the "eternal themes" of love, art, and death, and yet the novel reveals the extent to which Chraïbi was affected by the potent political atmosphere of Quiet Revolution–era Quebec, even as he expressed cynicism toward nationalisms and the comfort of Quebecois "revolutionaries." The novel mirrors this ambivalence, positioning the figure of the artist (Patrik) in contradictory ways: he simultaneously fails to understand Canada, experiences mystical metempsychosis through Canada, and remains in ideological harmony with the aims of Quebecois sovereigntist intellectuals. Analyzing the character's relationship to setting, then, both as an idealized space of romance and as a quotidian reality laden with political signification, is key to understanding the work of the novel in imagining various modes of relation.

In other words, Quebec as a space of renewal for Patrik is precisely linked to a political situation; Chraïbi's imagination of Quebec as a space for new types of connections suggests how strongly he was affected by the effervescence of 1970s Quebec. These new connections represent experiments in imagining solidarity, the first two models relying on an idealized, immanent connection detached from the reality of working through difference, and the last model accounting more carefully for difference and relying on it to structure the space of solidary relation. The novel inscribes the transformative space of Quebec as a place of francophone interconnection, a space where French represents difference, both from English and from France. Quebec offers a space to imagine new political and human energies, away from the colonial baggage haunting Chraïbi's early novels; in *Mort au Canada* it represents a place of radical renewal and artistic freedom. The narrative describes this sense of renewal explicitly:

"Mais ici, au Canada, il découvrit l'appel d'un puissant besoin: changer de pays, changer de peau, de mentalité et de croyance, de langue et de culture, changer de personnalité, à tout jamais, radicalement, afin qu'il n'y eût plus d'errance ou de souffrance" (91). As the novel reveals, Canada is the geographical place where transformations can occur, but Quebec is the reason they occur. Quebec's political undercurrent of cultural and linguistic resistance, portrayed as the backdrop of the novel, is precisely what animates Chraïbi's literary experiment with solidarity as he tries to imagine romance and artistic connection as solidary relations.

## Chraïbi's Canadian *La civilisation, ma mère!* . . .

Chraïbi's second Canadian novel, *La civilisation, ma mère!* . . . , was first imagined in Quebec, in the heat of a discussion with a Canadian educator who was interested in subsidizing a pedagogical edition of a novel that could be used in Canada to teach French to anglophones. Chraïbi narrates the invention of this pedagogical novel in his memoir:

> Un certain McDonnel, professeur de littérature comparée à McGill [in fact G. Robert McConnell, coordinator of modern-language education for the Scarborough school council in Ontario, as announced by the title page of the Quebecois edition of *La civilisation*],[18] vint me rendre visite. Il se proposait d'établir une version universitaire commentée d'un de mes livres, à l'usage des étudiants anglophones. . . . Aurais-je par hasard dans mes tiroirs ou en chantier un ouvrage plus facile à lire que les précédents, plus léger et plus tendre? L'imagination à bride abattue, j'inventai sur-le-champ. Je lui dis que j'avais en tête le sujet d'un roman dont le personnage principal serait une femme de chez nous confrontée aux emblèmes de la civilisation occidentale, mais que je ne savais pas par quel bout le prendre. Ses yeux brillèrent.
> —D'accord! J'achète. (*Le monde à côté* 131–32)

The resulting novel, first published in Paris with Chraïbi's usual editor, Denoël, before being reissued by Éditions Aquila in Montreal,[19] tells a story that at first seems far removed from Canada. It narrates the life of an unnamed Moroccan mother who, thanks to lessons she receives from her two sons, breaks free from housebound servitude. The novel takes place in the context of colonial Morocco; the family lives in Casablanca in the 1930s and 1940s, and the characters' main point of international reference is France. The younger son, the "petit loustic," leaves for France halfway through the novel, and the story concludes with the mother and her older son, Nagib, leaving Morocco to join him. References to

Canada within the novel, however, suggest that travel to that country has significantly shaped the younger son, who narrates his Moroccan childhood from a temporal and spatial remove. I argue that the novel's approach to personal transformation was inspired by Quebec, much as *Mort au Canada*'s boundless hope for human connection drew inspiration from the energy of French-language advocacy during the Quiet Revolution. In *La civilisation, ma mère!...*, Quebec's solidary political energy (and its pedagogical mission of teaching French) transforms the desolate and violent familial setting of Chraïbi's first novel, the Morocco of *Le passé simple,* into a comical stage teeming with possibilities for change. Quebec's nationalism may not have persuaded Chraïbi, but the province's effervescent political climate did inspire this radically hopeful revision of his own past. I propose that as a consequence of his sojourn in Canada and of his resulting purpose of teaching French, Chraïbi gained the distance required to reimagine his past in the style of comedy and to reframe it from a perspective of hope for transformation.

Scholars typically read *La civilisation* as the improbable tale of one woman's liberation from the constraints of traditional Moroccan gender roles through an idiosyncratic adoption of Western modes of learning and being in the world.[20] Recontextualizing it as a pedagogical text, however, requires a drastic shift in interpretive focus. If the text was created as a teaching tool for educators and their students, the mother's gradual opening up to the world, from her domestic servitude in Morocco to her departure for France, becomes an exemplar or a model for the transformations experienced by students during a much more banal process of language learning. As she learns to navigate new technologies and the vocabularies relevant to them, for instance, the mother comically symbolizes the methods by which students assimilate foreign words and concepts. In Chraïbi's Montreal edition of the novel, anglophone students are asked to assimilate idiomatic content via translations footnoted in the text, such as the expression *Pas de puces, pas de punaises,* translated at the bottom of the page into the English idiom "Don't let the bed bugs bite" (35). At the same time, however, these translated idioms convey clearly the ultimate "untranslatability" of the text and of a culture's expression of reality; *Pas de puces, pas de punaises* does not mean the same thing as "Don't let the bedbugs bight." Although these idioms are used in similar contexts for similar purposes and thus convey an equivalent *function* of sorts, the differences between them do remind learners that "no two languages are ever sufficiently similar to be considered as representing the same social reality. The worlds in which different societies live are distinct worlds, not merely the same world with different labels attached" (Edward Sapir, quoted in Bassnett 24).[21] The French-learning readers of *La civilisation*'s pedagogical edition thus arrive at the text from a perspective of cultural relativity; languages and cultures are incommensurable, in spite of (and perhaps especially from the perspective of) the possibility of learning them.

Chraïbi's text suggests, moreover, that this process of learning in the cultural breach is an enchanted and enchanting experience. When the mother calls the German Blaupunkt radio "Monsieur Kteu" (her sons having read out the label "Blo Punn Kteu"), for example, she imagines that the radio houses a magician. In this she is, like a classroom language learner, labeling a foreign concept and integrating it into her own imaginary, but she also invests the foreign object and the breach that separates her from understanding it fully with magical powers. The extraordinariness of the mother's educational journey suggests the wonders of language learning even as the edition's glossary and comprehension questions simultaneously facilitate the correlation of one language with another *and* point out the impossibility of any perfect such correlation. Chraïbi thus maps the practical project of teaching French in a Quiet Revolution Quebec that felt itself besieged by English onto a story of self-liberation in Morocco. Though he makes no overtly political statement linking these francophone spaces, his novel exercises a solidary practice, not only by connecting Quebec and Morocco via a shared French language but also by creating a feedback loop in which self-liberation (at the level of plot) and immersion in French (at the level of syntax, format, and paratext) generate each other—a stance that resonates with Quiet Revolution values. In the context of 1970s Quebec, indeed, teaching and learning French meant participating in the cultural revendication of this language in the otherwise English-speaking northern American continent, so that the process of translating the untranslatable and crossing cultural boundaries through education took on a political dimension.

This model of double reading implied by the Montreal edition's status as both a novel and a language-learning tool is one I revisit below, when I suggest that Chraïbi mixes narrative realism and tonal irony to simultaneously teach French and locate anticolonial possibilities in that imperial language. But double reading also informs other aspects of the novel. On the simplest level, even the title (*La civilisation, ma mère!* . . . ), because of its punctuated truncation, can be read two ways. *Ma mère* is in apposition to *la civilisation*, which makes the two terms equal (*la civilisation = ma mère*). *Ma mère* can also be read as an apostrophe, in which case *la civilisation* becomes the object being introduced *to* the mother (something like *Voilà la civilisation, ma mère!*).[22] The two meanings work together: the mother's self-realization is a progressive education, an introduction to civilization (the apostrophe) through which she realizes herself *as* civilization (the apposition), as she gathers knowledge, learns to communicate, organizes political rallies, and becomes a central node of Morocco's revolutionary change. The title's unusual terminal punctuation implies an energetic open-endedness that accords both with the novel's role as a language textbook—with the continual wonder and potential of discovering a new language—and with the hopeful politics of the narrative's tale of transformation. The double significance of the novel's title shows that the text constitutes an exercise in political imagination, one that reimagines the Moroccan body politic as a female body, and postcolonial autonomy for Morocco as that female body freed from the restraints of both patriarchy and colonialism.

## "As through a Canadian Fog": Quebec Inflects Morocco in *La civilisation, ma mère!* . . .

In order to illustrate how strains of Quiet Revolution political energy make themselves felt in the mode of double reading the novel prompts, and how that energy informs the political vision of Morocco as a freed female body, I begin by exploring the significance of Quebec both within the novel and as the context for its composition. Quebec structures the entire narrative, figuring in the novel as a space visited by the younger brother (the "petit loustic") between the narrators' writing periods. The poet and scholar Hédi Bouraoui (founder of the Canada-Maghreb Center at York University, in Toronto) has demonstrated the temporal complexity of *La civilisation,* arguing that the first section ("Être," a nonepistolary narration of the boys' early childhood, before 1936) is written by the "petit loustic" in 1972, *after* he has received the letter(s) from his brother, Nagib, that constitute the second section of the novel ("Avoir," an epistolary narration describing Nagib and his mother's life between 1936 and 1956, after the younger brother's departure to study in France).[23] The "petit loustic" narrative ("Être") thus comes simultaneously before and after Nagib's narrative, so that "Être" forms the frame and the determining voice for the novel. Of course, it is not the focus of Bouraoui's study as he examines the temporal complexities of *La civilisation* to account for the North American travels that have marked and influenced the "petit loustic" during the interim between his narrated childhood (before 1936) and his process of narration (in 1972). This interim period, however, has a significant structuring effect on the narrative.

Canadian influence is signified by a simile that appears in the early scenes of *La civilisation;* this structuring simile sets the perspective for the novel, suggesting—by way of the younger brother's experience of Quebec—that Canada *inflects* the Moroccan setting. Specifically, the "petit loustic" narrates seeing his mother as through a Canadian fog, a metaphorical intrusion that the older narrator introduces into memories of his childhood. The scene sets up an unlikely comparison between a hot stove in a small, enclosed Moroccan kitchen and the cold of a Canadian November day. The object of transnational comparison is the smoke produced as the "petit loustic" watches his mother rudimentarily repair the *brasero* she uses to cook at the beginning of the narrative, before her transformation: "Si ma mère toussa? Oui. À se fendre les poumons. . . . Je la voyais comme à travers le brouillard qui tombe en novembre sur le lac Beauport, au Canada. Entre deux quintes, elle soufflait sur le feu, de toutes ses forces" (39). The comparison is strikingly discordant. The Moroccan side of the equation is based on fire, on heat; the white, diaphanous suspension in the air results from burning, and it is noxious, making breathing difficult. On the Canadian side of the equation, however, the November fog is created by a plunge in air temperature. Northern lakes are foggy in the fall because the water retains the heat of summer longer than the air does; the image evokes a damp, shivering cold, and yet it also implies easy breathability, the clean purity of forest-washed air. The narrator's Morocco-Canada simile is structured to join opposing elements, a disjointed juxtaposition of entirely different experiences linked by a similar white visibility of the air. The difference between the two situations suggests the impossibility of comparison, an impossibility that the text de facto perverts by making it possible. This paradoxically possible impossibility parallels the language-learning context of the Montreal edition, which emphasizes that languages are simultaneously incommensurable and yet also learnable. In fact, just as language learning becomes possible through reading literature, the incongruous comparison of fog and smoke suggests that simile is eminently possible precisely because of the literary figure's ability to bridge difference.

The unexpected and jarring comparison structures the perspective of the novel. Foggy Canadian coolness marks the narrator's distance from his family's hearth—an anachronistic perspective, since, as a child, the narrator had not yet been to Canada. The Canadian simile marks, then, not the child's perspective but the narrator's point of view; the text contemplates a Moroccan childhood from the vantage of someone who knows Canada, who has experienced such specific Quebecois moments as fall on Lake Beauport. Moreover, we learn from Chraïbi's autobiographical text *Le monde à côté* that the environs of Beauport have a sentimental significance for the author, being where, after weeks of exploring the province by car, he and his student Marie became lovers during a November snowstorm: "Nous étions là, elle au volant, moi à son côté, . . . à deux ou trois kilomètres du lac Beauport. . . . Elle mit le moteur en marche, passa les vitesses. Et puis elle s'arrêta. Sans nous consulter, sans même nous regarder, nous mîmes pied à terre. Et sans dire un seul mot, nous nous étreignîmes à ciel ouvert. . . . Longtemps plus tard, nous nous relevâmes. Nous étions transis de froid et de joie" (135–37).[24] The kitchen of *La civilisation, ma mère!* . . . thus converges, through the Beauport simile, with the rejuvenating hope Chraïbi describes experiencing in the Quebecois storm with Marie. As I suggested above, the closeness Chraïbi felt to Quebecois hosts was politically inflected by their revolutionary energy; so, too, this episode of amorous renaissance must be understood against a backdrop of political discussion. In fact, Marie is the young woman Chraïbi describes earlier in his memoir as introducing him to Quebecois politics. She is, then as well, at the wheel of her car, and she explains the Quebec sovereignty struggle to him: "Elle m'expliqua les méandres des enjeux sociaux, la démographie des Canadiens francophones (et catholiques) face à leurs compatriotes protestants et de langue anglaise, les programmes versatiles du parti québécois et du parti 'créditiste' qui misaient sur la jeunesse" (124–25). Even though Chraïbi was dismissive of his students' revolutionary attitudes, his associations of personal rejuvenation with Beauport cannot be separated from the political currents that were animating the province during his time there. Indeed, the Quiet Revolution made possible such socially revolutionary possibilities (revolutionary compared with the social norms of pre-1960s Quebec) as a young woman driving her older professor around the province, among other liberties. Chraïbi's decision to compare the *brasero*'s smoke, incongruously, to a fog in Beauport highlights the social and political Quebecois energies that motivated *La civilisation*'s ebullient fictionalization of his Moroccan childhood.

Another key comparison in *La civilisation* sustains the idea that Chraïbi employs Canada as a prism for understanding Morocco. Describing his joy at his mother's learning how to spell, the narrator writes,

> Elle apprenait avec avidité, inscrivant des syllabes et des mots sur ses paumes et, tout en préparant un de ses fameux ragoûts, elle consultait ses mains, disait à toute vitesse:
> —Oui, il faut que j'ajoute maintenant du sel. S.E.L, sel. Le sel. Ceci, c'est du sel.
> Et elle riait, vidait distraitement toute la salière dans la marmite. À moi seul, j'ai mangé tout ce ragoût: depuis lors, France, Yougoslavie ou Canada, jamais je n'en ai goûté de semblable. (68)

Here again, Canada serves as a point of reference as the narrator recalls his childhood.[25] Nowhere else, the narration implies, can excitement about learning be so striking, so memorable, as in the Morocco of his childhood for the mother newly liberated from her servitude. The oversalted stew represents the epitome of educational elation, unparalleled in Canada, and yet Canada functions as a necessary parallel, one in a trio of comparisons that underscore the exceptionality of his mother's learning. These metaphors link unlikely elements, relying on references to Chraïbi's time in Quebec to inject ideals of self-realization into the mother's story. Smoke becomes fog, which becomes rebirth; oversalted stew suggests that a Moroccan kitchen, unlike other, undersalted travel destinations, is a center of civilization.

Another aspect that makes *La civilisation, ma mère!* . . . stand out in Chraïbi's oeuvre is the contrast between it and his two other autofictive narrations of his growing up, *Le passé simple* (1954) and *Succession ouverte* (1979).[26] That it has Quebec as a social revolutionary backdrop helps explain why *La civilisation* constitutes such a radically upbeat, major-key transformation of the other two semiautobiographical novels, both of which portray the cruelties of the father-patriarch, the inability of the boy to come to terms with his father's harshness, and the servitude and mistreatment of the mother. Janice Spleth, explaining the relation between Chraïbi's three semiautobiographical childhood novels, writes that *La civilisation* is "the third novel in which the author works through the patterns of his own childhood and family relationships by means of the catharsis of fiction, and it is the only one in which the son's fulfillment is linked to the mother's emancipation and personal growth" (66). Spleth does not investigate what causes this transformation in tone, the narrative strategy that locates the son's fulfillment in the mother's emancipation. I propose that the sympathetic and hopeful narration of the mother's liberation arises out of the construction of an analogy with Quebecois social and political energy.

One of the features that links *La civilisation* and *Le passé simple* specifically is the comedic anthropomorphosis, in the later novel, of the earlier novel's much-debated parallel between French colonization and Moroccan tradition. As Marx-Scouras so cogently argues, *Le passé simple* portrays Islamic fathers acquiescing to colonialism and mirroring colonial oppression in their own treatment of women and children (135). This link is made flesh in *La civilisation* when the mother notices a resemblance between her husband and de Gaulle. When she catches sight of de Gaulle ("un grand impavide coiffé d'un képi") during a World War II–era protest she leads to the military barracks, the mother asks, "Qui est-ce?" Finally understanding that it is the general, she says, pensively, "C'est étrange. J'ai cru voir ton père. Il lui ressemblait trait pour trait" (92). The resemblance between de Gaulle and her husband, the patriarch of *La civilisation*, recalls the parallel Chraïbi had dared to draw in *Le passé simple* between colonizing France and the Moroccan patriarchy. The in-the-flesh resemblance tells, in comedic form, the same tale of parallel oppression, although *La civilisation*'s patriarch does not perform the same oppressive function as the patriarch of *Le passé simple*.

The depiction of *La civilisation*'s patriarch as generous and pliable in fact warrants investigation. His character, and the woman-led household of which he is a willing inhabitant, begins to make sense when considered in parallel with Chraïbi's experience in Quebec, as narrated in his memoir. Indeed, contrasting the patriarch's household in *La civilisation* with that of Chraïbi's nontraditional boardinghouse host family in Quebec City elucidates why the tone of *La civilisation* remains so light and comedic. Chraïbi had explored his memories of the oppressed mother of his childhood in *Le passé simple;* in *La civilisation,* by contrast, he uses memories of his host family in Quebec to create a new version of his childhood family, this time imagined from the perspective of Quebecois countercultural liberation. Chraïbi in *Le monde à côté* writes of his boardinghouse family,

> Elle s'appelait Mme Poulin. Elle avait la cinquantaine triomphante, le verbe méditerranéen ... elle avait adopté une petite fille prénommée Denise qu'elle chérissait de toutes ses entrailles. ... L'enfant avait à présent une quinzaine d'années, gauche et timide à souhait. ... Un homme mûr à point et d'une jovialité gastronomique venait souvent partager notre souper. Denise l'appelait tonton. Mme Poulin l'entraînait ensuite dans sa chambre dont j'entraperçus une fois le vaste lit à baldaquin. Le dimanche matin, il en sortait vêtu d'une

soutane pour se rendre dans sa paroisse du centre-ville. Je les aimais bien l'un et l'autre. (119–20)

The bon vivant priest, his widowed lover, and her teenage adoptive daughter, all living apparently free from the imposed righteousness of societal pressures, model a departure from traditional roles that, I argue, became the background for *La civilisation,* and for Chraïbi's manipulation of the couple and of gender relations in the Moroccan context. Joan Monego called the second half of the novel, the narration of the mother's liberation, "quite improbable,"[27] but the entire premise of a permissive, detached, unoppressive Moroccan patriarch contrasts so sharply with *Le passé simple*'s family setting that the entire novel, not only the second half, is permeated with this "improbable" quality. I would not call it "improbable" any more than I would *Le passé simple* (in neither case does realistic probability seem a suitable criterion by which to evaluate fiction), but it is true that *La civilisation*'s mode of imagining the Moroccan family is quite distinct from that of *Le passé simple.*

I argue that *La civilisation* reimagines the Moroccan patriarch in the mold of the easygoing Quebecois priest. Both of these characters hold a position of male power, but they are portrayed as tolerant and gentle, their drives and instincts for pleasure overwhelming and defeating the oppressive potential of their positions. Toward the end of *La civilisation,* for example, when the mother announces her departure for France, the father, ever the assenting and supportive spouse, answers meekly, "Oui, chérie" (127). Moreover, the patriarch in *La civilisation* accepts the reversal of gender roles without grumbling. He is happy to eat the meat-only meals cooked by his son Nagib as the mother studies frenetically for her exams. Nagib narrates, "Parce qu'elle avait des devoirs, des thèmes, des versions—des problèmes algébriques!—elle montait dans son bureau.... C'est ainsi que j'ai ceint un tablier de cuisine—oui—et que je nous ai mijoté, à Pa et moi, des plats où je mélangeais toutes les viands.... C'est Pa qui était content!" (111). The narration's asides, between dashes, intensify the gender-role reversal (the mother even does *math,* Nagib really dons an *apron*), accentuating the enormity of the father's acceptance of this state of affairs. But the visceral pleasure the father takes in discussing the meat proportions ("Combien de bœuf aujourd'hui?") and in seasoning his own food ("Passe-moi le poivre rouge") serves as a key to interpret his lenience; it is reminiscent of the Quebecois priest's "jovial gastronomy." The patriarch's relinquishing of his role as all-powerful leader of the household represents a radical departure from *Le passé simple*'s Seigneur, whose cruel hypocrisy permeates the narrative. *La civilisation*'s tolerant patriarch functions as a transposition of the priest, both men having made significant concessions in terms of their positions of power; the Quebecois priest's general tolerance and kind participation in the household function, ironically, as a pattern of wholesome existence in the world, a pattern that Chraïbi applies to his revision of his Moroccan childhood. Mme Poulin, too, as head of household and boardinghouse proprietor freed from the moral expectations that might be imposed by a Catholic society, generates a model for *La civilisation*'s earnestly independent mother. Whereas *Le passé simple* highlights the repressions the Seigneur imposes on his sons and his wife, *La civilisation* subordinates a compliant father to an increasingly assertive mother, modeling female liberation on Chraïbi's Quiet Revolution–era Quebecois experience. An intricate link between Chraïbi's experiences in Quebec City, both with his nontraditional host family and with his lover Marie, allows the imagination of postcolonial autonomy for Morocco as a female body freed from patriarchal and colonial bonds.

Chraïbi's experience of Quebec thus enables him to create a scenario of personal (and national) liberation in Morocco, subtly linking two francophone spaces and modulating the function of the French language as a colonial tool by making a story of transformation the gateway to learning that language. It is also important to consider to what degree the influence of Quebec enables Chraïbi to revise—that is, to fictionally rewrite—his Moroccan childhood. Because the child Driss Chraïbi did not have the experiential knowledge of Canada that the author Chraïbi had as an adult, understanding the function of Quebec in the semiautobiographical novel necessitates an investigation into the nature of fictionality. It is here, in comparing Chraïbi's childhood with the invented childhood of *La civilisation,* that we find a knowledge of Canada that the author has transferred to his narrator and, through him, to the eyes of the child character, the "petit loustic" who represents young Driss.

Previous scholarship has questioned whether *La civilisation* represents fact or fiction, as Yacoubi's previously noted argument for its categorization as "autofiction" demonstrates. Taking into account the Quebecois energies that inspired the novel brings this question into sharp focus. On the side of autobiography, noticing Quebec in *La civilisation* highlights the similarity of the narrator's well-traveled perspective to Chraïbi's; on the side of fiction, though, the idea of reimagining Morocco from the space of revolutionary Quebec signifies that Chraïbi's (or the narrator's) memories have been altered, are changed from how the child originally experienced Casablanca. Similarly, Chraïbi's foreword to the Quebecois edition, which avers *La civilisation*'s autobiographical nature, adds yet another layer to the autofictionalization of his life. He claims, "J'ai cherché à être le plus simple, le plus vrai possible. . . . J'ai limité le nombre des personnages de ce roman à trois: la mère et ses deux enfants, moi et mon géant de frère, Nagib" (7). His statement "J'ai cherché à être" (meaning "I tried to be," but with a sense of *searching* for simplicity and truth), however, brings the problem of truthfulness to a head: there is no simple, true telling of the past, only a search for it. Chraïbi's continued insistence on the factuality of his tale is suspect: "Les faits parlent d'eux-mêmes. Et j'ai toujours estimé mon lecteur. Pourquoi aurait-il besoin d'un mode d'emploi?" (7). Quite to the contrary, literary "facts" do not speak for themselves. As I will show, *La civilisation, ma mère!* . . . is not as simple and truthful as Chraïbi claims it is; its tone remains hard to pin down, and readers taking its autobiographical nature for granted fall into a trap, one that hides precisely the Quebecois influences shaping the fictionalization of Chraïbi's life-telling.

Early European critics of the 1972 Parisian edition, unaware of the novel's conception as a French-as-a-second-language textbook and oblivious to its Quebecois references, did read *La civilisation* as an autobiography.[28] One Swiss critic writes, for example, "Il s'agit d'une chronique autobiographique mais qui dépasserait le cas particulier du narrateur, puisque à travers son récit apparaît le processus de libération des pays d'Afrique du Nord et plus généralement du tiers monde" (J.V., in *Tribune de Genève,* April 21, 1972, quoted in *La civilisation,* Montreal edition, 132). This reading seems problematic; it is difficult to parse to what extent the text is factual and to what extent the initial primitiveness of the mother, described with vivid hyperboles, merely answers to early critics' expectations of "une mère du temps ancien" (Jean Sulivan, *Le Monde,* June 9, 1972, quoted in *La civilisation,* Montreal edition, 132). Are the French critics performing here the clichéd error of projecting onto an "Oriental other" their conceptions of a more or less distant past? And are their expectations for a primitive "Oriental other" blinding them to the possibility that the text hovers on the sharp edge of irony? Hédi Bouraoui's analysis corroborates this claim, showing that in the French reviews of *La civilisation* the Maghrebi character functions as a banal and racist stereotype: "Le ton de l'article est condescendant; nous sommes en face d'un racisme à fleur de peau puisqu'on suggère que le Maghrébin est émotionnel et intuitif plutôt que rationnel" (Bouraoui 68).

If the Quebecois text itself supports a double mode of reading, as both a language-learning tool and a model of self-liberation (personal and national), the European reviews of the text suggest that yet another, "colonial" mode of reading shaped the European reception of *La civilisation*.

The Quebecois origin of Chraïbi's conception of the novel and the Quebecois perspective that haunts it suggest a different readerly position, one that does not begin from a position of "othering" the Moroccan characters as primitive and backward but rather from a perspective of linguistic and cultural discovery mirroring the mother's own development. Paradoxically, the Quebecois edition, which makes explicit the novel's pedagogical aspects and thus participates in a sincere project of transformative education linked to Quebec's linguistic and cultural struggle, in fact facilitates an *ironic* reading of the novel that contrasts with the naïve autobiographical reading apparently accepted by early European critics. Indeed, the narrative of *La civilisation* warrants an ironic reading precisely because it self-consciously emphasizes the linguistic construction of the story, something the pedagogical footnotes further enhance; the narrative's tropes, wordplay, and uses of hyperbole complicate the "autobiographical" and "realist" reading because they tell a different story, the story of the author's (and the language student's) continual linguistic reflection and amusement.[29] *La civilisation*'s treatment of the mother and her transformation thus emerge as a tongue-in-cheek interpellation of Western racism, a gesture of hyperbole that pushes European readers to accept at face value the mother's exaggeratedly described exploits in order to demonstrate their ignorance and their belief in the so-called Orient's essential and absolute (primitive) difference. The Canadian learners of French, however, offer a mode of language-focused reading that brings attention to the linguistic games of the text and allows for a pause at its hyperbolic aspects.

Let us take as an example the *cocasse* story of how the mother makes clothes: she fleeces a sheep in her kitchen, cards the wool using her son's slate studded with needles, spins it with only her fingers and toes, and weaves it using four nails shoe-hammered into the wall. This process represents a series of Herculean tasks described with offhand humor and savant flippancy, a tone that should leave readers at least considering incredulity, as the tropological work of the narration makes clear: "On passait un nœud coulant au cou du mouton.... L'animal dansait n'importe comment, sans aucun sens artistique, en s'accompagnant de bêlements si plaintifs que je cherchais autour de moi qui pouvait bien jouer de la flûte de Pan. Le rire de Nagib valsait et tanguait dans toute la maison" (22).

The image of a sheep dancing "with no artistic sense" preposterously implies that sheep otherwise *do* have an artistic aptitude; the comparison between the sheep's bleating and the sound of a Pan flute is ironic because although the sounds are entirely different, Pan himself, Greek mythology's inventor of the Pan flute, is half goat; Nagib's laugh simultaneously waltzes and pitches through the house, incongruously juxtaposing images of elegant dancers and reeling boats. The farcical and hyperbolic apposition of these descriptions makes it difficult to accept them as realistic, as early French readers did, and yet this is precisely the scene on which those early critics drew to discuss the text's truth to nature. The primitiveness of the sheep-shearing process seems to have been a matter of fascination for them, corresponding to their expectations of North African life. Although I do not want to discount the know-how and constrained circumstances of women in 1930s Morocco, I argue that Chraïbi's witty tropes erect an ironic distance between the narrator and any kind of direct truth; they clearly structure the text as a *novel,* not as an autobiographical, anthropological, or ethnographical record.

Indeed, the novel is filled with moments of humor that point out the linguistically constructed nature of the fictional world it represents. For instance, the *brasero,* originally *"made in Germany"* (the inscription is given in English in the text—a foreign intrusion in Chraïbi's prose as much as the brazier is in the mother's home), needs repair. The mother patches it up, ripping her apron into long shreds and dripping the shreds in clay. The narrator describes this process using a comparison: it is "comme des bandelettes de momie," he asserts (39). The simile in turn permits a pun: Nagib, the elder brother, carves into the newly repaired *brasero:* "Made in Casablanca, Morocco. By Mummy" (39, in English in original). The brazier is "mummified" in two ways: it is repaired in such a way that it resembles a mummy, and it is repaired by the mother, the "mummy." The pun functions not within the characters' lives (the child Nagib did not know English) but only in the narrator's text. In addition, the "momie/mummy" pun functions as a wink addressed to English readers emerging into bilingualism; the interlingual pun is specifically addressed to Chraïbi's intended audience, English Canadian learners of French. Such literary gestures clearly show the "writerliness" and the constructed nature of the narrated story, steering readers away from more straightforward ethnographic readings of the text, and suggest the perspective from which an alternative reading can be attained: one such as language-student readers may be expected to have, one that struggles with and is thus attuned to Chraïbi's linguistic complexities and interlingual games.

I am not arguing that the characters' mother was unable to make clothes from scratch, or that Chraïbi's own mother was unable to do that, or that the life of a woman in 1930s Morocco was easy. In addition, what the psychologist Jeanne Fouet writes about *Le passé simple* can also be applied to some extent to *La civilisation:* "Le roman installe le principe de vraisemblance, réfute le recours au merveilleux, s'enracine dans une Histoire" (226). In other words, the novel itself is structured so as to *dare* readers to believe its verisimilitude. The problem is that the ironic potentiality of Chraïbi's text removes from readers the ability to perform a conclusive reading. The book appears guilelessly open and simultaneously invites readers to tentatively doubt its details (small and great), consistently denying readers the ability to discern absolutely the authentic from the ironic. In order to perform this ambivalent reading, readers must be aware of its ironic potential, of its tropological complexities and interlingual puns.

Let us contrast a European critic's reading to an educator's reading based on the Canadian pedagogical edition. Jean-Paul Colin, a critic for *Nouvelles littéraires,* a French journal sponsored by the Librairie Larousse, described *La civilisation* as "un texte dont la sincérité et la simplicité sont les qualités dominantes" (quoted in *La civilisation,* Montreal edition, 135). This reading illustrates the trap Chraïbi lays for his French readers. As a writer of Moroccan origin writing in French and in France, he promises (or rather, his position seems to promise) a "translation" of his world of origin, an explanation of it for his curious readers, which his irony then belies. By contrast, a review of the Quebecois edition penned in 1976 by Nadine Dormoy Savage focuses on the difficulty and complexity of the text rather than on its supposed simplicity. Dormoy Savage's pedagogical perspective, geared to readers of the *French Review,* the publishing organ of the American Association of Teachers of French,[30] leads her to read the text with an eye to its potential intricacies: "Driss Chraïbi est un écrivain de tout premier plan, dont le style vivant, coloré, plein de bonhomie et d'humour, est tout à fait original. Mais sa langue est difficile" (818). She recognizes that Chraïbi's "language is difficult," on the one hand meaning that his way of writing is out of reach for all but advanced students (which she states explicitly) and on the other hand suggesting that his manipulation of language is not straightforward. Dormoy Savage's evaluation points to the tonal complexity of Chraïbi's language use, which makes precisely the elements she lists—liveliness, color, cordiality, and humor—tricky to pin down. Her consciousness of the difficulty of the text for learners of French allows her to approach the novel from a place of (relative) cultural and linguistic open-mindedness. From this perspective, she sees and discusses the opacity of the text, its unanswered questions, its unstable tone and unstraightforward construction.

In a sense, then, *La civilisation* reaches its fullest ambiguous interpretive potential in the context for which it was imagined, that is, in the Canadian classroom of French for English speakers. Similarly, it is significant that Hédi Bouraoui's finely nuanced and insightful analysis of *La civilisation* emerges not only from a reading of the Quebecois edition of the novel but also from the perspective of a French department at an English-language Canadian university. The novel was made for Canada, for educators and their students to puzzle over, closely, with the doubts and hesitations of interlinguistic distance,[31] although it also baits racist readings based on stereotyped expectations. *La civilisation* sustains these two modes of reading that confuse the binary opposition between sincerity and irony. European readers read the text as sincere, unaware of the irony of the stereotypes that blind them; Canadian readers, by contrast (these reviews suggest), are earnest in their study of language, and Quebec is sincere in its solidary sympathy, and yet the North American readerly position allows for an ironic reading.

If we consider the mother as a metaphor for the nation, the double reading (earnest and ironic) poignantly reveals, beyond the hopeful tale of anticolonial liberation, a cynical calling out of a less than perfectly progressive Moroccan postcolonial society. Chraïbi's intended audience, the English learners of French for whom the book was commissioned, are in a better position to perceive the ironic potential of *La civilisation* than European critics, since their attention is necessarily drawn to language, to tone, and to the unstraightforward relation between language and any kind of "reality." They are thus better placed to understand the combined celebration and critique of personal and national liberation that the novel represents, able to read Chraïbi's underlying discontent with Morocco's achieved freedoms. Paradoxically, then, the Quebecois liberatory context both inspired Chraïbi's hopeful reenvisioning of his childhood and, in the mode of reading that this Quebecois context makes possible, casts doubt on the validity and even possibility of national liberatory processes.

In fact, Chraïbi's quality of linguistic and stylistic in-betweenness was precisely what attracted G. Roberts McConnell, who commissioned *La civilisation* as a pedagogical text. As Chraïbi remembers in his memoir, *Le monde à côté*, McConnell "appréciait les thèmes abordés dans mes œuvres; ils n'étaient pas parisiens. [Le] style non plus d'ailleurs. . . . J'avais trouvé un créneau entre deux mondes, voire deux conceptions du monde" (131). Chraïbi's idiosyncratic usage of French fulfills McConnell's expectations of it as a teaching tool because it brings attention to the construction of the French language beyond clichés and metropolitan linguistic habits.[32] Writing from the "créneau," the creative "gap" between worlds, allows Chraïbi to reimagine space and language. As he invents *La civilisation* for McConnell, a reader and editor eager for specifically this type of linguistic *dépaysement,* Chraïbi envisions yet another way to defamiliarize space and language: by imposing the effervescent energies of a metamorphosing Quebec onto his world of origin, the Casablanca of his teenage years.

The defamiliarization of French implied by *La civilisation*'s role as a language textbook, and by its Quebecois inflections of Morocco, establishes Chraïbi's outsider position and maintains his in-betweenness—the refusal to take a political side that nonetheless reflects anticolonial ideals. Because *La civilisation* in many ways seems to valorize the "West" over Moroccan tradition, French's alienating defamiliarization in an anglophone context is key to the novel's ability to establish the in-between neutrality for which Chraïbi's work strives. This neutrality is not always foregrounded in the plot. Indeed, the mother's transformation is based on her sons' *French* education, and Chraïbi's "Mot de l'auteur" claims that the sons have birthed her into the "occidental world" ("mise au monde . . . occidental" [8]). Moreover, the transformation culminates in the mother's ordering new home furnishings from France before departing for the metropole. As Nagib narrates, "Les meubles arrivèrent de France, lits, literies, vaisselle, appareils ménagers, produits d'entretien, miroirs sur pied, bibelots, tapis et carpettes 'manufacturés à Lyon.' Trois camions, je les ai comptés—et déchargés: les déménageurs étaient un peu trop brusques pour les choses de la civilisation" (110). Nagib's acceptance of France as civilization ("*la* civilisation") and the mother's affirmation of her desire to transcend her horizons by going to France ("j'irai à la découverte de cet Occident, j'ai besoin de faire reculer mon horizon" [127]) are structured along an axis that leads directly to, and privileges, the colonial metropole.

This distinct valorization of French culture as "civilization," however, is inverted when we consider that the text is simultaneously straightforward and ironic and that, diegetically, French is not the language in which the narrative unfolds nor the native language of its intended readers. Bouraoui draws attention to the ambiguous nature of the text when he writes, "Cette femme du Tiers Monde totalement libérée sur le plan individuel n'opte pas pour une culture étrangère comme semblent le croire les critiques. L'énigme du livre réside dans les changements perpétuels de toutes les valeurs en cours. L'ambiguïté de la technique narrative, le jeu des perspectives culturelles, la manipulation constante du réel et de l'allégorique, du fictif et du vécu, du littéral et du symbolique, toutes ces techniques de l'écriture indiquent que la position de l'héroïne n'est pas catégoriquement fixée dans un camp ou dans un autre" (65). A double reading that makes allowances for both realism and irony transforms the extravagant enumeration of French items of luxury into a critique of consumer capitalism suspending Chraïbi's text outside both the "Occidental" and the "Oriental" camp. The critique of commodity fetishism aligns not only with Patrik Pierson's rejection of the consumer goods proffered to him in *Mort au Canada* but also with Chraïbi's own choice of living in humble circumstances, which interviewers and friends who visited him at home never failed to mention.[33] The novel performs a similar ironization of Western consumerism without necessarily anchoring itself in Moroccan tradition, embodying Chraïbi's refusal to take sides overtly in his portrayals of the postcolonial francophone world.

The novel's seeming valorization of French also changes when we consider that the characters' language is Arabic, *not* French. The novel is a translation without an original. The translatedness of *La civilisation* emerges, for example, when the mother says of de Gaulle, "J'ai lu ses discours . . . Nagib . . . m'a traduit quelques-uns de ses discours" (90). Nagib adds, "On a un gros dictionnaire, on l'a acheté au marché. J'ai sué sang et eau, mais je suis arrivé à saisir l'essentiel" (90). The big dictionary emblematizes *La civilisation*'s inner translation; it reminds us that the novel presents, in French, (fictional) dialogues and lives that unfold diegetically in an Arabic linguistic and cultural context. And the native language of the novel's intended audience is not French, but Canadian English. In this context, Nagib's big dictionary stands as a metonym for the readers' relation to the text: they decipher French along with Nagib. Moreover, the French these English readers decipher is not an imperial language in the context of Quebec; rather, it represents an anticolonial position. The irony destabilizing *La civilisation* finds linguistic instantiation in this double valuation of French, which is at once the apex of imperial civilization and a tool for overcoming imperialism.

Quebec's Quiet Revolution–era effervescence is at the heart of the playfulness and ambiguity, as well as the interest in liberation, of *La civilisation, ma mère!* . . . The interactions Chraïbi describes in his memoir, in spite of his lack of enthusiasm for the political positions of his students, were inspired precisely by the energy of the revolution's social transformations—and they inspired, in turn, his imagination of Morocco as a place of radical (though tongue-in-cheek) transformation and hope. Like *Mort au Canada*, *La civilisation* emphasizes "universal" human transformations and attachments, but it also demonstrates that these ideals stem from and contribute to more locally political efforts in Quebec.

Even as *La civilisation* uneasily maintains Chraïbi's typical outsider position with respect to the colonial relation between Morocco and France, it takes a clear political stance in Quebec's cultural struggle. As a textbook of French for English speakers in the Canadian context, *La civilisation* decontextualizes French as a language of conquest in the Maghreb and reconceptualizes it as a language of resistance in Quebec, relativizing the importance of racial and regional difference for French speakers in the face of the global domination of the English language. Chraïbi's insistence on being considered "un écrivain de langue française" ("Je suis d'une génération perdue" 42) in this context takes on a new dimension. Writing in French is no longer a "betrayal" of his origins or a form of alienation from the self, as some journalists had implied. Quebec's revendication of French against English encroachment allows Chraïbi to detach French from its Maghrebi colonial context; it becomes a global (not only an imperial) language with struggles of its own to fight.

The understanding Chraïbi reaches of French's connective possibilities in Quebec is expressed precisely as a literary solidarity. In *Le monde à côté*, he describes his francophone literature classes as follows: "Ensemble, nous . . . placions [French-language Maghrebi texts] dans la Belle Province, dans le contexte de la langue française" (124). The verb *placer* here operates a striking juxtaposition of concreteness and abstraction: the material texts exist concretely in the hands of Quebecois students, and the shared French language allows for the abstract insertion of the texts' significance into Quebec's cultural context. Above all, it is the intimacy of sharing a language—Chraïbi and his students do this work "ensemble"— that transmogrifies material objects into signifying objects. What develops between Chraïbi and his students is a "prise de contact" (*Le monde à côté* 122), facilitated both by the fact that he is not French (125) *and* by the fact that he defends the use of the French language against North American English: "J'opposais la plus grande résistance à l'emploi de la langue des Américains qui avaient colonisé même l'anglais" (125). Chraïbi sympathizes with the linguistic nationalist causes that define his students' political imaginary (determining Quebec's future as a French-language nation politically independent from Canada and culturally distinct from France). Ultimately, for all his skepticism in the face of nationalist movements, Chraïbi nevertheless participates, through his Canadian novels, in articulating the northern province's nationalist struggle for independence.

# Coda

Francophone Nostalgias and the
Afterlives of Independence-Era Solidarity

THE FRANCOPHONE literary solidarity this book examines articulated itself during and because of the independence era, an era marked not necessarily by an accession of all territories to independence but rather by a fomenting hope for change linked to ideas of independence. That roughly thirty-year period revolutionized the ways French speakers across different regions of the world imagined themselves, their separate but somehow common spaces, and their hopes for a more progressive future. Independence, as this book has gradually revealed, means not just the end of colonialism in its various forms. It also means the elaboration of scaffolding to support new kinds of liberties—for those who labor under the yoke of capitalism, as Césaire's plays explore; for people of color, as Césaire and Aquin's works examine; for those oppressed by neocolonial political economies, as Beti's essay analyzes; or for those who want the right to self-expression free from identitarian limits, as Chraïbi's novels celebrate. Writers imagined these liberties through textual experiments with solidarity—or rather, through a poetics that strove to express the solidarities necessary for these liberties to be contemplated.

With the end of the era of hope for and belief in independence, by and large the textual flashes of solidarity connecting intellectuals across the francophone world also ended. In Quebec, the first referendum of 1980, which the sovereigntists lost, winning only 40 percent of the vote, marked a setback in terms of the province's imagination of itself as desiring independence, and it weakened the connections to other French-speaking (post)colonies. And long before this North American event, the realities of independence had fossilized dreams for postcolonial progress on the African continent. Faced in some parts with the failure to achieve independence and in others with the failure to enact the transformations expected to be contingent on and to devolve from independence, intellectuals turned their creative energies away from imagining new postcolonial solidary liberties. This meant generally revolving away from *engagé* writing, a movement Odile Cazenave and Patricia Célérier have traced for the African continent in *Contemporary Francophone African Writers and the Burden of Commitment* (2011). But it also meant a much more fragmented understanding of the French-speaking world: with the beacons of the independence struggles and victories buried under a range of totalitarian experiences and the perpetuation of concerted pauperization in Africa, and with the growing hegemony of capitalism, resistances reverted to localisms; a global narrative of change no longer seemed imaginable, and the solidarity to which it gave rise and by which it simultaneously was inspired dissipated. Texts postdating the independence era frequently attest to a sense of disillusionment, and yet, as shown below, independence-era textual solidarities did leave a mark on francophone cultural production.

This coda examines the afterlife of the poetics of solidarity in francophone independence culture by analyzing the Tunisian filmmaker Nouri Bouzid's 1997 drama *Bent familia*. The film, set in then present-day Tunis, constructs geopolitical imaginaries that complicate received spectrums of geographical liberties explicitly in terms of how those imaginaries model solidarity. Sisterhood and feminine friendship emerge here as new models for solidarity, complicating the masculine and fraternal models analyzed earlier in this book. Indeed, the solidarities imagined by Césaire and Aquin and those surrounding Beti's text were almost exclusively masculine, relying heavily on metaphors of fraternity, at its root a gendered principle. These gendered models of textual solidarity reflect the overwhelmingly masculine configuration that structured imperial power and that anticolonial discourse tended to appropriate, as discussed in the chapter on Aquin's *Trou de mémoire*. The genius of Bouzid's *Bent familia* is that it manages to commemorate these earlier (masculine) models even as it critiques them, looking back nostalgically on the independence era and aligning present-day (1997) solidarities with older articulations. The metaphorical imbrication of past, present, and future francophone solidarities forms a network of memory, relying on nostalgia for the moments, always in the past, of seeming possible (the instant of dispossession right before a revolution or the euphoric moment of independence itself) and projecting forward (the anticipation of the population-to-be symbolized by Aquin's unborn baby, for example). The telescoped juxtaposition of elapsed solidarities to new, living solidarities emphasizes both the tenuousness and the potential longevity of these charged affective bonds and begins to answer the question, Wither solidarity?

## Siting Images, Citing Worlds: Nostalgic Francophone Solidarities in *Bent familia*

The trope within *Bent familia* that performs a gesture of criticism coupled with nostalgic recuperation of the hopes of independence is the trope of interpictorial reference, the inclusion of preexisting (and independently signifying) Quebecois images within the film's setting. The film functions differently from the literary texts studied in previous chapters. The Quebecois images refer to past literary solidarities—which were expressed in songs and a play—of the long independence era, but within the film the images appear as frozen relics rather than actual articulations (spoken or written) of solidarity. They are muted vestiges rather than functioning instruments of hope for transformation, symbolizing the past of the solidarities that can be articulated in the protagonists' 1997 present.

*Bent familia*, although it is rooted in the ultralocal of 1990s Tunis,[1] featuring its crowded streets, shops, and apartment buildings, and although it is in Arabic rather than French, relies on francophone Quebec as a signifying part of its setting. It does so by planting posters of 1970s Quebecois cultural icons in its *mise en scène:* a much-larger-than-life photograph of Pauline Julien (1928–1998), singer and feminist-nationalist activist, and a playbill advertising Michel Tremblay's 1971 play, *À toi, pour toujours, ta Marie-Lou*. These Quebecois posters present a temporal palimpsest by pointing to the transnational hopes linking Quebec and the Maghreb during the era of the independences, thus commemorating the possible futures that went unfulfilled. In addition, the past solidarities serve as metaphors for the contemporary solidarities uniting the film's characters. But the posters' metaphorical significance, and consequently also the articulation of the film's solidarities, is complex. On the surface, the Quebecois posters seem to enrich the visual space with references to transnational francophone feminism, secularism, and non-heteronormativities (Tremblay is one of Quebec's pioneers in queer cultural production), aligning with the solidarities that the film's characters value. In fact, however, the posters' referents problematize these progressive values, suggesting that there may be no outside to the difficulties faced by the protagonists within Tunisian patriarchy. "Siting" the Quebecois images, or grounding them in the local specificities of their origins, means "citing" an entire world, or, in other words, referring to an imagined network of transnational crosstemporal francophone connections that couch the narrative of the film and define the significance of its solidarities.

Whereas Quebec represented a stretching of the limits of solidarity in the 1970s for Césaire, whose texts raise the issues of inequality and misunderstanding in interracial solidarities, by the 1990s, Bouzid's film suggests, Quebec's independence-era attempts to articulate itself as solidarily linked to the recent French postcolonies signifies asymptotically as a promising alternative to the history that actually unfolded, a history that swallowed the hopes of independence and offered instead a continuation of oppressive patriarchal-capitalist structures. The film recuperates the era of the independences and elevates its attempts to articulate francophone solidarities, idealizing these solidarities as commemorative of a moment when the Maghreb could have been radically transformed for the better—and when it served as an inspiration for Quebec, where, for example, revolutionaries modeled the Front de libération du Québec (FLQ) on Algeria's Front de libération nationale (FLN).[2] From the nostalgic perspective of Bouzid's 1997 film, then, Quebec's solidary past appropriations and aspirations represent a climax of Maghrebi international influence, an influence based on that moment of independence-linked anticolonial hope for progressive change.

At the same time that *Bent familia* highlights the idealistic promises of the independence era, however, the posters in the film bring into sharp focus the independence era's unresolved machismo and heteronormativity. Bouzid's film highlights the fact that the anticolonial solidarities of the independence era were masculine—and indeed, they were often articulated as brotherhood or fraternity. While some authors confronted this explicitly (Aquin's *Trou de mémoire*, for instance, constitutes in some ways a satire of the machismo of revolutionary discourse), nonetheless revolutionary anticolonialism was overwhelmingly constituted as a masculine position.[3] In contradistinction, Bouzid's film proposes sisterhood and feminine friendship as models of solidarity by exploring the support that three women oppressed by Tunisian patriarchal structures can offer one another. In exposing the fragile balance of their lives, Bouzid indicts the exclusively masculine solidarity of the independence era: its progressive program failed, his film shows, and its hopes for positive transformation were betrayed precisely in the domain of women's rights. And yet the international solidarities that the independence era fostered still hold significance for the characters and offer scaffolding on which to construct new solidarities—solidarities that, while still aspirational or asymptotic, redress some of the old gender imbalances.

In the previous chapters, I have analyzed the linguistic tropes and figures of speech that articulated solidarity and its limits, the "master tropes" of solidarity, metaphor and simile, which are linked to its abstracting mechanism. Of course, a film does not function the same way that a novel, a play, or an essay does; the mechanics of the tropes that signify solidarity in *Bent familia* differ considerably from those discussed in Césaire's plays and lectures, in Aquin's or Chraïbi's novels, or in the prefaces surrounding Beti's essay. It is important to take a moment to explore what form the figures of speech or tropes of solidarity take in a film format. In Bouzid's film, the main symbols for solidarity appear in *interpictorial references* (i.e., visual equivalents of *intertextual references*), representations that refer to other works of art and that function as complex metaphors for solidarities onscreen. These interpictorial references—visual quotations of images that, in the case of *Bent familia*, are linked to other art forms (a music album and a play)—attempt to imagine possible constructions of solidarity in a way similar to the way that tropes such as metaphors and similes function in the chapters of this book. What I call interpictorial references are linked to what Carla Taban calls "inter-images" (11); she defines these as simply images about other images, a slightly broader definition than the term I prefer, which emphasizes the citational quality of the images in Bouzid's film.[4] Taban cites the art historian Leo Steinberg, whose approach broaches the question of artistic intent: "In their traffic with art, artists employ preformed images as they employ whatever else feeds into their work. . . . The varieties of artistic trespass or repercussion (or whatever you call it) are inexhaustible because there is as much unpredictable originality in quoting, imitating, transposing and echoing, as there is in inventing. The ways in which artists relate their works to their antecedents—and their reasons for doing so—are as open to innovation as art itself" (quoted in Taban 13). I contend that Bouzid quotes images of Quebec (or introduces interpictorial references) in *Bent familia* because he is trying, on the one hand, to reanimate and also criticize the transnational solidarities of the independence era and, on the other hand, to make these old solidarities function as signifying posts for the new solidarities his film constructs. Bouzid's Quebecois posters represent a mute presence, however; they are not discussed or otherwise referenced in the film, offering visual meaning without the verbal articulation of the texts discussed in previous chapters. They represent muted vestiges of the independence-era solidarities in which the new 1997 solidarities take root, a silent francophone backdrop to the film's Arabic dialogues.

The new solidarities in *Bent familia* develop among three thirty-something women in Tunis in the face of patriarchal oppression. Aida, a Tunisian divorcée, is denigrated because of her marital situation; Amina, who went to school with Aida when they were children, is married to an abusive man; and Fetiha recently escaped the gendered violence of Algeria's civil war. The women's life situations exemplify a microcosm of Maghrebi political and social circumstances. Indeed, as children of the independences, Aida, Amina, and Fetiha represent test subjects for the experiments in statehood of the nations where they were born, Tunisia and Algeria; they are Maghrebi "midnight's children" of sorts. As women who grew up concurrently with and under the aegis of President Habib Bourguiba's Code du statut personnel (CPS),[5] Amina and Aida test the limits of this code of law, which aimed at instituting equality between men and women in an attempt to blend local specificity and "Western"—for Bourguiba, specifically French—progressive aspirations. Amina and Aida test these limits by trying to assert their right to divorce, to make choices for themselves, and to be in control of their movements. The results of the test are abysmal: *Bent familia*'s Tunis is portrayed as oppressively patriarchal, a betrayal of the potential represented by the possibilities of independence.

Within the film, the disappointments of independence are articulated through disappointments in gender relations. Aida *is* divorced, a right that devolves directly from the CPS, but she is ostracized because of this and under constant surveillance by neighborhood boys. Amina is married to an abusive husband who forbids her leaving the house, cheats on her, rapes her, and cannot begin to understand her unhappiness; nor does he consider it his duty to do so. Fetiha, a refugee in Tunis, is a child of Algeria's War of Independence, scarred by the sexual violence she witnessed in Algeria's civil war.[6] *Bent familia*, then, is an indictment of the reactionary forces that derailed the progressive hopes of independence. The three women struggle to achieve a balance between, on the one hand, the liberty of body and mind that they have learned is their right and, on the other, their desire for a place within a society that does not willingly grant women that liberty; they want to be free to make their own choices, and they want society to respect these choices. Their solidary friendship both nurtures and is fostered by this struggle.

*Bent familia* creates a kind of geographical spectrum to map the sites of this struggle, the tension between a legally guaranteed Tunisian right to equality and a reactionary social resistance to the granting of this equality. Elaborated through visual cues and dialogue, this geographical spectrum maps locations in *Bent familia* as representations of the human relationships they allow. In other words, the film construes space (the indefinite volume of air, objects, and structures that covers the globe) as a conjunction of places (humanly defined and delimited as signifying entities), each enabling a different kind of community and social exchange. From this array of places arises a spectrum of relative liberties, a kind of ranking according to social permissiveness.[7] *Liberty*, of course, is itself a relative term; here, it serves as an abstraction conjoining the hopes for progressiveness and gender equality represented (and disappointed) by Tunisian independence.

On a micro level, the characters' living quarters reflect and structure the relations that develop within their walls. Amina's opulent house in a wealthy suburb, for example, shines with hard, cold marbled surfaces mirroring the psychological distance that separates Amina from her husband and that confers on her a dependent, inferior status. By contrast, the place that allows the richest and warmest relationships is Aida's homely apartment. Alive with warm yellows and bright blues and cluttered with statuettes, lamps, books, snapshots, paintings, colorful fabrics, and posters (including the Quebecois posters), it constitutes a cultural and actual refuge for the women. Not coincidentally, the visual array carries significations that project onto an exterior map, extending the horizons of Aida's apartment. In other words, the objects and images in her apartment, reaching beyond the apartment's walls and beyond the national borders of the Tunisian state, represent yet other, external places on the geographical spectrum of relative liberty.

On a macro level, then, the film constructs a patchy global map that sketches out a spectrum of liberty. More an affective concept than a cartographical representation, this geographical spectrum of relative liberties at first glance orients itself along old colonial lines. For Fetiha, who lives in Aida's apartment while in transit between Algiers and Paris, a unidirectional mapping of relative liberties emerges as she relives the traumas of the civil war behind her and imagines, without any of the disillusionments that are bound to come with actual lived experience, the transformative liberty awaiting her in France. And when Amina first visits Aida's apartment, she pulls from a shelf a small book recognizable as a specimen of Gallimard's poetry collection and opens it with a wistful smile. On the one hand, the book arouses her nostalgia for her past, for the French education she received and the close friendship that used to tie her to Aida before her quarantine of a marriage. On the other hand, the book figures on the geographical scale of relative liberty as a stand-in for an idea of France as the place of predilection for francophone freedom.

France serves as a foil to anticolonial solidary imaginations in most of the chapters in this book; it also frequently is a multivalent or shifting signifier. In Césaire's plays, for example, and in his choice to articulate Martinique's departmental autonomy, France emerges as a participant in the imagination of antiimperial liberty only to double back as the enforcer of empire and neocolonial influence. For Mongo Beti, France is a second home, his country of (contested) citizenship, and the place of publication for his oeuvre in collaboration with the exceptional editor François Maspero even as it proves to be a place of censorship and neocolonial collusion with Cameroonian authorities. And for Chraïbi, France represents a first (and last) exile, a fruitful place to work and write in French, but it is paradoxically a context that tends to emphasize his non-Frenchness. The imagination of France as a locale of francophone freedom in *Bent familia* attests to France's continued presence in francophone articulations of interregional solidarities; France remains a linguistic, cultural, and political monument with which francophone imaginaries must contend.

In *Bent familia*, however, as in the other texts studied in this book, the valence of France's crucial role in the French-speaking world is contested. The two images depicting Quebecois cultural icons that appear in the midst of the apartment's artfully encumbered *mise en scène* disrupt any straightforward colonial pattern of affective geography, evoking places whose signifying value destabilizes the spectrum of relative liberties. France is no longer the monolithic signifier of imagined francophone liberty, nor can it and its (post)colonies be considered apart from or opposite one another. Quebec in some senses literalizes what Homi Bhabha termed the "Third Space," or the spatiotemporal disjuncture between the act of cultural enunciation and any immanent meaning that makes "claims to the inherent originality or 'purity' of cultures . . . untenable" (Bhabha 21). Quebec similarly makes impossible the hierarchical discreteness of France and its Maghrebi (post)colonies, a disruption that takes the shape of imagined anticolonial solidarities and their contemporary echoes.

## Locating Pauline Julien and the Feminisms of *Bent familia*

The first Quebecois poster to appear is a larger-than-life portrait of a warmly wrapped woman shown from the waist up, inscribed with the name "Pauline Julien." This is the cover image of the album *Femmes de paroles*, produced in 1977 by Pauline Julien, the Quebecois singer, feminist, and sovereigntist who lived from 1928 to 1998. The image opens onto another world; it represents an alternative place available to the film characters' imagination, mapping out a French-language geographical connection potent with social and political significance. It also serves as a visual metaphor (a symbolic pictorial reference) that teases out the meanings of *Bent familia*'s solidary relationships.

The portrait appears most importantly during a discussion in which Fetiha tries to persuade Aida's much younger sister, Dalila, to stop dating an older married man.[8] The poster anchors the perambulating conversation during which Fetiha tries to draw Dalila away from Aida's eavesdropping; the camera's panning and zooming leave Julien's portrait always partly cut off by the frame, first in the upper left corner and then in greater focus in the upper center of the scene. In fact, for a few moments Pauline Julien constitutes the only human figure visible, becoming the lone inhabitant of the screen and our visual interlocutor as her gaze appears to be directed at the camera. This poster haunting the border of Bouzid's shot clearly sets Quebec as an offscreen referent for the events onscreen. Florence Martin calls attention to the importance of the offscreen space in Nouri Bouzid's work, citing his claim that "the essence of cinematic language resides in the off-screen space, for the latter must be constituted in the viewer's mind without him seeing it. . . . The power of cinema lies in its ability to convey at once what is on-screen and what is off-screen" (Martin, "Maghrebi Women's Cinema" 26). As Martin points out, "The only way such a semantic approach can function is if the viewer recognizes, at the faintest hint, the off-screen reference to which the on-screen narrative is referring" (26). The question then becomes, how does Julien—and all she represents—signify as a point of reference for the solidary relationships that develop during the film?

In the spectrum of relative freedom, Pauline Julien as a figure for Quebec would make the northern province at first appear to be, like France, a place of relative liberty—because the province is a settler colony, because it is perceived as "white," because it is "Western," because it belongs to the so-called first world. But the image's quirky presence in Aida's apartment suggests that these dichotomies were never that clear-cut. The reversal of expectations of modesty in this scene, for instance, complicates easy taxonomies: Pauline Julien's autumnal accouterment, an oversized woolen scarf completely hiding her neck, stands out in the palpable heat of the Tunisian afternoon, and it contrasts sharply with the three characters' light dresses and slips, making it seem as though she, and not they, comes from a world where women's bodies are policed. In addition, Julien is no whiter than Aida, Amina, and Fetiha, confounding any classification based on racial characteristics; indeed, as discussed earlier, Quebec during the sixties was at pains to redefine itself as a colonial victim, problematically borrowing the discourse of anticolonialism and antiracism to label itself a land of "white Negros." Quebec here operates a softening of the border between the "West" and its colonial other, bringing into question the dichotomies that structure it. Furthermore, the poster's era, dating back to Quebec's Quiet Revolution and its transformation from a conservative, Catholic province dominated by English financial and political interests into a secular, politically left-leaning region legally enforcing the primacy of French and straining toward independence, highlights the contingency of the established order that posits the "West" as static and as essentially and permanently isolated from non-Western others. The poster of Pauline Julien disrupts and shows the inadequacy of the basic binary colonial paradigm opposing France to its African colonies as a model for understanding the francophone world: the geographical and temporal detour represented by 1970s Quebec suggests a much denser network of interregional relations and affects that bears out the observations made in the chapters of this book.

The poster functions in the demesne of nostalgia, harking back to Aida's youth. The significance it adds to the solidarities elaborated in the film therefore has much to do with retrospection. Concretely, the poster outlines the intergenerational chasm that separates Aida from her younger sister, complicating their sisterly solidarity. If Aida is a product of Tunisia's independence and a test subject for its promises of equality, she hangs on to its idealism, to the hopes it represented; keeping Julien's poster is a sign of this wistfulness. Her sister, Dalila, on the contrary, is a young profiteer in the struggle for women's rights: she represents a postindependence generation that takes for granted certain gains—she wants to have a career—and accommodates the patriarchal system to get the most from it, adapting to its devaluation of women in order to gain value for herself by accruing personal capital in the form of gifts from her older lover. Aida, in spite of her divorce, still sees marriage, a happy egalitarian marriage to a man one loves, as the ultimate goal not only for herself but for all women. Part of her enormous energy comes from the excitement of being in love, and even as she supports Amina's rebellion against her husband, she advises her against divorce. Dalila, by contrast, although conceding that she may eventually marry, in the meantime wants to use the power of her young body (in this scene revealed by a close-fitting half-mesh dress) to entice men into giving her what she wants until she can earn her living through a career. Her casual sex appeal, her absolute assurance in controlling her older lover's sexual appetite, and her desire for luxury form, for her, part of the life of a career woman, someone who can earn her own living and provide for herself and her family.

This is all shocking to Aida, for whom the model of the husband as breadwinner is so ingrained that she fears that Dalila will suffer because of her addiction to luxury once she marries a poor man; she is unable to imagine a woman comfortably earning her own living. Aida, for all her desire for liberty, cannot see her sister's choices as a form of freedom. In fact, when Dalila calls out Aida for her hypocrisy on the question of marriage (how can a divorcée preach marriage?), she could also reproach her with her relationship to M'hamed, Aida's married Palestinian lover. Aida's double standards suggest that she has largely accepted tradition. She sees herself as social refuse because of her divorce, which allows her the sad freedom of not being able to sink any lower, but she still holds on to an ideal of purity that she wants to apply to her younger sister. In this sense, Aida is not that different from Amina's parents, who, in another scene, want to marry off their youngest daughter in spite of her desire to continue her studies. Aida carries the weight of the failed promises of independence, the yearned-for equality that evaporated when she tried to exercise it. Dalila, much younger, is blithely unaware of these past hopes. She represents a generation that takes for granted simultaneously the contemporary system's limited successes and gross failures, a postmodern capitalist collage of values that entitles Dalila to refuse to make sacrifices. On the one hand, she expects society to allow her to succeed in a career; on the other hand, she acknowledges the patriarchal structures that allow the kinds of illicit relationships that she considers lucrative. The Pauline Julien poster symbolizes a past that defines Aida but predates Dalila and is irrelevant to her, thus crystallizing the values that structure both the two sisters' relationship and Aida's relationship to her friends Amina and Fetiha.

The Pauline Julien image, however, fits uneasily into the interstices of Aida and Dalila's conflict because of the complexity of what the poster stands for. In the opposition between the two generations of "liberated" women (Aida and Dalila), the poster and the collection of songs it represents stage an uneasy amalgam of romance and political emancipation. In this context, Pauline Julien aligns with Aida; the songs she interprets in

*Femmes de paroles* despise the exploitation of women but extol the virtues of heterosexual love. She intones earnestly (she was nicknamed "the passionara of Quebec") in "Non tu n'as pas de nom,"

> Que savent-ils de mon ventre
> Pensent-ils qu'on en dispose
> Quand je suis tant d'autres choses . . .
> Quiconque se mettra entre
> Mon existence et mon ventre
> N'aura que mépris ou haine.

And then in "Urgence d'amour," just as earnestly,

> C'est par amour
> Que nous changeons d'histoire
> C'est par amour
> Que nous changeons l'histoire

She represents a feminism defined by women who demand control of their bodies but who still believe in the structural power of passionate relationships with men ("Urgence d'amour" establishes the lover's masculine gender with adjectives such as *beau*), seeing heterosexual love as a motive power for social change. "It is out of love/That we change history," she sings.

For Pauline Julien, however, the emancipation of women is linked to the emancipation of Quebec as a cause of the political Left. In the 1960s and 1970s, she militated on behalf of imprisoned members of the Front de libération du Québec and toured Cuba and the Soviet Union, where her interpretation of Gilles Vigneault's proindependence anthem "Les gens de mon pays" drew ovations. As activist and artist, she participated in the 1968 Mouvement Souveraineté-Association convention, which saw the conception of the sovereigntist Parti québécois. During the October Crisis of 1970, she and her partner, Gérald Godin, were among the first arrested after the instantiation of the War Measures Act. She was a "porte-parole du pays à venir" (Desjardins 189); in the French press, during a series of concerts in Paris in 1974, she became equated with Quebec's independence (268). Internationally, she was known as a committed artist whose songs and harangues sometimes seemed too radical for her staid publics. The poster on the wall of the Tunisian apartment thus exemplifies the hopes of Aida's youth, symbolizing her "coming of age" as a freethinking, educated young woman full of the hopes inspired by independence. As not only a feminist but also a nationalist icon, Pauline Julien would have embodied young Aida's ideals.

By 1997, however, the tone of that poster becomes nostalgic rather than hopeful. On the American side of the Atlantic, Pauline Julien's dreams for a free Quebec miscarried, especially following the bitter 1995 referendum, narrowly lost by the sovereigntists and leading to the divisive disclosure of feelings of anti-Semitism and racism within the Parti québécois.[9] And in *Bent familia*'s Maghreb, Aida has discovered by 1997 that the equality she had hoped for in marriage is illusory and that the right to divorce comes with serious social consequences. So the poster of Pauline Julien interposes itself in the argument between the two sisters by supporting Aida's former hopes but also by memorializing them. The image constitutes both a figure for idealism and its haunting memory, and in this way it defines symbolically the complicated relationship that we see developing between Aida and her younger sister. Sisterhood here is fraught with the radically uneven expectations of women who came of age at different ideological stages in the evolution of women's rights; the poster signifies both the hopes of the past and their contemporary irrelevance, paralleling Aida's and Dalila's positions.

Contemporary (1997) solidarity branches out in multiple directions from the prism of the Pauline Julien poster. Between the two sisters, solidarity exists asymptotically as a tense conversation, and the poster helps articulate their differences. They share a deep intimacy in the heat of the sunshiny afternoon, and they wish for themselves and for each other happiness and fulfillment, but they cannot agree on the terms of this happiness or on the best way to reach it. The poster also represents a feminist solidarity, as I have discussed above, and a past transnational solidarity uniting anticolonial Quebec with the Maghreb, something I will return to below. Both these past solidarities are culturally expressed through a passionate and iconic voice, in a musical register. Pauline Julien's voice, deep and vibrant, and the melodies she interpreted had the ability to align people, like the Soviet concertgoers. (There is an entire other project to be developed around the music of solidarity or the solidarity of music.)

The muted visual representation available in the poster, as a signifier for the voice, simultaneously participates in that transnational musical-solidary movement and serves as a reminder of its extinguishment. Pauline Julien's significance is firmly rooted in the 1970s; by the mid-nineties she was suffering from aphasia, a condition limiting her linguistic ability, and refusing to accept its progression, she took her own life in September 1998, the year after *Bent familia* was produced. The disease that caused her to end her life—physiologically inflicted silence—plays out as a cruel irony for someone whose life represented, internationally, the musical articulation of so many freedoms. The poster in Aida's apartment, then, serves as a reminder of past solidarities and of their collapse. This reminder itself constitutes a transtemporal solidarity, suggesting connections between different moments in time. Césaire's plays about the Haitian Revolution, written during the heat of anticolonial struggles, performed similar interepoch solidarities. The very fact that the Julien poster's significance informs our understanding of *Bent familia* shows something about how literary (cinematic) solidarity is constructed: it relies on past constructions of solidarity. Solidarity exists as a network of memory, either explicitly (as it does here) or implicitly (think not only of Césaire's Haiti plays but also of Hubert Aquin's allusions to the slave trade as mark of international connection; Beti's Quebecois documentary filmmakers' montage of past censorships; or Chraïbi's emphasis on preserving French, a temporal orientation toward language). Francophone solidarity spans both space and time. And yet, although present articulations of solidarity recuperate older variants in their construction, they do not simply reaffirm these older solidarities' modalities; they build from them, attempt to correct their flaws, and introduce new concerns and tropes to express them.

## Finding Nonheteronormative Solidarities

The second Quebecois poster, again appearing first as a fragment of an image and gradually fleshing out into a poster fully signifying clear cultural, historical, and social referents, performs the work of introducing a new concept to an old solidarity. The poster, a playbill publicizing the 1979 production of the Montreal writer Michel Tremblay's 1971 play *À toi, pour toujours, ta Marie-Lou*, features a black-and-white photograph of four young women staring into the camera. These four figures are meant to represent the fictional character Marie-Louise and her three sisters. The play is set in 1961 and 1971, and the photograph dates back to the (fictional) forties, before Marie-Louise's disastrous marriage. *À toi, pour toujours* appears prominently during the scene when Amina, having abandoned her husband's house for several days, rebuffs an advance from Aida's musician friend Slah. The attempted kiss troubles Amina but also seems to give her new confidence in herself. The entire ambiguous encounter gains interpretive depth against the backdrop of the Tremblay poster, which shifts from being a meaningless fragment at the bottom right corner of the screen to become a looming presence as Amina breaks free from Slah's embrace. Like Pauline Julien's photo, the poster even fills the screen for a fraction of a second after Amina runs out of the frame.

The poster's photograph seems full of camaraderie, and the title suggests devotion; the image and words represent a nostalgic vision of the past as idyll. But as we know from Tremblay's play (in which the characters discuss the photograph), that nostalgia is rooted in a lie: indeed, the idyllic image of the four girls in tank tops masks a misery so deep that Marie-Louise married the first comer—Léopold, a poor chap from a family marked with hereditary insanity—in order to get away from it. And the photograph hides also the fact that the mother (the photographer) and her daughters were all "pognées," as Léopold calls it, what he considered frigid, frozen by a puritanical, Catholic fear of sex that makes the mere thought of being sexually approached terrifying and painful. The play gradually reveals that over twenty years of marriage Marie-Louise had sex with her husband (or as she put it, was raped) only four times and that after each sexual encounter she became pregnant. So the words "à toi, pour toujours" of the title, written by Marie-Louise to her husband at the bottom of the photograph featured in the poster, constitute a strange promise of nonpossession; marriage is eternal in the Catholicism of 1950s Quebec, but the possession is coerced and thus incomplete. Or rather, it is complete and absolute but unsatisfactory because it breeds reticence, resentment, fear, and pain. The false innocence of youth, false because the fear of the carnal always already haunts the photographed girls' half smiles, highlights the hopelessness of Amina's position in the context of *Bent familia*. Any hope for change and even the youthful energy she remembers from her maidenhood are bound to be false in a system where women's pleasure and liberty are at the mercy of men and religion. In this light, Slah's advances do not liberate Amina or expand her self-worth but instead typify the kind of power granted to men, and the intimate solidarity that develops between Amina, Aida, and Fetiha is ever so fragile.

*À toi pour toujours,* haunting the solidary all-women friendships of *Bent familia*, constitutes a scathing critique of heterosexual normativity and the social and religious institutions that perpetuate its hegemony. Marie-Louise and Léopold's devastating relationship, with its forms of nondesire and repulsion, queers the hetero couple that Catholic Quebec required. Léopold's imagined alternative lives reinforce this queering. He tells Marie-Louise, "Moé aussi, si j'aurais su, j't'aurais pas mariée! J's'rais peut-être heureux, à l'heure qu'y'est! Dans l'armée . . . ou en prison . . . mais ailleurs, ciboire, ailleurs!" (40, ellipses in original). Léopold's hopeful counternarratives (the army, prison), on which he expounds in joual, the working-class Quebecois French spoken by the play's characters, happen to be two arenas among the array of options available within Catholic society that would have afforded him constant male companionship; Léopold regrets the homosocial relationships that his marriage has made impossible. À toi, pour toujours can here be read as an experiment in queering Catholic Quebec, showing the emptiness of the obligatory marriage's heteronormative promise.

Within the wider context of Tremblay's oeuvre, À toi, pour toujours inserts itself in the genre of the cycle of Les belles-soeurs, a series of works depicting "members of the Quebec working class grappling with an oppressive family life: la maudite vie plate" (Pigeon 28). But this maudite vie plate coexists with its contrapuntal opposite, the demimonde, or the fringes of society in which Tremblay sets his other works, portraying "characters who had managed to escape from the tyranny of the family, . . . social outcasts" (Pigeon 30). The hatred and repression of a life like Marie-Louise and Léopold's structurally necessitates the existence of an outlet, a marginal world affording individual freedom to those willing to brave society's rejection. À toi, pour toujours offers a glimpse of this marginal world as another model of solidarity, still structured within (and critiquing) the play's constraining social structures. Marie-Louise lives marriage as complete isolation, but her expression of this isolation raises other possibilities: "Nous autres, quand on se marie, c'est pour être tu-seuls ensemble. Toé, t'es tu-seule, ton mari à côté de toé est tu-seul, pis tes enfants sont tu-seuls de leur bord. . . . Pis tout le monde se regarde comme chien et chat. . . . Une gang de tu-seuls ensemble, c'est ça qu'on est!" (50). From her perspective, the social and Catholic pressures that make sex both necessary and sinful effect this total fragmentation, with each unit surveying the others with the hatred of cats and dogs. And yet the suggestive phrase *une gang de tu-seuls ensemble,* if we transplant it out of Marie-Louise's hatred-filled living room, emphasizes the companionship of outsiders within a limiting, heteronormative landscape—something like the solidary experience of the three protagonists of Bent familia. The ephemeral community of women and children living together in Aida's apartment, compelled into symbolic parallelism with À toi, pour toujours, founds a paradigm for solidary refuge against the pressures of patriarchal Tunisian society.

The reference to Michel Tremblay's play, however, also accentuates the portentousness latent in Bent familia's ambiguous conclusion, in that it furnishes new symbolic meaning for the appearance of Amina's little red

Peugeot at the end of the film. A car features thematically in the ending of *À toi, pour toujours,* which climaxes in the revelation of how Marie-Louise, her husband, and their young son Roger were killed: Léopold, deeply depressed by capitalist exploitation and abject penny-pinching poverty, not to mention his hopelessly unhappy marriage, took his wife and Roger on a car ride and purposely slammed into a pillar of the Metropolitan Highway in Montreal, a symbol for the urbanization of their despair. This murder-suicide figures particularly ominously against Amina's hopes for change because in her case as well a car serves as the agent of transformation: her husband, Majid, appears at Aida's apartment, where Amina has been hiding for a few days, and returns the car keys and driver's license that he had earlier confiscated in an attempt to limit her movements. In this moment she appears to triumph completely: her friends Fetiha and Aida congratulate her as she exchanges parting tokens with them. But the structural setup of the husband's delivery of keys articulates the couple as triangulated, with the car inserted as the locus of both contention and interaction. And indeed, the film ends with a shot of Amina's husband waiting at the bottom of the stairs to talk with her—"in the car," as promised.

The relation between *À toi, pour toujours*'s vehicular murder-suicide, which the poster offers as an offscreen referent, and *Bent familia* is not so straightforward as to imply that Majid will kill Amina, but it does suggest that attempts to achieve greater liberty will reach a limit in men's ownership of women, of capital, and of the bases of all relationships. In fact, it turns out that even Amina's token exchanges with Aida and Fetiha, although generous and symbolic of a continued spiritual and even physical link (Aida says, "Keep my dress; it'll give me an excuse to visit you"), rely entirely on a masculine structure of providing. Like Marie-Louise, who has to justify to her husband the six extra cents she spends on "crunchy" instead of "smoothy" peanut butter, Amina cannot have earned for herself the bracelet she gives Fetiha because she does not work except as Majid's wife, and Aida's dresses, we know from the earlier conversation with Dalila, have been bought with moneys given to Dalila by her married lover. Can these three women be considered to be revendicating their freedom from ties to masculine power by exchanging such tokens? Perhaps, but the exchange itself is only possible because of a structure of masculine power revolving around the possession—sexual and economic—of women's bodies. *À toi, pour toujours* as an offscreen referent devastates the possibilities for triumph and hope that *Bent familia*'s final scenes, in their ambiguity, seem to foster; the gift exchange articulating the solidary connection between Aida, Amina, and Fetiha is poisoned, as the interpictorial reference to Michel Tremblay's play highlights the destructiveness of the patriarchal structure on which the exchange rests.

Telescoping out from the interpictorial signification of the poster, the latent darkness that *À toi, pour toujours* brings out in *Bent familia* helps inscribe the film in a particular filiation of *engagé* cultural production. Michel Tremblay's play brings to life an inescapably bleak world of repression, exploitation, and resentment, but like much of Tremblay's work, it does so in the service of a militant social critique. Far-reaching and iconoclastic, the critique in *À toi, pour toujours* takes aim not only at the Catholic system of oppression and its complementary heteronormative regime but also at capitalism, which Léopold experiences as a mechanizing, alienating force driving him to destroy his family: "Hostie! Toute ta tabarnac de vie à faire la même tabarnac d'affaire en arrière de la même tabarnac de machine! . . . Tu viens que t'es tellement spécialisé dans ta job steadée, que tu fais partie de ta tabarnac de machine! C'est elle qui te mène! . . . Pis à part de ça, c'est même pas pour toé que tu travailles, non c'est pour ta famille! . . . Une autre belle invention du bon Dieu! Quatre grandes yeules toutes grandes ouvertes, pis toutes prêtes à mordre quand t'arrives, le jeudi soir!" (28). Léopold's misery anthropomorphizes the machine on which he works and reduces his family to a many-mouthed monster, a hungry machine. Léopold's complaint, whose rhythm of Quebecois *sacres* decelerates and peters out as he sums up the tale of his workweek with payday, imitates the tempo of industrial capitalism, whose beating pulse he experiences with such violence. Since by 1997 capitalism has all the trappings of hegemony, however, the critique of that socioeconomic system is subdued in *Bent familia*. The political theorist Alain Badiou marks the paces of the dialectic that has led to this hegemony:

> Because it has ended in failure all over the world, the communist hypothesis is a criminal utopia that must give way to a culture of "human rights," which combines the cult of freedom (including, of course, freedom of enterprise, the freedom to own property and to grow rich that is the material guarantee of all other freedoms) and a representation in which Good is a victim. Good is never anything more than the struggle against Evil. . . . As for Evil, it is everything that the free West designates as such, what Reagan called "the Evil Empire." Which brings us back to our starting point: the Communist idea, and so on. (2)

Bouzid's film reflects a world that is missing a leftist escape option, an option still very current and imaginatively productive during the independence era and the heyday of Tremblay's play. Although it could be argued that the conservative patriarchy that so constrains the women's lives in *Bent familia* coincides with a misogynistic system of accumulation of capital, these anticapitalist barbs remain subordinate in the film to a complex critique of the social and cultural effects of male dominance. So the poster in a way represents a nostalgia for a time when an openly anticapitalist critique formed part of mainstream popular culture; linking Bouzid to Tremblay is a kind of metasolidarity in a struggle that Bouzid imagines as common to both of them but that he understands, in 1997, they may have lost.

*Bent familia*'s various models of solidarity thus articulate solidary connection as asymptotic and abstract. Sisterhood promises intimacy but presents intergenerational misunderstandings. Even the companionship allowed by relocating to the margins of heteronormative, patriarchal society, as imagined in the phrase *une gang de tu-seuls ensemble,* although it affords moments of rich solidarity to Amina, Aida, and Fetiha, proves to rely on and thus be threatened by a system of providing very much rooted in patriarchal capitalism. And yet, the tropological presence of 1970s Quebec through interpictorial reference suggests that there is a thread linking these fragile 1997 Tunisian solidarities to past constructions of solidarity, themselves fragile and asymptotic. Rather than indicating the end of the currency of a poetics of solidarity with the close of the independence era, then, *Bent familia* asserts the afterlife of this poetics; it changes but survives. Kristin Ross writes, citing the Communard Élisée Reclus, "Solidarity . . . extends not only to one's living associates but to the dead as well—it exists 'between those who travel through the conscious arena and those who are no longer here'" (127). The tropological experiments with articulating French-language solidarity survive, illuminating a constellation of solidary clusters across time and space,[10] even as the nature of that solidarity alters.

The presence of the two Quebecois posters in Aida's Tunisian apartment implies a very specific solidary transtemporal French-language map—and this even though the characters speak Arabic. The images of Pauline Julien and *À toi, pour toujours* suggest an imbrication of Quebec with Tunisia's past, or rather of a past Quebec with Tunisia's 1997 present. The epoch of the posters, together with the sovereigntist leanings of Pauline Julien and Michel Tremblay, anchors the Quebec-Maghreb link in the era of independences that transformed both regions. As this book shows, the international connection runs deep: Quebec's participation in the anticolonialist and nationalist foment of the sixties and seventies was to a surprising extent inspired by anticolonial theory and practice on the African continent. Pauline Julien herself famously interrupted a speech at the 1969 Niamey international conference of francophonie with cries of "Vive le Québec libre!," symbolically bringing back to Africa a cause that was motivated in part by Africa's successes and insights. In this light, the posters immortalize a moment when the hopes of a newly independent Maghreb inspired revolutionary imaginaries elsewhere. The Quebecois images on the walls of Aida's apartment are something like the landmarks in Irish atlases described by Dudley Andrew in his article "An Atlas of World Cinema": "openings that allow [viewers] to tunnel into a past, in what amounts to an historical dictionary of the earth" (Andrew 16–17), or at least of the possible futures imagined on that earth. In addition to being reminders of international feminist solidarity, the posters represent something of a flattering mirror of the "new Tunisia" that *could have been,* that could have come to life with the end of colonialism, at that moment of immense potential and transformative hope. The discrete places and cultural events suggested by Aida's Quebecois posters morph into a kind of francophone spacetime, a relational universe integrating a network of memory that haunts the 1997 present, in this particular case with nostalgia for progressive hopes—a bittersweet figuring of francophone synchronicity across space as always in the past or future.

And yet, it is worth noting that the francophone spacetime of *Bent familia* recuperates past articulations of solidarity to enrich contemporary ones. I use the term *spacetime* as fruitfully delineated by the geographer David Harvey to mean a relational concept: "Matter and processes do not exist *in* spacetime or even affect it. . . . Space and time are internalized within matter and process. . . . It is impossible to disentangle space from time. They fuse into spacetime. . . . Memories and dreams are the stuff of such fusion" (137). Memories and past dreams are indeed the stuff of Bouzid's imagined solidarities across the space and time of global francophone history. Yet, in spite of francophone solidarity's focus on past moments of seeming possible and of hopeful projecting forward, there is something absolutely *present* about each articulation. It may refer to the past, it may refer to an imagined future (and, this book shows, as a rule it does one or both of those things), but the actual articulation, the tropological experimentation, is rooted in a specific contemporariness. Césaire's *Christophe* exhumes the circumstances of young Haiti's untenable position within global capitalism and shows its relevance not only to contemporary anticolonial struggles but also to Césaire's own relationship to the PCF. Aquin's *Trou de mémoire* anticipates the population to be, symbolized by Rachel Ruskin's unborn baby, but it roots its referents in contemporary Montreal revolutionary activities. Each chapter's author, like the filmmaker Bouzid, is concerned with struggles of an extreme contemporariness. Articulations of solidarity, the *poetics* analyzed in this book, asymptotically bridge the gap between solidarity's rootedness in the present and its structural need to refer to the past and to possible futures.

Literary (cinematic) solidarity's network of memory across francophone spacetime makes sense as a metaconstruction uniting the various articulations of solidarity analyzed in this book. Indeed, a network of memory functions as an abstracting mechanism similar to solidarity's (and language's) own modes of operation. Such a network presents a way to understand contemporary circumstances by culling from them whatever can serve as common ground with remembered circumstances and dreamed circumstances, cobbling together an edifice of imagined similarities and parallels conjoined by an affect of engagement—an edifice of solidarities. The independence era, through the lens of this network of memory, emerges as a particularly fertile period for articulations of solidarities, but the work of solidary poetics reaches beyond. The practice of solidary reading is the mode offered by *The Quebec Connection* to recover the past's unrealized anticipated futures, to begin to delineate the richly textured network of interlinked articulations of solidarity. Solidary reading, as this book shows, embraces and allows full expression to the text's imagined solidarities, while also revealing their limits and limitations, their failure to fulfill the asymptotic ideal for which they reach.

The question of language, finally, is the piece of *The Quebec Connection*'s puzzle that remains to be put in place. *Bent familia* brings this question to a head because although the French poetry book and the Quebecois posters suggest the importance of a shared French language in Tunisia's recent past, the film itself is in Arabic. It is considered to belong, by a consensus general to African film studies, to the francophone corpus because, as Roy Armes has explained, "those who write about African filmmaking . . . tend to use the shorthand of the language of the colonizer: anglophone cinema, francophone cinema, lusophone cinema" (11). Of course, *Bent familia* fits the pattern of many African films (a pattern that only reinforces the taxonomy Armes describes) in that it was coproduced by Tunisian and French companies (Cinétéléfilms in Tunisia, Lucie Films and La SFP Cinema in France). But in addition to these material conditions of production and to the questionable scholarly practice of perpetuating colonial divisions, the film itself is clearly invested in making cultural French-language-based connections—among them the glimpses of Quebecois posters—regardless of the Arabic that is spoken throughout. Quebec's past relevance to Tunisia was determined in part by their shared linguistic experience, which was intimately comingled with their anticolonial experience. And even if Aida, Amina, and Fetiha's relationships are articulated in Arabic, these contemporary (1997) solidarities are still tied to older, French-language solidarities. The anticolonial legacy raised against French colonialism continues to define articulations of solidarity. The example of *Bent familia* suggests that the French language endures, through the network of memory of past solidarities, and that it connects descendants of France's deep imperial history. But as past francophone solidarities continue to define current ones, conversely, the bundle of transtemporal solidarities also continues to work on the French language. In *Bent familia,* French-language solidarities are symbolically enmeshed with lived Arabic solidarities, suggesting the artificiality of fixed borders between languages. And the joual of Tremblay's anticapitalist, antipatriarchal homily haunts and distorts the "Frenchness" of the poster's image, stretching the signifying patterns of French even as it contests the social structures from before the 1789 revolution that France imported to the New World and bequeathed to the settlers who remained there after it relinquished the territory. The French language generates solidarities even as these solidarities regenerate the French language, slowly but certainly.

# Notes

**Introduction**

1. I am not the first to comment on the identification of Quebecois militants with non-Quebecois causes. The incongruous figure of a white Quebecois activist on a human-rights panel concerning an imprisoned African journalist, for instance, makes a comical appearance in Akin Adesokan's brilliant satirical short story "Knocking Tommy's Hustle" (2010).

2. Indeed, borrowing a militant anticolonial discourse was necessary to bring the idea of nationalism in line with progressive, leftist ideologies at a time when nationalism itself had been discredited by fascism in Europe and by Quebec premier Maurice Duplessis's conservative, reactionary patriotism (see Roy 34).

3. For a thorough examination of the emergence and late 19th- and early 20th-century political applications of the word *solidarité* within France, see Marie-Claude Blais's *La solidarité*. Blais's history focuses not on (anti)colonialism but rather on metropolitan French politics, arguing that solidarity emerged as a postrevolutionary concept to define French citizens' social relations as free and equal individuals.

4. The term *race* in the context of this study is used to refer to a sociolinguistic identifier that is embodied without being biological, essential, or innate; it is socially constructed through perception and structures of knowledge.

5. See the endlessly useful site of the Centre national de ressources textuelles et lexicales (CNRTL), https://www.cnrtl.fr/etymologie/solidaire.

6. For a discussion of this early modern shift to an imperial world system, see Jacques Lezra's recourse to Immanuel Wallerstein in his examination of the image of the "stage Turk" in early modern discourses (Lezra 164).

7. Featherstone argues similarly that "solidarities . . . [construct] relations between places, activists, diverse social groups," turning the focus of solidarity studies away from "likeness" and instead toward "the active creation of new ways of relating" (Featherstone 5).

8. In a broader context, the Canadian scholar Northrop Frye writes that "all our mental processes connected with words tend to follow the structure of the language we're thinking in" (72).

9. For a discussion of the Abbé Grégoire's abolitionism in light of the events in Saint Domingue, see Jean-François Brière; see also Sepinwall.

10. See Walsh 52.

11. For a history of anticolonialisms in France and in France's colonies in the interwar period, see Derrick; Dewitte; and Liauzu.

12. Vallières narrates the story of his activism and his imprisonment in *Nègres blancs*. See also part 2 of Louis Fournier's history of the Front de libération du Québec, *F.L.Q.*, or Daniel Samson-Legault's 2018 biography of Vallières, *Dissident—Pierre Vallières*.

13. David Austin has shown that Vallières later (in the 1990s) made explicit his antiracist stance, trying to redefine his use of *whiteness* and *blackness* as metaphorical rather than physiological. In the context of the late 1990s, Vallières was opposing himself to the Parti québécois's racist exclusionism surrounding the 1995 referendum on national sovereignty, to which I will return in the coda (Austin 71).

14. This black-white solidarity, and Quebec's solidarity more generally with African and Caribbean decolonization as well as with African American Black Power movements, goes against the grain of what the political scientist Juliet Hooker calls "the racialized contours of the politics of solidarity—how the social fact of race shapes the practice of solidarity" (Hooker 4). Hooker's project refers more broadly to democratic social formations and social justice than does *The Quebec Connection*, which isolates solidarity as an intellectual and cultural phenomenon, and yet the solidary expressions considered in this book do diverge significantly from broader movements of political alliance based on social constructions of race in that they seek to express transracial solidarities.

15. Alain Badiou in *The Communist Hypothesis* makes a similar connection between politics and poetics: "If politics is, as I think, a procedure of truth, just as poetry can be, then it is neither more nor less inappropriate to sacralize political creators than it is to sacralize artistic creators" (151).

16. Nick Nesbitt, in an extended discussion of Glissant's *Discours antillais*, points out that "Glissant's late texts [such as *Traité du tout-monde*] perform a symptomatic slippage from [the] affirmation of the aesthetic apperception of totality as a *prelude* to political action, to passages that '[give] the impression that this poetics is sufficient unto itself and, as a consequence, that it is not politicians, or people armed with principles, who will be of the most help to us in our dealings with the forces of globalization and Empire, but poets'" (*Caribbean Critique* 238, citing Chris Bongie's *Friends and Enemies* 337). I do not discount this oscillation between politics and aesthetics in Glissant's work. The particular passages I quote in the introduction and below, however, are drawn from a lecture Glissant gave at the Congrès du réseau des villes refuges in 1997, in which he makes explicit the seeming contradiction between his elevated definition of

*Relation* and the concrete political work of the congress: "Il paraît contradictoire d'employer ce terme, une Poétique, à propos d'une entreprise, le réseau des Villes refuges, qui a requis et qui nécessite encore tant d'aménagements administratifs, de décisions institutionnelles et appelle à surmonter tant de barrières dressées par les usages. . . . Mais je me porterai à cette audace. Car il ne s'agit pas ici et seulement d'une démarche humanitaire, quoique la chose eût pu se suffire. La Ville refuge . . . entretient avec l'hôte . . . des rapports de connaissance mutuelle, de découverte progressive, d'échange à long terme, qui font de cette entreprise un exercice véritablement militant, une participation active au rendez-vous généralisé 'du donner et du recevoir'" (Glissant 249). The francophone solidarities of the independence eras similarly bring together aesthetics and politics in their projects of imagining connections and political formations.

17. In her beautiful commentary and translation of Roland Barthes included in *This Little Art,* Kate Briggs quotes, "'Attention! When I speak of these writer-heroes, *I am identifying-with, not comparing-myself-to.*' There is a difference, insists Barthe: 'the great writer, like Dante, is not someone to whom one can compare oneself, but whom one can, and one wants to, more or less partially, identify with. (I don't have the right to compare myself with Dante but I have the right to identify with him)'" (179, emphasis in original). Briggs channels Barthes to establish the right to identify with others, quite apart from the question of comparison to others; as we will see, however, the tropes of solidarity sometimes blur the line between identification and comparison.

18. Lawrence Wilde in *Global Solidarity* contests the qualifier *utopic* that marks totally inclusive solidarity as an asymptotic ideal; he proposes instead a new radical humanism that attempts to lay the groundwork for the realization of global solidarity. Wilde's theorization (he offers a thorough overview of theories of solidarity) is oriented toward the realizability of solidarity rather than toward its philosophical or linguistic articulation as a concept.

19. Wilde also comments on this dual nature of solidarity, writing that "as well as being realized in multiple forms of association, it is felt as an inward pull, as an empowering affective force" (1).

20. *Master tropes* is a term Hayden White borrowed from Kenneth Burke to refer to "the archetypal form[s] of discourse itself," namely—in White's case—metaphor, metonymy, synecdoche, and irony (White 5, 12).

21. Similarly, Rachel Mesch writes in a different context, "Where language works toward precision, narrative allows for depth and complexity. Indeed, stories are a way to use language to express that which exceeds language" (10).

22. Writers and scholars have problematized this way of conceptualizing the field, proclaiming, for instance, the "death of francophonie" in the *Littérature-monde* manifesto of 2007. See Dominique Combe's productive valuation of the manifesto and of the edited volume that accompanied it.

23. The use of the term *francophone* must be context relevant. For example, Florence Martin, discussing a later period of cinema production in the Maghreb,

is quite correct to claim that the term *francophone* loses valence and significance in that context (Martin, "*Cinéma-monde*" 466), but in a (post-)French imperial 1950s–1970s sphere centered on Quebec, *francophone* is applicable and useful, whatever criticism may have been brought against it in other contexts.

24. Numerous recent studies problematize academic uses of *francophone* and *francophonie*. See, e.g., *Transnational French Studies*, edited by Alec G. Hargreaves, Charles Forsdick, and David Murphy; Lydie Moudileno's chapter in *Antillanité, créolité, littérature-monde*; Christopher L. Miller's chapter in *French Global*; and Nicolas Di Méo's chapter in *Literature, Geography, Translation*.

25. With the term *colonizing trick*, Kazanjian refers to the divergence between notions of equality that structure the American national myth and the actual racial inequalities and imperial tendencies revealed in eighteenth- and nineteenth-century texts.

26. Édouard Glissant, in *Poetics of Relation*, describes how "scales of value" are used to appraise usage of French: "a distinction is made between *la francophonie* of the north, the French spoken in France, Switzerland, Belgium, or Quebec; and *la francophonie* of the south, everything else" (114). Glissant's interest in linguistic distinction here steers his argument away from both the European assessment of Quebecois French as a dialect requiring translation and the racial dimension that is perceived to distinguish the "north" from the "south"—elements this book will take up as focal points.

27. An exception is the label "francophone cinema," which, in an incongruous but real extension of the meaning of the word *francophone*, includes cinema from the former French colonies in languages other than French—Arabic, Wolof, Diola, etc. I return to this subject when I discuss Nouri Bouzid's Arabic-language film in the coda.

28. Alec Hargreaves's excellent "pre-history" of francophone studies brings up the issue of race without naming it explicitly: "The distinction between 'French' and 'Francophone' does not map neatly onto former colonies in the Caribbean and elsewhere that are now officially classified as PTOM (pays et territoires d'outre-mer), i.e. integral parts of France, though their literatures are often classified as 'Francophone,' and it is ill-suited to accommodate migrant writers or those descended from migrants who sit astride that divide" ("Presaging the Francosphere" 133).

29. For an outline of Quebecois intellectuals' appropriation of anticolonial discourse, see Poulin.

30. See the introduction and first chapter of Anne McClintock's *Imperial Leather*.

31. See, e.g., Janis.

32. This gesture of trying to understand a text's possibilities parallels what Anthony Alessandrini has called "the need to appropriate" in his analysis of the importance of Fanon and Fanonian studies—"the need to appropriate" here representing a need for "bringing Fanon's work to bear on contemporary cultural

politics" (Alessandrini, *Frantz Fanon* 47), an effort to think with and act with Fanon's works. For an example of appropriative solidary reading, see Raja, whose article proposes a "praxis-oriented" reading of Sembene's *Bouts de bois de Dieu*.

## 1. "Interior Geographies"

1. For examinations of Césaire's influence on Quebecois sovereigntist literature, see Selao; Poulin; and Demers.

2. For a detailed analysis of Césaire's position with regard to departmentalization, autonomy, and emancipation, see Fonkoua.

3. See Gil, "Découverte de l'urtext de *Et les chiens se taisaient*," an in-depth study of the genesis of the text.

4. For an analysis of earlier literary accounts of the Haitian Revolution, see Daut.

5. It is interesting to compare this analysis of the unstable forest metaphor in *Et les chiens se taisaient* with Mireille Rosello's reading of the tree-planting metaphor in *La tragédie du roi Christophe*. She demonstrates that Christophe cites the English abolitionist Wilberforce in such a way that contradictory positions on emancipation are delineated: "What is crucial about this confrontation between two metaphorical constructions is that neither system is coherent enough to translate simply into a political platform" (Rosello 82).

6. The first 14 articles of the Code Noir, for example, deal specifically with the implications of the imposition of the Catholic faith on slaves within the French imperial territories.

7. A supplemental triangular trade was superimposed on the Africa-Antilles-France trade triangle meticulously described in Christopher L. Miller's *French Atlantic Triangle*. This supplementary triangle circulated salt cod (the play's "morue terreneuvienne") and timber from New France to the French Caribbean in exchange for slave-produced goods such as sugar, molasses, and rum; both colonies also traded their respective products with France for manufactured goods. The New France trade provided the raw supplies necessary for the slave trade.

8. Bénédicte Boisseron in her article "Afro-Dog" explains that "during slavery, bloodhounds imported from Cuba or Germany were trained to pursue escaping slaves in both the Caribbean and the American South. The white slaveholder trained the dogs to become ferocious only when in contact with blacks" (20). For a discussion of the ownership of dogs, see p. 21.

9. For an alternative reading, see Davis, which brings up a final barking of the dogs at the end of the play: "The barking of the dogs, invoked by the Rebel at the play's threnodic close, marks the end of the 'silence' imposed on, and internalized by, the oppressed slaves. . . . This barking signals both a coming liberation and a resuscitation, an access of power and a denial of death" (131).

10. Césaire himself explained, "C'est toujours plus facile de conquérir sa liberté—il ne faut que du courage—, seulement, une fois qu'elle est obtenue, il

faut savoir ce qu'on va en faire. La libération est épique, mais les lendemains sont tragiques. . . . J'ai eu l'idée de situer en Haïti le problème de l'homme noir assailli par l'indépendance. . . . Ce que le Congo, la Guinée, le Mali ont connu vers 56–60, Haïti l'a connu dès 1801" (quoted in Beloux 30). Césaire's explicit parallel between Haiti and the Congo, Guinea, and Mali suggests that there is a thread of solidarity that enables him to imagine a connection between past and present revolutionaries across physical space, an imagined geography of possible alliances that locates foundational moments and that survives, through hope and nostalgia, their turn to tragedy.

11. For a discussion of Césaire's time in Haiti, see Fonkoua 93–95 or Walsh 107–9.

12. Césaire emphasized the importance of Haiti's shift in allegiance (from being with France to being against France) during a press conference he gave in Quebec City in 1972, in which he underscored the fact that Haiti's decision to fight for independence from France was not really a choice: after participating in the revolution in parallel with French revolutionaries, against the planters, the ex-slaves were suddenly faced with reactionary military forces arriving from France "with slavery in their luggage" *(Conférence de presse)*.

13. See Robespierre, quoted in Nesbitt's *Caribbean Critique*: "The French Revolution is the first to be founded on the theory of the rights of humanity and on the principles of justice" (292n2).

14. Nesbitt, at the end of "From Louverture to Lenin," acknowledges that Césaire's poetry points toward a "future without a telos, rendered as the pure promise of the aesthetic" (144), but he does not analyze the plays, which stage worlds of fictional political possibilities. It seems to me that Césaire's plays, even more than his poetry, constitute experiments in political imaginaries.

15. *Kontikis* is an anachronism for Christophe's epoch; it came into use after 1946, when a Norwegian explorer crossed the Pacific in a raft of that name. Another anachronism in the text is the mention in act 2 of the "roman qui fait pleurer tout Paris" (*Tragédie* 81), *Ourika,* which was first published three years after the death of Henri Christophe. Roger Little, in "A Further Unacknowledged Quotation in Césaire," writes, "Césaire could count, it seems, . . . on the spectator's indulgence as regards his slight readjustment of history in the interest of his poetic theater" (15). John Patrick Walsh suggests, without alluding to the anachronism, that the reference to *Ourika* also serves to delineate the idea of a universal revolutionary "black" position, since Ourika is outraged by the racist treatment she undergoes in Paris but is disgusted by the revolutionary violence in Saint Domingue. (Walsh points out that the family of Claire de Duras, the author of *Ourika,* owned a plantation in Martinique and states that "in the evocation of Saint-Domingue, Duras's abolitionist leanings only went so far" [139].)

16. Or its profits will go to the "Whites of America," a possible allusion to the United States' profiteering occupation of Haiti (1915–34), another instance of racialized capitalism at work.

17. It is interesting to consider the unnamed *philanthropes* as structural ancestors of Maurice Thorez and his fellow Parti communiste français members, whom Césaire, in his 1956 letter of resignation from the PCF, accuses of being distant altruists who presume they understand how equality works without taking into account the trauma of the colonial context. Fonkoua explains, "Le député de la Martinique s'élève contre ce qu'il appelle le 'fraternalisme,' la version communiste du 'paternalisme'" (257). Césaire's neologistic "fraternalism" articulates precisely the uneven and opportunistic solidarity he sees in the PCF. In "Letter to Maurice Thorez" Césaire writes, "We are offered solidarity with the French people; with the French proletariat, and, by means of communism, with the proletarians of the world. . . . I do not want to erect solidarities in metaphysics. . . . And if alliance with the French proletariat is exclusive . . . then I say communism has done us a disservice in making us exchange living fraternity [with the rest of the Caribbean and with Africa] for what risks appearing the coldest of cold abstractions" (151–52). Césaire is concerned with the dehumanizing potential of solidarity's abstracting mechanism, which functions by drawing lifeless "metaphysical" or conjectural parallels without regard for the vast inequality in which these parallels are couched. He lists the specific tropes and abstractions that enable the PCF to discursively mask the inequalities of French communist solidarity with colonial subjects: "their inveterate assimilationism; their unconscious chauvinism; . . . their rarely avowed but real belief in civilization with a capital C and progress with a capital P (as evidenced by their hostility to what they disdainfully call 'cultural relativism') . . . the notion of 'advanced' and 'backward' peoples" (149). This critique parallels Christophe's critique of the *philanthropes,* who also philosophize about universal rights without being conscious of their privileged position.

18. Césaire's use of the word *philanthropes* rather than *abolitionistes* or *républicains* emphasizes the apolitical nature of the do-gooders' stance; they are imagined gazing charitably, compassionately at Christophe's court (*Tragédie* 116). As Lauren Berlant has suggested in a trenchant analysis of compassion as a mode of human relation, "Compassion and coldness are not opposite at all but are two sides of a bargain that the subjects of modernity have struck with structural inequality" (10).

19. See, e.g., the 1894 *Revue de l'Avranchin,* which offers etymologies for geographical names and labels.

20. See CNRTL, http://www.cnrtl.fr/definition/raque.

21. For a thorough comparison of Shakespeare's *Tempest* and Césaire's, see Arnold, "Césaire and Shakespeare."

22. Nick Nesbitt, in "History and Nation-Building," traces the Kojèvian Hegelianism structuring *La tragédie du roi Christophe;* a similar philosophical tapestry undergirds *Une tempête.*

23. Photo included in Fonkoua's biography of Césaire in unnumbered photography pages.

24. For an investigation into the death of Lumumba, see De Witte.

25. The exact nature of Césaire's attitude remains unspecified, but it can be considered as the continuation of his exploration of self-sacrifice's limits in *Et les chiens se taisaient*.

26. Lumumba's efforts parallel Christophe's in the *Tragédie*, which functions as an allegory for the African independences.

27. This fable, with its deploring fraternal reproof, echoes an article Fanon published in February 1961, a week after the announcement of Lumumba's actual death: "La mort de Lumumba: Pouvions-nous faire autrement?" In this article, Fanon blames African nations for not acting to support Lumumba outside the restrictive mandate of the United Nations.

28. Elsewhere, Césaire points specifically to the flamboyant as a tree that defines his Caribbean identity: "Quand je parle du flamboyant, du fromager, des arbres spécifiquement antillais . . . je veux parler . . . d'arbres qui sont à moi et à nul autre, d'arbres qui me définissent et m'enracinent, en qui je suis ce que je suis et qui sont ce que je suis" ("La situation du poète antillais," *Conférence de presse . . . [suite]*). Thus by inserting the "arbre flamboyant" in *Une saison au Congo*, Césaire affirms his own region's presence in Lumumba's dying words.

29. See, e.g., Kesteloot, "La tragédie du roi Christophe."

30. Césaire's Caribbean functions as a difficult node of solidary francophone exchanges: at once a French department and an American island, a European settler colony and an African slave work camp, it explodes geographical and racial taxonomies. This makes it an ideal testing ground for francophone solidarity, a kind of limit case where all boundaries are examined.

31. In her examination of Césaire's models of nation building ("'Césaire Effect'"), Mireille Rosello writes, "It is the combination of the cultural context as well as the meaning of the poet's words that create [*sic*] a context allowing or discouraging certain reappropriations, regardless of whether the man encourages them or not" (79).

32. Of Césaire's works, the poetry and essays were most influential in Quebec, although *La tragédie du roi Christophe* was played in Montreal during the 1967 Exposition universelle (Dorsinville, *Pays natal* 43).

33. Selao addresses the somewhat befuddling fact that Césaire inspired the Quebecois struggle for independence even though he also orchestrated the departmentalization of Martinique. She contrasts the Quebecois veneration of his work with the response of Martinican intellectuals, who reacted much more acutely to what they saw as Césaire's association with France and his "créolophobie."

34. This was the lecture Césaire had given at the Congrès des écrivains et artistes noirs in Paris in 1956. It was republished in Quebec in 1963 (Dorsinville, *Pays natal* 43). For a thorough reading of Césaire in Aquin's "La fatigue culturelle," see Demers.

35. It is interesting to compare Césaire's use of poetry to express solidarity with his Quebecois public with his speech asserting *poetically* the political impact of Senghor's poetry (see Wilder 49–50).

36. Kesteloot penned among the first monographs about Césaire's work, *Aimé Césaire: Une étude* (1962).

37. Césaire specifies that this is his second presentation of the day, a demanding itinerary for the author-politician.

38. Indeed, as Kate Briggs writes, "An analogy . . . works by pointing to something familiar or readily understood [for Césaire, the Caribbean as a colonial situation] in order to clarify or explain something more complex and less readily understood [Quebec as a putative colonial situation]. If the analogy is a good one then it should last long enough for the complex thing to be clarified or explained: for it to emerge, instructively, that *this* is indeed a bit like *that*. But . . . it is in the very nature of the analogy that at some point it will break down: the ways in which *this,* in fact, now you or I come to think of it, is actually quite unlike *that,* will always win out, eventually" (291, emphases in original).

39. It is interesting that Césaire uses *canadien* and *québécois* interchangeably. Not coincidentally, these identity terms were shifting during the era of the independences, from the original *canadien français* to *québécois,* associated with the sovereigntist movement but gradually gaining general ground.

40. Quebec's relation to France was in fact quite convoluted. In order to establish themselves as different from English Canadians, French Canadians reached out to France as a model and long-lost relative; and yet, at the same time, some French Canadians felt deep-seated resentment toward the country that had abandoned them centuries before. Quebec's alignment with France's (ex-)colonies only complicates the matter, wedging the North American province further away from France while keeping it in that imperial nation's orbit.

## 2. Interlace, Interrace

1. Mentioned in Giroud.

2. Magnant considers his struggle for an independent Québec an anticolonial struggle. Ghezzo-Quenum's struggle draws on both anticolonial and antineocolonial Ivoirian imaginaries; in a (fictional) letter dated 1966, he mentions that recently he participated in a (real) anti-French uprising that actually took place in 1948 (8), but he also refers to President Houphouët-Boigny (10), whose rule began with independence in 1960. The narrative thus amalgamates African colonialism and neocolonialism, facilitating a clean parallel with anticolonial Québec.

3. The first part of Martine-Emmanuelle Lapointe's *Emblèmes d'une littérature* ("La révolution tranquille ou le centre de l'histoire") provides an in-depth analysis of the Quiet Revolution as it relates to literature.

4. See Glen Sean Coulthard's authoritative *Red Skin, White Masks* for an analysis of First Nations self-determination in Canada. Coulthard's title points to another important network of anticolonial solidarity and identification functioning in North America.

5. Olympe Guezzo-Quenum was named after the Beninese writer Olympe Bhely-Quenum, whom Aquin interviewed in the early sixties and with whom he

collaborated briefly on the subject of the parallel progressive journals they each edited, *Liberté* for Aquin and *La vie africaine* for Bhely-Quenum. See Bhely-Quenum, detailing a phone call he had with Aimé Césaire, who agreed to have one of his articles republished in *Liberté*.

6. Notice, of course, that Ghezzo-Quenum undermines the dichotomy by the very act of adding the aside: if calling Magnant "mon frère" was an understatement based on Cartesian (European) modesty, allowing the parenthetical "jumeaux" represents the enthusiastic instinct Senghor had ascribed to Africans. Ghezzo-Quenum's letter, by explaining the dichotomy, also troubles it.

7. Aquin also traveled to Paris to meet with Memmi in the context of his work on the research and text for *À l'heure de la décolonisation* (1963), a short documentary produced by the National Film Board of Canada under the direction of Monique Fortier (see Aquin, *Journal*, n. 279). Memmi is surprisingly absent from the film, which focuses on the survival of the French language in the newly independent countries, a subject of primordial importance for Quebecois intellectuals preoccupied with the North American menace of English, as we saw in chapter 1. We will return to this question in chapter 4.

8. For a thorough overview of Aquin's essays in relation to anticolonialism, see Poulin.

9. *Biolectographical* is a useful neologism created by the scholar of Quebecois literature Marilyn Randall to describe *Trou de mémoire*.

10. Other passages narrate Joan's murder (poisoning and asphyxiation) more coherently, but they consistently slip into language that obfuscates the reality of her death and replaces it with Lagos. For example, "Étranglement, c'est beaucoup dire alors que j'ai simplement étrangé, de ma main masquée, l'inconnue de Lagos, la passagère voilée des vaisseaux fantômes qui continuent d'échouer dans les entrelacs de la lagune funèbre qui se découpe en dentelles de souvenirs" (103). Each of these passages detracts from Joan's suffering by diverting toward imagery of Lagos and the slave trade.

11. For a thorough explanation of the interweaving narratives of *Trou de mémoire*, see, among others, Söderlind.

12. *Laqueus*, in the context of the slave trade, evokes the capture and lynching of slaves, raising the specter of the violence that characterized the triangular commerce.

13. Actually, the novel makes explicit the connection between rape, murder, and colonial aggression: "L'Afrique toute entière est morte asphyxiée en même temps que son socle fragile en forme de Joan," writes Magnant (95).

14. Aquin was in point of fact quite interested in the figure of the double. See Wall 309.

15. Magnant's narrative refers to the Anglo-French struggle in the context of Joan's capitulation to Magnant's sexual advances: "Dès l'instant où je la réduisais à la défaite totale et irréversible, comment ne deviendrait-elle pas ma sœur selon la défaite? . . . D'un seul coup, Joan a épousé mon être-conquis" (Aquin, *Trou*

*de mémoire* 41). This pairing of sexual and colonial capitulation is the corollary of the trope of rape as colonization discussed by Katherine A. Roberts (see Roberts 25).

16. Roberts opens her article by acknowledging the difficulty of approaching Aquin's work: "It seems that at some point in her career, the feminist critic of Quebec literature is compelled to study Hubert Aquin, and in particular, his controversial and often violent rapport with all things female. It is not an altogether pleasant moment" (17).

17. Not to mention Aquin's own suicide in 1977. Aquin was himself a militant for the Rassemblement pour l'indépendance nationale (RIN). In 1964, he made public his departure from the RIN in favor of clandestine action, forming a group he named the Organisation spéciale after the first clandestine movement created in Algeria in 1947, the ancestor of the FLN. Aquin was arrested a month into his clandestine action and released in 1966 on grounds of inconclusiveness; his 1965 novel *Prochain épisode* is a fictionalization of this affair (Fournier 81–83; for *Prochain épisode*'s vexed relationship with history, see, among others, Purdy).

18. Cf. Fournier 102.

19. Aquin's published diaries list his eclectic readings. In August 1961, for example, he read Georges Hardy's *La géographie psychologique* (1939), Pierre Klossowski's *Le souffleur ou un théâtre de société* (1960), Luc Estang's *Le bonheur et le salut* (1961), Octave Mannoni's *Prospéro et Caliban: Psychologie de la colonisation* (1950), and Michel Leiris's *La possession et ses aspects théâtraux chez les Éthiopiens de Gondars* (1958) (Aquin, *Journal* 229).

20. In a footnote in the final pages of the novel during which she explains her own mendacious chapter, Rachel Ruskin specifically comments on Mullahy/Magnant's disingenuity: "On aura remarqué, au passage, que P.X. Magnant (transformé en éditeur) se surprend d'un passage de ses mémoires décrivant le littoral africain: ce pseudo-éditeur s'étonne de cette description parce que l'auteur-assassin ne serait jamais allé à Lagos. Ce brouillage de piste ne fait que donner une preuve supplémentaire de la capacité qu'avait P. X. Magnant de se dédoubler" (235). Rachel Ruskin's pedantic explanation (Magnant's ability to split himself in two) does little to explain the novel's fascination with falsehood; impersonation and disguise are skills in deceit.

21. So Magnant and Ghezzo-Quenum are pharmacists both literally and figuratively, as writers.

22. Valérie Loichot's 2007 *Orphan Narratives* examines a similar parallel between family and narrative structures, focusing on the fact that the traumas of life on plantations did not destroy the human ability to imagine narratives and family structures but instead led to the invention of new forms of literary, political, and familial imagination.

23. And also its *past* social body, something to which Aquin draws attention by linking Quebec to the slave trade.

24. See, e.g., Nakayama and Krizek, whose critique, "by naming whiteness, [displaces] its centrality and [reveals] its invisible position" (292). Within the novel, Ghezzo-Quenum is the only character who names the power of whiteness: he invests Magnant's and Rachel Ruskin's whiteness with significance in terms of their position in a racialized hierarchy of power relations.

25. The diary straddles two calendar years; some day-of-the-week or date combinations (this one, for example) coincide with the calendar for 1966, which is the year Ghezzo-Quenum provides in his diary, while others coincide with the calendar for 1967, the year Mullahy, in his "Note finale" following the diary, claims to be the year of the writing of the diary. If the rape by Magnant took place in 1966 and Rachel is pregnant in the summer of 1967, then Magnant clearly is not the baby's father, but her certainty regarding his paternity suggests that the events actually took place in 1967, meaning that Ghezzo-Quenum's diary is misdated.

26. This scene of desire for an inert woman's body reminds us of Magnant's harassment of Joan after reading *La femme frigide*, reinforcing the parallels between the two men.

27. The narrative makes this explicit: "Chaque fois que Rachel Ruskin recommence son récit, je me retrouve encore à Lausanne, quasiment sous la peau de Rachel Ruskin . . . et j'attends que Pierre X. Magnant m'aborde" (220). Roberts explains, "The African narrator becomes both victim and rapist as he oscillates between the idea of being violated—colonization as rape—and his desire to rape in turn, to punish the white man's woman, to take back and heal his masculinity that has been compromised by colonization" (Roberts 25).

28. Aquin's papers are housed in the Fonds Hubert Aquin, Université du Québec à Montréal.

29. The intepretation of *Trou de mémoire* that I have laid out thus far is grounded in the novel itself, specifically in the metaphors that structure its construction of interracial solidarity. While the analysis of "White Baby" forms a fascinating counterpoint to my study of *Trou de mémoire*, it is by no means necessary to support the chapter's argument. Hereafter, the play is cited in the text as "WB."

30. See Aquin, *Journal* 248.

31. The 1962 *avant-textes* are addended to the Critical Edition of *Trou de mémoire*, pp. 273–320.

32. See Anne McClintock's *Imperial Leather* for an analysis of the colonial imagination of the colonized other as cannibal (27).

### 3. Publishable Offense

1. Specifically, Article 14 of France's law concerning publication (Loi sur la Presse) gave the French government the right to prohibit any work of foreign origin. Beti explains the law's nineteenth-century origins and applications in his preface to the 1977 edition of the book. See "Préface de l'auteur à l'édition de 1977," 20.

2. Beti also documents his trajectory with respect to his citizenship in the preface to the 1977 edition of *Main basse,* 21–24. It is ironic that when Beti finally returned to Cameroon in 1991, the official media of then president Paul Biya discredited him by arguing that he was a "foreigner" in Cameroon, that he was *too* French to participate in political deliberation in his homeland (Kom, "Mongo Beti Returns to Cameroon" 417). In the face of this criticism, Beti "never tired of explaining his French citizenship—'I have French nationality, but that doesn't mean that I have renounced my country'" (418, citing *La Nouvelle Expression,* March 9–25, 1991, 3). For a more thorough examination of the question of Beti's citizenship, see Kemedjio, *Combattant fatigué* 110–31.

3. The useful compendium of censorship edited by Derek Jones tells the story of the censorship of *Main basse,* but it omits mention of the Canadian republication of the book (see Djiffack and Wynchank).

4. "Avec cette édition canadienne vendue en Belgique, nous avons eu de l'argent pour faire la revue *Peuples Noirs—Peuples Africains.* C'est avec cet argent-là qu'on a commencé la revue" (Beti, *Mongo Beti parle* 99).

5. Beti himself admitted, "L'interdiction, la censure est venue faire la fortune du livre. . . . À partir du moment où on saisit un livre en France, comme ce fut le cas pour *Main basse sur le Cameroun,* tout de suite, tous les militants s'y intéressent" (Beti, *Mongo Beti parle* 98).

6. This was in the same year that Beti and Maspero won their legal case against censorship and a year before the French second republication of *Main basse,* an event warranted by the 1972 disappearance of the text, its clandestine distribution, and its advertisement in the Quebecois documentary.

7. Immediately on publication, the book's reception was mixed, depending on the political position of each reviewer. Jean Copans, a French anthropologist and sociologist whose work was also published by Maspero in the 1970s, writes appreciatively in 1973 that Beti's "description du cynisme et de la violence néocoloniale ne pourra que surprendre ceux qui croient encore aux vertus de l'aide française et de la politique de coopération." By contrast, Jean-François Bayart, then emerging as a political scientist of Africa, writes a dismissive, single-sentence review: "[Beti's] sole concern is in the fact that he has been banned by the French government (at the instance of the Cameroun authorities?); [*Main basse sur le Cameroun*] is a tissue of fabrications and misrepresentations—notably in his treatment of the Ndongo [*sic*] affair, on which Le Vine shows himself better informed—which can only damage his reputation as a novelist" (454).

8. For a history of Cameroon's colonial and decolonial history, see Bouopda.

9. Beti writes, "Le forfait du prélat camerounais, c'est d'avoir ruiné les fondements psychologiques et socio-économiques d'un ordre des choses hypocrite et injuste, qui ne repose que sur le mensonge et l'oppression et que l'indépendance à la mode d'Ahidjo avait renforcé, loin d'y mettre fin"; he further describes Ndongmo as a "génial businessman africain" (*Main basse* 120), both asserting and seeing value in Ndongmo's business acumen.

10. Beti ends the section of *Main basse* that analyzes the courtroom proceedings with a poignant eulogy to Ouandié, imagining that on the accused's bench "le marxiste, l'homme maigre et gris, le maquisard préparé depuis toujours au sacrifice suprême, souriait, stoïque, attendant la mort avec sérénité" (189).

11. In a situation where facts are contested, Beti seeks to establish that the relation between Ndongmo and Ouandié originated first at the request of Ahidjo's government, as part of an effort to persuade revolutionaries to join the bureaucratic fold. Ahidjo himself denies ordering Ndongmo to spy on Ouandié, which begins to suggest the level of misinformation that researchers into the events in Cameroon must navigate: "Le président camerounais a démenti des affirmations répétées de l'évêque [Ndongmo] pendant le procès [that of Ndongmo], selon lesquelles ce sont les autorités camerounaises elles-mêmes qui lui ont demandé de nouer des contacts avec le chef révolutionnaire, son diocèse se trouvant au cœur de la zone la plus troublée, et le chef de la révolution camerounaise étant un Bamiléké, comme lui-même. Contredisant les dénégations présidentielles, plusieurs témoignages venus de tous horizons établissent que les premières rencontres se firent en effet à l'inspiration du gouvernement" (*Main basse* 117). Beti further contends that the witnesses who saw Ndongmo's official *laissez-passer* (a document allowing him to visit the maquis without questions) should be believed more than Ahidjo and that indeed Ndongmo was tasked with converting Ouandié politically, with bringing him out of the maquis and into public view. Beti brilliantly defines public presence as nonresistance: Cameroonians who were visible were deemed to support Ahidjo's single-party rule. Presence is acceptance; absence (invisibility) is the only form of resistance to Ahidjo's corrupt neocolonial regime (111). This is the "public presence" that Ndongmo was supposed to persuade Ouandié to adopt.

12. This is the case in spite of Ahidjo's purportedly weak grasp of the language. For a discussion of Ahidjo's education and his inability to speak French, which, Beti claims, the president masked with false modesty and would-be spiritual silence, see *Main basse* 36.

13. Beti's recourse to citing Chateaubriand's *Mémoires* here is complicated: Chateaubriand, himself an ultraroyalist, was miffed that Napoleon's social and political circles were still influential even after the deposition of the emperor. However, as a French nationalist, Chateaubriand also resented French society's flocking to the Russian invader, leader of the coalition that had just deposed Napoleon, and he deplored the scorn with which royalists were cast out of both imperial and coalition circles.

14. Beti in *Main basse* speaks specifically of the "pauperization" of former colonies.

15. Interestingly, Cilas Kemedjio, Pierre Tabue, André Djiffack, and Blaise Toualla, in "Mongo Beti: The Nobility of a Struggle," use the same term, *interested philanthropy,* to describe the "various imperialisms which keep Africans

and Black people in a state of undeclared slavery" (422). In the context of (post)colonialism, philanthropy is decidedly suspect.

16. As Jacques Michon, editor of the two-volume *Histoire de l'édition littéraire au Québec,* wrote, the paratext generally informs readers "sur le discours de l'éditeur, les transformations idéologiques" that shape the context of the text's publication (2:19). "Entre le lecteur et le public, l'éditeur crée un espace, un lieu d'échange à la fois économique et idéologique.... La médiation éditoriale inscrit le texte dans un projet d'entreprise et l'insère dans un processus de communication qui lui donne un sens" (1:17). For a general analysis of the functions of paratext, see also Genette.

17. See Rivière 70 for a narration of the publication and distribution of this incendiary and popular text (popular both because it sold well and because Bergeron insisted that it never be sold for more than one dollar, so it could be accessible to "the people.")

18. For the newspapers, see Beaulieu and Hamelin 27, 172. A telling example of an official Parti québécois project published by Journal Offset is *Prochaine étape: Quand nous serons vraiment chez nous* (1972). Journal Offset also produced Pierre Vallières's *L'urgence de choisir* (1971), published by Parti pris.

19. Beti writes, "La police du port [of Rouen] a ouvert le colis et a constaté qu'il s'agissait d'un livre interdit en lisant la quatrième de couverture où l'éditeur canadien affichait cette particularité en tant qu'argument de vente" (*Mongo Beti parle* 98).

20. The pagination of the Quebec edition of *Main basse* does not account for the presence of the "extra" prefatory material. I number these supernumerary pages i–iv, with i representing the beginning of Le Chêne's "Présentation."

21. This is reminiscent of Nesbitt's *Caribbean Critique,* in which he traces through French-language works a concern with universal justice.

22. Another similarity that the form of Le Chêne's simile obscures (even though it refers to it obliquely) is Quebec and Cameroon's shared French-English colonial heritage. Le Chêne's focus on anticolonialism forecloses further exploration of the bilingual legacy of Cameroon as it differs from Quebec's.

23. *Québec-Presse* was a radical Left Sunday weekly published from 1969 to 1974; for a history of the newspaper, see Keable.

24. See Dupont 10.

25. As Ngũgĩ wa Thiong'o termed the collaborating upper middle classes of African colonial occupation in *Decolonizing the Mind* 20–23.

26. The main text of *Main basse sur le Cameroun* also lays out how Western nations, Canada included, assert their presence in the third world through "gracious" donations that give them right of access. Beti lists "la route goudronnée de cent kilomètres, offerte (mais l'opinion ignore ce détail) 'gracieusement' par l'Allemagne fédérale, dans la région de Mbalmayo; ou le tronçon de chemin de fer transcamerounais offert 'gracieusement' lui aussi par les États-Unis; ou l'université offerte 'gracieusement' encore une fois par le Canada et construite

252  Notes to Pages 148–159

à Makak" (61). Beti's reproach is that "tout se passe . . . comme si le régime [d'Ahidjo], reprenant la tradition coloniale, tentait d'ériger les principales activités économiques, qui elles, demeurent en dehors de l'État, en un domaine réservé aux étrangers, c'est-à-dire évidemment aux Occidentaux et à ceux qu'on peut leur assimiler" (74). Beti accuses Ahidjo's government of taking credit for the "donations" of foreign governments, which "graciously" seem to benefit local populations but in fact transfer all power of determination to foreign actors.

27. See chap. 5, "The Opening Up to the Third World," in Christoph Kalter's carefully researched *Discovery of the Third World*. Kalter's bibliography on Maspero draws a full portrait of the man and the publishing house.

28. For example, Maspero had published, in 1960–61, a series of three essays collectively titled *Liberté*, each exposing French-sponsored murders and genocides related to colonialism. The third essay, *L'affaire Moumié*, written by Jean-Francis Held, investigated the poisoning of Félix Moumié. Maspero's publication of *Main basse* is thus inscribed in a longer project of revealing French colonial injustices.

29. Maspero's family were members of the Resistance during World War II. His father and brother died, the former at Buchenwald and the latter with the American army at the siege of Metz. As Maspero describes in his ruminative memoir *Les abeilles et la guêpe*, he felt deeply guilty for not being old enough to participate fully in the Resistance.

30. Beti does not even discuss the Cameroonian press, in which censorship was a matter of common knowledge. See, e.g., Bourdon-Higbee.

31. Beti returns to this simile (Cameroon / Santo Domingo / Ceylon / Guatemala) in his 1974 lecture at Dalhousie University in Halifax, where he theorizes these comparative situations as a "grille d'analyse" whose application in Cameroon the French press makes impossible by means of obfuscating lies. The lies of the Agence de Presse Française "étaient en effet la matière première d'une intoxication abominable visant à dénaturer le procès [Ndongmo's and Ouandié's] de telle façon que dans la confusion ainsi créée l'opinion publique européenne . . . ne puisse utiliser, pour s'y reconnaître, la grille traditionnelle pour l'Amérique latine ou pour l'Asie du sud-est" ("L'action des médias occidentaux" 106).

32. See Kemedjio, chap. 4; and Beti, *"Contrecensure."*

33. Le Chêne, in an interview with Cilas Kemedjio, shares that he and his collaborator used pseudonyms to preserve their liberty to travel to African states, Cameroon among them (Kemedjio 189).

34. Also discussed in Kemedjio 189.

35. The narrator, Bernard Derome, was an award-winning Quebecois radio and television news anchor.

36. It is telling that of all the people interviewed, the only ones who are not identified by name, role, or location are three Cameroonian young men who attest briefly and without specificity to the reality of summary executions and police repression. This anonymity accentuates the danger faced by Cameroonians but also points out that white people in Cameroon are necessarily disconnected from

the violence, never personally at risk of being tortured or executed. There arises from the film an understanding of the radical segregation existing in Cameroon, the white populations living separately and safely (in what one interviewee calls "le monde de la coopération" or "la colonie blanche française-canadienne"), the black populations constantly at risk of running afoul of the regime and being disappeared and tortured.

37. Éloïse Brière documents Beti's inability to attend the conference, where she had hoped to meet him: "Déception: Mongo Beti ne viendra pas au congrès. C'est l'époque de *Main basse sur le Cameroun*. J'apprendrai plus tard que le bras du gouvernement camerounais était très long. L'invitation avait, paraît-il, été annulée sur la demande du chef de l'État camerounais" (104).

38. Ironically, "le financement du film aurait été obtenu à partir d'un projet de faire un film sur les œuvres du Cardinal Léger," as Gérard Le Chêne explains to Kemedjio (Kemedjio 188).

## 4. As through a Canadian Fog

1. Chraïbi mentions this project, which was to have involved filmmaker Jacques Baratier but which was never completed, in a 1966 interview ("Je suis d'une génération perdue" 41). In 1973, he worked on another screenplay about madness with Jacques Baratier, an adaptation of Chraïbi's own novel *Un ami viendra vous voir* into a film titled *La raison folle*, which also did not bear fruit (Delayre 351–54).

2. On the near-censorship of *Le passé simple* and on its effect on Chraïbi's positioning of himself in French and Moroccan society, see Harrison 512.

3. For a history of France's presence in Morocco, see Rivet.

4. About his choice to write in French, Chraïbi says in his memoir *Le monde à côté* that unlike other Maghrebi writers, he never experienced writing in French as torment: "Certains d'entre eux [Kateb Yacine, Mohammed Dib, Mouloud Feraoun, Mouloud Mammeri], ici ou là, écrivaient dans les affres parce que le français était pour eux la langue du dominateur. Ce qui n'était pas mon cas. Ce ne le fut jamais" (124).

5. See Joan Monego: "The mutilation of French syntax . . . [and the dislocation of] the language of *the other* constitutes an act of vengeance against the French acculturation process. Chraïbi tries to be outrageous and obscene. . . . He tries to shock by whatever means possible" (112).

6. For a complete history of the October Crisis, see Fournier.

7. The concept of the French and the English as two "colonizing races" has historically been used to describe Canada. See, e.g., Lucas 347.

8. See the interview with Jamal Al Achgar, "Je suis d'une génération perdue": "Pour ma part, j'ai définitivement renoncé à ce régionalisme qu'implique l'expression 'littérature maghrébine de langue française.' . . . Je suis un écrivain d'expression française, un point c'est tout" (42).

9. This is one detail in *Le monde à côté* that dates Chraïbi's visit as later than it likely happened: Margaret Sinclair's marriage to Pierre-Elliott Trudeau

took place on March 4, 1971, after a secret courtship, so the students could only have worshiped the First Lady's skirts beginning in 1971. Fernando Lambert, by contrast, confidently dates Chraïbi's visit to before his own arrival at Laval in 1970.

10. Tétu favored and defended the term *francophone,* for example, in his article "Cousins proches et voisins lointains."

11. Marx-Scouras asserts that Chraïbi conceived of culture "as a relative notion . . . [which] eventually led him to adopt an unbiased, critical, and realistic point of view" (136).

12. The Tet Offensive, which took place in the winter of 1968, dates Chraïbi's Canadian sojourn to the late sixties, contradicting some other elements of the text.

13. See also Hervé Tchumkam's examination of the signification of the category "popular" (a category that includes romance novels, although Tchumkam focuses on whodunits) with regard to African detective fiction, "Of Murder and Love." For Tchumkam, "popularity" is a two-pronged concept referring both to the relation of a writer's oeuvre to "the people" and to the genre in which the writer chooses to write (39). In the crux of these two definitions of "the popular," social realism as a genre (for example) is popular according to the first definition of the term, but according to the second definition it becomes "canonical" in comparison with a genre like detective fiction or romance. *Mort au Canada* fits uneasily in the interstices of popularity and canonicity as it hovers at the limit of the romance.

14. Chraïbi's characters borrow names from his biography: the author had a child called Dominique, his second wife's name is Sheena McCallion, and *Mort au Canada* is dedicated to a Maryvonne Taupin.

15. Other characters also notice Patrik's relational genius: Sheena, his pregnant soon-to-be former lover, assesses that he is able to establish "un contact direct et spontané de sa vie privée et intime à leur vie privée et intime, par-delà les convenances-contraintes et les barrières des mots de la civilisation" (28).

16. These characters' names, unusual in French, bring attention to their lack of national or linguistic moorings. "Patrik Pierson" is not a name of French origin, although the character travels to Canada from France and has familial attachments in Paris. Some readers have identified Patrik as representing Chraïbi. Anne-Marie Guinoune, for example, comes to this conclusion by drawing a parallel between the childhood to which the narrator of *Mort of Canada* briefly alludes and Chraïbi's own childhood (as described in his first novel, *Le passé simple*) and because the name Pierson corresponds to the phonetic spelling of the French word *personne* (person, no one) as pronounced with an Arabic accent (Guinoune 77). Supporting this claim, Chraïbi himself explains in an interview that certain aspects of the novel are "autobiographical" (quoted in Guinoune 77). Moreover, as stated above, *Mort au Canada* is dedicated to a Maryvonne Taupin, and some passages echo events narrated in Chraïbi's autobiographical *Le monde à côté*: Patrik's affair

in Sweden, for example, which happened in the absence of a shared language, resembles a similar affair described briefly in *Le monde à côté* as Chraïbi's own experience. Chraïbi's claim that *some* aspects of the novel are autobiographical, however, suggests that other aspects are not. The names also remind us of the fictionality, the fabrication of *Mort au Canada*: the spelling of *Patrik*, without the *c*, recalls either a Swedish name or an Eastern European one, and *William* is an English variant of *Guillaume*.

17. Patrik is unable to answer questions on the driving exam: "QUESTION: 'Vous n'avez pas le droit de stationner sur la bande blanche de l'autoroute.' RÉPONSE A: 'Oui.' RÉPONSE B: 'Non.' ... J'ai répondu oui *et* non. C'était logique: 'Oui, je n'ai pas le droit de stationner . . .'—et: 'Non, je n'ai pas le droit . . .' Les deux réponses étaient valables, ça tombe sous le sens. Eh bien, semble-t-il, seule la réponse B comptait" (112–13; notice the Quebecism *stationner* for *garer*). Patrik refuses the logic of capital, which instrumentalizes language beyond language's own structures of coherence.

18. See also Irene Oktaba's biographical sketch of McConnell in the Sault Sainte Marie, Ontario, paper *Sault This Week*.

19. The two versions of the novel differ slightly in terms of content. The Aquila edition omits a few passages that appear in the Denoël edition, notably the very short first chapter, but it includes a more ample paratext: a preface written by Chraïbi that locates his text in Montreal, as well as supporting materials provided by others.

20. See Marx-Scouras 139 for a dexterous example.

21. For an overview of the problems with equivalence in translation, see Bassnett.

22. Hédi Bouraoui in his brilliant analysis of the novel comments on the polyvalence of the title and reveals Chraïbi's "intention" for the meaning of the title: Chraïbi "avoue lui-même dans une lettre adressée à H. Bouraoui que le titre est ironique, dérisoire: '(O ma mère, voilà ce qu'on appelle la civilisation !)'" (60). Bouraoui would agree, however, that the author's intention does not necessarily limit the polysemic nature of the title.

23. "Paradoxalement, les structures narratives de la première partie du livre sont fonction de la matière romanesque acquise dans la seconde" (Bouraoui 63).

24. The November date also marks the personal significance, for Chraïbi, of *Mort au Canada*'s insistence on November 17 as the date of Maryvonne and Patrik's meeting. Notice, too, that Marie is the driver, as Maryvonne is in *Mort au Canada*.

25. In one of many moments blurring the line between fiction and autobiography in *La civilisation*, France, Yugoslavia, and Canada are all places that Chraïbi, like the "petit loustic," had visited. See Déjeux 231.

26. El Hassan Yacoubi argues that Chraïbi's fictive retellings of his childhood should be labeled "autofiction": "[Le] pacte romanesque est . . . un pacte contradictoire qui affiche un récit romanesque déclaré par le générique et l'intégration

de faits certifiés authentiques, réels, dans la narration. . . . L'autofiction reste un compromis pour faire entendre la voix de l'auteur à l'abri de toute censure" (9–10).

27. "The novel begins in a realistic vein," writes Monego. "It depicts the typical bourgeois Moroccan housewife of the thirties, ignorant, entirely devoted to her children, her husband, and her housework, isolated from the outside world, and totally resigned to her condition. . . . The second half of the novel, which is quite improbable, translates with verve and amusement the total transformation of this simple peasant into an educated woman of the world who makes her voice heard in the political arena and who crusades for female liberation" (121).

28. Excerpts from these European reviews are given in an appendix to the Quebecois text, a publication that shows greater awareness of *La civilisation*'s place in the francophone publishing world. Hédi Bouraoui comments on the French reviews (68).

29. For Chraïbi, the novel is comic, hilarious: "Oh oui, je pleurais en écrivant ce roman, de rire!" (8).

30. Dormoy Savage's pedagogical perspective is evident from the opening of her review. She begins, "Après avoir découvert le Canada, l'Afrique noire et les Antilles, il est grand temps que nos étudiants puissent se familiariser avec les écrivains nord-africains d'expression française" (817).

31. Dormoy Savage's openness to the text's ironies is emblematic of North American readings, but these readings do not preclude entirely some "anthropological" leanings. Janice Spleth, for example, in her chapter on teaching *La civilisation, ma mère!* . . . (either in English translation or using the Québécois Editions Aquila's FSL version), similarly brings attention to the text's surrealism: "This text is a verbal feast in a much lighter vein [than Chraïbi's previous texts]. There is some kind of magic on almost every page" (65). And yet, despite her awareness of the text's "magical" departures from reality and its emphatic literariness, Spleth nevertheless points to "Mother's own natural abilities" as she introduces students to "the ingenuity of North African artisans" by using a "travel video" (67). Spleth's article reminds us that teaching African literature in North America means trying to achieve a balance between explaining the functioning of a text *and* introducing students to the text's cultural background, a tricky task in which we must avoid anthropologizing fiction while at the same time providing the necessary historical and cultural information for understanding it. This approach, while somewhat problematic, remains more open to the text's ironies than the French critics' wholesale "autobiographization" of *La civilisation*.

32. McConnell's resistance to "Parisian" French themes and style also has a political dimension: it participates in a certain revendication of French in Canada, which struggled to express Quebec's distance both from English Canada and from France. See, e.g., Maranda andWaddell.

33. Zohir El Mostafa, for example, writes, "La simplicité et la modestie . . . étaient exemplaires chez D. Chraïbi. . . . Il plaçait la littérature si haut qu'il dédaignait les biens matériels" (15).

## Coda

1. For an overview of Tunisian history, see Perkins.

2. There were purportedly contacts between the FLQ and the FLN: a FLQ militant named Gilles Pruneau claimed to have established contact with FLN militants, and the historian Louis Fournier reports that Ben Bella, the first president of the Algerian Republic (1963–65), acknowledged these contacts in a private communication and also said that French president de Gaulle had exhorted him to help the Quebecois in their "lutte de libération nationale" (90–91).

3. Susan Z. Andrade has analyzed the tendency in African women novelists' (and feminists') work of not writing explicitly about macropolitics but rather writing about the family as an allegory for the nation.

4. See also F. E. Pheasant-Kelly's chapter in Taban's volume, "Beyond Simulation." For Pheasant-Kelly, inter-imaging means "the reference of one image to another" and is embedded theoretically in the term *inter-textuality* (227).

5. See Camau and Geisser.

6. For an examination of the causes of the civil war in Algeria, see Schulhofer-Wohl.

7. The film's iconic scene, in which the three women drive out to a deserted beach and explore the dilapidated hull of a beached tanker, tests the limits of this paradigm of place as a reflection of human interactions: Aida, Amina, and Fetiha, dwarfed by the rusty, carbuncled interior of the tanker, become introspective. Mesmerized by the regular beat of the surf against the hull, they pare down the layers of conventions that structure everyday conversation and reach the bare, almost aphoristic anxieties that ceaselessly return to haunt them. "Every time I want to breathe I realize it's not the time," muses Fetiha. The bareness of the ship's hull and the inexorable violence of the waves allow the rawness of the women's emotions to surface in a cathartic exchange, carving out a space for the women to express the stifling of their very breath. The setting stands as a metaphor for their condition: they are caught in a restrained space, and the strength of their aspirations and emotions beats against these constraints. In the geographical spectrum of relative liberties, the beach scene symbolizes Tunis more generally, a place where the women's vibrant lives are stifled.

Amina's little red Peugeot holds a similar place on the geographical spectrum of relative liberties. At once an intimate and a public space (what John Urry calls a "private cocoon of glass and metal" "affording the possibilities for sociability" [128]), it fosters warm but ephemeral exchanges between the women. The movement of the vehicle, which is by nature finite, combined with the proximity enforced by the limits of the *carrosserie*, facilitates a certain type of exchange and conversation: the kind of intimacy that does not require eye contact, a closeness generated by a fixed temporal horizon. Time during travel in the car needs to be filled—by the women's singing, for example—and it is fillable because of the promise of its boundedness. Of course, however, the Peugeot belongs not to

Amina but to her husband, as he makes clear when he confiscates her keys and driver's license. The companionship that can exist inside the little red car is always contingent, the vehicle's very mobility representing in some ways the fragile and fluctuating social relations that make the women's access to it possible. It is no more a guarantor or a symbol of liberty than the beach was.

8. The portrait of Julien also appears, significantly, during the scene in which Fetiha relives the traumas of the Algerian civil war and Aida tries to comfort her while Amina looks on with sympathy. Here, Julien figures as another sympathetic feminine presence, a visual reprise of Amina and Aida's warmth.

9. For an analysis of the 1995 referendum (including a reference to Parizeau's postreferendum comment blaming the loss of the sovereigntists on "money and the ethnic vote"), see Clarke and Kornberg 681.

10. Ross's study on the *survivance* of the Commune sketches out this pattern of solidary moments echoing over time when she discusses William Morris's fascination with medieval Iceland: "Morris tended to call his references to ancient Iceland . . . a 'parable': 'To those that have the hearts to understand, this tale of the past is a parable of the days to come'" (75). Such past moments of solidary communities represent "'anticipatory designs,' 'novae,' or 'exemplary suggestions'" (75); they are germs found in the past for a possibly different (solidary) future.

# Bibliography

Adesokan, Akin. "Knocking Tommy's Hustle." *Agni Online*, 15 October 2010. http://agnionline.bu.edu/fiction/knocking-tommys-hustle.

Alessandrini, Anthony. *Frantz Fanon and the Future of Cultural Politics: Finding Something Different*. Lanham, MD: Lexington Books, 2016.

———. "Their Fight Is Our Fight: Occupy Wall Street, the Arab Spring, and New Modes of Solidarity Today." *Is This What Democracy Looks Like?* Ed. Cristina Beltrán, A. J. Bauer, Rana Jaleel, Andrew Ross. 2017. https://what-democracy-looks-like.org/their-fight-is-our-fight/.

Andrade, Susan Z. *The Nation Writ Small: African Fictions and Feminisms, 1958–1988*. Durham, NC: Duke UP, 2011.

Andrew, Dudley. "An Atlas of World Cinema." *Framework: The Journal of Cinema and Media* 45.2 (Fall 2004), 9–23.

Aquin, Hubert. *Journal, 1948–1971*. Ed. Bernard Beugnot. Montreal: Bibliothèque québécoise, 1999.

———. *Trou de mémoire*. Critical edition. Ed. Janet M. Paterson and Marilyn Randall. Montreal: Bibliothèque québécoise, 1993.

Armes, Roy. "The Context of the African Filmmaker." *A Call to Action: The Films of Ousmane Sembene*. Ed. Sheila Petty. Westport, CT: Greenwood, 1997.

Armitage, Anne. "The Debate over Literary Writing in a Foreign Language: An Overview of Francophonie in the Maghreb." "The Hybrid Literary Text: Arab Creative Authors Writing in Foreign Languages." Special issue, *Alif: Journal of Comparative Poetics* 20 (2000), 39–67.

Arnold, A. James. "Césaire and Shakespeare: Two Tempests." *Comparative Literature* 30.3 (Summer 1978), 236–48. http://www.jstor.org/stable/1770825.

———. "D'Haïti à l'Afrique: *La tragédie du roi Christophe* de Césaire." *Revue de littérature comparée* 60.20 (1 Apr. 1986), 133–48.

Austin, David. *Fear of a Black Nation: Race, Sex, and Security in Sixties Montreal*. Toronto: Between the Lines, 2013.

Bachelard, Gaston. *La poétique de la rêverie*. Paris: Presses universitaires de France, 1960.

Badiou, Alain. *The Communist Hypothesis*. Trans. David Macey and Steve Corcoran. London: Version, 2010.
Balibar, Étienne. "De la lutte des classes à la lutte sans classe?" *Race, nation, classe: Les identités ambiguës*. By Étienne Balibar and Immanuel Wallerstein. 1988. Reprint. Paris: La Découverte, 1997.
Barbery, Muriel, et al. "Le manifeste de quarante-quatre écrivains en faveur d'une langue française qui serait 'libérée de son pacte exclusif avec la nation'; Pour une 'littérature-monde' en français." *Le Monde des livres*, 16 March 2007.
Bassnett, Susan. *Translation Studies*. 4th ed. London: Routledge, 2014.
Bayart, J. F. "Review." *African Affairs* 72.289 (Oct. 1973), 453–54. http://www.jstor.org/stable/721160.
Beaulieu, André, and Jean Hamelin. *La presse québécoise: Des origines à nos jours*. Quebec: Presses de l'Université Laval, 1990.
Beloux, François. "Un poète politique: Aimé Césaire." *Le Magazine Littéraire* 34 (1969), 27–32.
Benjamin, Walter. "Paralipomena to 'On the Concept of History.'" *Selected Writings*. Vol. 4, *1938–1940*. Trans. Edmund Jephcott. Ed. Howard Eiland and Michael W. Jennings. Cambridge, MA: Harvard UP, 2006. 401–11.
Berlant, Lauren. "Introduction: Compassion (and Withholding)." *Compassion: The Culture and Politics of an Emotion*. Ed. Lauren Berlant. New York: Routledge, 2004. 1–13.
Beti, Mongo. "*Contrecensure:* Film d'Alain d'Aix (d'après *Main basse sur le Cameroun*, de Mongo Beti, F. Maspero édit.)." *Peuples noirs—Peuples africains* 23 (1981), 150–52. http://mongobeti.arts.uwa.edu.au/issues/pnpa23/pnpa23_14.html#haut.
———. "L'action des médias occidentaux en Afrique noire dite francophone." *Présence francophone* 8 (Spring 1974), 103–8.
———. *Main basse sur le Cameroun: Autopsie d'une décolonisation*. Montreal: Éditions québécoises, 1974.
———. *Mongo Beti parle: Testament d'un esprit rebelle. Entretiens avec Ambroise Kom*. Paris: Éditions Homnisphères, 2006.
———. "Préface de l'auteur à l'édition de 1977: Quatre années d'interdiction . . . ou de la censure, en connaissance de cause." *Main basse sur le Cameroun*. Paris: La Découverte, 2003.
Bhabha, Homi. "The Commitment to Theory." *New Formations* 5 (1988), 5–23.
Bhely-Quenum, Olympe. Letter to Hubert Aquin. 17 October 1962. 44p-030/2. Fonds Hubert Aquin, Université du Québec à Montréal.
Biyidi-Alama, A. [Mongo Beti, pseud.]. "Pourquoi?" *Peuples noirs—Peuples africains* 1 (1978), 1–26. http://mongobeti.arts.uwa.edu.au/issues/pnpa01/pnpa1.html#fnB4.
Blais, Marie-Claude. *La solidarité: Histoire d'une idée*. Paris: Gallimard, 2007.
Boisseron, Bénédicte. "Afro-Dog." "I Can Be Lightning." Special issue, *Transition* 18 (2015), 15–31. http://www.jstor.org/stable/10.2979/transition.118.15.

Bongie, Chris. *Friends and Enemies: The Scribal Politics of Post/Colonial Literature.* Liverpool: Liverpool UP, 2008.

———. *Islands and Exiles: The Creole Identities of Post/Colonial Literature.* Stanford: Stanford UP, 1998.

Bouopda, Pierre Kamé. *Cameroun du protectorat à la démocratie: 1884–1992.* Paris: L'Harmattan, 2008.

Bouraoui, Hédi. "Ambivalence stucturo-culturelle dans *La civilisation, ma mère!* . . . de Driss Chraïbi." *Modern Language Studies* 10.2 (Spring 1980), 59–68. http://www.jstor.org/stable/3194245.

Bourdon-Higbee, Helene Catherine. "The Cameroonian News Media." MA thesis, University of Montana, 1975. https://scholarworks.umt.edu/cgi/viewcontent.cgi?article=6078&context=etd.

Brady, Thomas F. "Lumumba Fans Racialism to Strengthen Position." *New York Times,* 21 August 1960, E4. ProQuest (Historical Newspapers 115071553).

Brière, Éloïse. "Lire, enseigner et rencontrer Mongo Beti." *Remember Mongo Beti: Mémorial.* Ed. Ambroise Kom. Bayreuth: Thielmann & Breitinger, 2003.

Brière, Jean-François. "Abbé Grégoire and Haitian Independence." "Haiti, 1804–2004: Literature, Culture, and Art." Special issue, *Research in African Literatures* 35.2 (Summer 2004), 34–43.

Briggs, Kate. *This Little Art.* London: Fitzcarraldo, 2017.

Camau, Michel, and Vincent Geisser, eds. *Habib Bourguiba: La trace et l'héritage.* Paris: Karthala, 2004.

Cardinal, Jacques. *Le roman de l'histoire: Politique et transmission du nom dans "Prochain épisode" et "Trou de mémoire" de Hubert Aquin.* Montreal: Éditions Balzac, 1993.

Cazenave, Odile, and Patricia Célérier. *Contemporary Francophone African Writers and the Burden of Commitment.* Charlottesville: U of Virginia P, 2011.

Césaire, Aimé. *Cahier d'un retour au pays natal.* Paris: Pierre Bordas, 1947.

———. *Conférence de presse avec Aimé Césaire.* 1972. Video recording. Archives Université Laval. S-1371. Fonds U-540.

———. *Conférence de presse avec Aimé Césaire (suite).* Interview by Michel Tétu, Lilyan Kesteloot, and Fernando Lambert followed by "La situation du poète antillais et les caractéristiques poétiques de l'Antillais." 1972. Video recording. Archives Université Laval. S-1372. Fonds U-540.

———. "Discours prononcé par Aimé Césaire à Dakar le 6 avril 1966." *Gradhiva: Revue d'anthropologie et d'histoire des arts* 10 (2009), 208–13. http://gradhiva.revues.org/1604.

———. *Discours sur le colonialisme suivi de Discours sur la négritude.* 1955. Paris: Présence Africaine, 2004.

———. *Et les chiens se taisaient: Tragédie.* Paris: Présence Africaine, 1956.

———. *La tragédie du roi Christophe.* Rev. ed. Paris: Présence Africaine, 1970.

———. "Letter to Maurice Thorez." Trans. Chike Jeffers. *Social Text 103* 28.2 (Summer 2010), 145–52.

———. "Société et littérature dans les Antilles." *Études littératires* 6.1 (1973), 9–20. http://id.erudit.org/iderudit/500264ar.

———. *Toussaint Louverture: La révolution française et le problème colonial.* Paris: Présence Africaine, 1961.

———. *Une saison au Congo.* Paris: Seuil, 1973.

———. *Une tempête.* Paris: Seuil, 1969.

Chraïbi, Driss. "Je suis d'une generation perdue." *Lamalif* 2 (Apr. 1966), 41–43.

———. *La civilisation, ma mère!* . . . Paris: Denoël, 1972.

———. *La civilisation, ma mère!* . . . *(avec des notes, des questions, des thèmes de discussion et un lexique bilingue par G. Robert McConnell, M.A. et une notice sur l'auteur et son œuvre par Jean Déjeux).* Montreal: Éditions Aquila, 1972.

———. *Le monde à côté.* Paris: Denoël, 2001.

———. *Mort au Canada.* Paris: Denoël, 1975.

———. *Une vie sans concessions: Interviews with Abdeslam Kadiri.* Léchelle: Zellige, 2009.

Clarke, Harold D., and Allan Kornberg. "Choosing Canada? The 1995 Quebec Sovereignty Referendum." *PS: Political Science and Politics* 29.4 (Dec. 1996), 676–82.

Cohen, William B. "The Colonial Policy of the Popular Front." *French Historical Studies* 7.3 (Spring 1972), 368–93.

Combe, Dominique. "Littératures francophones, littérature-monde en français." *Modern and Contemporary France* 18.2 (May 2010), 231–49.

Copans, Jean. Review of *Main basse sur le Cameroun*, by Mongo Beti. *Cahiers d'études africaines* 13.49 (1973), 167–68. http://www.jstor.org/stable/4391202.

Coulthard, Glen Sean. *Red Skin, White Masks: Rejecting the Colonial Politics of Recognition.* Minneapolis: U of Minnesota P, 2014.

Dash, J. Michael. *The Other America: Caribbean Literature in a New World Context.* Charlottesville: U of Virginia P, 1998.

Daut, Marlene. *Tropics of Haiti: Race and the Literary History of the Haitian Revolution in the Atlantic World, 1789–1865.* Liverpool: Liverpool UP, 2015.

Davis, Gregson. *Aimé Césaire.* Cambridge: Cambridge UP, 1997.

Déjeux, Jean. *Dictionnaire des auteurs maghrébins de langue française.* Paris: Karthala, 1984.

Delayre, Stéphanie. *Driss Chraïbi, une écriture de traverse.* Pessac: Presses universitaires de Bordeaux, 2006.

Demers, Martin. *"Prochain épisode" et La fatigue culturelle.* MA thesis, McGill University, 2011. http://digitool.library.mcgill.ca/R/?func=dbin-jump-full&object_id=106274&local_base=GEN01-MCG02.

Derrick, Jonathan. *Africa's 'Agitators': Militant Anti-Colonialism in Africa and the West, 1918–1939.* New York: Columbia UP, 2008.

Desjardins, Louise. *Pauline Julien: La vie à mort.* Montreal: Leméac, 1999.

De Witte, Ludo. *The Assassination of Lumumba*. Trans. Ann Wright and Renée Fenby. London: Verso, 2001.

Dewitte, Philippe. *Les mouvements nègres en France, 1915–1939*. Paris: L'Harmattan, 1985.

Di Méo, Nicolas. "From *Francophonie* to World Literature in French: A Contextual Analysis." *Literature, Geography, Translation: Studies in World Writing*. Ed. Stefan Helgesson. Cambridge: Cambridge Scholars, 2011.

Diop, Boubacar Boris. "Mongo Beti et nous." *Remember Mongo Beti: Mémorial*. Ed. Ambroise Kom. Bayreuth: Thielmann & Breitinger, 2003.

Djiffack, André, and Anny Wynchank. "Mongo Beti." *Censorship: A World Encyclopedia*. Ed. Derek Jones. London: Routledge, 2001. 224–25.

Dor, Georges. "La chanson difficile." *Georges Dor*. Montreal: Gamma Records, 1966.

Dormoy Savage, Nadine. Review of *La civilisation, ma mère! . . .* , by Driss Chraïbi. *French Review* 45.5 (Apr. 1976), 817–18.

Dorsinville, Max. *Le pays natal: Essais sur les littératures du Tiers-Monde et du Québec*. Dakar: Nouvelles éditions africaines, 1983.

———. "L'influence d'Aimé Césaire au Québec." *Soleil éclaté: Mélanges offerts à Aimé Césaire à l'occasion de son soixante-dixième anniversaire*. Ed. Jacqueline Leiner. Tübingen: Gunter Narr Verlag, 1984. 115–23.

Dubois, Laurent. *Avengers of the New World: The Story of the Haitian Revolution*. Cambridge, MA: Harvard UP, 2004.

Dupont, Pierre. *How Levesque Won*. Trans. Sheila Fischman. Toronto: Lorimer, 1977.

El Mostafa, Zohir. *Hommages à Driss Chraïbi*. Paris: L'Harmattan, 2013.

El-Tayeb, Fatima. "The Forces of Creolization: Colorblindness and Visible Minorities in the New Europe." *The Creolization of Theory*. Ed. Shu-Mei Shih and Françoise Lionnet. Durham, NC: Duke UP, 2011.

Fanon, Frantz. *Black Skin, White Masks*. Trans. Charles Lam Markmann. New York: Grove Press, 1967.

———. "La mort de Lumumba: Pouvions-nous faire autrement?" Reprinted in *Pour la révolution africaine: Écrits politiques*. Paris: La Découverte & Syros, 2001. 217–23.

Featherstone, David. *Solidarity: Hidden Histories and Geographies of Internationalism*. London: Zed, 2012.

Foesser, Guitte. Review of *Mort au Canada*, by Driss Chraïbi. *Books Abroad* 50.2 (Spring 1976), 360.

Fonkoua, Romuald. *Aimé Césaire (1913–2008)*. Paris: Perrin, 2010.

Fortier, Monique, dir. *À l'heure de la décolonisation*. Montreal: National Film Board of Canada, 1963.

Fouet, Jeanne. "La fabrication du roman familial dans les passages autobiographiques." *Écritures de soi: Secrets et réticences. Actes du colloque international de Besançon (22, 23, 24 novembre 2000)*. Ed. Marie Miguet-Ollagnier and Bertrand Degott. Paris: L'Harmattan, 2002. 219–36.

Fournier, Louis. *F.L.Q.: Histoire d'un mouvement clandestin*. Montreal: Québec Amérique, 1982.

Frye, Northrop. *The Educated Imagination*. Toronto: House of Anansi Press, 2002.

Genette, Gérard. *Paratexts: Thresholds of Interpretation*. Trans. Jane E. Lewin. Cambridge: Cambridge UP, 1997.

Gil, Alex. "Découverte de l'urtext de *Et les chiens se taisaient*." *Aimé Césaire à l'œuvre*. Ed. Marc Cheymol and Philippe Ollé-Laprune. Paris: EAC, 2010. 145–56.

———. "La représentation en profondeur de *Et les chiens se taisaient* d'Aimé Césaire: Pour une édition génétique en ligne." *Genesis: Manuscrits—recherche—invention* 33 (2011), 67–77. http://genesis.revues.org/605.

Giroud, Françoise. "Terrorisme et ordinateur." Online archives, http://prix francoisegiroud.com/archives/terrorisme-et-ordinateur. Originally published in *L'Express*, 2–8 March 1970.

Glissant, Édouard. *Poetics of Relation*. Trans. Betsy Wing. Ann Arbor: U Michigan P, 1997.

———. *Traité du tout-monde: Poétique IV*. Paris: Gallimard, 1997.

Guinoune, Anne-Marie. *De l'impuissance de l'enfance à la revanche par l'écriture: Le parcours de Driss Chraïbi et sa représentation du couple*. PhD diss., University of Groningen, 2003.

Hargreaves, Alec G. "Presaging the Francosphere: Politics, Culture, and the End of Empire." *Francosphere* 2.2 (2013), 121–34.

Hargreaves, Alec G., Charles Forsdick, and David Murphy, eds. *Transnational French Studies: Postcolonialism and Littérature-monde*. Liverpool: Liverpool UP, 2010.

Harrison, Nicholas. "Driss Chraïbi." *Censorship: A World Encyclopedia*. Ed. Derek Jones. London: Routledge, 2015. 512–13.

Harvey, David. *Cosmopolitanism and the Geographies of Freedom*. New York: Columbia UP, 2009.

Held, Jean-Francis. *L'affaire Moumié*. Paris: François Maspero, 1961.

Hiddleston, Jane. *Decolonising the Intellectual: Politics, Culture, and Humanism at the End of the French Empire*. Liverpool: Liverpool UP, 2014.

Hooker, Juliet. *Race and the Politics of Solidarity*. Oxford: Oxford UP, 2009.

Hugo, Victor. *Le Rhin*. https://fr.wikisource.org/wiki/Le_Rhin_(Victor_Hugo).

Janis, Michael. "Remembering Sembene: The Grandfather of African Feminism." *CLA Journal* 51.31 (Mar. 2008), 248–64.

Janvier, Louis Joseph. *Les constitutions d'Haïti, 1801–1885*. Vol I. Paris: Marpon & Flammarion, 1886. http://gallica.bnf.fr/ark:/12148/bpt6k61426252/f17.image.r=Louis-Joseph+Janvier.

Joseph-Gabriel, Annette. *Reimagining Liberation: How Black Women Transformed Citizenship in the French Empire*. Urbana-Champaign: U of Illinois P, 2020.

Julien, Pauline. *Femmes de paroles*. Montreal: Kébec-Disc, 1977.
Kakish, Shereen. "Énonciation fictive au service de la réalité sociale dans les romans africains d'expression française." *Dalhousie French Studies* 101 (Spring 2014), 3–11. http://www.jstor.org/stable/43487404.
Kalter, Christoph. *The Discovery of the Third World: The French Radical Left and the International Struggle against Colonialism, c. 1950–1970*. Trans. Thomas Dunlap. Cambridge: Cambridge UP, 2016.
Kazanjian, David. "Charles Brockden Brown's Biloquial Nation: National Culture and White Settler Colonialism in *Memoirs of Carwin the Biloquist*." *American Literature* 73.3 (Sept. 2001), 459–96.
———. *The Colonizing Trick*. Minneapolis: U of Minnesota P, 2003.
Keable, Jacques. *Québec-Presse, un journal libre et engagé*. Montreal: Éditions écosociété, 2015.
Kemedjio, Cilas. *Mongo Beti: Le combattant fatigué. Une biographie intellectuelle*. Berlin: LIT Verlag, 2013.
Kemedjio, Cilas, Pierre Tabue, André Djiffack, and Blaise Toualla. "Mongo Beti: The Nobility of a Struggle." *Critical Perspectives on Mongo Beti*. Ed. Stephen H. Arnold. Boulder, CO: Lynne Rienner, 1998. 421–24. Originally published in *African Literature Association Bulletin* 18.4 (Fall 1992).
Kesteloot, Lilyan. *Aimé Césaire: Une étude*. 1962. Reprint. Paris: Pierre Seghers, 1970.
———. "La tragédie du roi Christophe ou les indépendances africaines au miroir d'Haïti." *Aimé Césaire, l'homme et l'œuvre*. By Lilyan Kesteloot et Barthélémy Kotchy. Paris: Présence Africaine, 1973. 158–72.
Kom, Ambroise. Introduction to *Remember Mongo Beti: Mémorial*. Ed. Ambroise Kom. Bayreuth: Thielmann & Breitinger, 2003.
———. "Mongo Beti Returns to Cameroon: A Journey into Darkness." *Critical Perspectives on Mongo Beti*. Ed. Stephen H. Arnold. Boulder, CO: Lynne Rienner, 1998. 413–19.
———. "Remember Mongo Beti." Trans. R. H. Mitsch. *Research in African Literatures* 33.2 (Summer 2002), 1–3.
———. *Université des Montagnes: Pour solde de tout compte*. Rouen: Éditions des peuples noirs, 2017.
Lambert, Fernando. Email exchange with author. 28 June 2018.
Lapointe, Martine-Emmanuelle. *Emblèmes d'une littérature: "Le libraire," "Prochain épisode," et "L'avalée des avalés."* Montreal: Fides, 2008.
Leiner, Jacqueline. *Aimé Césaire: Le terreau primordial*. Vol. 1. Tübingen: Gunter Narr Verlag, 1993.
Lezra, Jacques. "Translated Turks on the Early Modern Stage." *Theater Crossing Borders: Transnational and Transcultural Exchange in Early Modern Drama*. Ed. Robert Henke and Eric Nicholson. Aldershot: Ashgate, 2008. 159–80.
Liauzu, Claude. *Aux origines des tiers-mondismes: Colonisés et anticolonialistes en France (1919–1939)*. Paris: L'Harmattan, 1982.

Lionnet, Françoise. "Continents and Archipelagoes: From 'E Pluribus Unum' to Creolized Solidarities." *PMLA* 123.5 (Oct. 2008), 1503–15.

Lionnet, Françoise, and Shu-Mei Shih. "The Creolization of Theory." Introduction to *The Creolization of Theory*. Ed. Shu-Mei Shih and Françoise Lionnet. Durham, NC: Duke UP, 2011.

———, eds. *Minor Transnationalism*. Durham, NC: Duke UP, 2005.

Little, Roger. "Césaire, Hammarskjöld and an Unattributed Quotation in *Une saison au Congo*." *French Studies Bulletin* 35 (June 1990), 13–17.

———. "A Further Unacknowledged Quotation in Césaire: Echoes of Ourika." *French Studies Bulletin* 43 (June 1992), 13–16.

Loichot, Valérie. *Orphan Narratives: The Postplantation Literature of Faulkner, Glissant, Morrison, and Saint-John Perse*. Charlottesville: U of Virginia P, 2007.

Louis XIV. "Le code noir: Édit du roi sur les esclaves des îles de l'Amérique (1680)." *L'esclavage aux Antilles françaises avant 1789: D'après des documents inédits des archives coloniales*. By Lucien Peytraud. Paris: Hachette, 1897. http://classiques.uqac.ca/collection_documents/louis_XIV_roi_de_France/code_noir/code_noir.pdf.

Lucas, Sir Charles Prestwood. *A Historical Geography of the British Colonies: Canada—Part 1 (New France)*. Vol. 5. London: Oxford Clarendon, 1901.

Lumumba, Patrice. *La pensée politique de Patrice Lumumba*. Ed. Jean Van Lierde. Paris: Présence Africaine, 1963.

Maranda, Pierre, and Éric Waddell. "Imposer la bâtardise francophone." *Anthropologie et sociétés* 6.2 (1982), 1–3. https://www.erudit.org/fr/revues/as/1982-v6-n2-as498/006076ar/.

Martin, Florence. "*Cinéma-monde*: De-Orbiting Maghrebi Cinema." *Contemporary French Civilization* 41.3–4 (Dec. 2016), 461–75.

———. "The Whiles of Maghrebi Women's Cinema." *Visions of Struggle in Women's Filmmaking from the Mediterranean*. Ed. Flavia Laviosa. New York: Palgrave Macmillan, 2010. 23–41.

Marx-Scouras, Danielle. "A Literature of Departure: The Cross-Cultural Writings of Driss Chraïbi." *Research in African Literatures* 23.2 (Summer 1992), 131–44.

Maspero, François. *Les abeilles et la guêpe*. Paris: Seuil, 2002.

McClintock, Anne. *Imperial Leather: Race, Gender, and Sexuality in the Colonial Contest*. New York: Routledge, 1995.

McDonald, Russ. *Shakespeare and the Arts of Language*. Oxford: Oxford UP, 2001.

Memmi, Albert. *Portrait du colonisé suivi de Les Canadiens français sont-ils des colonisés?* Montreal: L'étincelle, 1972.

Mesch, Rachel. *Before Trans: Three Gender Stories from Nineteenth-Century France*. Stanford: Stanford UP, 2020.

"Michel Tétu: Faculté des Lettres." Website of Université Laval. http://www.rec.ulaval.ca/rectorat/Honneuretdistinctions/Professeursemerites/notesbio2006/biomtetu2006.htm.
Michon, Jacques, ed. *Histoire de l'édition littéraire au Québec au XXe siècle*. 2 vols. Quebec: Fides, 1999.
Miller, Christopher L. *The French Atlantic Triangle: Literature and Culture of the Slave Trade*. Durham, NC: Duke UP, 2008.
———. "The Slave Trade, *La Françafrique*, and the Globalization of French." *French Global: A New Approach to Literary History*. Ed. Christie McDonald and Susan Rubin Suleiman. New York: Columbia UP, 2011.
Mills, Sean. *The Empire Within: Postcolonial Thought and Political Activism in Sixties Montreal*. Montreal: McGill-Queens UP, 2010.
———. *A Place in the Sun: Haiti, Haitians, and the Remaking of Québec*. Montreal: McGill-Queens UP, 2016.
Monego, Joan Phyllis. *Maghrebian Literature in French*. Boston: G. K. Hall, 1984.
Moudileno, Lydie. "From *Pré-littérature* to *Littérature-monde*: Postures, Neologisms, Prophecies." *Antillanité, créolité, littérature-monde*. Ed. Isabelle Constant, Kahiudi C. Mabana, and Philip Nanton. Cambridge: Cambridge Scholars, 2013. 13–26.
———. "The Troubling Popularity of West African Romance Novels." "Positively Popular: African Culture in the Mainstream." Special issue, *Research in African Literatures* 39.4 (Winter 2008), 120–32. http://www.jstor.org/stable/30135307.
Nakayama, Thomas K., and Robert L. Krizek. "Whiteness: A Strategic Rhetoric." *Quarterly Journal of Speech* 81 (1995), 291–309.
Nesbitt, Nick. *Caribbean Critique: Antillean Critical Theory from Toussaint to Glissant*. Liverpool: Liverpool UP, 2013.
———. "From Louverture to Lenin: Aimé Césaire and Anticolonial Marxism." *Small Axe* 19.3 (Nov. 2015), 129–44. https://muse.jhu.edu/article/602416.
———. "History and Nation-Building in Aimé Césaire's *La tragédie du roi Christophe*." *Journal of Haitian Studies* 3/4 (1997–98), 132–48. http://www.jstor.org/stable/41715051.
Ngũgĩ wa Thiong'o. *Decolonising the Mind: The Politics of Language in African Literature*. 1981. Reprint. Nairobi: East African Educational Publishers, 1986.
Oktaba, Irene. "Sault Native G. Robert McConnell Now a Practising Linquist [*sic*], Writer, Publisher." *Sault This Week*, 3 July 2008.
Parti Québécois, Conseil exécutif. *Prochaine étape: Quand nous serons vraiment chez nous*. Montreal: Éditions du Parti québécois, 1972.
Perkins, Kenneth. *A History of Modern Tunisia*. Cambridge: Cambridge UP, 2014.
Pheasant-Kelly, F. E. "Beyond Simulation: Inter-Textuality, Inter-Imaging and Pastiche in *The Artist*." *Meta- and Inter-Images in Contemporary Visual Art and Culture*. Ed. Carla Taban. Leuven: Leuven UP, 2013.

Pierre, Samuel, ed. *Ces Québécois venus d'Haïti: Contribution de la communauté haïtienne à l'édification du Québec moderne.* Montreal: École polytechnique, 2007.

Pigeon, Elaine. "Hosanna! Michel Tremblay's Queering of National Identity." In *a Queer Country: Gay and Lesbian Studies in the Canadian Context.* Ed. Terry Goldie. Vancouver: Arsenal Pulp Press, 2001.

Poulin, Mathieu. *Citer la révolte: La reprise québécoise du discours de la décolonisation francophone.* MA thesis, Université de Montréal, 2009. http://hdl.handle.net/1866/3753.

Purdy, Anthony. "The Politics of Incoherence: Narrative Failure and the Invention of History in Hubert Aquin's *Prochain épisode.*" *A Certain Difficulty of Being: Essays on the Quebec Novel.* Montreal: McGill-Queen's UP, 1990. 83–108.

Raja, Masood Ashraf. "Ousmane Sembène's *God's Bits of Wood*: The Anatomy of a Strike and the Ideologeme of Solidarity." *Spheres Public and Private: Western Genres in African Literature.* Ed. Gordon Collier. New York: Rodopi, 2011. 423–40.

Randall, Marilyn. "L'homme et l'œuvre: Biolectographie d'Hubert Aquin." *Hubert Aquin en revue.* Ed. Jacinthe Martel and Jean-Christian Pleau. Quebec: U of Quebec P, 2006. 123–42.

*Revue de l'Avranchin: Bulletin trimestriel de la société d'archéologie, de littérature, sciences et arts d'Avranches et de Mortain.* Tome VII. Avranches: Jules Durand, 1894. https://play.google.com/store/books/details?id=B6gTAAAAYAAJ&rdid=book-B6gTAAAAYAAJ&rdot=1.

Rivet, Daniel. *Le Maghreb à l'épreuve de la colonisation.* Paris: Hachette, 2002.

Rivière, Sylvain. *Léandre Bergeron, né en exil.* Trois-Pistoles: Éditions Trois-Pistoles, 2007.

Roberts, Katherine A. "Making Women Pay: Revolution, Violence, Decolonizing Québec in Hubert Aquin's *Trou de mémoire.*" *Québec Studies* 30 (Fall/Winter 2000), 17–27.

Rorty, Richard. *Contingency, Irony, and Solidarity.* Cambridge: Cambridge UP, 1989.

Rosello, Mireille. "The 'Césaire Effect,' or How to Cultivate One's Nation." *Research in African Literatures* 32.4 (Winter 2001), 77–91.

Ross, Kristin. *Communal Luxury: The Political Imaginary of the Paris Commune.* London: Verso, 2015.

Roy, Fernande. "Nègres blancs d'Amérique?" *Liberté* 51.3 (Sept. 2009), 34–52. https://www.erudit.org/fr/revues/liberte/2009-v51-n3-liberte1038708/34736ac.pdf.

Saint-Martin, Lori. "Pur polyester." *Nuit blanche, magazine littéraire* 73 (1998–99), 35–37. http://id.erudit.org/iderudit/19312ac.

Samson-Legault, Daniel. *Dissident—Pierre Vallières (1938–1998): Au-delà de "Nègres blancs d'Amérique."* Montreal: Québec Amérique, 2018.

Schulhofer-Wohl, Jonah. "Algeria (1992–Present)." *Civil Wars of the World: Major Conflicts since World War II*. Ed. Karl Derouen Jr. and Uk Heo. Vol. 1. Santa Barbara, CA: ABC-CLIO, 2007.

Sekora, Karin. "'Il y avait un tabou à lever'; Intertextualité dans *Une saison au Congo* d'Aimé Césaire." *Œuvre et critiques* 19.2 (Jan. 1994), 243–65.

Selao, Ching. "Les fils d'Aimé Césaire: De la Martinique au Québec." *Tangence* 98 (2012), 35–56. https://www.erudit.org/fr/revues/tce/2012-n98-tce0290/1012486ar/.

Sembene, Ousmane. *Les bouts de bois de Dieu: Banty mam yall*. Paris: Le livre contemporain, 1960.

Senghor, Léopold Sedar. "Ce que l'homme noir apporte." *L'homme de couleur*. By S. E. Cardinal Verdier et al. Paris: Librairie Plon, 1939. 291–313.

Sepinwall, Alyssa Goldstein. *The Abbé Grégoire and the French Revolution: The Making of Modern Universalism*. Oakland: U of California P, 2005.

Sherrington, Robert. "The Use of Mongo Beti." *Critical Perspectives on Mongo Beti*. Ed. Stephen H. Arnold. Boulder, CO: Lynne Rienner, 1998. 393–404. Originally published in *Francophone Studies*, ed. Anne-Marie Nisbet (Kensington, Australia: New South Wales UP, 1981).

Söderlind, Sylvia. *Margin/Alias: Language and Colonization in Canadian and Québécois Fiction*. Toronto: U of Toronto P, 1991.

Spleth, Janice. "Chraïbi's *Mother Comes of Age*." *African Novels in the Classroom*. Ed. Margaret Jean Hay. Boulder, CO: Lynne Rienner, 2000. 63–74.

Suret-Canale, Jean. "Mon ami Mongo Beti." *Remember Mongo Beti: Mémorial*. Ed. Ambroise Kom. Bayreuth: Thielmann & Breitinger, 2003.

Taban, Carla. Introduction to *Meta- and Inter-Images in Contemporary Visual Art and Culture*. Ed. Carla Taban. Leuven: Leuven UP, 2013.

Tchumkam, Hervé. "Of Murder and Love: Peregrinations of the African Detective Writer." "Measuring Time: Karin Barber and the Study of Everyday Africa." Ed. Onookome Okome and Stephanie Newell. Special issue, *Research in African Literatures* 43.4 (Winter 2012), 38–49. http://www.jstor.org/stable/10.2979/reseafrilite.43.4.38.

Tétu, Michel. "Cousins proches et voisins lointains: La francophonie." *Annuaire français des relations internationales* 1.1 (2000), 407–11. http://www.afri-ct.org/article/cousins-proches-et-voisins/.

Tremblay, Michel. *À toi pour toujours, ta Marie-Lou*. Paris: Actes Sud-Papier, 2007.

Urry, John. *Mobilities*. Cambridge: Polity Press, 2007.

Vallières, Pierre. *L'urgence de choisir*. Montreal: Parti pris, 1971.

———. *Nègres blancs d'Amérique: Autobiographie précoce d'un "terroriste" québécois*. Montreal: Parti pris, 1968.

Wall, Anthony. "Prisonnier dans ce trou, ce *Trou de mémoire*." *Voix et images* 14.2 (Winter 1989), 301–20.

Walsh, John Patrick. *Free and French in the Caribbean: Toussaint Louverture, Aimé Césaire, and Narratives of Loyalist Opposition*. Bloomington: Indiana UP, 2013.
Warren, Jean-Philippe. "L'opération McGill français: Une page méconnue de l'histoire de la gauche nationaliste." *Bulletin d'histoire politique* 16. 2 (Winter 2008), 97–116. https://www.bulletinhistoirepolitique.org/le-bulletin/numeros-precedents/volume-16-numero-2/l%E2%80%99operation-mcgill-francais-une-page-meconnue-de-l%E2%80%99histoire-de-la-gauche-nationaliste/.
Webster, David. "Foreign Policy, Diplomacy, and Decolonization." *Canada and the Third World: Overlapping Histories*. Ed. Karen Dubinsky, Sean Mills, and Scott Rutherford. Toronto: U of Toronto P, 2016.
"White Baby." Fonds Hubert Aquin, Université du Québec à Montréal. 44p-660:06/1.
White, Hayden. *Tropics of Discourse: Essays in Cultural Criticism*. Baltimore: Johns Hopkins UP, 1978.
Wilde, Lawrence. *Global Solidarity*. Edinburgh: Edinburgh UP, 2013.
Wilder, Gary. *Freedom Time: Negritude, Decolonization, and the Future of the World*. Durham, NC: Duke UP, 2015.
Yacoubi, El Hassan. "L'autofiction comme alternative à l'autobiographie chez les écrivains marocains." *Nouvelles études francophone* 31.1 (Spring 2016), 7–19. https://doi.org/10.1353/nef.2016.0016.
Yanacopoulo, Andrée. Telephone interview. 16 June 2016.
Zand, Nicole. "Entretien avec Aimé Césaire." *Le Monde* 7071 (7 Oct. 1967), 13. http://www3.carleton.ca/francotheatres/entretiens_Theatre_Aime_Cesaire.html.
Zeilig, Leo. *Patrice Lumumba: Africa's Lost Leader*. London: Haus, 2008.

# Index

abolitionism, 5
Adesokan, Akin, "Knocking Tommy's Hustle," 237n1
Afana, Osendé, 151
Ahidjo, Ahmadou, regime of, 118, 119, 121, 122–29, 138, 150–51, 155, 157, 159–63, 250nn11–12, 252n26
Alessandrini, Anthony: *Frantz Fanon and the Future of Cultural Politics,* 240–41n32; "Their Fight Is Our Fight," 8
Algeria, 140, 148, 218–20
*À l'heure de la décolonisation* (documentary), 246n7
analogies, 66, 71–72, 201, 245n38
Andrade, Susan Z., *The Nation Writ Small,* 19, 257n3
Andrew, Dudley, "An Atlas of World Cinema," 234
Aquin, Hubert, 15, 20; Césaire's influence on, 76; essays of, 84; fascination with colonization, 83–84; "La fatigue culturelle des Canadiens français," 63, 76; *Prochain épisode,* 247n17; published diaries, 247n19; suicide of, 247n17. See also *Trou de mémoire;* "White Baby"
Armes, Roy, "The Context of the African Filmmaker," 235
Association canadienne d'études africaines (1975 conference), 159–60
asymptote, 8–10. See also solidarity, francophone
Austin, David, *Fear of a Black Nation,* 5–6, 77, 238n13

Bachelard, Gaston, *La poétique de la rêverie,* 1, 7, 21

Badiou, Alain, *The Communist Hypothesis,* 232, 238n15
Balibar, Étienne, "De la lutte des classes à la lutte sans classe?," 112–13
Baratier, Jacques, 253n1
Barthes, Roland, 239n17
Barton, Nathalie, 157–58
Basque Country, 150, 151, 159
Bayart, Jean-François, "Review," 249n7
Ben Bella, Ahmed, 257n2
Benjamin, Jacques, "Préface à l'édition québécoise," 139–48, 149, 150, 151, 163
Benjamin, Walter, "Paralipomena to 'On the Concept of History,'" 8–9
Benoist, Jean, 70–71
*Bent familia* (film), 19–20, 216–36, 240n27; critique of heterosexual normativity, 229–33; gender relations in, 220–21, 222–28; geographical spectrum in, 220–22; gift exchange in, 231–32; interpictorial references in, 217–20, 232–33, 234, 235–36; Julien poster in, 217, 222–28, 233, 258n8; nostalgic francophone solidarities in, 19, 215–34; paradigm of place in, 257n7; producers of, 235; Tremblay poster in, 217, 228–33
Bergeron, Léandre, 133, 136, 137–38, 155, 160
Berlant, Lauren, "Introduction: Compassion (and Withholding)," 243n18
Berque, Jacques, 62
Beti, Mongo, 15, 16, 18, 20; "Avertissement," 153–55; French citizenship of, 118, 222, 249n2; influence on white

Beti, Mongo (*continued*)
  Quebecois intellectuals, 120, 129–31; *Main basse* in career trajectory of, 119–20, 121–22; press conference with Bergeron, 159–60; treated as martyr of censorship, 159–60, 253n37. See also *Main basse sur le Cameroun*
Bhabha, Homi, "The Commitment to Theory," 222
Bhely-Quenum, Olympe, 245–46n5
biloquism, 84
Biya, Paul, 249n2
Black Liberation Front, 1–2, 21, 92–93
Blais, Marie-Claude, *La solidarité*, 237n3
Boisseron, Bénédicte, "Afro-Dog," 241n8
Bongie, Chris, *Islands and Exiles*, 95–96
Bouraoui, Hédi, "Ambivalence structuro-culturelle dans *La civilisation, ma mère!* . . . de Driss Chraïbi," 198–99, 205, 209, 210–11, 255n22
Bourassa, Robert, 142
Bourguiba, Habib, 220
*bouts de bois de dieu* trope, 13–14
Bouzid, Nouri, 15, 19, 20, 216. See also *Bent familia* (film)
Brière, Éloïse, "Lire, enseigner et rencontrer Mongo Beti," 253n37
Briggs, Kate, *This Little Art*, 239n17, 245n37
Burke, Kenneth, 239n20

Cameroon, 222; Ahidjo regime crimes and atrocities, 160–63; Beti's *Main basse* concerning, 118–64; contextualization for Quebecois readers, 131–32, 134–36, 140, 148–52; French neocolonialism in, 119, 120–29, 135–36, 137–41, 150–51, 157–58
capitalism: Canada's neocolonial involvement, 162, 180, 190–92, 251–52n26; consumerism and commodity fetishism, 176, 180, 192–93, 211; foreign investment in Quebec, 141–46; global colonial, 2, 26, 29, 31–47, 234; global neocolonial, 16, 119, 123–29, 137–38, 143, 151–52, 160–63, 216, 251–52n26; grassroots, 146; hegemony of, 231–33; Marx's description of, 2; "native" elites and, 142–43, 145–47; racialized, 35–47, 49, 72, 242n16

Cardinal, Jacques, *Le roman de l'histoire*, 97–98, 99–100
Caribbean: Césaire's *Et les chiens* and, 33–34; Césaire's *Une tempête* and, 47–52. See also Haitian Revolution; Martinique
Cazenave, Odile, *Contemporary Francophone African Writers and the Burden of Commitment* (with Célérier), 216
Célérier, Patricia, *Contemporary Francophone African Writers and the Burden of Commitment* (with Cazenave), 216
Césaire, Aimé, 15, 20, 118; *Cahier d'un retour au pays natal*, 76; filmed interview with, 64, 65; gendered nature of metaphorical language defining influence of, 19, 29–30, 50–51, 88–89, 216; influence on white Quebecois intellectuals, 24, 62–75, 76, 244nn32–33; interest in Haiti, 36, 241–42n10, 242n12; interview (1967), 24; involvement in Martinique national determination, 51, 59, 222, 244n33; lectures and essays of, 18, 23, 25, 26, 62–75, 244n34; nation-building models, 244n31; pharmacist brother of, 76; plays of, 18, 23–61, 64, 74–75, 222, 228, 242n14; press conference (1972), 51, 64, 65, 70, 242n12; "La situation du poète antillais et les caractéristiques poétiques de l'Antillais," 72–73; "Société et littérature dans les Antilles," 64, 66–72; tropes and metaphors used by, 24, 28–34, 37–39, 48, 58–61, 66, 219; use of abstraction, 24, 75; views on class questions, 72–73; visit to Quebec, 63–64, 169–70, 218. See also *Discours sur la négritude*; *Et les chiens se taisaient*; *tragédie du roi Christophe, La*; *Une saison au Congo*; *Une tempête*
Ceylon uprising, 153–54
Chad, 151, 152, 159, 164
Charte des valeurs québécoises, 80
Chateaubriand, François-René de, 250n13
Chraïbi, Driss, 15, 18, 20; autofictions of, 201, 204–5, 255–56n26; Berber trilogy, 172; *Les boucs*, 167; choice of French for writings, 166–67; "Je suis d'une génération perdue," 171–72; nationalism viewed by, 171–72; as person

"in-between," 165–67, 169–71, 209–10, 222; Quebec city sojourn, 167–74, 193; *Succession*, 201; *Un ami viendra vous voir*, 253n1; *Une vie sans concession*, 166. See also *civilisation, ma mère!, La; monde à côté, Le; Mort au Canada; passé simple, Le*
Christophe, Henri, 35–47, 61
Cinétéléfilms, 235
*civilisation, ma mère!, La* (Chraïbi), 18, 173–74, 195–213; critics of Parisian edition, 205–6; double reading of, 197–98, 206, 209–11; foreword in Quebecois edition, 205; gender-role reversal in, 203–4, 209–10; ironic reading of, 206–8, 209, 211; Morocco–Canada simile in, 199–201, 207; *Le passé simple* and *Succession* compared with, 201, 202–4; as pedagogical novel, 195, 196–97, 205–9, 210, 212–13; political stance in Quebec's cultural struggle, 212–13; setting of, 195–96; significance of Quebec in, 198–212; tone of, 202; translated nature of, 211
Code du statut personnel (CPS), 220
Code Noir, 4, 30–31, 42, 241n6
Colin, Jean-Paul, 208
colonialism as infectious disease metaphor, 76, 120
"colonizing trick," 17, 240n25
Combe, Dominique, "Littératures francophones, littérature-monde en français," 239n22
Comité de défense de la race nègre, 5
Concordia University, 145
Congolese independence, 23, 52–61, 151
Congrès du réseau des villes refuges (1997), 238–39n16
*Contre-censure* (film), 121, 130, 136, 155–63, 228; Beti's presence in, 160; Catholic Church's complicity depicted in, 161–63; as display of solidarity, 155; montage in, 158–59; parallel interviews in, 159–61; pseudonyms in, 156, 157–58; puns in, 156–57; similes in, 156–59; structure of, 156
Copans, Jean, review of *Main basse sur le Cameroun*, 249n7
Coulthard, Glen Sean, *Red Skin, White Masks*, 245n4
Cuba, 226

d'Allemagne, André, *Le colonialisme au Québec*, 140–41
Dash, J. Michael, *The Other America*, 7
Davis, Angela, 129
Davis, Gregson, *Aimé Césaire*, 241n9
decolonization: in Aquin's *Trou de mémoire*, 76, 78, 82–84, 89–93, 97; Beti's *Main basse sur le Cameroun* as autopsy of, 120; Quebec's parallels and differences with African and Caribbean countries, 136, 143, 148, 238n14
de Gaulle, Charles, 149, 202
Denoël publishing firm, 174, 195
Derome, Bernard, 252n35
Descartes, René, *Discourse on Method*, 81
Desjardins, Louise, *Pauline Julien*, 226
*Discours sur la négritude* (Césaire), 24, 63–64
Djiffack, André, "Mongo Beti: The Nobility of a Struggle," 250–51n15
dogs trope, 34–35
Domazon, Lina, 161
Dor, Georges, "La chanson difficile," 10–11
Dormoy Savage, Nadine, review of *La civilisation, ma mère!...*, by Driss Chraïbi, 208–9, 256nn30–31
Dorsinville, Max, "L'influence d'Aimé Césaire au Québec," 63
Dubois, Laurent, *Avengers of the New World*, 44
Duclos, Michèle, 92–93
Duplessis, Maurice, 79, 237n2
Duras, Claire de, *Ourika*, 242n15

économie-monde, 112–13
Éditions Aquila, 195
Éditions Maspero, 118, 148
Éditions Parti pris, 134
El Mostafa, Zohir, *Hommages à Driss Chraïbi*, 256n33
El-Tayeb, Fatima, "The Forces of Creolization," 80
*entrelacs* trope, 78, 85–88, 106–7, 117
Estang, Luc, *Le bonheur et la salut*, 247n19
*Et les chiens se taisaient* (Césaire), 23, 25, 26–35; bishops in, 32–33, 53; concept of unity in destruction, 27–28, 32, 48, 59; forest/wood trope in, 28–34, 241n5; meaning of title, 34–35; narrators' role in, 33–34; slavery portrayed in, 27–34
*Études littéraires*, 66

Fanon, Frantz, 62, 98, 240–41n32; *L'an V de la révolution algérienne*, 148; *Black Skin, White Masks*, 81, 88–89, 91, 108; *Les damnés de la terre*, 148; "La mort de Lumumba," 244n27
*fatigue culturelle* notion, 63, 76
Featherstone, David, *Solidarity*, 3, 237n7
*Femmes de paroles* (Julien album), 222–23, 226
First Nations people of Canada, 173
Fochivé, Jean, 128
Foesser, Guitte, review of *Mort au Canada*, 174
Fonkoua, Romuald, *Aimé Césaire (1913–2008)*, 25, 40, 243n17
forest/wood trope, 28–34, 241n5
Fortier, Monique, 246n7
Fouet, Jeanne, "La fabrication du roman familial dans les passages autobiographiques," 208
Fournier, Louis, *F.L.Q.*, 257n2
francophone (as term), 235–36, 239–40n23, 240nn27–28, 254n10
francophone literatures, 16–18; male domination of, 18–19. See also *specific authors, works, countries, and regions*
fraternity metaphors, 19, 29–30, 48, 82–84, 125–26, 130, 216, 218, 243n17
French Equatorial Africa, 150
French imperialism, 2, 4–5, 16, 17, 21, 23, 26–29, 47–52, 60, 66–67, 129, 150
French Occidental Africa, 150
French Revolution, 4–5, 36
Front de libération du Québec (FLQ), 140, 168, 218, 226, 257n2
Front de libération nationale (FLN), 218, 257n2
Frye, Northrop, *The Educated Imagination*, 238n8

gendering of anticolonial resistance, 19–20, 29–30, 50–51, 77, 82–83, 85–93, 101–6, 175, 216, 218–19
Glissant, Édouard: *Discours antillais*, 238–39n16; *Poetics of Relation*, 240n26; *Traité du tout-monde*, 7, 164, 238n16
Godin, Gérald, 226
Grande Noirceur era, 79
Grégoire, Abbé, 4
*griffe*, 95–96

Guatemala, U.S. interference in, 153–54
Guevara, Che, 169
Guinoune, Anne-Marie, *De l'impuissance de l'enfance à la revanche par l'écriture*, 254n16

Haeffely, Claude, 73
Haitian Revolution, 4–5, 23, 25, 60, 228, 234; aftermath of, 25, 35–47; importance of, 36, 242n12; portrayed in Césaire's *Et les chiens se taisaient*, 26–35
Hammarskjöld, Dag, 52–53, 54–56
Hardy, Georges, *La géographie psychologique*, 247n19
Hargreaves, Alec, *Transnational French Studies*, 240n28
Harvey, David, *Cosmopolitanism and the Geographies of Freedom*, 234
Held, Jean-Francis, *L'affaire Moumié*, 252n28
"hermeneutics of suspicion," 20
Hiddleston, Jane, *Decolonising the Intellectual*, 34–35
Hitler, Adolf, 151, 152
Hooker, Juliet, *Race and the Politics of Solidarity*, 238n14
Houphouët-Boigny, Félix, 245n2
Hugo, Victor: *Bug-Jargal*, 96; *Le Rhin*, 9

"interior geography" concept, 24, 26, 28
interpictorial reference trope, 217–20, 232–33, 234, 235–36

Jacobins, 4
Jones, Derek, 249n3
Joseph-Gabriel, Annette, *Reimagining Liberation*, 19
Journal Offset, 134
Julien, Pauline, 217, 222–28, 233, 234, 258n8
Jutra, Claude, 191

Kalter, Christoph, *The Discovery of the Third World*, 148, 252n27
Kasa-Vubu, Joseph, 52–53
Kazanjian, David: "Charles Brockden Brown's Biloquial Nation," 84; *The Colonizing Trick*, 17, 240n25
Kemedjio, Cilas: *Mongo Beti*, 119, 121–22, 132, 155–56, 252n33; "Mongo Beti: The Nobility of a Struggle," 250–51n15

Kesteloot, Lilyan, *Aimé Césaire*, 64, 65, 245n36
Klossowski, Pierre, *Le souffleur ou un théâtre de société*, 247n19
Kom, Ambroise: introduction to *Remember Mongo Beti*, 121; *Mongo Beti parle*, 134; "Mongo Beti Returns to Cameroon," 126; *Université des Montagnes*, 143–44, 148
Krizek, Robert L., "Whiteness" (with Nakayama), 248n24

La Joie de Lire, 148
Lambert, Fernando, 6, 64, 168, 171, 193
Lapointe, Martine-Emmanuelle, *Emblèmes d'une littérature*, 245n3
La SFP Cinema, 235
law 21 (La loi sur la laïcité de l'État, 2019), 80
Le Chêne, Gérard: as director of *Contre-censure*, 136, 155, 157–58; "Présentation," 136–39, 148, 150, 151, 155, 163; sovereigntist views of, 138–39
Legault, Gilles, 92–93
Léger, Alexis (Saint-John Perse), *Vents*, 54–55
Léger, Paul-Émile, 161, 162
Leiner, Jacqueline, *Aimé Césaire*, 64
Leiris, Michel, *La possession et ses aspects théâtraux chez les Éthiopiens de Gondars*, 247n19
Lesage, Jean, 79
Les Éditions Québécoises, 133–34, 136, 148, 155
Lezra, Jacques, "Translated Turks on the Early Modern Stage," 237n6
*Liberté*, 246n5
Librairie des Peuples Noirs, 119
"linguistic trick," 17–18
Lionnet, Françoise: "Continents and Archipelagoes," 9–10; *The Creolization of Theory* (with Shih), 17, 80, 155
literary ventriloquism trope, 78, 81–84
*Littérature-monde* manifesto (2007), 239n22
Little, Roger: "Césaire, Hammarskjöld and an Unattributed Quotation in *Une saison au Congo*," 54, 55, 56; "A Further Unacknowledged Quotation in Césaire," 242n15
Loichot, Valérie, *Orphan Narratives*, 247n22

long independence era, 15–19, 25, 149–50; aftermath of, 19–20, 120, 215–36. *See also specific countries, regions, authors, and works*
Louis XIV, King of France, 30
Louverture, Toussaint, 4–5, 26–27, 36, 61
Lucie Films, 235
Lumumba, Patrice, 52–61, 151, 244nn26–28; speech on francophone solidarity (1959), 3

*Main basse sur le Cameroun* (Beti), 118–64; "Avertissement," 132, 153–55; censorship in France, 118–19, 121–22, 130, 132, 134, 136, 139, 148, 153–55, 157–60, 248n1, 249n3; contextualization of, 132–36, 140–48; film *Contre-censure* and, 121, 130, 136, 155–63; Montreal edition, 118–20, 130–31, 132–34, 136, 148, 164; "Note de l'éditeur," 132, 148–52; order of prefaces, 148; paratexts for, 18, 119–20, 121, 131–36, 163–64, 219; "Préface à l'édition québécoise," 132, 134, 139–48; Preface to 1977 edition, 248–49nn1–2; "Présentation," 132, 136–39; publishing history of, 118–20; Quebec Left's reaction to, 129–31; Quebecois edition's role within local networks and personalities, 133–36; simile trope in, 120–64; solidarity in, 121–29; subject and structure of, 122–26
Mannoni, Octave, *Prospéro et Caliban*, 247n19
Martin, Florence: *Cinéma-monde*, 239–40n23; "The Whiles of Maghrebi Women's Cinema," 223
Martinique, 5; Césaire's views on, 66, 67, 68, 70, 72, 74, 222; national determination deliberations, 23, 51, 59, 61, 244n33
Marx, Karl, 2, 8–9
Marxism, 5
Marx-Scouras, Danielle, "A Literature of Departure," 171, 172, 174, 202, 254n11
Maspero, François: *Les abeilles et la guêpe*, 252n29; as Beti's French editor, 118, 129, 132, 137, 139, 148, 164, 222, 249nn6–7; family of, 252n29; Far Right violence against, 148; *Liberté* essays published by, 252n28; "Note de l'éditeur," 136, 148–52

master tropes, 15, 59, 219, 239n20
McClintock, Anne, *Imperial Leather*, 33, 89
McConnell, G. Robert, 172–73, 195, 209–10, 256n32
McGill University, 145
Memmi, Albert, 62, 88–89, 130, 246n7; *Portrait du colonisé suivi de Les Canadiens français sont-ils des colonisés?*, 83
Mesch, Rachel, *Before Trans*, 239n21
metaphors. *See* tropes and metaphors
*métissage*, 96–98
Michon, Jacque, *Histoire de l'édition littéraire au Québec au XXe siècle*, 251n16
Miller, Christopher L., *The French Atlantic Triangle*, 241n7
Mills, Sean, *The Empire Within*, 77
Miron, Gaston, 66–68, 73
Mobutu, Joseph Désiré, 53, 151
*monde à côté, Le* (Chraïbi), 165–66, 168–73, 193; dismissal of Quebec sovereigntist sentiment in, 169–71; on McConnell, 209–10; *Mort au Canada* compared with, 188; personal connections in, 172–73, 200, 202–3
Monego, Joan, *Maghrebian Literature in French*, 168, 203, 253n5, 256n27
*Mon oncle Antoine* (Jutra film), 191
Montreal Congress of Black Writers (1968), 77
Moreau de St. Méry, Médéric-Louis-Elie, *Description de la partie française de l'Isle de Saint-Domingue*, 44–45, 96
Morocco, 165–66, 172; in Chraïbi's *La civilisation, ma mère!*, 195–212
Morris, William, 258n10
*Mort au Canada* (Chraïbi), 173–95; characters' names in, 254n14; consumerism and commodity fetishism in, 176, 180, 192–93, 211; doublings in, 175–76; first instantiation of Canada in, 185–86; importance of Canadian setting, 175, 176, 177–80, 186–88, 196; interchangeability of Canada and Quebec in, 171–72; metaphors in, 178–79, 184–89; metempsychosis in, 175–77, 186–90, 194; misunderstandings and misreadings in, 177–86, 194; *Le monde à côté* compared with, 188; "parallel universe" in, 174, 175, 183–84; plot of, 175–76; Quebecization of text, 189–90, 192; second instantiation of Canada in, 186–89; third instantiation of Canada in, 186, 189–95; touristic stereotypes of Canada in, 177–80, 182, 184, 185, 194; versions of novel, 255n19; viewed as romance novel, 174–75, 177, 182–83, 186, 254n13
Moudileno, Lydie, "The Troubling Popularity of West African Romance Novels," 174, 175, 182–83, 186
Moumié, Félix, 151, 252n28
Mouvement de libération populaire, 133
Mouvement Souveraineté Association convention (1968), 226

Nakayama, Thomas K., "Whiteness" (with Krizek), 248n24
Napoleon, Emperor of the French, 36
Nazism, 150, 158, 159
Ndongmo, Albert, 122–26, 130–31, 135, 140, 146, 152, 161, 164, 249n9, 250n11
*nègres blancs* trope, 2, 5–7, 12, 24, 52, 63–64, 98–99, 117, 224
*négritude*, 6, 24, 25, 51–52, 62, 63, 68, 72, 75
Nesbitt, Nick: *Caribbean Critique*, 4, 36, 37, 51, 64, 238n16, 251n21; "From Louverture to Lenin," 242n14; "History and Nation-Building," 243n22
Ngũgĩ wa Thiong'o, *Decolonizing the Mind*, 251n25
Niamey international conference of francophonie (1969), 234
*Nouvelles littéraires*, 208

Organisation spéciale, 247n17
otherness, 10, 70, 80, 83, 84
Ouandié, Ernest, 122–26, 130–31, 140, 150, 151, 161, 164, 250nn10–11
outside observers, impartiality and, 54–56, 126–28
Oyono, Ferdinand, 118

paratext, functions of, 251n16
Paris Commune of 1871, 5, 12, 233, 258n10
Parizeau, Jacques, 79
Parti communiste français (PCF), 5, 234, 243n17

*Parti pris* (sovereigntist journal), 63
Parti québécois, 134, 142, 226; racial discrimination in, 79–80, 227, 238n13
*passé simple, Le* (Chraïbi), 166, 167, 172, 201, 202–4, 208
Peters, Fritz, *The World Next Door*, 165
Pettiti, Louis, 126–28
*Peuples noirs—Peuples africains*, 119, 161–62
Pheasant-Kelly, E. E., "Beyond Stimulation," 257n4
*philanthropes*: in Césaire's *La tragédie du roi Christophe*, 40–46, 51, 53, 72, 127, 128–29, 243nn17–18; French Left and, 128–29, 137–38, 250–51n15; Pettiti seen as, 127–28; Quebec and, 62, 243n17
Pierre, Samuel, *Ces Québécois venus d'Haïti*, 77
Pigeon, Elaine, "Hosanna!," 230
Pilon, Claude-Guy, 161
Pilon, Jean-Guy, 69
Plato, 95
Pruneau, Gilles, 257n2

Quebec: appropriations of *négritude*, 2, 5–7, 12, 24, 25, 52; Catholic Church in, 163; Césaire in, 63–64, 169–70; Césaire's influence on solidarity views in, 18, 62–75; Chraïbi in, 167–74, 193; francophone studies and, 18, 80; Grande Noirceur era, 79; history of modern, 79–80; independence movement, 23, 65, 70, 74, 79–80, 120, 163–64, 168–69, 215, 226–27; involvement in slave trade, 241n7; language politics, 144–46; October Crisis of 1970, 168; Quiet Revolution in, 1, 79, 118–19, 166, 168–69, 173, 176, 190–95, 196–213, 224; racial and religious discrimination in, 79–80, 227, 238n13; racial demographics of, 2, 5–6, 62, 79–80, 116; referendum of 1980, 215; referendum of 1995, 227, 258n9; relationship to France, 245n40; status viewed by intellectuals as colonized, 129–30, 139–48, 190–92, 224; strikes and protests in, 77; as "third space," 136–39, 166, 169–70, 177–78, 194–95, 222; unmoored nature of, 107; as "white space," 18, 76–77, 98–99, 109, 117

*Québec-Presse*, 142
Quiet Revolution era. *See under* Quebec

race, 237n4; "francophone studies" and, 17–18, 240n28; *nègres blancs* trope, 5–7; Quebec's demographics, 2, 5–6, 62, 76–77, 79–80, 116
*raison folle, La* (film), 253n1
Randall, Marilyn, "L'homme et l'oeuvre," 97, 246n9
Rassemblement pour l'indépendance nationale (RIN), 247n17
Reclus, Élisée, 233
Reich, Wilhelm, 158
Ricoeur, Paul, 20
Roberts, Katherine A., "Making Women Pay," 82, 88, 91, 247n16
Robespierre, Maximilien, 4, 242n13
Rorty, Philip, *Contingency, Irony, Solidarity*, 9
Rosello, Mireille, "The 'Césaire Effect' or How to Cultivate One's Nation," 19, 241n5, 244n31
Ross, Kristin, *Communal Luxury*, 12, 233, 258n10
Roy, Fernande, "Nègres blancs d'Amérique?," 5

Saint-Martin, Lori, "Pur polyester," 79–80
Santo Domingo, civil unrest in, 153–54
Sapir, Edward, 197
Schoelcher, Victor, 5
Selao, Ching, "Les fils d'Aimé Césaire," 62–63, 244n33
Sembene, Ousmane, *Les bouts de bois de Dieu*, 13–14
Senghor, Léopold Sedor, "Ce que l'homme noir apporte," 81, 244n35, 246n6
Shakespeare, William, *The Tempest*, 47
Sherrington, Robert, "The Use of Mongo Beti," 122
Shih, Shu-Mei, *The Creolization of Theory* (with Lionnet), 17, 80, 155
simile trope (in Beti's *Main basse*), 120–21; as accusation, 153–55; Cameroon–Quebec likeness, 130–31, 149–50, 163–64; French language as solidarity, 121–29, 164; paratexts used for, 135–48; recentering around Cameroon, 148–52; in solidarity, 163–64; as structural element, 155–63

slavery: decree abolishing, 5; dogs' use in, 241nn8–9; French Revolution and, 4; Haitian Revolution and, 4–5; portrayed in Césaire's plays, 25, 27–51, 61, 74–75; status of former slaves, 40–47; transnational trade in, 93, 127, 228, 241n7, 246n10, 246n12, 247n23
Slavery Abolition Decree (1848), 5
Söderlind, Sylvia, *Margin/Alias*, 89
solidarity, francophone: as abstraction, 13–15, 36, 75; archetypes of, 48–52; as asymptotic unity, 4, 8–12, 20, 26–35, 41, 46, 47, 160, 164, 227, 235; Césaire's critique of, 24–25, 36, 60–61; Césaire's influence on Quebecois thought, 62–75; Césaire's metaphors of, 28–34; Chraïbi's rejection of, 169–71; as community of interests, 2–3; Congo Crisis and, 52–61; construction of, 228; creolized, 9–10; critical reading of, 20–21; in destruction, 27–28, 32, 48, 49–50; dissipation of, 216; dual nature of, 239n19; failure and, 12; foundational moments of, 25; French imperialism and, 2, 4–5, 16, 17, 21, 23, 26–29, 47–52, 60, 66–67, 129, 150; gendering of, 19–20, 29–30, 50–51, 77, 82–83, 85–93, 175, 216, 233; idea of, 2; as method rather than goal, 9–12; music and, 227; *nègres blanc* trope and, 5–7; neutrality contrasted with, 54–56; poetics of, 1–21, 24, 26, 63–64, 71, 74–75, 77, 117, 164, 215, 216, 233–36, 238nn15–16; post-independence era, 215–36; simile as avenue for, 147–48; sisterhood and feminine friendship as, 216–36; through language, 3–8, 11–12, 23–24, 67–68, 79, 197, 212–13, 222, 228, 235–36; through long independence era, 15–17; utopic visions of, 3, 239n18
Soviet Union, 226
spacetime concept, 234, 235
Spleth, Janice, "Chraïbi's *Mother Comes of Age*," 201, 256n31
Statue of Liberty vandalism plot, 1–2, 20–21, 92–93
Steinberg, Leo, 219
Stekel, Wilhelm, *La femme frigide*, 89–90
Sulivan, Jean, 205
Suret-Canale, Jean, "Mon ami Mongo Beti," 121

Taban, Carla, introduction to *Meta- and Inter-Images in Contemporary Visual Art and Culture*, 219
Tabue, Pierre, "Mongo Beti: The Nobility of a Struggle," 250–51n15
Tchumkam, Hervé, "Of Murder and Love," 254n13
Tétu, Michel, "Cousins proches et voisins lointains," 64, 170, 171, 254n10
Tétu de Labsade, Françoise, *Le Québec—Un pays, une culture*, 171
Thorez, Maurice, 243n17
Tobner, Odile, 119
Toualla, Blaise, "Mongo Beti: The Nobility of a Struggle," 250–51n15
*tragédie du roi Christophe, La* (Césaire), 23, 25, 35–47, 59, 234, 241n5; image of spitting (*crachat*) in, 39, 42, 43–44, 45, 72; paradox in, 37; *philanthropes* in, 40–46, 51, 53, 72, 127, 128–29, 243n17; water metaphors in, 37–39, 43–46
transnational francophone solidarity, 2, 23–24; nonpolitical, 174, 176–77, 188–89, 193–95; between Quebec and African nations, 120, 148–52, 155, 195–212, 216–36; transatlantic connections, 25, 242n10, 244n26, 244n30. *See also specific authors and topics*
transracial francophone solidarity, 2, 5–7; in Aquin's *Trou de mémoire*, 77–117; Césaire's influence on Quebecois thought, 62–75; futility of hopes for, 35–47, 64; "interior geography" and, 24, 26, 28; power relations and, 113–15; Quebec edition of Beti's *Main basse* and, 137, 139–48. *See also specific authors and topics*
Tremblay, Michel: *À toi, pour toujours, ta Marie-Lou*, 217, 228–33; *Les bellessoeurs*, 230
tropes and metaphors: as abstraction, 13–15, 75, 219; as basic units of discourse, 7–8; as essential to expressing solidarity, 8–12; in film, 219–20; French-specific, 4; gaps in, 12; master, 15, 59, 219, 239n20; mechanism of, 4, 5–7, 165. *See also specific tropes, authors, and works*
*Trou de mémoire* (Aquin), 18, 76–117, 118, 175, 234–35; ambiguous paternity